JOURNAL FOR THE STUDY OF THE OLD TESTAMENT SUPPLEMENT SERIES
188

Editors
David J.A. Clines
Philip R. Davies

Executive Editor
John Jarick

Editorial Board
Richard J. Coggins, Alan Cooper, Tamara C. Eskenazi,
J. Cheryl Exum, John Goldingay, Robert P. Gordon,
Norman K. Gottwald, Andrew D.H. Mayes, Carol Meyers,
Patrick D. Miller

Sheffield Academic Press

Concentricity
and
Continuity

The Literary Structure of Isaiah

Robert H. O'Connell

Journal for the Study of the Old Testament
Supplement Series 188

Copyright © 1994 Sheffield Academic Press

Published by
Sheffield Academic Press Ltd
Mansion House
19 Kingfield Road
Sheffield, S11 9AS
England

Typeset by R.H. O'Connell, using Nota Bene 4.1
(with Frank Ruehl Hebrew fonts)
and
Printed on acid-free paper in Great Britain
by Bookcraft
Midsomer Norton, Somerset

British Library Cataloguing in Publication Data

A catalogue record for this book is available
from the British Library

ISBN 1-85075-521-3

תִּכְרַע כָּל־בֶּרֶךְ

CONTENTS

Preface 11
Abbreviations 13

Introduction 15
The Need for This Study 15
Procedure and Methodology Used in This Study 21
Complex Frameworking in Isaiah 23
Limitations and Objectives of This Study 29

Chapter 1
ISAIAH 1:1–2:5: CAMEO OF A COVENANT DISPUTATION 31
Structural Delineation of Isaiah 1:1–2:5 33
Covenant Disputation Pattern and Complex
Frameworking in Isaiah 1:1–2:5 38
Persuasion as a Function of Structure in Isaiah 1:1–2:5 51
Covenant Disputation Pattern and the Continuity of
Isaiah 1:1–2:5 with its Context 53

Chapter 2
ISAIAH 2:6-22: THREAT OF JUDGMENT ON IDOLATERS 57
Structural Delineation of Isaiah 2:6-22 57
Complex Frameworking in Isaiah 2:6aγ-21 59
Persuasion as a Function of Structure in
Isaiah 2:6aγ-21 65
The Continuity of Isaiah 2:6-22 with its Context 67

Chapter 3
ISAIAH 3:1-4:1: THREAT OF JUDGMENT ON THE UNJUST 69
Structural Delineation of Isaiah 3:1-4:1 70
Complex Frameworking in Isaiah 3:1-4:1 70
Persuasion as a Function of Structure in Isaiah 3:1-4:1 75
The Continuity of Isaiah 3:1-4:1 with its Context 77

Chapter 4
ISAIAH 4:2–12:6: THE SYRO-EPHRAIMITE-ASSYRIAN
SCHEME FOR ZION'S JUDGMENT AND RESTORATION   81
   Structural Delineation of Isaiah 4:2–12:6   81
   Asymmetrical Concentricity in Isaiah 4:2–11:16   82
   Complex Frameworking in Isaiah 4:2–11:16   88
   Selected Substructural Complexes in Isaiah 4:2–11:16   96
   Persuasion as a Function of Structure in
    Isaiah 4:2–11:16   101
   The Continuity of Isaiah 4:2–12:6 with its Context   106

Chapter 5
ISAIAH 13:1–39:8: THE ASSYRIAN-BABYLONIAN SCHEME
FOR ZION'S JUDGMENT AND RESTORATION   109
   Structural Delineation of Isaiah 13:1–39:8   110
   Asymmetrical Concentricity in Isaiah 13:1–39:8   111
   Complex Frameworking in Isaiah 13:1–39:8   116
   Selected Substructural Complexes in Isaiah 13:1–39:8   121
   Persuasion as a Function of Structure in
    Isaiah 13:1–39:8   135
   The Continuity of Isaiah 13:1–39:8 with its Context   144

Chapter 6
ISAIAH 40:1–54:17: YHWH'S EXONERATION   149
   Structural Delineation of Isaiah 40:1–54:17   150
   Complex Frameworking in Isaiah 40:1–54:17   151
   Selected Substructural Complexes in Isaiah 40:1–54:17   162
   Persuasion as a Function of Structure in
    Isaiah 40:1–54:17   209
   The Continuity of Isaiah 40:1–54:17 with its Context   212

Chapter 7
ISAIAH 55:1–66:24: FINAL ULTIMATUM   215
   Structural Delineation of Isaiah 55:1–66:24   216
   Asymmetrical Concentricity in Isaiah 55:1–66:24   216
   Substructural Complexes in Isaiah 55:1–66:24   221
   Persuasion as a Function of Structure in
    Isaiah 55:1–66:24   232
   The Continuity of Isaiah 55:1–66:24 with its Context   233

Conclusion   235
  The Literary Structure of Isaiah   235
  Literary Networking in the Light of the Literary
    Structure of Isaiah   239
  Genre Competence in the Light of Isaiah's Literary Form   242
  The Message of Isaiah in the Light of its Literary Form   243

Bibliography   247
Index of References   255
Index of Authors   271

PREFACE

This work represents the culmination of seven years of study and teaching in the book of Isaiah. I am grateful for the opportunity to have revised various details of the study over that period, yet that experience has prompted me to realize how subject to improvement even its present form may be. I would like to admit from the outset, therefore, that it is with a little apprehension that I offer up this work for publication, for I suspect that there are many points in my analysis that might benefit from further study and reflection. Nevertheless, its present issuance seems warranted, less on the grounds that I claim to present in it anything that yet approaches a definitive study of the literary form of Isaiah, than by the assurance that one may profitably proceed toward a better understanding of it by following such lines of investigation. It is in the sincere hope of serving the latter alternative that I offer this book to its readers.

It will be evident to many readers where I have taken the liberty of traversing the bounds of strict form-critical categorizations in my delineation of the broader formal structures in Isaiah. This I have done, with due respect for the value of form criticism, on the basis of my pursuit of a balance between concern for the form and concern for how the form may have been altered or adapted to function in its present, broader context. Thus, although my approach may seem to slight some conventional regularities of certain prophetic speech forms (e.g., the covenant disputation, whose rhetoric, I argue, governs the whole of Isaiah), my departure from recognized norms has only been such as seemed warranted by a rhetorical strategy that inheres in the patterns of repetition that appear throughout the book as a whole.

As a further caveat, I would also beg the reader's forgiveness for a number of pages in the book where the lower portion of the page had to be left blank. This was done only where a diagram might otherwise have been broken over the page at a point where the pattern of correspondences would not have remained as clear to the reader.

For several suggestions for improvement on an earlier version of Chapter 6 in this study, read informally in Denver in the Winter of 1992, I would like to thank Dr Peter D. Miscall, who responded to the paper, as well as Dr Robert L. Alden, Dr Frederick E. Greenspahn, Dr Robert L. Hubbard, Jr, and Dr David L. Petersen, whose presence and insights were appreciated. I derived further insights from queries and comments made by several who responded to my paper on the use of complex frameworking in Isaiah, read for the Biblical Hebrew Poetry Section at the AAR/SBL Annual Meeting in Washington, D.C., among whom Dr J. Kenneth Kuntz and Dr Roy F. Melugin deserve special mention.

I also wish to thank my colleague, Robert G. Buller, for his careful editing of the final draft, and Dr J. Webb Mealy, of Sheffield Academic Press for his patience and guidance in helping me to prepare the camera-ready copy. I especially wish to thank Professor D.J.A. Clines for consenting to publish this study in the JSOT Supplement Series.

Finally, I would like to express my gratitude and love to my wife, Mina, for her unfailing support during the many hours that I devoted to this work.

Denver, Autumn 1994   Robert H. O'Connell

ABBREVIATIONS

AcOr	*Acta orientalia*
ALUOS	Annual of Leeds University Oriental Society
AnBib	Analecta biblica
ANET	J.B. Pritchard (ed.), *Ancient Near Eastern Texts*
ARI	A.K. Grayson, *Assyrian Royal Inscriptions*
ATD	Das Alte Testament Deutsch
AUSS	*Andrews University Seminary Studies*
BA	*Biblical Archaeologist*
BEvT	Beiträge zur evangelischen Theologie
BHS	*Biblia hebraica stuttgartensia*
Bib	*Biblica*
BKAT	Biblischer Kommentar: Altes Testament
BLS	Bible and Literature Series
BWANT	Beiträge zur Wissenschaft vom Alten und Neuen Testament
BZAW	Beihefte zur *ZAW*
CBC	Cambridge Bible Commentary
CBQ	*Catholic Biblical Quarterly*
CBSC	Cambridge Bible for Schools and Colleges
ConBOT	Coniectanea biblica, Old Testament
EBib	Etudes bibliques
ET	English translation
EvT	*Evangelische Theologie*
FTL	Forum Theologiae Linguisticae
HDR	Harvard Dissertations in Religion
HKAT	Handkommentar zum Alten Testament
HUCA	*Hebrew Union College Annual*
ICC	International Critical Commentary
Int	*Interpretation*
ISBL	Indiana Studies in Biblical Literature
JBL	*Journal of Biblical Literature*
JCS	*Journal of Cuneiform Studies*
JNES	*Journal of Near Eastern Studies*
JSOT	*Journal for the Study of the Old Testament*
JSOTSup	*Journal for the Study of the Old Testament*, Supplement Series
JSS	*Journal of Semitic Studies*
JTS	*Journal of Theological Studies*
KAT	Kommentar zum Alten Testament
KEHAT	Kurzgefaßtes exegetisches Handbuch zum Alten Testament
KHAT	Kurzer Hand-Commentar zum Alten Testament
NCB	New Century Bible
NEB	*New English Bible*
NICOT	New International Commentary on the Old Testament
NIV	*New International Version*
OBO	Orbis biblicus et orientalis
OTL	Old Testament Library

RB	*Revue biblique*
RevExp	*Review and Expositor*
RivB	*Rivista biblica italiana*
RSV	*Revised Standard Version*
SBL	Society of Biblical Literature
SBLDS	SBL Dissertation Series
SBT	Studies in Biblical Theology
ScrHier	Scripta Hierosolymitana
SEÅ	*Svensk exegetisk årsbok*
ST	*Studia theologica*
TBT	*The Bible Today*
TBü	Theologische Bücherei
TynBul	*Tyndale Bulletin*
VT	*Vetus Testamentum*
VTSup	*Vetus Testamentum*, Supplements
WBC	Word Biblical Commentary
WMANT	Wissenschaftliche Monographien zum Alten und Neuen Testament
ZAW	*Zeitschrift für die alttestamentliche Wissenschaft*
ZTK	*Zeitschrift für Theologie und Kirche*

INTRODUCTION

The Need for This Study

To one degree or another, scholars who have endeavored to understand the overall form and rhetoric of large prophetic books, like the book of Isaiah, have had to admit of a less than sufficient familiarity with the genre conventions that made those books sensible to their authors and compilers. As long ago as 1976, J.W. Rogerson remarked:

> In the case of the so-called Wisdom Literature, and especially a book like Proverbs, we can read it in the light of comparable literature from the ancient Near East, and understand it as an instance of a wider class of writing. Again, in the case of books like Daniel, we can learn something about the 'enabling conventions' of what we call 'apocalyptic'. It would be fair, though, to say that although we know much about the individual items which might make up a prophetic book, we do not know how to read a prophetic book as a whole ...[1]

It is interesting to realize that this awareness of methodological poverty was coming about at a time when genre-critical studies had been burgeoning for a decade, under the guise of form criticism.[2] As a method, form criticism had long since proven itself inadequate for treating larger literary entities, such as the book of Isaiah, as unified compositions.[3] Its programmatic focus had been on smaller speech

[1]J.W. Rogerson, 'Recent Literary Structuralist Approaches to Biblical Interpretation', *The Churchman* 90 (1976), p. 173.

[2]Cf. R. Knierim's comment on form criticism that, 'to the extent that genre is by definition a "conventional structure" and a conventional structure a "form," form criticism is by definition genre criticism' ('Old Testament Form Criticism Reconsidered', *Int* 27 [1973], p. 456). This article is a particularly insightful treatment of the problematic criteria for determining genre. See also W.G. Doty, 'The Concept of Genre in Literary Analysis', in L.C. McGaughy (ed.), *The Society of Biblical Literature, 1972 Proceedings* (2 vols.; Missoula, MT: SBL, 1972), II, pp. 413-48; J.A. Baird, 'Genre Analysis as a Method of Historical Criticism', in *SBL, 1972 Proceedings*, II, pp. 385-411; W. Richter, *Exegese als Literaturwissenschaft* (Göttingen: Vandenhoeck & Ruprecht, 1971), pp. 125ff. On the prophetic genre in particular, see K. Koch, *The Growth of the Biblical Tradition: The Form-Critical Method* (trans. S.M. Cupitt; New York: Charles Scribner's Sons, 1969), pp. 210-20.

[3]A. Berlin has said that 'the primary axiom in form criticism is that the present text is composed of smaller literary units that once existed independently' (*Poetics and Interpretation of Biblical Narrative* [BLS, 9; Sheffield: Almond Press, 1983], p. 122). Indeed, this is the assumption that underlies the first step of form

16   Concentricity and Continuity

forms, the product of orally conditioned compositional conventions.¹
Although Gunkel, the pioneer of form criticism, did not work in Isaiah,
others contributed significant studies that carried out his lines of
analysis.² Then, form critics themselves, increasingly aware that the
criticism, to delimit each literary unit from its larger literary context.
Although this assumption proved productive when applied to biblical hymnic literature, where
psalms already existed as independent literary units, one may justifiably wonder
whether this was a fair assumption to make of the longer works to which form
criticism was applied. Truly, one may query whether the assumption that gave rise
to the predisposition to work with shorter subunits—namely, that most of what now
appears in written form once existed as oral forms—should remain valid (cf.
Berlin, *Poetics*, p. 123).

¹See H. Gunkel, 'Die Propheten als Schriftsteller und Dichter', in H. Schmidt
(ed.), *Die grossen Propheten übersetzt und erklärt* (Die Schriften des Alten Testaments, II/2; Göttingen: Vandenhoeck & Ruprecht, 1915), pp. xxxvi-lxxii; T.H.
Robinson, *Prophecy and the Prophets in Ancient Israel* (Studies in Theology; New
York: Charles Scribner's Sons, 1923); Koch, pp. 84-86. H.F. Hahn commented
that 'the process of breaking up the extensive "orations" into separate oracles and
poetical compositions ... appeared entirely justified in the light of the hypothesis
that prophetic oracles, like other "literary types" in their original form, were
always brief utterances confined to the statement of single ideas' (*The Old Testament in Modern Research* [Philadelphia: Fortress Press, 1954], p. 134). Under the
rubric of this hypothesis the prophetic 'books' were to be regarded as compilations
of independent speech forms from diverse historical and circumstantial origin
rather than as literary works conceived in their entirety by writing authors.

²Form-critical analyses of sections of Isaiah have been offered by
H. Gressmann, 'Die literarische Analyse Deuterojesajas', *ZAW* 34 (1914),
pp. 254-97; S. Mowinckel, 'Die Komposition des deuterojesajanischen Buches',
ZAW 49 (1931), pp. 87-112, 242-60; idem, 'Neuere Forschungen zu Deuterojesaja, Tritojesaja und den Äbäd-Jahwä-Problem', *AcOr* 16 (1938), pp. 1-40;
O. Eissfeldt, *Einleitung in das Alte Testament unter Einschluss der Apokryphen und
Pseudepigraphen* (Neue theologische Grundrisse; Tübingen: Mohr, 3d edn, 1964),
pp. 377ff.; ET of 3d German edn: *The Old Testament: An Introduction* (trans. P.R.
Ackroyd; Oxford: Basil Blackwell; New York: Harper & Row, 1965), pp. 332ff.;
P. Volz, *Jesaja: Zweite Hälfte Kapitel 40–66 übersetzt und erklärt* (KAT, IX/2;
Leipzig: Deichert, 1932); J. Begrich, *Studien zu Deuterojesaja* (BWANT, 4; Folge
Heft 25 [77]; Stuttgart: Kohlhammer, 1938; repr., TBü, 20; Munich: Chr. Kaiser
Verlag, 1963); C. Westermann, *Grundformen prophetischer Rede* (BEvT, 31;
Munich: Chr. Kaiser Verlag, 1960); ET: *Basic Forms of Prophetic Speech* (trans.
H.C. White; Philadelphia: Westminster Press, 1967), treating judgment-speeches;
idem, 'Sprach und Struktur der Prophetie Deuterojesajas', in *Forschung am Alten
Testament: Gesammelte Studien, I* (TBü, 24; Munich: Chr. Kaiser Verlag, 1964),
pp. 92-170 (reprinted as *Sprache und Struktur der Prophetie Deuterojesajas*
[Calwer Theologische Monographien, Reihe A (Bibelwissenschaft), 11; Stuttgart:
Calwer Verlag, 1981]); R.F. Melugin, *The Formation of Isaiah 40–55* (BZAW,
141; Berlin: de Gruyter, 1976; cf. PhD diss., Yale University, 1968); A. Schoors,
I am God Your Saviour: A Form-critical Study of the Main Genres in Is. XL–LV
(VTSup, 24; Leiden: Brill, 1973); D.L. Christensen, *Transformations of the War
Oracle in Old Testament Prophecy* (HDR, 3; Missoula, MT: Scholars Press,
1975). Cf. A. Graffy, *A Prophet Confronts His People: The Disputation Speech in
the Prophets* (AnBib, 104; Rome: Biblical Institute Press, 1984).

predisposition of their method to working with shorter literary units precluded any attempt to understand larger literary forms as rhetorically designed organizational schemes, began to call for a methodological shift that would redress some of the fundamental misconceptions regarding the nature of the relationship between genre and formal structure.[1] Today, precisely because of an increase in literary sensibilities and the absence of a definitive accounting for the form of Isaiah as a whole, concern with the question of the rhetorical coherence and message of the book of Isaiah has become a major focus of scholarly endeavor.[2]

The present study constitutes a contribution to the discussion around the question of the form of Isaiah since there is, in recent form-critical

[1] See Knierim, pp. 449-55, 458-63. Cf. also Doty, pp. 433-36.

[2] Consider the foci of the 'Formation of the Book of Isaiah Consultation' of the SBL Annual Meeting at Kansas City (§S19, 'Reading the Book of Isaiah'; cf. E.H. Lovering, Jr [ed.], *SBL 1991 Seminar Papers* [Atlanta: Scholars Press, 1991]), and of the 'Formation of the Book of Isaiah Seminar' at San Francisco (§S158, 'Structure and Tradition History of the Book of Isaiah'; cf. Lovering [ed.], *SBL 1992 Seminar Papers* [Atlanta: Scholars Press, 1992]) and at Washington, D.C. (§S60, 'Issues in the Interpretation of the Book of Isaiah'; cf. Lovering [ed.], *SBL 1993 Seminar Papers* [Atlanta: Scholars Press, 1993]). Some scholars propose that the unity of Isaiah's message derives from 'reciprocal relationships' (so R. Rendtorff) between the amalgamated collections of chs. 1-39, 40-55 and 56-66. Such a unity, in fact, is the product of a diachronic synthesis of allegedly diverse 'Isaianic' literary traditions. Cf. B.S. Childs, *Introduction to the Old Testament as Scripture* (Philadelphia: Fortress Press, 1979), pp. 325-38, whose leveling of alleged diachronic distinctions, out of concern for the final ('canonical') form of the text, highlights his departure from the hermeneutical axiom of historical criticism that 'a biblical book could only be properly understood when interpreted in the light of its original historical setting' (p. 317). See also the criticisms of Childs's approach by J. Barr, *Holy Scripture: Canon, Authority, Criticism* (Philadelphia: Westminster Press, 1983), pp. 75-104, 158-62; and Childs's review of Barr's work in *Int* 38 (1984), pp. 66-70.

For relatively recent treatments of the coherence of the book of Isaiah, see R.E. Clements, 'The Unity of the Book of Isaiah', *Int* 36 (1982), pp. 117-29 (reprinted in J.L. Mays and P.J. Achtemeier [eds.], *Interpreting the Prophets* [Philadelphia: Fortress Press, 1987], pp. 50-61); idem, 'Beyond Tradition History: Deutero-Isaianic Development of First Isaiah's Themes', *JSOT* 31 (1985), pp. 95-113; J.H. Eaton, 'The Isaiah Tradition', in R. Coggins, A. Phillips and M. Knibb (eds.), *Israel's Prophetic Tradition: Essays in Honour of Peter R. Ackroyd* (Cambridge: Cambridge University Press, 1982), pp. 58-76; R. Rendtorff, 'Zur Komposition des Buches Jesaja', *VT* 34 (1984), pp. 295-320; W.J. Dumbrell, 'The Purpose of the Book of Isaiah', *TynBul* 36 (1985), pp. 111-28; C.R. Seitz, 'Introduction: The One Isaiah // The Three Isaiahs' and 'Isaiah 1-66: Making Sense of the Whole', in C.R. Seitz (ed.), *Reading and Preaching the Book of Isaiah* (Philadelphia: Fortress Press, 1988), pp. 13-22, 105-26.

scholarship, no treatment available that concerns itself with an analysis of pervasive patterns of repetition in the book.[1] Further, the present study constitutes an example of the kind of method that may be deemed appropriate to discovering extensive patterns of repetition in the larger sections of prophetic poetry elsewhere in the Hebrew Bible.

[1] A recent study of repetition patterns in Isaiah was made by A. Gileadi, 'A Holistic Structure of the Book of Isaiah', (PhD diss., Brigham Young University, 1981). His bifid model comprises two parts of thirty-three chapters each (p. 14):

I. Ruin and Renascence, Chapters 1–5; 34–35.
II. Biographical Material, Chapters 6–8; 36–40.
III. Agents of Divine Deliverance and Judgment, Chapters 9–12; 41–46.
IV. Oracles Against Foreign Powers, Chapters 13–23; 47.
V. Suffering and Salvation, Chapters 24–27; 48–54.
VI. Sermons on Loyalty and Disloyalty, Chapters 28–31; 55–59.
VII. Dispossession of the Wicked, Inheritance by the Righteous, Chapters 32–33; 60–66.

The prototype for this model was proposed by W.H. Brownlee (*The Meaning of the Qumrân Scrolls for the Bible* [New York: Oxford University Press, 1964], pp. 247-49) and was inspired by a gap between chs. 33 and 34 in 1QIsa[a]:

I. The Ruin and Restoration of Judah (1–5)	I. Paradise Lost and Regained (34–35)
II. Biography (6–8)	II. Biography (36–40)
III. Agents of Divine Blessing and Judgment (9–12)	III. Agents of Deliverance and Judgment (41–45)
IV. Anti-foreign Oracles (13–23)	IV. Anti-Babylonian Oracles (46–48)
V. Universal Judgment and Deliverance of God's People (24–27)	V. Universal Redemption through *yhwh's* Servant, also the Glorification of Israel (49–54[55])
VI. Ethical Sermons, Indicating Israel and Judah (28–31)	VI. Ethical Sermons, the Ethical Conditions for Israel's Redemption (56–59)
VII. The Restoration of Judah and the Davidic Kingdom (32–33)	VII. Paradise Regained: The Glories of the New Jerusalem and the New Heavens and the New Earth (60–66)

This bifid scheme was also endorsed by J.A. Callaway ('Isaiah in Modern Scholarship', *RevExp* 65 [1968], pp. 403-407), by R.K. Harrison (*Introduction to the Old Testament* [Grand Rapids: Eerdmans, 1969], pp. 787-89), who thought that this design evidenced single authorship of the book, and, more recently, by C.A. Evans ('On the Unity and Parallel Structure of Isaiah', *VT* 38 [1988], pp. 129-47). However, what one sees in these bifid models of the structure of Isaiah is not so much the result of close analysis of literary patterning as the result of thematic summarizations over broad sections of the book. Despite the citation of key word collocations between allegedly parallel sections, their structural divisions are much too broad to represent a pattern verifiable from vocabulary repetitions alone.

The attempt of E.W. Bullinger to arrange the materials of Isaiah, indeed, of the whole Bible, according to concentric schemata (*The Companion Bible* [N.p., 1900; repr., Grand Rapids: Zondervan, 1964]) must be regarded as of limited value because his methodology did not establish sufficient criteria for assessing the probability that his proposed concentric patterns were the result of the author's deliberate design.

This study is concerned with more than just the question of formal patterning, however, for it also seeks to make an advance on the problem of determining what set of genre conventions might account for the rhetoric implied by the form of Isaiah. Rhetorical criticism, though not yet so-named, began in Isaiah with the commentary of J. Muilenburg on Isaiah 40–66.[1] It was there argued that the arrangement of materials in chs. 40–66 could not be delineated according to conventional form-critical genres, since the materials were so integrated into the larger stanzas comprising the argument as to dissolve recognizable units. This study was followed by several key contributions worked out along similar lines from M. Haran, E. Hessler and Y. Gitay.[2] To these studies, R.J. Clifford has added a rhetorical treatment of Isaiah 40–55, which proposes that seventeen sections together comprise an integrated argument,[3] and G.J. Polan has contributed an analysis of Isaiah 56–59 from a rhetorical perspective.[4] However, none of these rhetorical-critical studies have overcome the obstacle of describing the book as a coherent design, for all are limited to analyzing within one, or at most two, of the three major sections of the book of Isaiah, whether chs. 1–39, 40–55 or 56–66. The effect has been that rhetorical critics have presented few studies that treat the entire book of Isaiah as an integrated entity.

The thesis of the present study is twofold: that the formal structure of the book of Isaiah comprises seven asymmetrically concentric

[1] J. Muilenburg, 'The Book of Isaiah: Chapters 40–66: Introduction and Exegesis', in G.A. Buttrick et al. (eds.), *The Interpreter's Bible* (12 vols.; Nashville: Abingdon Press, 1956), V, pp. 381-773. For an outline of the programmatic concerns of rhetorical criticism, see Muilenburg, 'Form-Criticism and Beyond', *JBL* 88 (1969), pp. 1-18. See also the criticism by Knierim (p. 458 n. 91) that Muilenburg's meritorious article neglects to set forth precisely where his proposed rhetorical criticism goes 'beyond' form criticism—a deficiency made up for in Melugin, 'The Typical versus the Unique among the Hebrew Prophets', in *SBL, 1972 Proceedings*, II, pp. 331-41.
[2] See M. Haran, 'The Literary Structure and Chronological Framework of the Prophecies in Is. xl–xlviii', in *Congress Volume, Bonn* (VTSup, 9; Leiden: Brill, 1963), pp. 127-55; E. Hessler, 'Gott der Schöpfer: Ein Beitrag zur Komposition und Theologie Deuterojesajas' (PhD diss., Greifswald, 1961); idem, 'Die Struktur der Bilder bei Deuterojesaja', *EvT* 25 (1965), pp. 349-69; Y. Gitay, 'Rhetorical Analysis of Isaiah 40–48' (PhD diss., Emory University, 1978); idem, 'Isaiah and His Audience', *Prooftexts* 3 (1983), pp. 223-30, treating only Isa. 1–9.
[3] R.J. Clifford, *Fair Spoken and Persuading: An Interpretation of Second Isaiah* (New York: Paulist Press, 1984).
[4] G.J. Polan, *In the Ways of Justice toward Salvation: A Rhetorical Analysis of Isaiah 56–59* (American University Studies, Series VII: Theology and Religion, 13; New York: Peter Lang, 1986).

sections, each of which presents a complex frameworking pattern of repetitions among its subunits, and that the rhetoric of the book is closest to that of the prophetic covenant disputation. As to the second claim, it may be inferred that the book best manifests its structural unity, thematic coherence and rhetorical emphasis when read as an exemplar of the prophetic covenant disputation genre. An aggregate of constituent elements sampled from among covenant disputation exemplars of the ancient Near East and elsewhere in the Hebrew Bible can be seen to align with the aggregate of elements in the book of Isaiah as a whole. Indeed, it seems only under the rhetoric of a prophetic covenant disputation that the major sections and subsections of Isaiah can be seen to cohere. Under the recognition that Isaiah's exordium (1:1–2:5) functions as an introductory cameo of the form of the book, the virtual absence from the exordium of the expected exoneration (i.e., the case for the innocence of the offended party) should be seen as setting up a delay in the fulfillment of genre expectations, which is designed to intensify the impact of the exoneration section when it finally arrives in 40:1–54:17.

The claim of my main thesis, which relates to the formal structure of the book of Isaiah, is that the book comprises an architectural scheme whereby corresponding blocks of prophetic material have been arranged into seven asymmetrically concentric sections. The patterns of repetition among these form-critical subunits, which almost always frame a central axis, may involve two-, three- or fourfold repetitions that combine to make up complex framework configurations. The book of Isaiah, comprising the seven concentric sections that employ this frameworking pattern, is arranged, with transitional materials (i.e., 2:6aαβ, 22; 12:1-6), into a continuous development of the themes and elements that make up the book's rhetoric of prophetic covenant disputation (hence, the title of this study). The seven main sections of the book include: an exordium, which focuses on an appeal for covenant reconciliation (1:1–2:5), two structurally analogous accusatory threats of judgment (2:6aγ-21 denouncing cultic sins; 3:1–4:1 denouncing social crimes), two structurally analogous schemes for the punishment and restoration of Zion and the nations (4:2–11:16; 13:1–39:8), an exoneration of YHWH (40:1–54:17) and a final ultimatum, which again appeals for covenant reconciliation (55:1–66:24). Perhaps as a means of lending coherence to the whole, the hierarchical branching pattern of 40:1–54:17 permutes the structural schemata of 2:6aγ-21 and 3:1–4:1; likewise, the concentric pattern of 55:1–66:24 echoes the schemata of 4:2–11:16 and 13:1–39:8.

Procedure and Methodology Used in This Study

Although the primary concern of this study is to describe the rhetorical
form of the book of Isaiah, from a procedural standpoint the unity of
the book had to be assumed as a working hypothesis and standard by
which to assess the possible contribution that its constituent parts might
make toward a coherent design.[1] Thus, those formal patterns of repetition that best coincided with the rhetorical arrangement of materials in
the book were viewed as patterns that the (implied) author(s) of the
book used to arrange the blocks of materials in the book. Form and
rhetoric were thus assumed to cohere with each another.

The arrangement of materials in the book was understood to cohere
under the rhetoric of prophetic covenant disputation. It would be mis-
taken, however, to infer from this that I am claiming that the book of
Isaiah contains no elements other than those that would be typical of a
covenant disputation (rîb-pattern). Form critics have rightly discerned
the presence of a variety of speech forms (e.g., woe oracles, judgment
speeches, salvation oracles, hymnic invocations, etc.) that would not
normally be associated with a covenant disputation form. Nevertheless,
it seemed reasonable to infer that the overall rhetoric of the book is that
of a prophetic covenant disputation, that it is the covenant disputation
that forms the basis of the book's rhetorical strategy. Hence, woe
oracles and judgment speeches may function rhetorically as threats of
punishment, while salvation oracles and hymnic invocations function as
motivating appeals, typical of the rhetoric of covenant disputation. Cor-
roboration for this thesis was found in the fact that Isaiah's exordium
(1:1–2:5) appears to be a truncated version of the biblical covenant disputation form and in the fact that an aggregate of rhetorical elements
typical of ancient Near Eastern and biblical covenant disputation forms
aligns with the rhetorical strategy of the book of Isaiah as a whole.[2] On

[1]To this end, I have endorsed J. Culler's set of conventions for the reading of
poetry as equally applicable to the reading of all literary texts: 'The primary convention is what might be called the rule of significance: read the poem as express-
ing a significant attitude to some problem concerning man and/or his relation to the
universe ... [Other important conventions are] the conventions of metaphorical
coherence—that one should attempt through semantic transformations to produce
coherence on the levels of both tenor and vehicle ... More important, however, is
the convention of thematic unity ...' (*Structuralist Poetics: Structuralism,
Linguistics and the Study of Literature* [Ithaca, NY: Cornell University Press,
1975], p. 115).

[2]Explicit references in Isaiah to YHWH's entering into disputation, sometimes
against his people (e.g., יָבוֹא בְמִשְׁפָּט יְהוָה עַמִּים לָדִין וְעֹמֵד יְהוָה לָרִיב נִצָּב in 3:13-
14aα; cf. 27:8; 45:9; 57:16), sometimes to vindicate his servant before his people

this basis, it seemed warranted to infer that the controlling set of rhetorical conventions in Isaiah was that of the prophetic covenant disputation genre.

The formal patterning of the book was assessed according to the following strategy. Each block of text, which I shall call a 'tier', was delimited on the basis of both observable similarities within the tier and dissimilarities with the context of the tier, and similar tiers were correlated with one another so as to determine any larger pattern of repetitions that might exist among them. The recognition of patterns of repetition among the tiers was based upon information concerning the presence and structural function of: (1) 'structural delineators' such as superscriptions, formulaic introductions or conclusions, and changes of person, addressee, point of view, subject matter, referent, disposition or discourse mode; (2) 'corresponding devices' such as internal allusions, cross-referencing, repetitions (of key terms, subject matter, themes, imagery, modes, type-scenes, or recognized form-critical subgenres), collocations, inclusio, paneling, frameworking, and concentric patterning; and (3) 'developmental devices' such as the development of *Leitwörter*, varied restatements of subject matter, theme, mode or scenarios, and permutations of recognizable formal structures. The less the probability that patterns and their recurrences could have come about by chance, the greater became the probability that they reflected a controlling design. As it became evident that certain patterns of repetition recurred within the book, it seemed warranted to allow the predictability of such patterns to play a role in searching for aspects of similarity among ostensibly coordinate tiers. While this procedure thus became somewhat circular, it provided a system of checks and balances between the set of criteria for determining similarity and difference among the tiers and the set of criteria for recognizing patterns of repetition among the tiers.

(49:25; 50:8) and sometimes to vindicate his people before the nations (51:22; cf. 2:4; 41:11), demonstrate both the author's awareness of the disputation form and his intention to portray YHWH in disputation with both his covenant people and the nations. These explicit examples of a strategy in Isaiah to portray YHWH in covenant disputation may lend further support to the thesis, confirmed on other grounds, that it is the genre of covenant disputation that best defines the controlling rhetorical strategy of the book.

Complex Frameworking in Isaiah

Other than at the macrostructural level (i.e., among the seven main sections of the book) and in shorter narrative reports (e.g., Isa. 6:1–9:6; 36:1–37:38), the architecture of Isaiah reflects little concern for temporal sequencing.[1] Instead, the apparently disparate arrangement of blocks of text in Isaiah invokes the readers' context sensitivities to a desire to make sense of the relationship among these blocks. Perhaps the most basic obstacle to interpreting the book of Isaiah as a whole is that of discerning the scheme by which the author(s) arranged the blocks of material that make up the main sections of the book. My primary task, then, was to discover whether it was possible to discern a recognizable pattern of arrangement among the blocks of text that make up the book of Isaiah.

For the purposes of this study of Isaiah, I proceeded under the assumption that the blocks of text or 'tiers' were indeed arranged according to recognizable patterns of repetition. The scheme of repetition patterns formed by these tiers could then be called 'tiered architecture'. An assumption that a scheme of tiered architecture is the means by which blocks of material had been arranged in Isaiah offered multiple possibilities for recognizing the controlling patterns by which the book may have been arranged. Thus, it remained an assumption of this study that the book of Isaiah had been arranged according to recognizable patterns of repetition among the tiers that comprise the book.

My search for pervasive patterns of repetition in Isaiah stemmed from a desire to discover what are the broad structural contours of the book. The binary opposition set up between tiers in a simple palistrophic pattern, for instance, is one of the most obvious uses of tier repetitions to form broad contours of structure (e.g., in Isa. 14:4b–21).[2] Indeed, the principle of concentricity is dominant in some

---

[1]On the relation of narrated time to real time, see P. Ricoeur, *Time and Narrative* (trans. K. [McLaughlin] Blamey and D. Pellauer; 3 vols.; Chicago: University of Chicago Press, 1984–1988). More in keeping with the structure of Isaiah, R. Alter describes an 'episodic narrativity' inherent in the structure of biblical poetry whereby biblical verse creates the effect of consequentiality through thematic sequencing—analogous to chronological sequencing within plot-based narrative (*The Art of Biblical Poetry* [New York: Basic Books, 1985], pp. 61, 171–72). While this principle may be at work in the arrangement of some materials in Isaiah, the controlling principle used to arrange repeated materials seems to exceed the bounds of simple juxtaposition.

[2]Cf. R.H. O'Connell, 'Isaiah xiv 4b-23: Ironic Reversal through Concentric Structure and Mythic Allusion' *VT* 38 (1988), pp. 407-18.

writings of the ancients.[1] Most likely, concentricity was thought to give to such works an aura of formal proportion and balance, but it was more than just a structuring device. It had rhetorical force in that concentricity not only serves to signal interrelationships among corresponding tiers within a concentric structure but also tends to focus the reader's attention on the axes at the center of such structures and on the interrelationships among formally correspondent tiers.

It would appear that the main sections of Isaiah were constructed according to a formal pattern of repetition that I call 'complex frameworking'. In the Isaianic structuring of materials, complex frameworking involves the use of both triadic and quadratic repetition patterns. This is merely a permutation of the binary pattern of correspondence (inclusio) that one typically finds in symmetrical concentric structures. A 'triadic frame' comprises a triple statement of a key word, phrase or thematic block in which two of the statements lie near or next to one another but are separated from the third by some major structural barrier.[2] The materials that separate the two (ostensibly) juxtaposed statements from the third statement could be viewed as the axis of an asymmetrically concentric pattern. This might appear schematically as in the following example (describing the pattern among the imperative edicts of proclamation in Isa. 40:1-11), where the double row of dots represents an ellipsis of material where the axis is to be found:

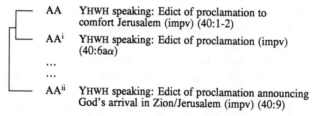

  AA YHWH speaking: Edict of proclamation to comfort Jerusalem (impv) (40:1-2)

  AAⁱ YHWH speaking: Edict of proclamation (impv) (40:6aα)

  ...
  ...

  AAⁱⁱ YHWH speaking: Edict of proclamation announcing God's arrival in Zion/Jerusalem (impv) (40:9)

Alternatively, the pattern may be inverted (as, e.g., among the repetitions of the doubled imperative forms of עוּרִי in Isa. 51:9–52:2):

---

[1] Cf. J.W. Welch (ed.), *Chiasmus in Antiquity: Structures, Analysis, Exegesis* (Hildesheim: Gerstenberg, 1981); N.W. Lund, *Chiasmus in the New Testament* (Chapel Hill: University of North Carolina, 1942).

[2] J. Muilenburg commented on Isaiah's rhetorical grouping of materials into triadic series, of which the final member was often climactic ('The Book of Isaiah: Chapters 40–66: Introduction and Exegesis', pp. 388, 389, 390-91). According to Muilenburg, such triadic patterns relate to the repetitions of particles, key words and the internal arrangement of strophes. He commented, 'the question must be raised whether this triadic organization may extend even farther. It is obvious that some of the poems seem to fall in groups' (p. 391).

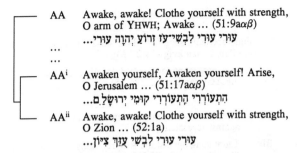

AA   Awake, awake! Clothe yourself with strength,
     O arm of YHWH; Awake ... (51:9aαβ)

     עוּרִי עוּרִי לִבְשִׁי־עֹז זְרוֹעַ יְהוָה עוּרִי...

AAⁱ Awaken yourself, Awaken yourself! Arise,
     O Jerusalem ... (51:17aαβ)

     הִתְעוֹרְרִי הִתְעוֹרְרִי קוּמִי יְרוּשָׁלִַם...

AAⁱⁱ Awake, awake! Clothe yourself with strength,
     O Zion ... (52:1a)

     עוּרִי עוּרִי לִבְשִׁי עֻזֵּךְ צִיּוֹן...

Isaiah also presents several cases of complex frameworking where
four repetitions are bifurcated by intervening material that serves as a
structural axis, as in the following example taken from Isa. 43:16-21
(where references to YHWH's past and future acts of redemption
brought about by means of water make up the fourfold frame):

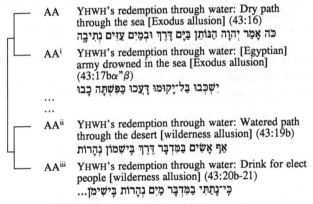

AA   YHWH's redemption through water: Dry path
      through the sea [Exodus allusion] (43:16)

      כֹּה אָמַר יְהוָה הַנּוֹתֵן בַּיָּם דָּרֶךְ וּבְמַיִם עַזִּים נְתִיבָה

AAⁱ   YHWH's redemption through water: [Egyptian]
      army drowned in the sea [Exodus allusion]
      (43:17bα"β)

      יִשְׁכְּבוּ בַּל־יָקוּמוּ דָּעֲכוּ כַּפִּשְׁתָּה כָבוּ

AAⁱⁱ YHWH's redemption through water: Watered path
      through the desert [wilderness allusion] (43:19b)

      אַף אָשִׂים בַּמִּדְבָּר דֶּרֶךְ בִּישִׁמוֹן נְהָרוֹת

AAⁱⁱⁱ YHWH's redemption through water: Drink for elect
      people [wilderness allusion] (43:20b-21)

      כִּי־נָתַתִּי בַמִּדְבָּר מַיִם נְהָרוֹת בִּישִׁימֹן...

In the present study, this fourfold repetition pattern will be designated a
'quadratic frame'.

     Throughout Isaiah these complex frames (both triadic and quadratic)
are combined to create a variety of configurations. In some instances,
one complex frame may be superimposed upon another, resulting in an
interlocking pattern. Paired triadic frames may be superimposed upon
one another in a receding inverse pattern (as, e.g., in Isa. 4:2–11:16
and 13:1–39:8), resulting in a schema such as that of the paired triadic
frames that enclose 13:1–39:8 (the outer triadic frame addressing
Babylonian interests, the inner, Assyrian interests):

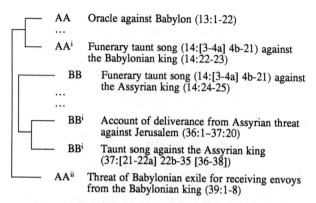

AA   Oracle against Babylon (13:1-22)
...

AA[i]   Funerary taunt song (14:[3-4a] 4b-21) against the Babylonian king (14:22-23)

BB   Funerary taunt song (14:[3-4a] 4b-21) against the Assyrian king (14:24-25)
...
...

BB[i]   Account of deliverance from Assyrian threat against Jerusalem (36:1-37:20)

BB[i]   Taunt song against the Assyrian king (37:[21-22a] 22b-35 [36-38])

AA[ii]   Threat of Babylonian exile for receiving envoys from the Babylonian king (39:1-8)

Note how the taunt song of Isa. 14:4b-21 in this pattern serves double duty, depending on which of the two alternative endings functions as the closing tier (14:22-23, addressing the song to the king of Babylon; 14:24-25, addressing it to the Assyrian king).[1]

Alternatively, as in the following schema (of Isa. 41:21–42:17), one quadratic frame (here comprising the 'AA' tiers, whose theme is YHWH's denunciation of idols/idolaters) may be superimposed upon another quadratic frame (here comprising the 'BB' tiers, whose theme is YHWH's election/summons of his warrior/servant to conquer/rule).

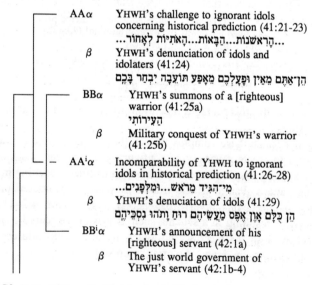

AAα   YHWH's challenge to ignorant idols concerning historical prediction (41:21-23)
...הָרִאשֹׁנוֹת...הַבָּאוֹת...הָאֹתִיּוֹת לְאָחוֹר...

β   YHWH's denunciation of idols and idolaters (41:24)
הֵן־אַתֶּם מֵאַיִן וּפָעָלְכֶם מֵאָפַע תּוֹעֵבָה יִבְחַר בָּכֶם

BBα   YHWH's summons of a [righteous] warrior (41:25a)
הַעִירוֹתִי

β   Military conquest of YHWH's warrior (41:25b)

AA[i]α   Incomparability of YHWH to ignorant idols in historical prediction (41:26-28)
...מִי־הִגִּיד מֵרֹאשׁ...וּמִלְּפָנִים...

β   YHWH's denuciation of idols (41:29)
הֵן כֻּלָּם אָוֶן אֶפֶס מַעֲשֵׂיהֶם רוּחַ וָתֹהוּ נִסְכֵּיהֶם

BB[i]α   YHWH's announcement of his [righteous] servant (42:1a)

β   The just world government of YHWH's servant (42:1b-4)

[1] Cf. R.H. O'Connell, 'Isaiah xiv 4b-23: Ironic Reversal through Concentric Structure and Mythic Allusion', pp. 417-18.

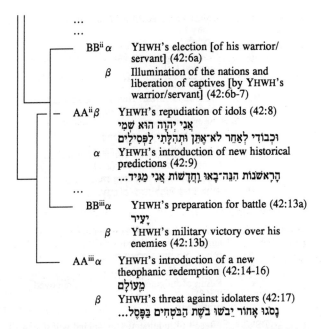

BBⁱⁱ α   YHWH's election [of his warrior/servant] (42:6a)

β   Illumination of the nations and liberation of captives [by YHWH's warrior/servant] (42:6b-7)

AAⁱⁱ β   YHWH's repudiation of idols (42:8)

אֲנִי יְהוָה הוּא שְׁמִי

וּכְבוֹדִי לְאַחֵר לֹא־אֶתֵּן וּתְהִלָּתִי לַפְּסִילִים

α   YHWH's introduction of new historical predictions (42:9)

הָרִאשֹׁנוֹת הִנֵּה־בָאוּ וַחֲדָשׁוֹת אֲנִי מַגִּיד...

BBⁱⁱⁱ α   YHWH's preparation for battle (42:13a)

יָעִיר

β   YHWH's military victory over his enemies (42:13b)

AAⁱⁱⁱ α   YHWH's introduction of a new theophanic redemption (42:14-16)

מֵעוֹלָם

β   YHWH's threat against idolaters (42:17)

נָסֹגוּ אָחוֹר יֵבֹשׁוּ בֹשֶׁת הַבֹּטְחִים בַּפָּסֶל...

Note how all the tiers in the foregoing example are bifid (two-part) in structure, a phenomenon that recurs frequently in the tiered architecture of Isaiah.

One may call the two preceding configurations 'compound frames' because they are unified configurations made up of more than one complex frame. Compound frames are, indeed, the usual context in which one finds complex (triadic or quadratic) frames in the book of Isaiah. Often in Isaiah, two triadic frames in such compound configurations are arranged inversely in pairs (as in the excerpt from Isa. 13:1–39:8) so that the imbalance resulting from the two tiers of one triadic frame appearing before the axis is counterbalanced by the two tiers of the other triadic frame appearing after the axis. The resulting compound frame may conveniently be called a 'compound inverse frame'. Thus, although the concentricity generated by the triadic frameworking in such configurations is asymmetrical, on the whole it remains balanced.

Sometimes in Isaiah (e.g., 2:6aγ-21; 3:1–4:1; or the macrostructure of chs. 40–54), a quadratic frame may be superimposed upon a triadic frame. Note again, in the following outline of 2:6aγ-21, how most tiers are essentially bifid:

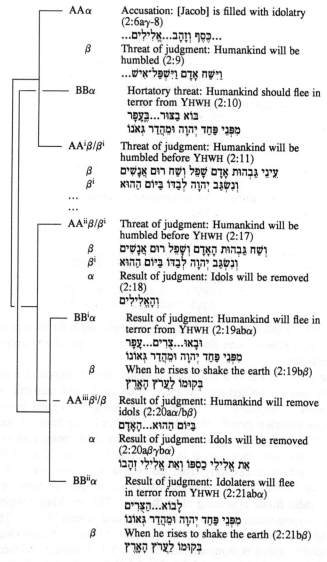

AAα	Accusation: [Jacob] is filled with idolatry (2:6aγ-8) ...אֱלִילִים...וְזָהָב...כֶּסֶף...
β	Threat of judgment: Humankind will be humbled (2:9) ...וַיִּשַּׁח אָדָם וַיִּשְׁפַּל־אִישׁ...
BBα	Hortatory threat: Humankind should flee in terror from YHWH (2:10) בּוֹא בַצּוּר...בֶּעָפָר מִפְּנֵי פַּחַד יְהוָה וּמֵהֲדַר גְּאֹנוֹ
AAⁱβ/βⁱ	Threat of judgment: Humankind will be humbled before YHWH (2:11)
β	עֵינֵי גַבְהוּת אָדָם שָׁפֵל וְשַׁח רוּם אֲנָשִׁים
βⁱ	וְנִשְׂגַּב יְהוָה לְבַדּוֹ בַּיּוֹם הַהוּא
...	
...	
AAⁱⁱβ/βⁱ	Threat of judgment: Humankind will be humbled before YHWH (2:17)
β	וְשַׁח גַּבְהוּת הָאָדָם וְשָׁפֵל רוּם אֲנָשִׁים
βⁱ	וְנִשְׂגַּב יְהוָה לְבַדּוֹ בַּיּוֹם הַהוּא
α	Result of judgment: Idols will be removed (2:18) וְהָאֱלִילִים
BBⁱα	Result of judgment: Humankind will flee in terror from YHWH (2:19abα) וּבָאוּ...צֻרִים...עָפָר מִפְּנֵי פַּחַד יְהוָה וּמֵהֲדַר גְּאוֹנוֹ
β	When he rises to shake the earth (2:19bβ) בְּקוּמוֹ לַעֲרֹץ הָאָרֶץ
AAⁱⁱⁱβⁱ/β	Result of judgment: Humankind will remove idols (2:20aα/bβ) בַּיּוֹם הַהוּא...הָאָדָם
α	Result of judgment: Idols will be removed (2:20aβγbα) אֵת אֱלִילֵי כַסְפּוֹ וְאֵת אֱלִילֵי זְהָבוֹ
BBⁱⁱα	Result of judgment: Idolaters will flee in terror from YHWH (2:21abα) לָבוֹא...הַצֻּרִים מִפְּנֵי פַּחַד יְהוָה וּמֵהֲדַר גְּאוֹנוֹ
β	When he rises to shake the earth (2:21bβ) בְּקוּמוֹ לַעֲרֹץ הָאָרֶץ

A variety of other permutations of complex frameworking may be found throughout Isaiah and elsewhere in the Hebrew Bible.[1] Indeed,

---

[1]Other examples of complex frameworking appear in Deut. 7 and 9:7–10:11 (cf. R.H. O'Connell, 'Deuteronomy vii 1-26: Asymmetrical Concentricity and the Rhetoric of Conquest', *VT* 42 [1992], pp. 248-65; idem, 'Deuteronomy ix 7–x 7,

the various permutations of complex frameworking that one encounters in Isaiah may constitute a heretofore unrecognized convention of semantic parallelism in the Hebrew Bible.

Limitations and Objectives of This Study

This study is primarily a rhetorical-critical analysis, not a form-critical nor redaction-critical analysis, of the book of Isaiah, though it will, of necessity, take account of some findings of other approaches as a basis for discerning literary subgenres and sublevels within the book.[1] An evaluation of the past contribution of such approaches to an understanding of the literary structure of Isaiah constitutes a necessary ground of departure but, of course, the nature and scope of this study forbids restating the results of previous contributions in anything but a summary fashion.

The main concern of this study is not so much with the matter of authorship as with that of literary form. Therefore, the main aim of the succeeding chapters is to demonstrate, by survey and synthesis of the book of Isaiah, what recurrent literary patterns (discernible in the arrangement of repetitions of vocabulary and thematic materials) govern the book as a whole and thereby give it unity, coherence and rhetorical emphasis. The focus is on discovering the literary form (not forms) of Isaiah with a view to discerning its rhetorical emphasis. The task will also entail explaining something of the rhetorical inter-relationships among the various sections of the book as they relate to the whole.

Corollary to the search for literary patterns in Isaiah is the question of what rhetorical function the present arrangement of materials may

10-11: Panelled Structure, Double Rehearsal and the Rhetoric of Covenant Rebuke', *VT* 42 [1992], pp. 492-509) and in Jer. 3:12-4:2.

[1]In a study that entails providing a manageable formal model for the structure of a literary work as vast and complex as the book of Isaiah, the method of analysis must necessarily be synthetic. While the ideal heuristic question to pose during the survey of the text might justifiably be: 'Who or what social groups acted at what point of time by what means for what purpose under what media conditions towards whom or what social groups and with what effect?' (so B. Wiklander, *Prophecy as Literature: A Text-Linguistic and Rhetorical Approach to Isaiah 2–4* [ConBOT, 22; Stockholm: Gleerup, 1984], p. 26 and n. 3), to represent the results of such a close reading of the whole of Isaiah would generate so unmanageable a volume of information as to complicate unnecessarily the structural model. The type of rhetoric with which I will be most concerned is that which effects persuasion or motivation (i.e., the means by which the author moves the reader toward desired ideals or actions).

have been intended to serve in the political–historical world of its (implied) author(s). These matters will involve a re-examination of the unity, coherence and emphasis of Isaiah with a view to understanding its rhetorical design. The question of rhetorical function will be addressed for each section of analysis and will be summarized for the whole book in the concluding chapter.

What is presented in this study is a proposed model of the structure of Isaiah. I shall not attempt to explain or illustrate fully the verbal and thematic correlations among all the coordinated tiers of each substructure. Instead, what is offered with the proposed structural schemata is a selection of words from the Hebrew text wherever it was thought that such would facilitate the readers' validating the suggested correlations among the tiers. A brief summary of the proposed rhetorical structure of Isaiah as a whole will conclude the study.

Chapter 1

ISAIAH 1:1–2:5: CAMEO OF A COVENANT DISPUTATION

BECAUSE OF IDOLATRY AND INJUSTICE, YHWH URGES
ZION'S CITIZENS TO BE FAITHFUL AND JUST
IN ACCORDANCE WITH ZION'S FUTURE

From the opening call for witnesses (1:2a) to the closing condemnation
of the wicked (66:24), the book of Isaiah denounces the injustice of all
who oppose YHWH and summons to future Zion all who would be
reconciled. The opening accusatory denunciations (1:2b-3, 4), which
attribute Israel's despoiled condition to punishment from YHWH for
covenant crimes, move with all the pathos of a family lawsuit.[1] In Isa.
1:18-19 and 2:2-5 one sees appeals for reconciliation that express a
response to the sense of estrangement that implicitly forms the background to the accusations of 1:2b-3, 4. Throughout Isa. 1:1–2:5, the
language and imagery emotes according to a rhetoric of covenant disputation. The rhetoric and imagery of covenant disputation continues
through the following accusatory threats of 2:6-21 and 3:1–4:1 and, for
the most part, dominates the book of Isaiah as a whole. In fact, it is one
thesis of this study that the rhetorical strategy that governs the book of

[1]Some, indeed, have reflected upon the mixture of lament and 'lawsuit' (*rîb*-
pattern) elements in the opening chapter of Isaiah. E.g., C. Westermann (*Basic
Forms of Prophetic Speech* [trans. H.C. White; Philadelphia: Westminster Press,
1967]) says that Isa. 1:2-3 equivocates between lament and lawsuit forms (pp. 202-
203), that 1:4-9 is an announcement of judgment formulated as a lament (p. 203),
that the prophetic torah of 1:10-17 is interrupted by the accusation 'your hands are
full of blood' (1:15b), that 1:18-20 is a lawsuit form (pp. 79, 199-200), that 1:21-
23 is an accusation composed as a lament (p. 203), and that 1:24-26 is an
announcement of judgment introduced with the messenger formula. Cf.
J. Vermeylen, *Du prophète Isaïe à l'apocalyptique: Isaïe, i–xxxv, miroir d'un
demi-millénaire d'expérience religieuse en Israël* (EBib; 2 vols.; Paris: Gabalda,
1977, 1978), I, pp. 42-49, 77-78; O. Kaiser, *Isaiah 1–12: A Commentary* (trans.
J. Bowden; OTL; Philadelphia: Westminster Press, 2d edn, 1983), pp. 12-13, 15-
16, 18-19, 41. It is doubtful whether either a strictly lyrical or strictly forensic
process should be understood to lay behind this exordium. What should be
observed of the language of prophetic disputation in Isa. 1:1–2:5, however, are
conventional rhetorical patterns that may be identified as summons to dispute,
accusation and ultimatum.

32   Concentricity and Continuity

Isaiah is ostensibly that of a prophetic covenant disputation. It should
come as no surprise, therefore, that the opening of Isaiah's book-length
covenant disputation (i.e., 1:1–2:5) should make numerous allusions to
Israel's founding document of covenant loyalty, the book of
Deuteronomy, and especially to that portion of Deuteronomy where the
rhetoric of covenant disputation is most evident, the Song of Moses.[1]

In the book of Isaiah, the author's main rhetorical concern seems to
lie within the sphere of the divine–human covenant. This is why the
author renders the prologue (Isa. 1:1–2:5) in the form and style of a
covenant disputation.[2] By setting up covenant morality as the fulcrum

[1]Cf. L.G. Rignell, 'Isaiah Chapter I', *ST* 11 (1957), pp. 140-58. This article
focuses on similarities between Isa. 1 and Deut. 28 and 32. It is not by coincidence
that the opening section of Isaiah and Deut. 32 share elements in common with the
covenant disputation (i.e., *rîb*) genre. On the biblical use of the covenant disputation genre, see H.B. Huffmon, 'The Covenant Lawsuit in the Prophets', *JBL* 78
(1959), pp. 285-95; J. Harvey, 'Le "Rîb-Pattern", réquisitoire prophétique sur la
rupture de l'alliance', *Bib* 43 (1962), pp. 172-96; idem, *Le plaidoyer prophétique
contre Israël après la rupture de l'alliance: Etude d'une formule littéraire de
l'Ancien Testament* (Studia, 22; Paris: Desclée de Brouwer; Montreal: Les Editions
Bellarmin, 1967); G.E. Wright, 'The Lawsuit of God: A Form-Critical Study of
Deuteronomy 32', in B.W. Anderson and W. Harrelson (eds.), *Israel's Prophetic
Heritage: Essays in Honor of James Muilenburg* (New York: Harper & Row,
1962), pp. 26-67; D.J. McCarthy, *Old Testament Covenant: A Survey of Current
Opinions* (Richmond, VA: John Knox, 1972), pp. 38-39.

Despite Kaiser's contention that Isa. 1:4-9 and 1:10-17 derive from successive
post-exilic stages of Deuteronomistic redaction (*Isaiah 1–12*, pp. 16 n. 18, 22, 27-
28), one may at least agree with Rignell that the nucleus of Deuteronomy antedates
the work of eighth-century BCE Isaiah. The pattern of formal elements in
Deuteronomy's overall literary structure seems to conform most closely to the patterns of second-millenium BCE suzerain–vassal treaties and law codes. Support for
this view may be found in G.E. Mendenhall, 'Law and Covenant in Israel and the
Ancient Near East', *BA* 17 (1954), pp. 26-46; idem, 'Covenant Forms in Israelite
Tradition', *BA* 17 (1954), pp. 50-76; idem, *Law and Covenant in Israel and the
Ancient Near East* (Pittsburgh: Biblical Colloquium, 1955); W. Moran, 'The
Ancient Near Eastern Background of the Love of God in Deuteronomy', *CBQ* 25
(1963), pp. 77-87; J.A. Thompson, 'The Significance of the Ancient Near Eastern
Treaty Pattern', *TynBul* 13 (1963), pp. 1-6; E.C. Lucas, 'Covenant, Treaty and
Prophecy', *Themelios* 8/1 (1982), pp. 19-23. For the view that the Sinai covenant
was not originally expressed in treaty form but that the treaty form of
Deuteronomy was a later (seventh-century BCE) development, see D.J. McCarthy,
*Treaty and Covenant: A Study in Form in the Ancient Oriental Documents and in
the Old Testament* (AnBib, 21; Rome: Biblical Institute Press, 1963; rev. edn,
1978); E.W. Nicholson, *Exodus and Sinai in History and Tradition* (Oxford: Basil
Blackwell, 1973). For the view that the covenant concept was not determinative for
Israel before the seventh century BCE, see G. Fohrer, *History of Israelite Religion*
(trans. D.E. Green; Nashville: Abingdon Press, 1972; London: SPCK, 1973);
R.E. Clements, *Prophecy and Tradition* (Oxford: Basil Blackwell, 1975).

[2]See A. Mattioli, 'Due schemi letterari negli oracoli d'introduzione al libro di
Isaia', *RivB* 14 (1966), pp. 345-64; S. Niditch, 'The Composition of Isaiah 1', *Bib*

of the balance, with Zion's condemnation or exaltation teetering on the scales, Isa. 1:1–2:5 sets forth the prophecy's major paradoxes. These paradoxes serve not only as adumbrations of the book's subsequent ideological tensions but are so arranged as to present a cameo of the genre and structural patterns of the book of Isaiah—with the calculated omission of one essential element of the covenant disputation.[1] Thus one can discern something of Isaiah's genre and main themes even from a delineation of Isa. 1:1–2:5.

Structural Delineation of Isaiah 1:1–2:5

When delineating literary substructures, one should not be so concerned with circumscribing only the external limits of the subunit (as

61 (1980), pp. 522-23; J.T. Willis, 'The First Pericope in the Book of Isaiah', *VT* 34 (1984), pp. 63-77. I have already referred to Rignell's study ('Isaiah Chapter I'), which demonstrates how Isa. 1 echoes, in both form and function, the covenant disputation (*rîb*-pattern) of Deut. 32. Cf. A. Condamin, 'Les chapitres I et II du livre d'Isaïe', *RB* 13 (1904), pp. 7-26.

Whereas the term 'lawsuit' presupposes a trilateral (juridical) case in which an arbiter decides between two parties, for bilateral legal cases I prefer the designation 'disputation'. In the prophetic *rîb*-oracles, one finds that, 'the harmed party seeks restitution by his own means, according to his own concept of justice. He does not ask a third party to mediate, nor does a judge issue a binding decision' (so M. de Roche, 'Yahweh's *Rîb* against Israel: A Reassessment of the So-called "Prophetic Lawsuit" in the Preexilic Prophets', *JBL* 102 [1983], p. 570). However, passages that evidence a trilateral legal procedure (e.g., Isa. 5:1-7; 41:21–42:9; 42:14–44:22), where one party appeals to an arbiter against an offender, might appropriately be called 'lawsuits'.

[1]See Fohrer, 'Jesaja 1 als Zusammenfassung der Verkündigung Jesajas', *ZAW* 74 (1962), pp. 251-68 (reprinted in *Studien zur alttestamentlichen Prophetie [1949-1965]* [BZAW, 99; Berlin: Töpelmann, 1967], pp. 148-66); H. Wildberger, *Jesaja, Kapitel 28-39* (BKAT, X/3; Neukirchen–Vluyn: Neukirchener Verlag, 1982), p. 1554; O. Loretz, *Der Prolog des Jesaja Buches (1,1-2,5)* (Ugaritologische und kolometrische Studien zum Jesaja-Buch, 1; Altenberg: CIS-Verlag, 1984), pp. 15-16. In Wildberger's objection to Fohrer's view that Isa. 1 constitutes an introductory summary of the message of the whole book of Isaiah, the former seems correct in observing that Isa. 1 lacks such essentials as the admonitions against disastrous political alliances, the appeal to the faithful and the 'messianic' hope. However, Wildberger's second objection may be allayed by observing an appeal in 1:18 and, as I shall argue, by including 2:1-5 as forming a part of Isaiah's exordium. As to the omission of disastrous alliances, there may be some hint of this in 1:2b-3, 4b though, admittedly, in the most general language (for no introductory synopsis should be expected to summarize in detail the themes that it was designed only to introduce). However, it must be conceded that the absence of the 'messianic' theme—indeed, all the themes central to the purpose of chs. 40–54—is a significant omission from the exordium of Isa. 1:1–2:5.

early form critics asserted) as with discerning the subunit's rhetorical function and relative position within the larger context. Writing and reading are both temporally linear (time-conditioned) and logically associative processes. Accordingly, in the book of Isaiah, one finds that successive literary subunits, which may be distinguished from each other on the basis of a linear process of reading through the intermittent repetitions and changes, may retroactively be associated with one another to form an interlocking web of thematic interconnections. It may be averred that such interlocking patterns in Isa. 1:1–2:5, if conforming to a regular pattern of complex frameworking, are the main determinants of structure and that these need to be described and delineated. This I shall do in the succeeding section of the chapter, but it seemed more prudent to begin by concerning myself with the function of the more obvious superscriptions of 1:1 and 2:1 and by describing their function within Isaiah's prologue.

In formal character, Isa. 1:1 is a typical prophetic superscription and stands in apposition to the material that follows.[1] Determining how much material in Isaiah it governs depends on one's view of the logical organization of the book. Some think that it introduces the whole book,[2] while others claim that it governs only chs. 1–39,[3] chs. 1–12,[4]

---

[1]Cf. G.M. Tucker, 'Prophetic Superscriptions and the Growth of a Canon' in G.W. Coats and B.O. Long (eds.), *Canon and Authority: Essays in Old Testament Religion and Theology* (Philadelphia: Fortress Press, 1977), p. 58. The superscriptions can be helpful as indicators of point of view. For instance, while the author sometimes represents the figure Isaiah as a narrative character addressing his own audience (usually the Judean king) within narrative discourse (e.g., Isa. 7; 20; 37–39), the material in the rest of the book usually constitutes oratory in which the author, as prophet, directly addresses his readers or, as messenger, relays YHWH's word by means of quotation. Never does one find extended indirect discourse, which would weaken the impression that the author is speaking directly to his people (the implied readers; cf. M. Sternberg, *The Poetics of Biblical Narrative* [ISBL; Bloomington: Indiana University Press, 1985], p. 58). Exceptionally, the author will even include a report from the first person perspective (e.g., Isa. 6:1-4, 5-7, 8-10, 11; 8:11-15, 16-17, 18; 22:14; 24:16aβ; 40:6aβ) that functionally equivocates between being a quotation of Isaiah (the character) and the words of the author—implying that Isaiah and the author are the same person. However, it is only in three superscriptions (Isa. 1:1; 2:1; 13:1) that the author's presence emerges functioning as the arranger of materials. Otherwise the author speaks through the persona of the prophet, directly addressing the readers or mediating quotations only enough to insert formulaic expressions of divine authorship (e.g., 'thus says YHWH'). Apart from these instances of first-person report, and the three superscriptions just mentioned, the strategy never varies throughout the book of Isaiah, despite abrupt shifts in chronological point of view by which 'the prophet' rhetorically demonstrates YHWH's control of history.

[2]E.g., H. Wildberger, *Jesaja, Kapitel 1–12* (BKAT, X/1; Neukirchen-Vluyn: Neukirchener Verlag, 2d edn, 1980), p. 2; Kaiser, *Isaiah 1–12*, p. 1; G. Fohrer,

or merely ch. 1.[1] It should be stressed, however, that it does not automatically follow that the superscription in 1:1 was intended to serve as the title for the whole of Isaiah (1:2–66:24) simply because the book is presented in the canon as a literary unity. The role of the superscription in 1:1 is complicated by its modified restatement in 2:1[2] and by the appearance of another (major) superscription introducing the denunciation of Babylon in 13:1.[3]

'The Origin, Composition and Tradition of Isaiah i–xxxix' (ALUOS, 3; 1961–1962), p. 6; E.J. Kissane, *The Book of Isaiah: Translated from a Critically Revised Hebrew Text with Commentary* (2 vols.; Dublin: Browne and Nolan, rev. edn, 1960), I, p. 8; Franz Delitzsch, *Biblical Commentary on the Prophecies of Isaiah* (trans. from the 3d German edn by J. Martin; 2 vols.; Edinburgh: T. & T. Clark, 1873), I, p. 72; Clements, *Isaiah 1–39* (NCB; Grand Rapids: Eerdmans, 1980), p. 29; E.J. Young, *The Book of Isaiah* (NICOT; 3 vols.; Grand Rapids: Eerdmans, 1965–1972), I, p. 27. For a concise statement of the main arguments, see M.A. Sweeney, 'Isaiah 1–4 and the Post-Exilic Understanding of the Isaianic Tradition' (PhD diss., Claremont Graduate School, 1983), pp. 94-96.
[3]R.B.Y. Scott, 'The Book of Isaiah, Chapters 1–39: Introduction and Exegesis', in G.A. Buttrick et al. (eds.), *The Interpreter's Bible* (12 vols.; Nashville: Abingdon Press, 1956), V, p. 165. This view may find support in the fact that all the kings mentioned in the date formula of 1:1 are explicitly mentioned within chs. 1–39: Uzziah in 6:1; Ahaz, Jotham and Uzziah in 7:1; Ahaz in 7:2, 3, 10, 12 and 14:28; and Hezekiah throughout chs. 36–39. Chapters 40–66 contain no such references to Judean monarchs.
[4]E.g., B. Duhm, *Das Buch Jesaia übersetzt und erklärt* (HKAT, 3/1; Göttingen: Vandenhoeck & Ruprecht, 4th [repr.] edn, 1922), p. 23; K. Marti, *Das Buch Jesaja* (KHAT, 10; Tübingen: Mohr, 1900), p. 1; J. Skinner, *The Book of the Prophet Isaiah, Chapters I–XXXIX* (CBSC; Cambridge: Cambridge University Press, rev. edn, 1905), p. 1; I.W. Slotki, *Isaiah* (Soncino Books of the Bible; London: Soncino, 1949), p. 1; G.B. Gray, *A Critical and Exegetical Commentary on the Book of Isaiah I–XXVII* (ICC; Edinburgh: T. & T. Clark, 1912), p. 1; O. Procksch, *Jesaia I* (KAT, IX/1; Leipzig: Deichert, 1930), p. 29 (though he includes chs. 28–35).
[1]E.g., Wildberger, *Jesaja, Kapitel 1-12*, p. 6; Vermeylen, I, p. 41, n. 4. This view finds support in the introduction of a new superscription at 2:1. Cf. Sweeney, (PhD diss.), pp. 97-98.
[2]On the relation of the superscription in 2:1 to that in 1:1, see Sweeney (PhD diss.), pp. 98-100. Sweeney argues that 2:1 governs chs. 2–4. In support of the unity of 2–4, he cites Delitzsch, I, p. 110; Skinner, pp. 12-13; Slotki, p. 9; Duhm, p. 36. Cf. also Sweeney (PhD diss.), pp. 315-17. However, P.R. Ackroyd has argued that the superscription in 2:1 applies only to 2:2-4 ('A Note on Isaiah 2:1', ZAW 75 [1963], pp. 320-21; cf. also R. Rendtorff, 'Zur Komposition des Buches Jesaja', VT 34 [1984], p. 305 n. 32, in support of Ackroyd). This seems closer to the actual state of things, though it may be argued that 2:1 has resumptive force in relation to 1:1.
[3]The superscription in Isa. 13:1 may serve to introduce not simply the oracles against Babylon and its king in chs. 13 and 14, the first two of a series of oracles against the nations (as Sweeney argues for chs. 13-23, [PhD diss.], pp. 97-98), but all the materials within chs. 13-39. This is supported by the fact that prophetic oracles concerning Babylon serve to frame this section (cf. chs. 13-14 and 39),

At the very least, the superscription of 1:1 governs the material from 1:2 until the second superscription in 2:1, delimiting the material for the first section to that contained within 1:2-31. However, there is good reason for coordinating the superscription in 2:1 with that in 1:1, so that 2:1 assumes a resumptive force.[1] Apart from the difference of the roster of Judean kings, the complementarity of the two superscriptions is plainly evident:

a	חֲזוֹן
b	יְשַׁעְיָהוּ בֶן־אָמוֹץ
c	אֲשֶׁר חָזָה
d	עַל־יְהוּדָה וִירוּשָׁלָ͏ִם
e	(1:1) בִּימֵי עֻזִּיָּהוּ יוֹתָם אָחָז יְחִזְקִיָּהוּ מַלְכֵי יְהוּדָה:
aⁱ	הַדָּבָר
cⁱ	אֲשֶׁר חָזָה
bⁱ	יְשַׁעְיָהוּ בֶן־אָמוֹץ
dⁱ	(2:1) עַל־יְהוּדָה וִירוּשָׁלָ͏ִם

In the case of Isa. 2:1, the resumptive repetition of formulae from 1:1 has the effect both of highlighting 2:2-5 against the background of materials subsumed under the first superscription (1:2-31) and of showing that the author's ultimate vision/word for Judah/Jerusalem is less one of punishment (1:2-31) than one of final exaltation (2:2-5).

Many take Isa. 1:18-20 to be a discrete unit, reading it as the conclusion to the preceding section (1:2-17), which contrasts pretentious

thus delineating it as a separate entity. Moreover, it seems that 13:1, as a superscription governing chs. 13–39, was intended to serve as the resumptive marker of a rhetorical substructure within the whole of Isaiah. It introduces a section that has the same general concern for the fate of Jerusalem as had the superscriptions of 1:1 and 2:1. Not only do the songs of Zion's exaltation (e.g., 24:21-23; 25:6-8; 26; 27:2-11; 30:19-26; 32–33; 35) form significant part of chs. 13–39, but the concern with denouncing foreign nations in chs. 1–39 grows out of the strategy to exalt Jerusalem, after punishment, as the pinnacle of world rule and religion.

[1] Various rhetorical functions for the resumptive force of 'framing repetition' have been observed in biblical narrative by S. Talmon ('The Presentation of Synchroneity and Simultaneity in Biblical Narrative', in J. Heinemann and S. Werses (eds.), *Studies in Hebrew Narrative Art through the Ages* [ScrHier, 27; Jerusalem: Magnes, 1978], pp. 9-26) and B.O. Long ('Framing Repetitions in Biblical Historiography', *JBL* 106 [1987], pp. 385-99). Resumptive repetitions may indicate the synchroneity of successively narrated events, mark a gap-filling analepsis (i.e., flashback), introduce a commentarial excursus (i.e., digression) that didactically converges story time and narrating time. However, such functions as relate narrating time to time in the story world do not operate where tiered architectural design nullifies the temporal sequentiality conventionally associated with plot-based narrative.

cultic ritual with true moral righteousness.[1] Both the appeal and threat contained in 1:18-20 spring from a situation of apostasy, which is implied also by the accusations of the previous context (1:2b-3, 4, 11-15). What is presented in these verses, however, seems to commence a new rhetorical departure within the exordium. Indeed, Isa. 1:18-20 may be seen to have two different connections, though its main rhetorical function seems to lie in the way that these verses cohere with the section that follows (1:21–2:5). Isa. 1:18–2:5, read as the sequel to 1:1-17, sets forth an appeal to the citizens of Zion to join with all who reconcile to YHWH and who not only escape the judgment against apostates but will enjoy the benefit of citizenship in future Zion. Isaiah 1:18 seems to set forth YHWH's invitation to negotiate a reconciliation, while vv. 19 and 20 present, alternatively, either an offer of absolution or a threat of destruction.[2]

For several reasons, the limits of Isaiah's exordium probably should not extend beyond Isa. 2:5. First, Isa. 2:6a$\alpha\beta$ marks a sharp turn in stance from what precedes. It is, in fact, an apostrophe.[3] For the first

---

[1]Among those who view Isa. 1:18-20 as the conclusion to the preceding section (1:10-17), is J.N. Oswalt, *The Book of Isaiah, Chapters 1-39* (NICOT; Grand Rapids: Eerdmans, 1986), pp. 100-101. While supporting this connection, some think that 1:18-20 is a later addition, e.g., W.L. Holladay, *Isaiah: Scroll of a Prophetic Heritage* (Grand Rapids: Eerdmans, 1978), p. 7; Clements, *Isaiah 1-39*, p. 34; Kaiser, *Isaiah 1-12*, pp. 36-38.

[2]Westermann described Isa. 1:18-20 as a judgment-speech unit in which an introductory announcement (1:18) is followed by an accusation (1:19-20) (p. 79). Isa. 1:18 is not really an announcement, however, but an invitation to negotiate an agreement (note the cohortative; cf. 2:3a$\beta\gamma$, 5). But just what that negotiation entails depends on one's interpretation of 1:19, 20, and this has always been a matter of controversy. If 1:19-20 constitutes an accusation, as Westermann suggests, then the parallel cola in 1:18 would need to be read as rhetorical questions: 'If your sins are like scarlet, are they white like snow? If they are red like crimson, are they like wool?' (so also Holladay, p. 92; Kaiser, *Isaiah 1-12*, p. 36). On the other hand, it may be preferable to understand 1:18b not as the announcement of an accusation but as an offer of absolution for the offenses described in 1:2b-4, 11-15. It is Zion's alternative responses to this offer (1:19a, 20a) that deserve the alternative consequences of either blessing or destruction (1:19b, 20b). In such a case, 1:18b presents parallel offers of purification, each introduced by a concessive clause: 'Though your sins are like scarlet, they can become as white as snow; though they are as red as crimson, they can become like wool' (so Oswalt, p. 100). Thus, the offers of purification in 1:18b complement the offer of restored blessing in 1:19. Coincidentally, the latter reading better conforms to a complex frameworking pattern in Isa. 1:1–2:5.

[3]An 'apostrophe', according to T.O. Sloan, is 'a turning from one's immediate audience to address another, who may be present only in the imagination' (T.O. Sloan and C. Perelman, 'Rhetoric', in M.J. Adler, et al. [eds.], *The New Encyclopaedia Britannica* [30 vols.; Chicago: Encyclopaedia Britannica, 1982], XV, p. 799).

time, the author addresses YHWH directly: 'but/surely [כִּי] you have forsaken your people, the house of Jacob'. This shift is strategic not only because it is so rare in the book of Isaiah for the author to address YHWH in direct speech but because, in Isaiah, the author's direct address of YHWH is dedicated to enveloping the book structurally and, thereby, to conditioning its rhetorical stance.[1]

Second, after the turn of stance in 2:6aαβ, one finds in 2:6aγ-21 a prolonged series of accusations and threats relating to idolatry. Such a prolonged and negative concern with cultic apostasy breaks from the balance of themes and moods represented in 1:1–2:5, which both alternates between concern with ritual impurity and social injustice and modulates between negative accusations and threats and positive offers of exaltation. Indeed, the balance between prolonged concern with cultic apostasy in Isa. 2:6aγ-21 and with social injustice in 3:1–4:1 reflects the balance between the more cursory concern about forms of apostasy relating to cult and social justice in Isa. 1:2b-3, 4, 11-15 and 21-23.

Covenant Disputation Pattern and Complex Frameworking in Isaiah 1:1–2:5

In most respects, Isa. 1:1–2:5 conforms to the genre qualifications of the covenant disputation, which is evidenced in both the Hebrew Bible and ancient Near Eastern texts.[2] Recognition of the *rîb*-form began

---

[1]Compare the direct address of YHWH in Isa. 2:6-8, the prophet's acknowledgement of Zion's guilt, to its structural complement in the closing petitions and confessions (63:15–64:11). The closing prayer rounds off the form of Isaiah and marks a transition to the dénouement (65:8–66:24), which echoes the very themes and terminology that opened the prophecy (1:1–2:5). For a list of key terms and themes common to Isa. 1 and 65–66, see R. Lack, *La symbolique du livre d'Isaïe: Essai sur l'image littéraire comme élément de structuration* (AnBib, 59; Rome: Biblical Institute Press, 1973), pp. 139-41.

[2]There has been much dispute over the origin, genre and function of the biblical covenant disputation, with the most recent contributions arguing for a distinction between the *rîb*-pattern (as a prophetic genre portraying bilateral disputes) and the juridical lawsuit (which portrays a trilateral process wherein the offended party appeals to an arbiter against the offender). Cf. E. Würthwein, 'Der Ursprung der prophetischen Gerichtsrede', *ZTK* 49 (1952), pp. 1-16 (reprinted in *Wort und Existenz: Studien zum Alten Testament* [Göttingen: Vandenhoeck & Ruprecht, 1970], pp. 111-26); F. Hesse, 'Wurzelt die prophetische Gerichtsrede im israelitischen Kult?', *ZAW* 65 (1953), pp. 45-53; B. Gemser, 'The *Rîb*- or Controversy-Pattern in Hebrew Mentality', in M. Noth and D.W. Thomas (eds.), *Wisdom in Israel and in the Ancient Near East* (Festschrift H.H. Rowley; VTSup, 3; Leiden: Brill, 1955), pp. 120-37; Huffmon; Wright; Harvey, 'Le "Rîb-Pattern"'; idem, *Le plaidoyer prophétique contre Israël après la rupture de l'alliance*;

with H. Gunkel and J. Begrich.[1] Their description of the basic *Gattung* of the *Gerichtsrede* was later outlined by Huffmon as follows:

I. A description of the scene of judgment
II. The speech of the plaintiff
   A. Heaven and earth are appointed judges
   B. Summons to the defendant (or judges)
   C. Address in the second person to defendant
     1. Accusation in question form to the defendant
     2. Refutation of the defendant's possible arguments
     3. Specific indictment[2]

A. Bentzen concurred that this *rîb*-form was at work in such biblical passages as Isa. 1:2-3, 18-20; 3:12-15; Mic. 6:1-8; and Jer. 2:4-9, 10-13.[3] Yet it should be pointed out that in early form analyses, such as those of Gunkel–Begrich and Bentzen, Isaiah 1 was customarily fragmented into a series of 'speech forms'.[4] In a similar way, Harvey, in his comparative analysis of biblical and extrabiblical patterns of the *rîb*-structure, found it necessary to segment Isaiah's prologue (though not Mic. 6:1-8) into disparate sections, which he categorized as follows:

[1] H. Gunkel and J. Begrich, *Einleitung in die Psalmen: Die Gattungen der religiösen Lyrik Israels* (Göttingen: Vandenhoeck & Ruprecht, 1933), pp. 329-81.

[2] Huffmon, p. 285. Cf. Gunkel–Begrich, p. 329. Wright suggests that another section be appended to this outline: 4. 'The verdict or sentence of the heavenly Judge' (p. 43).

[3] A. Bentzen, *Introduction to the Old Testament* (2 vols.; Copenhagen: Gad, 1948, 1949), I, pp. 198-99. Huffmon (pp. 286-89) expanded the roster to include other passages that open with a summons to the elements of nature (i.e., Deut. 32 and Ps. 50).

[4] See Bentzen, I, pp. 199-200. No doubt this segmentation resulted from the axiom of form criticism, which then assumed an oral background for such forms, that the original prophetic speeches were terse, independent sayings. Cf. Westermann, p. 24.

		Isaiah	Micah
I:	Introduction (appel à l'attention, appel au ciel et à la terre)	1:2a, 10	6:1-2
II:	Interrogatoire (et première accusation implicite)	1:11-12	6:3
III:	Réquisitoire (déclaration de la faute, qui a rompu l'alliance; rappel des bienfaits de Yahweh et des ingratitudes d'Israël)	1:2b-3, 15aγ	6:4-5
IV:	Référence à la vanité des compensations rituelles (ou des cultes étrangers)	1:13-15aαβ	6:6-7
V:	Déclaration de culpabilité et menaces de destruction totale		
ou			
V:	Avertissement, déterminant le changement de conduite exigé par Yahweh	1:16-20	6:8[1]

There is no accounting in this analysis for Isa. 1:4, 5a, 5b-6, 7-9, much less for 1:21-27, 28-31; 2:2, 3a, 3b-4, 5. Indeed, of the five biblical passages from which Harvey generates his *rîb*-pattern, his model conforms fully only to Mic. 6:1-8.[2]

Although Harvey proposed two distinct forms of the *rîb*-pattern, one used for condemnation (*rîb à condamnation*) and the other for warning (*rîb à avertissement*), it may be argued that what one has in these varying samples is a single genre whose exemplars vary in form according to the rhetorical strategy of their authors.[3] The design of the covenant disputation genre, whether in biblical or extrabiblical settings,

[1]Adapted from Harvey, 'Le "Rîb-Pattern"', p. 178.

[2]Using the same five headings, Harvey segments the other three passages (Deut. 32; Ps. 50; Jer. 2:5-37) as follows ('Le "Rîb-Pattern"', p. 178):

		Deuteronomy	Psalm	Jeremiah
I:	Introduction	32:1-2	50:1-7a	2:12
II:	Interrogatoire	32:6	50:16b	2:5-6
III:	Réquisitoire	32:7-14, 15-18	50:17-20, 21, [7b, 8-13]	2:7-13, 14-19 20-28, 29-30
IV:	Référence à la vanité des compensations rituelles	32:16-17	[50:8-13]	2:26-28
V:	Déclaration de culpabilité et menaces de destruction totale	32:19-25	50:22-23	2:31-37
ou				
V:	Avertissement, déterminant le changement de conduite exigé par Yahweh		[50:14-15]	

There is no accounting here for Deut. 32:3-5, 26-43; Ps. 50:16a; or Jer. 2:4 (though the latter suits category I. Introduction).

[3]Harvey, 'Le "Rîb-Pattern"', p. 178.

seems to urge the accused to be reinstated to the terms of the covenant whether the urging was made explicit through appeals or implied in the response that threats of destruction were intended to engender. The purpose is invariably to elicit covenant reconciliation from an apostatizing vassal—whether through appeals, warnings or the rhetorical threat of certain 'irrevocable' destruction. From among several known ancient Near Eastern treaties, Harvey cites two examples of a *Rîb à condamnation*: the Assyrian treaty from Tukulti-Ninurta I (1244–1208 BCE) to the Kassite Kashtiliash IV (1242–1235 BCE) and a treaty from Yarîm-Lim of Mari to Yashub-Yahad, king of Dir (ca. 1700 BCE).[1] As exemplars of the *Rîb à avertissement*, Harvey cites four documents: a letter from King Muwatillish of Hatti (1320–1294 BCE) to a subject Milavata, a disputation against Madduwattash (ca. 1200 BCE), a treaty from a Hittite king to Mita of Pahhawa (ca. 1200 BCE), and a Cappadocian text from King Anum-Hirbi of Mama to King Warshama of Kanish (nineteenth century BCE).[2]

[1]Harvey, 'Le "Rîb-Pattern"', pp. 180-83 and 183-84, respectively. On the use/adaptation of the *rîb*-genre within the Epic of Tukulti-Ninurta I (i.e., especially in columns IIA 13'-24', and D obv 9-18-Gap-IIIA 1'-20'), see P.B. Machinist, 'The Epic of Tukulti-Ninurta I: A Study in Middle Assyrian Literature' (PhD diss., Yale University, 1978), pp. 40, 76-79, 86-91, 215-19, and 247-48. He outlines IIA 13'-24' as a covenant disputation form that parallels the form of the international suzerain–vassal treaty on which it was based:

(1)	*13'-14'*	Tukulti-Ninurta's plea to Shamash of his faithfulness to the treaty [= Historical prologue]
(2)	*15'-16'*	Historical reminder of the making of the treaty [= Historical prologue]
(3)	*17'-18'*	Praise of Shamash as the vigilant overseer of the treaty [= List of divine witnesses and guarantors]
(4)	*19'-21'*	Indictment of Kashtiliash for violating the treaty [= Treaty stipulations]
(5)	*22'-24'*	Call on Shamash for battle that will give victory to the upholder of the treaty and defeat to the violator [= Treaty sanctions: curses and blessings]

The form of the segment contained in columns D obv 9-18-Gap-IIIA 1'-20', Machinist gives as follows:

(1)	*IIIA 1'-8'*	Review of Kashtiliash's treaty violations
(2)	*IIIA 9'-10'*	Appeal to Shamash against Kashtiliash for his crimes
(3)	*IIIA 11'-12'*	Tukulti-Ninurta's defense of his own treaty loyalty with examples of Assyrian goodwill to the Kassites
(4)	*IIIA 13'-20'*	Call for judgment against Kashtiliash by the ordeal of battle

Thus, the aggregate of elements in this work's covenant disputation genre would include: (1) accusation against the offender: (a) declaration of violations, (b) declaration of culpability; (2) exoneration of the offended: (a) claim of initiating the covenant and of loyalty to the covenant, (b) claim of the right to vindication by combat; and (3) ultimatum: threat of total destruction.

[2]Harvey, 'Le "Rîb-Pattern"', pp. 186-88.

If one were to arrange the elements of Isa. 1:1–2:5 according to the aggregate of *rîb*-genre variables represented in the aforementioned biblical and ancient Near Eastern texts, one might arrive at the following formal analysis of Isaiah's exordium:

I.	Summons to dispute	
	Call of covenant witnesses[1]	1:2a
	Call to attention of accused	1:10
II.	Accusation against the offender	
	Declaration of obligations/interrogation	1:5a
	Declaration of violations	1:2b-3, 4 [21-23]
	Declaration of culpability	
	Rejection of ritual compensation	1:11-15
III.	Exoneration of the offended	
	A. Covenant innocence	
	1. Voluntary initiation of the covenant	
	2. Loyalty to the covenant	
	Recount of past benefits	
	Present offer of reinstatement	
	B. Right to vindication	
	Trial by combat	
IV.	Ultimatum	
	A. Threat	
	Repeal of covenant benefits	
	Continued/partial/total destruction	1:20 [24-25] 28-31
	B. Appeal	
	1. Appeal proper	1:18a; 2:3a, 5
	2. Motivation	
	Description of present distresses	1:5b-6, 7-9
	Renewal of covenant benefits	1:18b-19 [26-27];
		2:2, 3b-4
	3. Condition	
	Terms of reinstatement/reparations	1:16-17

[1]Some have inferred that this reference to 'heaven and earth' illustrates a mythopoeic fiction of personified natural elements functioning as covenant witnesses or executors (not judges) among YHWH's divine entourage. Cf. H.W. Robinson, 'The Council of Yahweh', *JTS* 45 (1944), pp. 151-55; F.M. Cross, 'The Council of Yahweh in Second Isaiah', *JNES* 12 (1953), pp. 274-77. Huffmon describes a covenant-forensic function for such language and couples this with the ancient Near Eastern milieu of international law (pp. 285-95; so also Harvey, 'Le "Rîb-Pattern"', pp. 180-96). However, note Daniels's contention that the biblical appeal to heaven and earth is not elsewhere exemplified in ancient Near Eastern treaties (pp. 355-59). In biblical covenant and covenant disputation, however, 'heaven and earth' probably do not represent hypostatic witnesses of the covenant; rather, they merely form, through parallelism, a metonymical (realm-for-inhabitants) merismus signaling all inhabitants of heaven and earth—ostensibly, all who had witnessed the inauguration of YHWH's covenant with Israel (cf. Deut. 30:19; 31:28; 32:1).

Although Isa. 1:1–2:5 conforms to the covenant disputation pattern evident in ancient Near Eastern and other Old Testament contexts, one significant formal component is missing, namely, the exoneration of the offended party. The rhetorical strategy underlying this omission will be discussed below. My attention for the moment, however, is on the insight that one may gain from observing the conformity of Isa. 1:1–2:5 to the covenant disputation pattern.

Each of the three accusations, in Isa. 1:2b-3, 4, and 11-15, and the three invitations, in 1:18a, 2:3a, and 5, forms a separate triadic frame. The four descriptions of destruction, comprising two descriptions of present distress (1:5b-6, 7-9) and two threats of total destruction (1:20, 28-31), form one quadratic frame. This quadratic frame interlocks structurally with each of the previously mentioned triadic frames so as to form a single compound framework comprising three complex frames. The two superscriptions (1:1; 2:1), four structural insets (1:2a, 5a, 10, 21-27), and the main axis (1:16-17) serve both to delimit and bridge the tiers of this compound framework. The entire construction, both formally and rhetorically, serves as an expositional cameo for the main sections of the book of Isaiah that follow. Its schema may be outlined as follows:

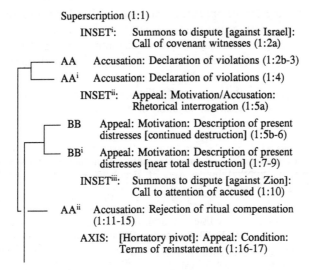

Superscription (1:1)

    INSET^i: Summons to dispute [against Israel]:
                  Call of covenant witnesses (1:2a)

  AA   Accusation: Declaration of violations (1:2b-3)
  AA^i Accusation: Declaration of violations (1:4)

    INSET^{ii}:   Appeal: Motivation/Accusation:
                  Rhetorical interrogation (1:5a)

  BB   Appeal: Motivation: Description of present
              distresses [continued destruction] (1:5b-6)
  BB^i Appeal: Motivation: Description of present
              distresses [near total destruction] (1:7-9)

    INSET^{iii}: Summons to dispute [against Zion]:
                  Call to attention of accused (1:10)

  AA^{ii} Accusation: Rejection of ritual compensation
              (1:11-15)

    AXIS: [Hortatory pivot]: Appeal: Condition:
               Terms of reinstatement (1:16-17)

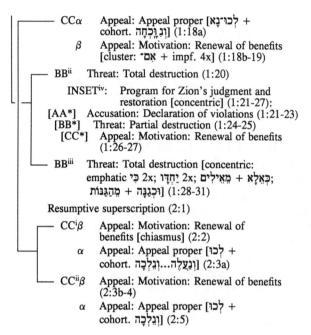

In the following outline appears a translation of Isaiah's exordium in which matching tiers have been similarly labeled and aligned in columns according to the pattern of complex frameworking presented in the preceding schema. Hebrew words thought to be rhetorically significant are given in square brackets though, in Isaiah's exordium, key word collocations among corresponding tiers are less determinative of the form than the rhetorical function of each tier within a covenant disputation.

Superscription (1:1)

The vision that Isaiah ben-Amoz saw concerning Judah and Jerusalem [עַל־יְהוּדָה וִירוּשָׁלָ͏ִם] in the days of Uzziah, Jotham, Ahaz, and Hezekiah the kings of Judah:

INSET[i]:   Hear [שִׁמְעוּ], O heavens,
              and listen [וְהַאֲזִינִי], O earth!
              For YHWH has spoken: (1:2a)

AA   'Though I have raised and brought up children
            they have rebelled against me.
      The ox may know its owner,
         and the ass its master's manger,
      but Israel does not know;
         my people do not understand'. (1:2b-3)

AA[i]   Woe [הוֹי], sinful nation,
         people weighed down with guilt,
         race of evildoers,
             corrupt children!
         They have forsaken [עָזְבוּ] YHWH,
             spurned the Holy One of Israel [קְדוֹשׁ יִשְׂרָאֵל],
             turned [נָזֹרוּ] [their] back! (1:4)

    INSET[ii]:   Why would you be beaten [תֻכּוּ] further
                 that you persist in rebellion? (1:5a)

  BB   The whole head [כָּל־רֹאשׁ] is injured,
             the whole heart faint.
         From the sole of the foot to the head [וְעַד־רֹאשׁ]
             there is no soundness therein.
         Wound, and welt, and open cut [וּמַכָּה טְרִיָּה]
             not compressed [לֹא־זֹרוּ], nor bandanged,
             nor moistened with oil. (1:5b-6)

  BB[i]   Your country is a wasteland [שְׁמָמָה],
             your cities burned with fire!
         Your land, aliens [זָרִים] devour it in front of you!
             A wasteland [וּשְׁמָמָה], like the upheaval at [Sodom]![1]
         The daughter of Zion is left [וְנוֹתְרָה]
             like a shelter in a vineyard,
         like a hut in a melon field,
             like a city left preserved [נְצוּרָה]!
         Unless Warrior YHWH had left [הוֹתִיר] us a remnant
             we would have become like Sodom [כִּסְדֹם],
             we would have resembled Gomorrah [לַעֲמֹרָה]. (1:7-9)

    INSET[iii]:   Hear [שִׁמְעוּ] the word of YHWH,
                   O rulers of Sodom [קְצִינֵי סְדֹם];
                 Listen [הַאֲזִינוּ] to the law of our god,
                   O people of Gomorrah [עַם עֲמֹרָה]! (1:10)

AA[ii]   'What is the abundance of your sacrifices to me?'
             says YHWH.
         'I am sated with offerings of rams
             and the fat of well-fed animals;
         with the blood of bulls, lambs, and goats
             I have no pleasure!
         When you come to see my face
             who has required this from your hand—
             this trampling of my courts?

[1]The MT has זָרִים, a possible dittography from the preceding colon. Given formal similarity between זרים and סדום, emendation to the latter seems warranted because elsewhere מַהְפֵּכָה ('overthrow, upheaval') is used only with reference to סְדֹם וַעֲמֹרָה (Isa. 13:19; Deut. 29:22; Amos 4:11; Jer. 49:18; 50:40) and because both סְדֹם and עֲמֹרָה are repeated in this context (1:9b, 10). Moreover, the emendation heightens the emotive effect that results from linking the 'description of [Zion's] present distresses' with those of an archetypal unholy city.

Stop bringing the worthless offering;
    incense, it offends me!
New moon [חֹדֶשׁ] and Sabbath, calling convocations—
    I cannot stand the assembly of solemn iniquity!
Your new moons [חָדְשֵׁיכֶם] and appointed feasts
    I hate!
They have become for me a burden
    I am weary of bearing.
When you spread out your hands
    I will turn my eyes from you;
even if you increase prayer
    I am not listening—
    your hands are full of blood! (1:11-15)

AXIS: [Hortatory joint] (1:16-17)
          'Wash and cleanse yourselves;
            remove [הָסִירוּ] from my sight
            the evil [רֹעַ] of your deeds [מַעַלְלֵיכֶם];
          cease from evil [חִדְלוּ הָרֵעַ],
            learn what is right;
          seek justice [מִשְׁפָּט],
            set oppression straight;
          defend the fatherless [שִׁפְטוּ יָתוֹם],
            contend for the widow [רִיבוּ אַלְמָנָה].

CCα   'Come now [לְכוּ־נָא], let us negotiate [וְנִוָּכְחָה]',
        says YHWH [יֹאמַר יְהוָה]. (1:18a)

   β   'Though [אִם־] your sins are like scarlet
        they can be as white as snow;
      though [אִם־] they are as red as crimson
        they can be like wool.
      if [אִם־] you are willing and obey
        you may [continue to] eat [תֹּאכֵלוּ] the good of the land,
      (1:18b-19)

BB^ii   but if [וְאִם־] you resist and rebel
        you will be eaten [תְּאֻכְּלוּ] by the sword',
        for the mouth of YHWH has spoken [יְהוָה דִּבֵּר]. (1:20)

INSET^iv: [concentric] (1:21-27):
[AA*]   A   a   How the faithful city [קִרְיָה נֶאֱמָנָה] has become
               a harlot!
            b   She was filled with justice [מִשְׁפָּט],
            b^i   righteousness [צֶדֶק] resided within her—
          a^i   but now murderers! (1:21)
        B   Your silver has become dross [לְסִיגִים],
            your wine is dilluted with water. (1:22)
          C   Your rulers are rebels,
            friends of thieves;
           they all love a bribe
            and pursue gifts. (1:23a)

D   They grant no justice [לֹא יִשְׁפֹּטוּ] to the fatherless
    [יָתוֹם];
    the widow's case [רִיב אַלְמָנָה] never gets to them.
    (1:23b)

[BB*]   Axis: Therefore the Lord, Warrior YHWH
                      [יְהוָה צְבָאוֹת],
                      the Mighty One of Israel [אֲבִיר יִשְׂרָאֵל],
                      declares: (1:24a)

        Dⁱ 'Woe [הוֹי]! I will get relief from my foes
            and avenge myself on my enemies! (1:24b)
      Bⁱ I will turn [וְאָשִׁיבָה] my hand against you;
          I will utterly purge your dross [סִיגָיִךְ]
          and remove [וְאָסִירָה] your alloy! (1:25)
[CC*]   Cⁱ Then I will restore [וְאָשִׁיבָה] your judges [שֹׁפְטַיִךְ]
            and your counselors as at the beginning (1:26a)
      Aⁱ Afterward you will be called the city of righteousness
          [עִיר הַצֶּדֶק],
          the faithful city [קִרְיָה נֶאֱמָנָה]. (1:26b)
          Zion [צִיּוֹן] will be redeemed with justice [בְּמִשְׁפָּט],
          her repentant [וְשָׁבֶיהָ] with righteousness [בִּצְדָקָה].
          (1:27)

BBⁱⁱⁱ   [concentric] (1:28-31):
      A   But transgressors and sinners will be broken together
          [יַחְדָּו],
          and apostates from YHWH will expire. (1:28)
        B   You will certainly become ashamed [כִּי יֵבֹשׁוּ]
            of the sacred oaks [מֵאֵילִים]
            in which you delighted, (1:29a)
          C   and you will be disgraced by the gardens [מֵהַגַּנּוֹת]
              that you chose. (1:29b)
        Bⁱ You will certainly become [כִּי תִהְיוּ] like an oak
            [כְּאֵלָה] with withered leaves [עָלֶהָ] (1:30a)
          Cⁱ and like a garden [וּכְגַנָּה] with no water. (1:30b)
      Aⁱ The mighty man will become kindling, and his work
          a spark;
          both of them will burn together [יַחְדָּו]
          with no one to extinguish'. (1:31)

Resumption of superscription (2:1)
    The matter that Isaiah son of Amoz saw concerning Judah and
Jerusalem [עַל־יְהוּדָה וִירוּשָׁלָ͏ִם]:

CCⁱβ   [chiasmus?] (2:2):

In the last days [וְהָיָה בְּאַחֲרִית הַיָּמִים]:

    A   the mountain of YHWH's temple [הַר בֵּית־יְהוָה] will be established

       B   as the chief among the mountains [בְּרֹאשׁ הֶהָרִים];

       Bⁱ it will be more elevated than the hills

       Aⁱ so that all the nations [כָּל־הַגּוֹיִם] will flow [וְנָהֲרוּ] to it.

    α   Then many peoples [עַמִּים רַבִּים] will come and say:
'Come [לְכוּ], let us go up [וְנַעֲלֶה] to the mountain of YHWH [אֶל־הַר־יְהוָה],

to the temple of Jacob's god [אֶל־בֵּית אֱלֹהֵי יַעֲקֹב]

that he may teach us his ways,

so that we may walk [וְנֵלְכָה] in his paths'. (2:3a)

CCⁱⁱβ   For [כִּי] the law will go forth from Zion [מִצִּיּוֹן],
and the word of YHWH [וּדְבַר־יְהוָה] from Jerusalem [מִירוּשָׁלָ͏ִם];

it will judge [וְשָׁפַט] between the nations [הַגּוֹיִם]
and will negotiate [וְהוֹכִיחַ] for many peoples [לְעַמִּים רַבִּים].

They will forge their swords [חַרְבוֹתָם] into plowshares
and their spears into pruning hooks.

Nation will not lift up sword against nation
[לֹא־יִשָּׂא גוֹי אֶל־גּוֹי חֶרֶב],

and never again will they learn [וְלֹא־יִלְמְדוּ עוֹד] warfare. (2:3b-4)

    α   Come [לְכוּ], O house of Jacob [בֵּית יַעֲקֹב],
let us walk [וְנֵלְכָה] in the light of YHWH [בְּאוֹר יְהוָה]
(2:5)

The complex frameworking in this passage gives structural cohesion to the exordium as a whole.[1] INSETⁱ and INSETⁱⁱⁱ (1:2a, 10), which

---

[1]J.D.W. Watts (*Isaiah 1–33* [WBC, 24; Waco, TX: Word Books, 1985], pp. 15-16) has proposed that 1:2-23 comprises a symmetrical concentric unit:

A   'I reared my children—but they rebelled against me' (1:2)

  B   'An ox knows—Israel does not know' (1:3)

    C   'Ah! Sinful nation! Why more?' (1:4-5)

      D   'Only wounds left—countryside desolate' (1:6-7a)

KEYSTONE Daughter of Zion isolated, like a city under siege—
except for the remnant left by Yahweh, would be like Sodom (1:7b-9)

      D' Empty, useless worship (1:10-15a)

    C'   'Hands full of blood! Wash yourselves' (1:15b-17)

  B'   'Come, let us test each other' (1:18-20)

A'   'How has the faithful city become a harlot?' (1:21-23)

However, this symmetrical palistrophe seems to have less to justify it, either from correspondences of vocabulary or of the rhetorical function of its tiers, than does the schema proposed above in which a complex framework arrangement of tiers is based mainly upon the function of its tiers within a covenant disputation.

contain elements of the summons to dispute, introduce two subdivisions: one addressed to Israel in general (1:2b-9), the other to Zion in particular (1:11–2:5). The whole exordium presents a scenario by which Israel is shown to have been pared down by successive military judgments (1:5-6) until Zion alone was left standing, a mere remnant of Israel's former glory (1:7-9). Now, even Zion comes under threat of total annihilation (1:20, 28-31) unless its citizens repent (1:18-19; 2:2-5) and adhere to YHWH's terms of reconciliation (1:16-17). Hence, in Isaiah's prologue, Zion is being addressed not only as the seat of state for Judah (cf. 1:1; 2:1) but as the last remnant of Israel, the covenant nation of YHWH.

All the 'AA' tiers constitute accusations against Israel/Zion for covenant apostasy. In each instance, their disloyalty is related directly to YHWH himself. The first inset (1:2a) opens the disputation with a summons to the inhabitants of 'heaven and earth'. After this, Israel is accused of unjustifiable rebellion (AA, 1:2b-3). The AA[i]-tier (1:4) heightens one's distaste for Israel's insolence by accusing them of having spurned their holy one. After a summons of the accused to attention (1:10), the AA[ii]-tier (1:11-15) outlines YHWH's surpassing repugnance at Zion's hypocritical overtures to appease him through the cult, a cult that he has rejected as an impure sham.

The 'BB' tiers make explicit Israel/Zion's alienation from YHWH in that all these tiers contain statements that outline the implications of Israel/Zion's negative response to accusations of sin. A motivational rhetorical question (1:5a) introduces the first two 'BB' tiers, the first of which (BB, 1:5b-6) describes the present effects of YHWH's punishment on Israel, and the second of which (BB[i], 1:7-9) details, with heightened intensity, how close to complete destruction Israel came. The third 'BB' tier (BB[ii], 1:20) threatens the complete destruction of a potentially unrepentant Zion, the last remnant of Israel. The BB[iii]-tier (1:28-31) presents the certainty of this consequence of judgment on those in Zion who refuse to repent from their present disloyalty to YHWH. Despite the difference in rhetorical function among the 'BB' tiers—the first two being 'descriptions of present distress', the last two, 'threats of total destruction'—my coordination of these 'BB' tiers so as to form one quadratic frame seems justified since, thematically, all describe the negative effects of YHWH's judgment (whether present or future) and all engender a response (whether remorse or fear) that is designed to impel Zion toward renewed covenant loyalty.

The structural axis of 1:1–2:5 appears to lie in 1:16-17, the only place where the author states the conditions of reinstatement to covenant blessing. This axis stands out not only because it is the hub of an asymmetrically concentric pattern but because of its erratic con-catenation of commands—three single commands (about purity) fol-lowed by three paired commands (about righteous conduct, social jus-tice, and mercy). These verses encapsulate the ideals of Isaiah's prologue—indeed, of the whole book—and highlight the fact that Zion's covenant responsibilities to YHWH exist in both the cultic and social spheres.

All the 'CC' tiers pertain to the issue of the possibility of restoration to YHWH. The 'CCα' tiers all contain invitations (from various speakers) to be reconciled to YHWH, implying that those addressed have been alienated from him. Each 'CCα' tier contains the interjection לְכוּ followed by a cohortative that appeals either to Zion's (1:18a; 2:5) or the nations' (2:3a) populaces. There is variance in the point of view expressed among the 'CCα' tiers but this only heightens the persuasive effect by portraying a sense of unanimity among the multiple voices.[1] As a complement to the 'CCα' tiers, the 'CCβ' tiers depict Zion purified and blessed in the land (1:18b-19) and the future state of the world under Zion's religious and political dominion (2:2 and 2:3b-4). The posterior position and conciliatory theme of the 'CC' tiers within the complex framework of 1:1–2:5 seem to imply that, after punish-ment, the peoples (of Zion and the nations) who would hearken to YHWH's invitation to be reconciled (tiers 'CCα') could expect to share in the blessings of his new world order (tiers 'CCβ').[2]

Others have already noted a concentric structure in the inset that separates the BB[ii]- and BB[iii]-tiers (i.e., 1:21-27).[3] In fact, it is very pos-sible that 1:21-27 was written on another occasion and was incorporated secondarily into the complex framework structure because of its conformity to the sequence and rhetorical patterning of the *rîb-*

---

[1]Here is a good illustration of the biblical phenomenon of ascending order of repetition effected through shifts in point of view (cf. Sternberg, *The Poetics of Biblical Narrative*, pp. 105-109, 138-52).

[2]The perception of Kaiser (*Isaiah 1–12*, p. 50), that, '2.(1)2ff. interrupts the theme of the future judgment on Jerusalem and Judah which governs these chapters as a whole', was right, though this alone is no argument for its being a redactional insertion, as he suggested. The repeated conformity of such 'thematic interrupt-ions' to the pattern of tiered architecture in this and the following chapters suggests rather that the present arrangement is the product of deliberate design.

[3]Vermeylen, I, pp. 71-76; W.G.E. Watson, *Classical Hebrew Poetry: A Guide to its Techniques* (JSOTSup, 26; Sheffield: JSOT Press, 1984), p. 206.

genre that are represented in this context: accusation (AA*, 1:21-23) is followed by ultimatum (comprising threat [BB*, 1:24-25] and appeal [CC*, 1:26-27]). Moreover, the accusation contained in 1:21-23 focuses more upon social injustice than does either of the general accusations in 1:2b-3 or 4 and complements the accusation of cultic hypocrisy in 1:11-15. The position of 1:21-27 within the complex framework structure of 1:1–2:5, at two thirds of the way through the section, offers an ideal point of climax for this peroration of the key vocabulary, themes and argument of the exordium as a whole. To this end, 1:21-27 emphasizes the ideal that Zion, as YHWH's regal city, ought to be a city of justice and righteousness. Thus, an idealized past and utopian future for Zion are portrayed as interrupted by YHWH's intervention to purge his city of impurity.[1]

Persuasion as a Function of Structure in Isaiah 1:1–2:5

Determining the rhetoric of the opening section of Isaiah's prophecy is crucial for understanding the major issues that the author will continue to address throughout the book. As an exordium, it presents two major lines along which the prophecy develops: one related to punishment, the other to restoration. Along the first line is presented the incongruity between Israel's privilege as YHWH's chosen people (cf. בָּנִים גִּדַּלְתִּי וְרוֹמַמְתִּי, 1:2bα) and their inexplicable continuance in unjustified rebellion (1:2b-3, 4), a rebellion that even their experience teaches them can only elicit the prolongation of the suffering that has already resulted in Israel's reduction to a single city (1:5-6, 7-9). It is this incongruity that impels the reader to form the judgment, in agreement with YHWH, that Israel, unwilling to respect either the hand that feeds them or the hand that disciplines them, deserves to be irrevocably rejected.[2]

---

[1] See J.H. Hayes and S.A. Irvine, *Isaiah the Eighth-century Prophet: His Times and His Preaching* (Nashville: Abingdon Press, 1987), pp. 54-56.

[2] The description of present distresses in this exordium, and especially the situation described in 1:7-9, seems to suit best the situation of Jerusalem after Sennacherib's campaign of 701 BCE, when it was left surrounded by a ring of razed environs. Note the prior threat of 8:6-8, which had predicted that the Assyrian flood would reach 'up to the neck' of Judah, conquering every major city but its elevated capital, Jerusalem. Correspondingly, the imagery in 1:8 emphasizes the solitary preservation of Jerusalem as left standing alone in a wasteland (in contrast to Sodom and Gomorrah, 1:9b). This was not the situation in the aftermath of the campaign of Nebuchadnezzar II, in 586 BCE. Therefore, 1:1–2:5 seems to describe the aftermath of Sennacherib's campaign rather than that of Nebuchadnezzar's campaign of 586 BCE. How long after 701 BCE this material came to be positioned within the prologue of the book would be difficult to say with precision, though one may venture to posit, because of formal and thematic

Once this judgment has been induced in the reader by the rhetorical strategy of 1:2-9, the author introduces a second line of development, namely, that which shows the incongruity between Zion's present irreconcilability (1:10-15) and YHWH's injunctions (1:16-17) and appeals (whether mediated by prophet [1:18a], by international consensus [2:3a] or by the author [2:5]) whereby he invites the repentant to enjoy the benefits of citizenship in future Zion (2:2, 3b-4). If the first incongruity left one with the impression that YHWH was right to punish Israel, the second introduces what seems to be an incongruity in the author's rhetorical strategy. One can understand why YHWH would subject a religiously unfaithful and socially unjust Zion to purging before restoring her to her former faithful and just condition (1:21-27) but, in view of Zion's perpetual rebellion, why would YHWH want to restore her at all? Does YHWH lack a sense of propriety in matters of justice? There is, as yet, not the slightest indication of repentance on the part of Zion—no willingness to acknowledge either the injustice of her social misconduct or the insolence of her religious infidelity. Would YHWH punish, then pardon the hardened? Such incongruity forces the reader to search for coherence. If YHWH is to remain just while vindicating Zion's recalcitrant rebels, what must be implied in the promise of Zion's exaltation is that YHWH would, among some future generation of Zion's descendants, bring about the repentance required for Zion's restoration. Yet, it remains inscrutable, from an examination of the prologue alone, just how and when YHWH would vindicate himself by restoring to himself a purged remnant of Zion's citizens.

It is crucial to see that this rhetorical strategy is apparent not only from incongruities in the lines of reasoning within 1:1–2:5 but that it is reinforced by the exordium's lack of conformity to the genre conventions of a covenant disputation. Isaiah 1:1–2:5 lacks precisely those rhetorical elements of a covenant disputation that vindicate the offended party. Thus, just where one expects to find an exoneration of YHWH's covenant faithfulness to be weighed against the descriptions of offenses committed by his covenant people, one is met with silence.

Those who understand Isaiah's prologue to be limited to ch. 1 may infer that it should be divided into sections represented by 1:1-17/20 and 1:18/21-31. It is understandable why this bifurcation has come about in the history of Isaiah's interpretation. Even in the structural

correspondences within the exordium as well as the continuity of the exordium with the rhetorical strategy of rest of the book, that it came into its present position only during the final stages of the book's compilation.

model of 1:1–2:5 offered here, 1:2-15 appears unified in structure and
accusatory tone: the declarations of Israel's violations (1:2b-3, 4) and
of YHWH's concomitant rejection of Zion's ritual compensation (1:11-
15) seem to frame two vivid portrayals of Israel's present distresses
(1:5b-6, 7-9), which are designed to engender a sense of desperation in
their readers—a sense met in 1:16-17 with commands for concrete
action. It may even seem to follow that the ultimatum in 1:18-20
anticipates Zion's expected alternative responses to the injunctions in
1:16-17. Concomitantly, on condition of Zion's response to the injunctions of 1:16-17, in 1:18–2:5 one finds both appeals to and threats
against YHWH's guilty people in which the invitations (1:18a; 2:3a, 5)
appear to frame, in juxtaposition, the tiers that promise blessing to
Zion (1:18b-19; 2:2, 3b-4). These bifid tiers, in turn, seem to frame
tiers that threaten destruction (1:20, 28-31). Finally, at the core of this
complex appears 1:21-27, a concentric peroration of the rhetorical elements that frame it.

Such alternative correlations among tiers only show the extent to
which the argument of the prologue may be made to cohere under a
tiered analysis of disputational language. It is my contention, however,
that it is through coupling a tiered analysis of elements that make up a
covenant disputation—albeit one from which an exoneration of the
offended party has been left out—together with a recognition of patterns
of complex frameworking that one discovers the controlling rhetorical
design of Isaiah's exordium.

Covenant Disputation Pattern and the Continuity of Isaiah 1:1–2:5 with its Context

A thoroughgoing interpretation of the composite structure of Isaiah's
exordium must be made with an eye not only to its content but also to
its continuity with what follows in the remainder of the prophecy.[1] The

---

[1]Cf. Ackroyd, 'Isaiah i–xii: Presentation of a Prophet', in *Congress Volume, Göttingen, 1977* (VTSup, 29; Leiden: Brill, 1978), pp. 16-48; W.J. Dumbrell, 'The Purpose of the Book of Isaiah', *TynBul* 36 (1985), p. 113. Following Ackroyd, Dumbrell (p. 113) says that,

> the content of Isaiah 1–12 moves alternately between the motifs of promise and threat. In this way is the outline of 1–39 introduced as mainly threat, and 40–66 as predominantly promise. Thus Isaiah 1 plainly contains a threat against Jerusalem while Isaiah 2:1-4 outlines the pro-phetic hope for Zion ...

Because of the continuity of 1:1–2:5 with the rest of the book, I infer that it is not just ch. 1 but 1:1–2:5 that best constitutes the full exordium of Isaiah's prophetic themes and overall structure.

reason why the importance of 2:2-5 is heightened under the force of the resumptive repetition of 2:1 (cf. the superscription of 1:1) becomes clearer in the light of the strategy that governs the whole book of Isaiah. Apart from 1:16-19 and 26-27, Isa. 1:2-31 is permeated by a tone of condemnation. What 2:2-5 portrays is an all-glorious Zion, the envy of the nations and the focus of their adoration and hope. Since the exaltation of Zion is the ultimate goal of setting forth what it is that 'Isaiah son of Amoz saw concerning Judah and Jerusalem', it makes sense that this vision should be held in balance with the vision that sets forth Zion's intermediate punishment. Thus, the overall strategy of the book of Isaiah is the same as that which one finds in the exordium: accusation and threat of punishment (emphasized in 1:1-15, 20-25, 28-31 and 2:6-39:8) essentially precede the offer of exaltation (emphasized in 1:18-19, 2:2-5 and chs. 55-66). Indeed, the view that accusations and threats of punishment are a means to covenant reconciliation and the renewal of covenant benefits is in keeping with the rhetorical strategy of all known exemplars of the covenant disputation genre.

Nevertheless, it is important to reiterate at this point that, despite the basic conformity of Isa. 1:1-2:5 to the rhetorical strategy of the covenant disputation, one essential component is noticeable by its absence: that of the offended party's plea of innocence. It is no coincidence, then, that one of the most striking structural dissimilarities between Isaiah's exordium (1:1-2:5) and the sections that follow becomes evident when the reader encounters 40:1-54:17. These chapters comprise the only major section of the book for which there is no explicit adumbration in the prologue. This is not, however, without justification on the author's part. Because the case for the innocence of the wronged party was a standard feature of the covenant disputation genre, its absence from Isaiah's exordium, which otherwise bears all the standard features of this genre, would seem to be a glaring omission.[1] The absence of a case for YHWH's innocence frustrates genre expectations. In fact, the delay of the exoneration seems deliberately protracted, chapter after chapter. When it finally appears in 40:1-54:17, at the position in the book normally reserved for a literary climax (two thirds or more into the prophecy), the reader senses relief both at the fulfillment of genre expectations and at the long-awaited vindication of YHWH before the offending citizens of Zion. In their

---

[1] The reference to YHWH's past benefits of fatherhood to Israel in 1:2b is so disproportionately small that it hardly constitutes more than a reminder that a proper exoneration of YHWH as the offended covenant party is wanting.

deliberations over the extent of Isaiah's exordium, neither Wildberger nor Fohrer perceived the extent to which the frustration of genre expectations in Isa. 1:1–2:5 sets up a rhetoric of delay in the book that heightens the emotive force of the case for YHWH's innocence when it is finally reached in 40:1–54:17.

It is also interesting to note that the delay in the fulfillment of genre expectations in the book (as one reads it) parallels the delay of the fulfillment of the prophecy in history, for which Zion's citizens had to wait from the time of the prophet (eighth to early seventh century BCE) until Cyrus' edict that allowed the Jews to return from Babylon (ca. 538 BCE). Thus, in either world of interpretative context (in the book or in history), the case for YHWH's exoneration was made to depend on the fulfillment of a promised return from Babylon—a fulfillment that was to be significantly delayed. Viewed from a rhetorical perspective, this retardation of fulfillment works in two opposing directions at once: first, by its delay, it escalates one's doubts, in sympathy with Israel/Zion, about whether YHWH will fulfill his promise to restore Zion, and second, when the case for YHWH's innocence is finally made, its delay has engendered so much sympathy for YHWH, who has so long awaited its disclosure (thirty-eight chapters in reading time; a century and a half in history) that it infuses 40:1–54:17 with compelling emotive force.[1] Isaiah 40:1–54:17 uses very emotive language and figures (e.g., images of childbirth, marital love and divorce), but the retardation of genre expectations for an exoneration of YHWH as the offended covenant party charges this language with even more persuasive power.

[1] Isa. 40:1–54:17 uses the three main types of rhetorical appeal (i.e., ethical, logical, and emotional) to make the important case for YHWH's innocence. Once convinced of YHWH's control of history, through the fulfillment of Zion's predicted emancipation from Babylon, the estranged citizens of Zion could be expected to infer that they had been exiled only as a result of YHWH's decree. Thus, not until the author had made a case for YHWH's justification in punishing his people could the author entertain the notion of presenting YHWH's appeal to all 'exiles' to be reconciled to himself (55:1–66:24).

Chapter 2

ISAIAH 2:6-22: THREAT OF JUDGMENT ON IDOLATERS

IMPENITENT IDOLATERS WILL HAVE NO HOPE
IN YHWH'S DREADFUL DAY

Within Isa. 2:6-22 one finds the clearest example of complex frame-working in the book of Isaiah. The passage forms a single structural unit that, under the rhetoric of covenant disputation established by the exordium of Isa. 1:1-2:5, functions as a specification of the accusations and threats against those who apostasize cultically from YHWH and defer reconciling until it is already too late.

Structural Delineation of Isaiah 2:6-22

The density of key word collocations in Isa. 2:6-22 has prompted many scholars to recognize the rhetorical cohesion of this subunit.[1] The

[1]E.g., T.R. Birks, *Commentary on the Book of Isaiah: Critical, Historical and Prophetical* (Cambridge: Rivingtons, 1871), pp. 28-30; C. von Orelli, *The Prophecies of Isaiah* (trans. J.S. Banks; Edinburgh: T. & T. Clark, 1889), pp. 35-36; A. Dillmann, *Der Prophet Jesaja* (KEHAT, 5; Leipzig: S. Hirzel, 5th edn, 1898), pp. 24-28; G.W. Wade, *The Book of the Prophet Isaiah with Introduction and Notes* (Westminster Commentaries; London: Methuen, 2d edn, 1911), pp. 16-20; K. Fullerton, 'The Original Form of the Refrains in Is. 2:6-21', *JBL* 38 (1919), pp. 64-76; G. Fohrer, *Das Buch Jesaja* (Zürcher Bibelkommentare; 3 vols.; Zürich: Zwingli-Verlag, 1964–1966), I, pp. 52-58; R. Davidson, 'The Interpretation of Isaiah ii 6ff', *VT* 16 (1966), pp. 1-7; A.S. Herbert, *The Book of the Prophet Isaiah: Chapters 1-39* (CBC; Cambridge: Cambridge University Press, 1973), pp. 36-40; R. Lack, *La symbolique du livre d'Isaïe: Essai sur l'image littéraire comme élément de structuration* (AnBib, 59; Rome: Biblical Institute Press, 1973), pp. 38-39; H.W. Hoffmann, *Die Intention der Verkündigung Jesajas* (BZAW, 136; Berlin: de Gruyter, 1974), pp. 107-24; J. Vermeylen, *Du prophète Isaïe à l'apocalyptique: Isaïe, i–xxxv, miroir d'un demi-millénaire d'expérience religieuse en Israël* (EBib; 2 vols.; Paris: Gabalda, 1977, 1978), I, pp. 133-44; K.J. Cathcart, 'Kingship and the "Day of YHWH" in Isaiah 2:6-22', *Hermathena* 125 (1978), pp. 48-59; R.E. Clements, *Isaiah 1-39* (NCB; Grand Rapids: Eerdmans, 1980), pp. 42-46; H. Wildberger, *Jesaja, Kapitel 1-12* (BKAT, X/1; Neukirchen-Vluyn: Neukirchener Verlag, 1972; 2d edn, 1980), pp. 91-115; J. Blenkinsopp, 'Fragments of Ancient Exegesis in an Isaian Poem (Isa 2:6-22)', *ZAW* 93 (1981), pp. 51-62; O. Kaiser, *Isaiah 1-12: A Commentary* (trans. J. Bowden; OTL; Philadelphia: Westminster Press, 2d edn,

section opens with a statement in 2:6aαβ that contrasts with the divine favor and entreaty offered in 2:2-5. For a moment, it seems that the author is charging YHWH with neglect of his people.[1] The jarring effect of this allegation derives from the seeming incongruity between YHWH's rejection of his people and the future held in store for those who heed the invitation to be reconciled (cf. 1:18b-19; 2:2, 3b-4). As one continues, however, 2:6aαβ is seen to function not as a charge against YHWH but as a description of a divine stance justified by the house of Jacob's multiple covenant violations. Thus, 2:6aγ-21 gives the reason for YHWH's aversion to his people (cf. 2:6aγ, causal כִּי) by bringing into the foreground the greedy motivations for and idolatrous effects of the house of Jacob's foreign alliances.[2]

Prompted by a desire for improved foreign trade relations and for the resultant benefits of economic and military security, YHWH's people sought out cultural ties with foreign nations; however, the cultic practices modeled by those nations concurrently became a source of moral and religious decay. Without explicitly saying so, the accusation of Isa. 2:6aγ-8 may imply that these were matters that fell under the jurisdiction of the king and, hence, should accrue to his condemnation. This accusation outlines the same prohibitions leveled against kings of Israel in Deut. 17:16-17, namely, prohibitions against accumulating vast amounts of silver and gold, amassing horses and contracting

1983), pp. 56-66; J. Jensen, *Isaiah 1-39* (Old Testament Message, 8; Wilmington, DE: Michael Glazier, 1984), pp. 59-66; J.F.A. Sawyer, *Isaiah* (Philadelphia: Westminster Press, 1984), I, pp. 26-31; J.N. Oswalt, *The Book of Isaiah, Chapters 1-39* (NICOT; Grand Rapids: Eerdmans, 1986), pp. 119-29; J.H. Hayes and S.A. Irvine, *Isaiah the Eighth-century Prophet: His Times and His Preaching* (Nashville: Abingdon Press, 1987), pp. 83-88; M.A. Sweeney, *Isaiah 1-4 and the Post-Exilic Understanding of the Isaianic Tradition* (BZAW, 171; Berlin: de Gruyter, 1988), pp. 139-46.

[1] Cf. Hayes-Irvine, p. 86. It may be that YHWH's forsaking of his people here refers to his neglect of defending Zion's perimeters from the Assyrian siege of 701 BCE, in which case the threat of total destruction in the following verses (2:9-21) is made against a city already nearly so destroyed. If so, 2:6-21 may find its situation of origin in the same aftermath of Sennacherib's destruction of Jerusalem's environs as is implied by the prologue. Evidence for this proposed situation of composition remains inferential, but such a situation would be amenable to the particulars of the text (see below).

[2] It may be argued that 2:6aαβ marks the transition not only to the accusations of apostasy (2:6aγ-21[22]) but also to the accusations against social injustice (3:1-4:1). Indeed, 2:6aαβ may be seen to function as the demarcator between the exordium (1:1-2:5) and the remainder of the book (2:6aγ-66:24), which expresses the nature of YHWH's stance against the citizens of Zion.

foreign (marriage) alliances, since these would lead to idolatry and apostasy from YHWH.[1] Here again one sees the prophet's strategy of reticence openly to criticize the Judean monarchy. The remainder of the section (Isa. 2:9-21) functions as a threat of total destruction against humans who persist in the arrogance of worshiping idols of their own creation. It is appropriate, therefore, that the hortatory transition in 2:22 should mark the end of this subunit with a prohibition against trusting in humanly devised economical, military or religious measures.

Complex Frameworking in Isaiah 2:6aγ-21

The collocations of key words/clauses in Isa. 2:6aγ-21 appear to form a single compound frame, made up of one quadratic and one triadic frame, that surrounds a central axis. The complex frameworking pattern in this section may be schematized in the following way:

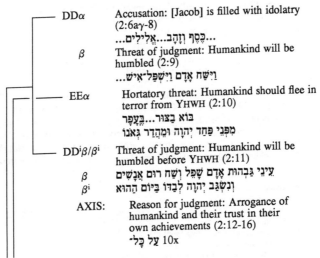

DDα		Accusation: [Jacob] is filled with idolatry (2:6aγ-8)
		...כֶּסֶף וְזָהָב...אֱלִילִים...
	β	Threat of judgment: Humankind will be humbled (2:9)
		וַיִּשַּׁח אָדָם וַיִּשְׁפַּל־אִישׁ...
EEα		Hortatory threat: Humankind should flee in terror from YHWH (2:10)
		בּוֹא בַצּוּר...בֶּעָפָר
		מִפְּנֵי פַּחַד יְהוָה וּמֵהֲדַר גְּאוֹנוֹ
DDⁱβ/βⁱ		Threat of judgment: Humankind will be humbled before YHWH (2:11)
	β	עֵינֵי גַּבְהוּת אָדָם שָׁפֵל וְשַׁח רוּם אֲנָשִׁים
	βⁱ	וְנִשְׂגַּב יְהוָה לְבַדּוֹ בַּיּוֹם הַהוּא
AXIS:		Reason for judgment: Arrogance of humankind and their trust in their own achievements (2:12-16)
		עַל כָּל־ 10x

---

[1]These were the very offenses that distinguished the reign of Solomon (1 Kgs 10:14-25, 26-29; 11:1-13) from that of his father David (1 Kgs 11:4, 6). As it turned out, Solomon, fully expected to fulfill the ideals of the promised 'son of David', was prototypical of a series of David's descendants for whom these condemnations became characteristic. As in the book of Kings, so in Isaiah, the reign of David is idealized and considered paradigmatic for the assessment of later Judean kings.

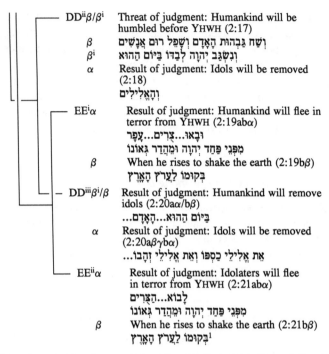

DDⁱⁱβ/βⁱ	Threat of judgment: Humankind will be humbled before Y<small>HWH</small> (2:17)
β	וְשַׁח גַּבְהוּת הָאָדָם וְשָׁפֵל רוּם אֲנָשִׁים
βⁱ	וְנִשְׂגַּב יְהוָה לְבַדּוֹ בַּיּוֹם הַהוּא
α	Result of judgment: Idols will be removed (2:18)
	וְהָאֱלִילִים
EEⁱα	Result of judgment: Humankind will flee in terror from Y<small>HWH</small> (2:19abα)
	וּבָאוּ...צֻרִים...עָפָר
	מִפְּנֵי פַּחַד יְהוָה וּמֵהֲדַר גְּאוֹנוֹ
β	When he rises to shake the earth (2:19bβ)
	בְּקוּמוֹ לַעֲרֹץ הָאָרֶץ
DDⁱⁱⁱβⁱ/β	Result of judgment: Humankind will remove idols (2:20aα/bβ)
	בַּיּוֹם הַהוּא...הָאָדָם...
α	Result of judgment: Idols will be removed (2:20aβγbα)
	אֵת אֱלִילֵי כַסְפּוֹ וְאֵת אֱלִילֵי זְהָבוֹ...
EEⁱⁱα	Result of judgment: Idolaters will flee in terror from Y<small>HWH</small> (2:21abα)
	לָבוֹא...הַצֻּרִים
	מִפְּנֵי פַּחַד יְהוָה וּמֵהֲדַר גְּאוֹנוֹ
β	When he rises to shake the earth (2:21bβ)
	בְּקוּמוֹ לַעֲרֹץ הָאָרֶץ[1]

[1]The tiers of this schema continue the alphabetical labelling of tiers from the previous section (i.e., 'AA', 'BB', 'CC') with tiers labeled 'DD' and 'EE'. This practice will facilitate cross-referencing throughout the present study. It may be appropriate to cite here B. Wiklander's concentric analysis of Isa. 2:1–4:6 (*Prophecy as Literature: A Text-Linguistic and Rhetorical Approach to Isaiah 2–4* [ConBOT, 22; Stockholm: Gleerup, 1984], pp. 225-26), which may be represented as follows:

A   Restoration (2:1-4)
   B   Conversion (2:5)
     C   Lawsuit as an instrument of conversion and restoration [Concentric] (2:6–3:26):
       aa   Lawsuit (2:6-8)
         bb   Argumentation regarding 'god' (2:9-10)
           cc   Theophany [paneling] (2:11-21):
             a   Humiliation of humanity and exaltation of Y<small>HWH</small> (2:11)
             b   The day of Y<small>HWH</small> and its effects upon the earth as a whole (2:12-16)
             a'   Humiliation of humanity and exaltation of Y<small>HWH</small> (2:17)
             b'   The day of Y<small>HWH</small> and its effects upon idols (2:18-19) and humanity (2:20-21)
         bb'   Argumentation regarding 'humanity' (2:22)
       aa'   Lawsuit (3:1-26)
   B'   Conversion (4:1)
A'   Restoration (4:2-6)

Alternatively, Wiklander proposed a similar pattern of inclusios in Isa. 2:6–4:1 based upon the stepwise compositional structure of its rhetoric (p. 234):

The following outline presents an English translation of Isa. 2:6-21, with common tiers labeled and aligned in columns according to the preceding schema and with rhetorically significant words given in square brackets.

Transition (2:6aαβ):
But [כִּי] you have forsaken your people [עַמְּךָ],
   the house of Jacob [בֵּית יַעֲקֹב],

DDα   for [כִּי] they are full [מָלְאוּ] of fortune-tellers
       and soothsayers, like the Philistines.
    They join hands with foreigners.
    Their land is full [וַתִּמָּלֵא אַרְצוֹ] of silver and gold [כֶּסֶף וְזָהָב];
       there is no limit [וְאֵין קֵצֶה] to their treasures.
    Their land is full [וַתִּמָּלֵא אַרְצוֹ] of horses;
       there is no limit [וְאֵין קֵצֶה] to their chariots.
    Their land is full [וַתִּמָּלֵא אַרְצוֹ] of idols;
       to the work of their [own] hands they bow down [וַיִּשְׁתַּחֲווּ],
       to that which their [own] fingers have made. (2:6aγ-8)

β   So humanity [אָדָם] will be brought low [וַיִּשַּׁח],
       and each one humbled [וַיִּשְׁפַּל]—
      but do not forgive [וְאַל־תִּשָּׂא] them. (2:9)

EEα   Enter the rock [בּוֹא בַצּוּר],
       hide in the ground [בֶּעָפָר],
       away from the terror of YHWH [מִפְּנֵי פַּחַד יְהוָה]
       and the splendor of his majesty [וּמֵהֲדַר גְּאוֹנוֹ]. (2:10)

DD^iβ   The eyes of human arrogance [גַּבְהוּת אָדָם] will be humbled [שָׁפֵל],
       and the loftiness of humans [רוּם אֲנָשִׁים] brought low [וְשַׁח] (2:11a)

β^i   so that YHWH alone will be exalted [וְנִשְׂגַּב יְהוָה]
       on that day [בַּיּוֹם הַהוּא]. (2:11b)

A   Abandoning the covenant community (2:6a)
  B   Abundance of foreigners, apostates and tokens of foreign authority (2:6-7)
    C   Abundance of idols and idol worshipers (2:8; cf. 2:7)
      D   Exhortations on 'god' (2:9-10)
    C'   Removal of idols and idol worshipers (2:11-21)
      D'   Exhortation on 'humanity' (2:22)
  B'   Removal of foreigners, apostates and tokens of foreign authority (3:1-26)
A'   Conversion to covenant community (4:1)

For the purposes of this study, however, it seems difficult to substantiate, without the support of patterns of key word repetition, which of these two structural models most accurately reflects the author's controlling criteria for the section.

AXIS: Reason (2:12-16):

For [כִּי] Warrior YHWH [לַיהוָה צְבָאוֹת] has a day [יוֹם]

for all [עַל כָּל־] the proud and lofty [וָרָם],

for all [וְעַל כָּל־] that is exalted [נִשָּׂא] to be humbled [וְשָׁפֵל];

for all [וְעַל כָּל־] the cedars of Lebanon, lofty [הָרָמִים] and exalted [וְהַנִּשָּׂאִים],

for all [וְעַל כָּל־] the oaks of Bashan;

for all [וְעַל כָּל־] the lofty mountains [הֶהָרִים הָרָמִים],

for all [וְעַל כָּל־] the exalted [הַנִּשָּׂאוֹת] hills;

for every [וְעַל כָּל־] high [גָּבֹהַּ] tower,

for every [וְעַל כָּל־] fortified [בְצוּרָה] wall;

for every [וְעַל כָּל־] sea-going ship,

and for every [וְעַל כָּל־] stately vessel.

DD^ii β   Human arrogance [גַּבְהוּת הָאָדָם] will be brought low [וְשַׁח],

and the loftiness of humans [רוּם אֲנָשִׁים] will be humbled [וְשָׁפֵל] (2:17a)

β^i   so that YHWH alone will be exalted [וְנִשְׂגַּב יְהוָה לְבַדּוֹ]

on that day [בַּיּוֹם הַהוּא], (2:17b)

α   and the idols [וְהָאֱלִילִים] will entirely disappear. (2:18)

EE^i α   They will enter [וּבָאוּ] the caves in the rocks [צֻרִים]

and the holes in the ground [עָפָר],

away from the terror of YHWH [מִפְּנֵי פַּחַד יְהוָה]

and the splendor of his majesty [וּמֵהֲדַר גְּאוֹנוֹ] (2:19abα)

β   when he rises to shake the earth [בְּקוּמוֹ לַעֲרֹץ הָאָרֶץ]. (2:19bβ)

DD^iii β^i/β'   On that day [בַּיּוֹם הַהוּא] humanity [הָאָדָם] will throw away (2:20aα)

α   their idols of silver [אֶת אֱלִילֵי כַסְפּוֹ]

and their idols of gold [וְאֵת אֱלִילֵי זְהָבוֹ],

which they made for themselves to worship [לְהִשְׁתַּחֲוֹת], (2:20aβγbα)

β"   to the rats and to the bats, (2:20bβ)

EE^ii α   so that they enter [לָבוֹא] the caverns in the rocks [הַצֻּרִים]

and the overhanging crags,

away from the terror of YHWH [מִפְּנֵי פַּחַד יְהוָה]

and the splendor of his majesty [וּמֵהֲדַר גְּאוֹנוֹ] (2:21abα)

β   when he rises to shake the earth [בְּקוּמוֹ לַעֲרֹץ הָאָרֶץ]. (2:21bβ)

A number of structural features of this unit deserve special mention. First, the 'DDα' and 'DDβ' tiers, which always occur in structural juxtaposition, appear in nearly reverse order about the axis of the section. This further emphasizes the asymmetrical concentricity of this section and so directs one's focus to the ten reasons for YHWH's judgment listed at the center. The 'DDα' tiers show a correspondence on the basis of a repetition (with variation) of three key words (זָהָב, כֶּסֶף, אֱלִילִים; 'silver', 'gold', and 'idols'):

DDα   כֶּסֶף וְזָהָב 'silver and gold' (2:7a)
                אֱלִילִים 'idols' (2:8a)

DDⁱⁱα   וְהָאֱלִילִים 'and the idols' (2:18a)

DDⁱⁱⁱα   אֵת אֱלִילֵי כַסְפּוֹ ‖ וְאֵת אֱלִילֵי זְהָבוֹ (2:20aβγ)
              'their idols of silver
              and their idols of gold'

There is a sense of both irony and poetic justice in placing the second to last clause of the DDα-tier, 'to the work of their [own] hands they bow down [יִשְׁתַּחֲווּ]' (2:8b), just before the first clause of the following DDβ-tier, 'so humanity will will be brought low [וַיִּשַׁח]' (2:9). This theme is taken up again in 2:20 where humans are finally seen to despise the idols 'which they made for themselves to worship [לְהִשְׁתַּחֲוֹת]'.

The three key words of the 'DDβ' tiers are: אָדָם 'humanity', שׁחח 'to be brought low', and שׁפל 'to be humbled'. The latter two verbs exchange positions as A- and B-words in the parallelism of these tiers:

DDβ   וַיִּשַׁח אָדָם ‖ וַיִּשְׁפַּל־אִישׁ (2:9)
         'Thus humanity will be brought low,
         and each one humbled'

DDⁱβ   עֵינֵי גַבְהוּת אָדָם שָׁפֵל ‖ וְשַׁח רוּם אֲנָשִׁים (2:11a)
         'The eyes of human arrogance will be humbled,
         and the loftiness of humans brought low'

DDⁱⁱβ   וְשַׁח גַּבְהוּת הָאָדָם ‖ וְשָׁפֵל רוּם אֲנָשִׁים (2:17a)
         'Human arrogance will be brought low,
         and the loftiness of humans will be humbled'

Furthermore, after the second and third occurrences of 'DDβ' tiers appears the newly added parallelism: בַּיּוֹם הַהוּא ‖ וְנִשְׂגַּב יְהוָה לְבַדּוֹ, 'YHWH alone will stand in that day'; however, בַּיּוֹם הַהוּא appears alone, in the fourth 'DDβ' tier. These accretions to the DDβ tiers have been given the siglum 'βⁱ' in the diagram.

DDβ	וַיִּשַׁח אָדָם	‖ (2:9) וַיִּשְׁפַּל־אִישׁ
DDⁱβ	עֵינֵי גַּבְהוּת אָדָם שָׁפֵל	‖ (2:11a) וְשַׁח רוּם אֲנָשִׁים
βⁱ	וְנִשְׂגַּב יְהוָה לְבַדּוֹ	‖ (2:11b) בַּיּוֹם הַהוּא
DDⁱⁱβ	וְשַׁח גַּבְהוּת הָאָדָם	‖ (2:17a) וְשָׁפֵל רוּם אֲנָשִׁים
βⁱ	וְנִשְׂגַּב יְהוָה לְבַדּוֹ	‖ (2:17b) בַּיּוֹם הַהוּא
DDⁱⁱⁱβⁱ		(2:20aα) בַּיּוֹם הַהוּא
β'		(2:20aα) הָאָדָם

This pattern of accumulation among the DDβ tiers, where the second
and following occurrences add a new phrase, appears again among the
'EE' tiers. The final two 'EE' tiers add the paronomastic colon: בְּקוּמוֹ
לַעֲרֹץ הָאָרֶץ ('when he rises to shake the earth'). Both of these accretions are labeled 'EEβ' in the diagram.

EEα	בּוֹא בַצּוּר	‖ (2:10a) בֶּעָפָר
	מִפְּנֵי פַּחַד יְהוָה	‖ (2:10b) וּמֵהֲדַר גְּאֹנוֹ
EEⁱα	וּבָאוּ בִּמְעָרוֹת צֻרִים	‖ (2:19a) וּבִמְחִלּוֹת עָפָר
	מִפְּנֵי פַּחַד יְהוָה	‖ (2:19bα) וּמֵהֲדַר גְּאוֹנוֹ
β		(2:19bβ) בְּקוּמוֹ לַעֲרֹץ הָאָרֶץ
EEⁱⁱα	לָבוֹא בְּנִקְרוֹת הַצֻּרִים	‖ (2:21a) וּבִסְעִפֵי הַסְּלָעִים
	מִפְּנֵי פַּחַד יְהוָה	‖ (2:21bα) וּמֵהֲדַר גְּאוֹנוֹ
β		(2:21bβ) בְּקוּמוֹ לַעֲרֹץ הָאָרֶץ

One may also observe that the 'DDα' and 'DDβ' tiers reverse order
about the axis of the section in the same manner as the 'CCα' and
'CCβ' tiers did in the previous section.[1] Not only is the passage
granted structural unity through a complex frameworking pattern, by
which asymmetrical concentricity is achieved, but emotional escalation
is effected by its cumulative pattern of repetitions. The accumulation of
repetitions added to the 'DDβ' and 'EEα' tiers escalates the emotional
effect of YHWH's threats of judgment described there: to the 'DDβ'
tier's threat that 'humanity will be humbled', the 'DDβⁱ' addition
counters that 'YHWH alone will be exalted on that day'; to the 'EEα'
tier's threat that people will 'flee to the rocks from the dread of
YHWH', the 'EEβ' tiers specify that YHWH will 'rise to shake the
earth'.

The rhetorical emphasis falls upon the structural axis, which lists no
less than ten manifestations of human arrogance, each a reason for

---

[1]Cf. a similar pattern of reversal about the axis among the bifid elements of tiers
'GGα' and 'GGβ' in the following section (Isa. 3:1–4:1). Here, exceptionally, the
'DDⁱⁱⁱβ-tier' has been segmented syntactically between DDⁱⁱⁱβ' (2:20aα) and
DDⁱⁱⁱβ" (2:20bβ).

YHWH's judgment, each beginning with עַל כָּל־ 'for all/every ...' This
tenfold denunciation adds emphasis to an axis already made the focal
point of the surrounding framing repetitions. The structural axis is
framed by both the tier repetitions and by the reversed order of bifid
tiers, by which the 'DDα' tiers ostensibly frame the 'DDβ' tiers about
the axis. Considering also the patterned alternation between שׁחח and
שׁפל as A- and B-words in the first three 'DDβ' tiers, it seems
reasonable to conclude that the intricate form of Isa. 2:6-21 is the product of a deliberate rhetorical strategy whose aim is to denounce the
arrogance of idolaters.

Persuasion as a Function of Structure in Isaiah 2:6aγ-21

It is difficult to assign a precise date of composition to this section of
Isaiah though, along with 3:1–4:1, its thematic concerns appear to
relate to the widespread idolatry and social injustices of pre-exilic
times. Perhaps the prophet Isaiah wrote some elements of this section
during the turbulent early years of Manasseh's reign (ca. 686–642 BCE)
though it is plausible that its structural patterning is the result of later
editing.[1] Considering the relative brevity of this and the following section (3:1–4:1) among the seven main concentric divisions of Isaiah, and
in view of the fact that these two sections, both comprising accusations
and threats, complement one another according to the same two themes
of accusation that were introduced in the exordium (namely, problems
of cult and social injustice), one may infer that 2:6aγ-21 came to be
positioned at the front of the book of Isaiah, in juxtaposition with 3:1–
4:1, during the final stages of the book's compilation. The final author
may have had two reasons for doing so. First, in terms of structure, the
complex frameworking presented in Isa. 2:6aγ-21 offers the most lucid
and verifiable example of this repetition pattern in the book of Isaiah
and, thus, presents an ideal paradigm by which to introduce the complex frameworking pattern to be used in the rest of the book. Second,
in terms of the book's rhetoric, Isa. 2:6aγ-21 and 3:1–4:1 establish,
more explicitly than did the exordium, the grounds for YHWH's use of
the rhetoric of covenant disputation throughout the remainder of the
book.

Although the culpability of the monarchy for the aberrations listed in
the accusation (2:6aγ-8) and for the subsequent threats of punishment

[1]See the summary of historical implications of the situation implied by 2:6aγ-21
and 3:1–4:1 under the same subheading in Chapter 3, below.

(2:9-21) remains unstated, it is nonetheless present under the force of the allusion to prohibitions contained in Deut. 17:16-17. The condemnation of Judah's royalty in Isa. 2:6aγ-8 remains obscured by the covenant imagery for perhaps two reasons. First, such indirectness might afford the prophet some measure of insulation against reprisal at the hands of the king(s) he was thus incriminating. Second, by refraining from specifying the social class that was the object of these denunciations, as well as of the threats that follow, they could be seen to apply equally well to those who followed misdirection as to those who misled. Thus, it is the lack of a specific addressee that extends culpability both to those who followed apostate policies and to the king and judicial heads who instituted them.

Equally effective for communicating the threats of impending doom is the triple repetition of בַּיּוֹם הַהוּא in the last three 'DDβ' tiers (2:11, 17, 20aα). The 'Day of YHWH' is foremost a day of justice but, for the house of Jacob, this becomes a two-edged sword. While this day may deliver and vindicate the helpless, it will also execute punishment on those disloyal to YHWH's covenant stipulations.[1] In this section, however, the certainty of doom escalates with every repetition; there is no sense of the 'deliverance' of that day offered here. Isaiah 2:6aγ-21 outlines only the negative aspect of YHWH's day, without counterbalance.

The ascending order of repetitions is a key rhetorical device in this section, which heightens the readers' mood of apprehension through a series of repetitions with additions. The accumulation of new material to the repetitions mimics the worsening effect of the cataclysm portrayed in YHWH's coming judgment. Indeed, the additions to the 'DDβ' tiers and of the 'EEβ' tiers may combine to form a broken couplet: 'YHWH alone will be exalted on that day' (2:11, 17) 'when he rises to shake the earth' (2:19, 21). This vindication of YHWH before covenant violators represents the antithesis of the people's exaltation of the lofty objects enumerated in the axis (2:12-16)—the only other tier of 2:6aγ-21 where יוֹם is used, again in reference to the time of YHWH's coming judgment.

---

[1] Cf. G. von Rad, 'The Origin of the Concept of the Day of Yahweh', *JSS* 4 (1959), pp. 97-108; M. Weiss, 'The Origin of the "Day of the Lord"—Reconsidered', *HUCA* 37 (1966), pp. 29-72; A.J. Everson, 'The Days of Yahweh', *JBL* 93 (1974), pp. 329-37; J. Gray, 'The Day of Yahweh in Cultic Experience and Eschatological Prospect', *SEÅ* 39 (1974), pp. 12-16; Y. Hoffmann, 'The Day of the Lord as a Concept and a Term in the Prophetic Literature', *ZAW* 93 (1981), pp. 37-50.

One instance of what appears to be deliberate rhetorical ambiguity occurs in the use of the 3 masc. pl. form of בוא 'to enter' in 2:19a. It may be taken to refer to the idols just mentioned in 2:18 or, on the basis of the parallelism between the EEⁱα-tier (2:19abα) and the EEα-tier (2:10), to the idolaters themselves. Through this ambiguity, which is only later clarified as referring to the idols (2:20), the reader is subtly prompted to equate the fate of people with the fate of their idols. In the end, this is precisely the rhetorical equation that results from the correlation of all three 'EE' tiers.

The Continuity of Isaiah 2:6-22 with its Context

Isaiah 2:6aγ-21 functions as a single rhetorical unit and seems to be a further specification of the accusations (cf. 2:6aγ-8) and threats of destruction (cf. 2:9-21) deserved by those against whom the earlier accusations (1:2b-3, 4), threats (1:20, 28-31), and appeals (1:18-19, 2:2-5) were made. In this respect, there is rhetorical continuity between these major sections of Isaiah. The latter continues the covenant disputation rhetoric introduced by the former. However, within the strategy of covenant disputation that governs the book of Isaiah, this section, like its complement that follows (3:1–4:1), is limited to the negative aspects of the disputation form, namely, accusation and threat of destruction. Together these two sections form a double series of accusations and threats within Isaiah's covenant disputation. Further, this doubling may correspond to the coupling of accusations of cultic and social violations in the exordium (there are two general accusation in 1:2b-3, 4, one accusation implied by the rejection of the cultic reparations in 1:11-15, and one accusation related to social injustices in 1:21-23).

The structural axis (2:12-16) is thematically important in that it focuses on a tenfold denunciation (grouped in five parallel pairs) of everything humanly exalted against the glory of YHWH. This axis thematically contrasts with 2:2 of the preceding section. Whereas it is only the mountain of YHWH's temple that is exalted in 2:2, every humanly exalted thing mentioned in 2:12-16 is to be debased. In the light of the covenant imagery invoked by the prologue's disputation pattern (1:1–2:5), it is probably not by chance that the towering objects denounced in 2:12-16 all pertain to key matters regulated and conditioned by the covenant—cult, military defense and commerce—and here only measure the degree of the people's abandonment of YHWH in their search for human means to attain national wealth, security and identity.

The paired list enumerates the material bases of the nation's spiritual aberration. At the same time, however, viewed as five paired hypocatastases, they may also serve to represent the haughtiness of those who esteem such matters to be more reliable than YHWH himself. The covenant violations implied here adumbrate the denunciations of Israel's false worship, foreign alliances and self-indulgences, which are articulated with greater specificity in the chapters that follow.

It must be borne in mind that, despite the consistent negativity of the accusatory and threatening tone in this section, there is overall an implicit appeal for repentance. What would be the use of chiding the house of Jacob for covenant apostasy and idolatry if not to warn them (in which case the section has a future orientation)? In any case, 2:6aγ-21 is only the first part of a double denunciation and focuses on the atrocities (chiefly idolatry) that have come about as a result of foreign alliances, and foreign alliances imply regal culpability.

Isaiah 2:22 serves as a hortatory joint between the related and similarly structured sections of 2:6aγ-21 and 3:1–4:1. It appropriately links the problems of covenant apostasy and social injustice that are emphasized in each of these sections, respectively, by showing the basic fault of YHWH's people to have been their inappropriate level of reliance upon human measures for achieving national wealth, security and identity.

Chapter 3

ISAIAH 3:1–4:1: THREAT OF JUDGMENT ON THE UNJUST

MISPLACED VALUES WILL BE INVERTED WHEN
YHWH OVERTURNS SOCIETY IN ZION

In Isaiah's exordium (1:1–2:5), YHWH's accusations against the
citizens of Zion contended against the unwarrantedness of their
covenant rebellion (1:2aγ-3, 4), the resultant impropriety of their cult
worship (1:11-15[16-17]), and their leadership's social injustices (1:21-
23). Although the prologue presents these in summary fashion, they
constitute the essential covenant violations that subsequent sections of
the book of Isaiah will particularize. In the section immediately following the exordium (2:6aγ-21[22]), one may surmise that the root of
apostasy, at which YHWH's prophet hacks with accusations and threats,
sprouted into the failure of Zion's monarchy to adhere to YHWH's
regal prohibitions, namely, in their arrogant confidence in foreign
alliances (cf. 2:6aγδb). Indeed, it was probably from such covenant
disloyalties among Zion's leaders that widespread religious and social
apostasy from YHWH diffused to permeate all echelons of society.
Thus, the threats of judgment in the section now under consideration
(3:1–4:1) redress social wrongs in a manner similar to that by which
the threats of the preceding section (2:9-21) redressed religious
infidelities. However, the interest in Isa. 3:1–4:1 focuses upon the form
that YHWH's judgment would take against the nonregal upper classes in
Zion's society, and its accusations and judgments appropriately concern
matters of economics. The passage outlines the removal of valuable
commodities and official personnel from Zion. This was YHWH's
means of inverting Zion's social structure so that both the corrupt leaders and judges, as well as the self-indulgent women, of Zion would no
longer be able to continue their callous injustices. Only the bare neces-
sities of life would be procurable once YHWH had brought judgment
upon them.

Structural Delineation of Isaiah 3:1–4:1

Isaiah 3:1–4:1 effectively commences with the hortatory joint of 2:22, which, because of its prohibition against trusting in human achievement, not only epitomizes the theme of the previous section but sets the mood for the present section as well:

> Stop [חִדְלוּ] trusting in humanity
>> whose breath is in their nostrils.
> Of what account are they?

The threats of judgment (3:1-7, 9b-11; 3:17–4:1) issue from the social abuses outlined in the accusations against self-indulgent youths and women, and unjust leaders (3:8-9a, 12-16). The section ends precisely where there is a shift from the negative disposition that characterizes it (except for 3:10) to the more positive disposition of the description of future Zion in 4:2-6.[1] Moreover, it is probably no coincidence that 3:1–4:1 opens and closes by setting into the foreground the thematic motif of 'removal', a motif that characterizes the whole section (מֵסִיר, 3:1aβ; and אָסֹף, 4:1bβ; cf. יָסִיר, 3:18α).

Complex Frameworking in Isaiah 3:1–4:1

The following schema presents a complex frameworking pattern by which this section may be arranged. Its overall contour, like that of Isa. 2:6aγ-21, is asymmetrically concentric, and one set of tiers (marked 'GG') is essentially bifid.

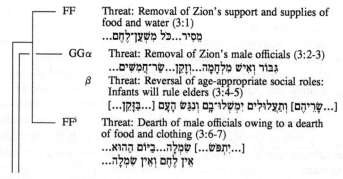

FF   Threat: Removal of Zion's support and supplies of food and water (3:1)
מֵסִיר...כֹּל מִשְׁעַן־לָחֶם...

GGα   Threat: Removal of Zion's male officials (3:2-3)
גִּבּוֹר וְאִישׁ מִלְחָמָה...וְזָקֵן...שַׂר־חֲמִשִּׁים...

β   Threat: Reversal of age-appropriate social roles: Infants will rule elders (3:4-5)
[...שָׂרֵיהֶם] וְתַעֲלוּלִים יִמְשְׁלוּ־בָם וְנִגַּשׂ הָעָם [...בַּזָּקֵן]

FFⁱ   Threat: Dearth of male officials owing to a dearth of food and clothing (3:6-7)
[...יִתְפֹּשׂ...] שִׂמְלָה...בַּיּוֹם הַהוּא...
אֵין לֶחֶם וְאֵין שִׂמְלָה...

---

[1] Recently, B. Wiklander (*Prophecy as Literature: A Text-Linguistic and Rhetorical Approach to Isaiah 2–4* [ConBOT, 22; Stockholm: Gleerup, 1984]) contended for the cohesion of Isa. 4:2-6 with its preceding context (2:1–4:1; especially 3:16–4:1) on the basis of syntax (pp. 100-105), semantics (pp. 112-14, 140-

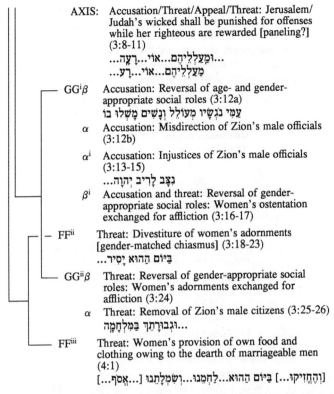

AXIS: Accusation/Threat/Appeal/Threat: Jerusalem/
        Judah's wicked shall be punished for offenses
        while her righteous are rewarded [paneling?]
        (3:8-11)
        ...רָעָה...אוֹי...וּמַעַלְלֵיהֶם...
        ...רָע...אוֹי...מַעַלְלֵיהֶם

GG^{i}β   Accusation: Reversal of age- and gender-
        appropriate social roles (3:12a)
        עַמִּי נֹגְשָׂיו מְעוֹלֵל וְנָשִׁים מָשְׁלוּ בוֹ

α   Accusation: Misdirection of Zion's male officials
        (3:12b)

α^i Accusation: Injustices of Zion's male officials
        (3:13-15)
        ...נִצָּב לָרִיב יְהוָה

β^i Accusation and threat: Reversal of gender-
        appropriate social roles: Women's ostentation
        exchanged for affliction (3:16-17)

FF^{ii} Threat: Divestiture of women's adornments
        [gender-matched chiasmus] (3:18-23)
        ...בַּיּוֹם הַהוּא יָסִיר

GG^{ii}β   Threat: Reversal of gender-appropriate social
        roles: Women's adornments exchanged for
        affliction (3:24)

α   Threat: Removal of Zion's male citizens (3:25-26)
        ...וּגְבוּרָתֵךְ בַּמִּלְחָמָה

FF^{iii} Threat: Women's provision of own food and
        clothing owing to the dearth of marriageable men
        (4:1)
        [...וְהֶחֱזִיקוּ] בַּיּוֹם הַהוּא...לַחְמֵנוּ...וְשִׂמְלָתֵנוּ [...אֱסֹף]

Below appears an English translation of this section outlined according to the previous schema, with common tiers aligned in columns and
rhetorically significant Hebrew words given in square brackets. Since,
in the present section, it is the selfish greed of Zion's elite that forms
the basis of their acts of injustice, YHWH appears in judgment to
remove from Zion the very commodities and desirable materials that
formed the basis of their false system of values. Appropriately, this
complex framework commences with a description of YHWH that uses
his epithet of judgment (יְהוָה צְבָאוֹת):

42), and rhetoric (pp. 158-67), and I admit that there are points of continuity
between 4:2-6 and the foregoing material. Similarly, M.A. Sweeney (*Isaiah 1–4
and the Post-Exilic Understanding of the Isaianic Tradition* [BZAW, 171; Berlin:
de Gruyter, 1988]), who contended for the redactional unity of 2:1–4:6 (pp. 35-36,
134-84), sought to demonstrate the cohesion of 4:2-6 with the preceding context
(pp. 179-81). Yet, the preponderance of key word collocations and the triadic patterning of subunits between 4:2-6 and 11:1-9, 10-16 seem to indicate more
strongly that 4:2-6 was intended to be read as introducing the following section
(4:2–11:16). See the discussion in Chapter 4.

FF   For now the Lord [הָאָדוֹן], Warrior YHWH [יְהוָה צְבָאוֹת],
        is about to remove [מֵסִיר] from Jerusalem and Judah
        [מִירוּשָׁלַ ִם וּמִיהוּדָה]
        both supply and support [מַשְׁעֵן וּמַשְׁעֵנָה]:
        the whole supply of food [מִשְׁעַן־לֶחֶם]
        and the whole supply [מִשְׁעַן] of water; (3:1)

GGα   warrior [גִּבּוֹר] and man of battle [מִלְחָמָה],
        judge and prophet,
        soothsayer and elder [וְזָקֵן],
        commander of fifty [שַׂר־חֲמִשִּׁים] and nobleman,
        counselor, clever artisan and expert enchanter.
        (3:2-3)

β   Then I will appoint youths as their commanders [שָׂרֵיהֶם],
        and infants [וְתַעֲלוּלִים] to rule over them [יִמְשְׁלוּ־בָם].
        The people will oppress [וְנִגַּשׂ הָעָם] one another:
        each one against another,
        each one against a neighbor.
        The youth will be brash against the elder [בַּזָּקֵן],
        and the base against the honorable. (3:4-5)

FFⁱ   When someone seizes [כִּי־יִתְפֹּשׂ] one of his brothers
        at his father's house [בֵּית], [saying:]
        'You have clothing [שִׂמְלָה];
        you be our ruler [קָצִין]
        and bring this ruin under your control!'—
        He will respond in that day [בַּיּוֹם הַהוּא], saying:
        'I will not undertake to remedy [this]
        when in my [own] house [וּבְבֵיתִי]
        there is neither food [לֶחֶם] nor clothing [שִׂמְלָה]!
        You shall not make me ruler [קָצִין] of the people!' (3:6-7)

AXIS: [paneling?] (3:8-11):
        A   For Jerusalem [יְרוּשָׁלַ ִם] is staggering,
                Judah [וִיהוּדָה] is falling!
                Their speech and their deeds [וּמַעַלְלֵיהֶם] are before
                YHWH,
                        an offense in the sight of his glory.
                The very look on their faces testifies against them;
                        their sin, like Sodom, they vaunt without
                                hiding.
        B   Woe [אוֹי] to them:
                        they have dealt [גָּמְלוּ] disaster [רָעָה] to
                                themselves!
        [1/]Aⁱ Happy the righteous,
                        for [it will be] well!
                For they will eat from the fruit of their deeds
                [מַעַלְלֵיהֶם].
        Bⁱ   Woe [אוֹי] to the wicked—
                        disaster [רָע]!
                For what was done [גְּמוּל] by their hands
                        shall be done to them!

GGⁱβ   My people's oppressors [עַמִּי נֹגְשָׂיו] are infants [מְעוֹלֵל]!
        Women [וְנָשִׁים] rule over them [מָשְׁלוּ בוֹ]! (3:12a)

α   O my people [עַמִּי], your guides mislead,
        they confound the course of your paths. (3:12b)

αⁱ YHWH takes a stand to accuse;
        he stands up to judge the peoples [עַמִּים].
        YHWH enters into judgment [בְּמִשְׁפָּט]
            with the elders of his people [זִקְנֵי עַמּוֹ] and their
                officials [וְשָׂרָיו].
        'It is you who have ruined the vineyard [הַכֶּרֶם];
            the plunder of the poor [הֶעָנִי] is in your houses
                [בְּבָתֵּיכֶם]!
        What do you mean by crushing my people [עַמִּי]
            and grinding the faces of the poor [עֲנִיִּים]?', (3:13-15a)
        declares the Lord [נְאֻם־אֲדֹנָי], Warrior YHWH
            [יְהוָה צְבָאוֹת]. (3:15b)

βⁱ YHWH says:
        'Because Zion's daughters [בְּנוֹת צִיּוֹן] are haughty [גָּבְהוּ]
            and walk with necks outstretched,
        flirting with the eyes,
            ogling and mincing along
                with anklets on their feet,
        the Lord will bring scabs on the scalps of Zion's
            daughters [בְּנוֹת צִיּוֹן],
        and YHWH will make bare their pates!' (3:16-17)

FFⁱⁱ In that day [בַּיּוֹם הַהוּא], the Lord will remove [יָסִיר] [their]
            finery [אֵת תִּפְאֶרֶת]: (3:18α)
        A   the anklets, sunbursts and crescents;
          B   the pendants, bracelets and veils;
            Axis: the headdresses, ankle chains, cinctures,
                        perfume boxes and amulets;
                    the signet rings and nose rings;
          Bⁱ the robes, capes, cloaks,
        Aⁱ purses, mirrors, linen tunics,
        Closure: turbans and shawls.
        [gender-matched chiasmus] (3:18β-23)

GGⁱⁱβ There will be stench instead [תַּחַת] of perfume;
            instead [וְתַחַת] of a sash, a rope;
        instead [וְתַחַת] of a coiffure, baldness;
            instead [וְתַחַת] of a rich robe, sackcloth;
        indeed, instead [תַּחַת] of beauty, [shame]! (3:24)

α   Your men will fall by the sword [בַּחֶרֶב],
            and your warriors [וּגְבוּרָתֵךְ] in battle [בַּמִּלְחָמָה].
        Her gates will lament and mourn;
            destitute, she will sit on the ground. (3:25-26)

FF[iii]   Seven women [נָשִׁים] will take hold [וְהֶחֱזִיקוּ]
          of a single man, in that day [בַּיּוֹם הַהוּא], saying:
          'We will eat our own food [לַחְמֵנוּ נֹאכֵל]
          and provide our own clothing [וְשִׂמְלָתֵנוּ נִלְבָּשׁ]—
          only let us be called by your name;
          remove [אֱסֹף] our disgrace!' (4:1)

In each case, the 'GG' tiers describe some group affected by
YHWH's judgment against the elite of Zion's society. Also, each of
these tiers is thematically bifurcated. The 'GGα' tiers deal with male
officials and citizens of Zion who are about to be removed from
society. The 'GGβ' tiers describe the reversal of some aspect of Zion's
social order, whether it involves distinctions of age (i.e., the promotion
of youths over elders) or of gender (i.e., the dominance, then humiliation, of women in relation to men). The 'FF' tiers link the 'GG' tiers
together by focusing on the antipolar tension between the human obses-
sion with seizing wealth and the divine removal of such basic commodities as 'food' and 'clothing'. In violation of YHWH's covenant,
luxurious commodities were being unjustly seized by Zion's officials
through extortion of the poor and then were being worn proudly by
their women. After YHWH's inversion of this unjust economic order,
however, self-indulgent women would have to provide their own food
and clothing just to be able to 'take hold' of some man who might help
them overcome the shortage of marriageable males.

One may note again the reverse-order pattern of the bifid tiers
'GGα' and 'GGβ' that frame the axis. The only variation from the pattern (which I have noted already among the bifid 'CC' and 'DD' tiers
in the previous two sections of Isaiah) occurs in the GG^i-tier (3:12-17).
This tier opens with the expected reverse order GG^{i}β–GG^{i}α (3:12a, b)
but then is followed immediately by another reversal, GG^{i}α^i–GG^{i}β^i
(3:13-15, 16-17), that reverts to the original bifid order. What is presented in this instance is a superimposed strategy of accusation: a
chiastic pattern (β-α-α^i-β^i), based upon an interchange among the elements of the bifid 'GG' tiers, is superimposed upon a series of divisions demarcated by changes of stance. In other words, YHWH first
indirectly decries the abuses committed by Zion's elite women and
infants (3:12a), then decries directly to his people the abuses of Zion's
male officials (3:12b), then directly accuses (and, in the second
instance, threatens) the same two groups of Zion's elite (3:13-15,
16-17).

The presence of gender-matched parallelism in 3:18β-23 has already been noted by W.G.E. Watson, but the following schematization shows a structural symmetry that represents all the words in the inset:[1]

```
        ┌─── m m m (3:18β)
        │ ┌─── f f f (3:19)
  Axis: │ │  m f m   m-f m   f m-m (3:20-21)
        │ └─── f f f (3:22αβⁱ)
        └─── m m m (3:22βⁱⁱ-23α)
              f m (3:23β)
```

Not only does the end-rhyme (ם־ִ, ם־ִ, ם־ִ; וֹת־, וֹת־, וֹת־) effect cohesion, but the structure of this inset, which is based upon gender alignment, is basically chiastic. A string of three masculines (3:18β) and another of three feminines (3:19) are mirrored by their own inversions (3:22αβⁱ; 22βⁱⁱ-23α) across a mixed, but gender-symmetrical, axis (3:20-21). The final line, with only one feminine and one masculine (3:23β), serves as an appropriate closure.

Persuasion as a Function of Structure in Isaiah 3:1–4:1

From all indications of subject matter, it would appear that the thematic core of Isa. 3:1–4:1 first appeared, in conjunction with 2:6aγ-21(22), in pre-exilic times, though the complex frameworking of the materials in the passage may be a result of the book's later editing. The situation described in the present section is one of social injustice and popular unrest, but there is no intimation that the anticipated military threat to Jerusalem was imminent or that it would come in the aftermath of the Neo-Babylonian conquest of Nineveh in 612 BCE. It may be that the situation presupposed in Isa. 3:1–4:1, as in 2:6aγ-21(22), best suits what we can to discern of the early years of Manasseh's long reign (ca. 686-642 BCE), during which cultic and social abuses purportedly irrupted in Jerusalem with unprecedented suddenness and force.[2] This

---

[1]W.G.E. Watson, *Classical Hebrew Poetry: A Guide to its Techniques* (JSOT-Sup, 26; Sheffield: JSOT Press, 1984), pp. 231-32. Cf. also E.E. Platt, 'Jewelry of Bible Times and the Catalog of Isa 3:18-23', *AUSS* 17 (1979), pp. 71-81, 189-201.

[2]Cf. Wiklander, pp. 175-82. Wiklander assigns 2:1–4:6 to the period of 'national-cultural renaissance' that emerged in the days of Hezekiah (ca. 715-686 BCE) but prior to its climactic reemergence under Josiah (ca. 640-609 BCE; especially after the reforms of 622 BCE). Thus, Wiklander purports a date of composition, within the period of Assyrian sovereignty over Jerusalem, between ca. 715 and 622 BCE.

remains a difficult matter to substantiate, however, since neither of these sections contains specific historical references by which one could date them.

It may be significant that there are changes of rhetorical function among the repetitions of tiers in which the two groups (male officials versus their dependants, i.e., youths and women) are alternatively threatened (GG, 3:2-3, 4-5), accused (GG^i, 3:12a, b, 13-15, 16-17), and then threatened (GG^{ii}, 3:24, 25-26). Moreover, it is noteworthy that the feminine gender, which applies to 'Zion's daughters' in the GG$^i\beta$-, GG$^i\beta^i$- and GG$^{ii}\beta$-tiers, comes to apply also to 'the daughter of Zion' (i.e., the city of Jerusalem personified) in the GG$^{ii}\alpha$-tier (3:25-26).

Contrariwise, the 'FF' tiers all function as threats in that they all describe the situation that would result from YHWH's coming judgment. The FF-tier (3:1) is a summary threat that introduces the motif of the removal of valued commodities from Jerusalem. The FF^i-tier (3:6-7) relates to the male population, which is portrayed as refusing to refill the deficit of leaders that would result from the coming judgment. Appropriately, the gender-matched chiasmus of the FF^{ii}-tier (3:18-23) pertains to the former officials' female dependants, whose adornment has been forfeited either by force of need or lack of value.[1] In the final tier (FF^{iii}, 4:1), the interests of both male and female citizens of Zion combine in that the problem portrayed there is one that would affect both genders—the shortage of men, owing to the casualties of warfare and deportation, would mean a dearth of marriageable men for the remaining women.

The main axis of the structure (3:8-11) begins with a description of present distresses accompanied by an accusation (A, 3:8-9a), which may be matched by the antithetical description of blessings on the righteous ([1/]A^i, 3:10). These tiers alternate with two woes (B, 3:9b; and B^i, 3:11), which function as threats. The rhetorical crux of the axis section is the promise (implicitly, appeal) to the righteous—

---

[1] J.H. Hayes and S.A. Irvine suggest that the luxury items may have been given up to pay tribute in time of national emergency (*Isaiah the Eighth-century Prophet: His Times and His Preaching* [Nashville: Abingdon Press, 1987], p. 95). This would seem to anticipate a situation in which the deprivations would be in excess of those of the siege of 701 BCE and would comport with the suggestion that the subject matter of Isa. 3:1–4:1 may derive from the early years of Manasseh's reign. In any case, the stance of this passage is futuritive and concerns a siege of Jerusalem yet to come.

significantly, the only positive note in the whole section—that they will be vindicated against the abuses of their unjust officials (3:10).[1]

It appears that Wiklander may have been correct in perceiving the elements of a 'lawsuit genre' in 2:6-8 and 3:1-15, 16-17, though he argued that this was only a subgenre (like the subgenre of 'prophetic vision report' in 2:11-21; 3:1-7, 13-14a and 3:18–4:6) within the over-all 'revelation text' subgenre that allegedly governs 2:1–4:6.[2]

The Continuity of Isaiah 3:1–4:1 with its Context

The prohibitive hortatory pivot of 2:22 both links and epitomizes the rhetorical concerns of the matching compound frames of 2:6aγ-21 and 3:1–4:1. Moreover, it alludes to the language of the axis of Isa. 1:1–2:5 (i.e., 1:16-17), wherein one finds a similar prohibition (beginning with חִדְלוּ, 1:16b) issued in commands to uphold social justice:

> Stop doing [חִדְלוּ] wrong;
>> learn to do right.
> Seek justice,
>> encourage the oppressed,
> vindicate the fatherless,
>> contend for the widow.

It may be tenable to suggest that 2:22, which is a hortatory joint between the twin flanking sections of 2:6aγ-21 and 3:1–4:1, and thereby ostensibly the axis of a bifid symmetrical structure, serves a function similar to that served by 1:16-17, the axis of 1:1–2:5.

[1]Cf. W.L. Holladay, 'Isa iii 10-11: An Archaic Wisdom Passage', *VT* 18 (1968), pp. 481-87.
[2]Wiklander, pp. 212-21. He states: 'Although the genre of "lawsuit" has a larger capacity to explain 2:6–4:6 as a unit, it nevertheless fails to include the dis-course as a whole, for it does not include the prophetic vision in 2:1-4, not the hortatory peak in 2:5, and not the theme of "restoration" in 4:1-6' (p. 217). Obviously, these inconsistencies are removed if one applies Wiklander's criteria for the 'lawsuit genre' only to the sections delineated above (i.e., 2:6aγ-21[22]; 3:1–4:1), but one should also observe that his criteria for the 'lawsuit genre' (cf. pp. 127-28) are limited to selected elements (i.e., accusation, threat, [appeal]) from among those that seem to have constituted the prophetic covenant disputation genre (see the discussion in Chapter 1). Cf. also Sweeney's remarks as to the difficulty of the joint (2:5) between 2:2-4 and 2:6-22, passages that seem to have little in common (p. 164). On the 'revelation text genre', see further J. Lindblom, *Die literarische Gattung der prophetischen Literatur: Eine literargeschichtliche Untersuchung zum Alten Testament*, in *Uppsala Universitets Arsskrift (1924)* (2 vols.; Uppsala: Lundeqvist, 1924), I, pp. 1-122. For a survey of research on prophetic genres, see L. Alonso-Schökel, *Estudios de Poética Hebrea* (Barcelona: Juan Flors, Editor, 1963), pp. 338-45.

An example of the continuity of 3:1–4:1 with its context may be found where the man of meager means is asked to take up rulership in 3:6-7. His reply is:

> I will not undertake to remedy [this]
> when in my [own] house [וּבְבֵיתִי]
> there is neither food [לֶחֶם] nor clothing [שִׂמְלָה]!
> You shall not make me ruler [קָצִין] of the people!

He uses the same term for ruler (קָצִין) by which his brother had prompted him to take up this position (cf. 3:6aδ). It may be by design that this use of the term echoes that in 1:10aβ, in the vocative phrase 'rulers of Sodom', by which YHWH accused Zion's leaders of practicing Sodom's excesses. Thus, by implication, YHWH may be portrayed here as threatening Zion with becoming a heap of destruction like that which resulted from Sodom's judgment. There is poetic justice in the present scenario in that once Zion, which had acted like Sodom, had come to resemble the ruin of Sodom, no one would seek further to govern it. Such would be the result of YHWH's judgment on the unjust of Zion.

Many aspects of the judgment threatened in Isa. 3:1–4:1 appear to flow from Inset[iv] (1:21-27) of Isaiah's exordium—especially 1:24-25 (tier 'BB*'). Both segments begin their threats of judgment with the same divine title of judgment (הָאָדוֹן יְהוָה צְבָאוֹת, 1:24aα; 3:1aα), and both employ the motif of removal (וְאָסִירָה, 1:25b; cf. מֵסִיר, 3:1aβ, which opens the unit; יָסִיר, 3:18α, which commences the gender-matched chiasmus of 3:18-23; and אָסֹף, 4:1bβ, which both closes and, together with מֵסִיר of 3:1aβ, frames 3:1–4:1). Moreover, these two segments contain very similar rhetorical interests: accusations of injustice against male officials (cf. 1:21-23 [tier 'AA*'] with 3:12b, 13-15), threats of disaster upon unjust leaders (cf. 1:24-25 [tier 'BB*'] with 3:2-3, 4-5, 25-26), and consoling promises for the righteous (cf. 1:26-27 [tier 'CC*'] with 3:10). It may follow that the editor responsible for the juxtaposition of Isa. 2:6aγ-21(22) and 3:1–4:1 was also responsible for the insertion of Inset[iv] (1:21-27) into the exordium, if not also the exordium's axis (1:16-17), whose prohibitions and injunctions likewise presuppose the existence of widespread social injustice in Zion.

What seems evident from the fact that Isa. 2:6aγ-21(22) and 3:1–4:1 are smaller in proportion to the longer sections that follow, from the fact that 2:6aγ-21(22) and 3:1–4:1 have analogous patterns of complex

frameworking (both sections comprising a quadratic frame superimposed upon a triadic frame), and from the fact that their frameworking patterns are comparable to patterns of repetition used elsewhere in Isaiah, is that 2:6aγ-21(22) and 3:1–4:1 were probably
designed, juxtaposed and positioned at the head of the book of Isaiah
during the finishing stages of its composition. Because of their smaller
size and position at the front of the book, they offer ideal micro-
structural models of the macrostructural patterns to come in later chapters. Because the patterns of complex frameworking that one finds in
2:6aγ-21(22) and 3:1–4:1 are analogous (as are also the structures of
Isa. 4:2–11:16 and 13:1–39:8—see below), they mutually confirm that
their formal structures resulted more from design than from accident.
Finally, it should be emphasized that, from a rhetorical vantage point,
Isa. 2:6aγ-21(22) and 3:1–4:1 play the complementary roles of setting
into the foreground the two main covenant offenses against which
YHWH contends throughout the remainder of the book: the offenses of
religious apostasy and social injustice.

Chapter 4

ISAIAH 4:2–12:6: THE SYRO-EPHRAIMITE-ASSYRIAN SCHEME FOR ZION'S JUDGMENT AND RESTORATION

AFTER PUNISHMENT YHWH WILL RESTORE A REMNANT IN ZION

Isaiah 4:2–11:16 constitutes a distinct structural entity in that it is patterned on an asymmetrically concentric model that gives it unity, coherence and emphasis. The concentric structure purported here is an elaborate permutation of the complex framing pattern already encountered in the asymmetrically concentric structures of 2:6aγ-21 and 3:1–4:1.

In the present section of Isaiah, one returns to a consideration of YHWH's ideal prospects for Zion (cf. Isa. 1:18-19; 2:2-3a, 3b-5). Herein YHWH is portrayed as setting forth his program for the purgation of Zion. It is a program that involves the judgment of present Zion as the prerequisite to the restoration of a righteous remnant in future Zion.[1] The first and preeminent focus, however, remains fixed on the progress of the Davidic line toward the fulfillment of YHWH's ideal for Zion's kingship.

Structural Delineation of Isaiah 4:2-12:6

The section comprising 4:2–11:16 commences with the reaffirmation of hope for a day in Israel when YHWH's 'branch' (the first of three references to a scion) and land would be glorious (4:2). This verse marks a sudden shift from the negative mood of accusation and threat in Isa. 2:6aγ-21, 22 and 3:1–4:1 to a positive mood of hope. The positive disposition of hope continues with the portrayal of a remnant living

---

[1]Since Isa. 4:2-6 corresponds to 11:1-9, 10-16 is such a manner as to frame the whole of 4:2–11:16, perhaps what O. Kaiser said in regard to 4:2-6 could be taken to pertain to the whole section: 'Yahweh's last word to his people is not judgment but his saving will; indeed, judgment is the means of realizing his saving will' (*Isaiah 1-12: A Commentary* [trans. J. Bowden; OTL; Philadelphia: Westminster Press, 2d edn, 1983], p. 84).

in future Zion and safeguarded by YHWH's promise to glorify and protect them (4:3-6). The section begins to close in two passages (11:1-5, 10) with a reiteration of the scion motif. Whereas the scion in 4:2 refers to the resurgence of the remnant of Israel, in 11:1-5 and 10 it becomes more specifically identified with the royal remnant of David's line. The first of the latter two repetitions of the scion motif (11:1-5) is immediately followed by the portrayal of an Edenlike era of peace in the realm of nature (11:6-9). The second repetition of the scion motif (11:10) is likewise followed by the idealized portrayal of Israel's national restoration (11:11-16), which correlates structurally and thematically to the previous idealized portrayals. Indeed, when the three corresponding portrayals of the future resurgence of a scion (4:2; 11:1-5, 10) are taken in combination with the three idealized portrayals of the world of future Zion (4:3-6; 11:6-9, 11-16), they comprise a triadic frame made up of bifid tiers. It is this triadic frame that best serves to delimit 4:2-11:16 as a single unified section. The whole section is then fully demarcated, after its conclusion, by the two-part hymn of Isa. 12:1-6, which forms a transition to 13:1-39:8.

Asymmetrical Concentricity in Isaiah 4:2-11:16

The asymmetrical concentricity is more extended in this section than in the previously described sections, but the triadic patterning is the same. Here one finds several paired compound inverse frames recessed within one another like the ever diminishing structures of a Chinese box. The six outer triadic frames appear to have been arranged so as to form three pairs, each pair comprising two triadic frames arranged inversely in relation to each other. The overall pattern of this section appears as follows:

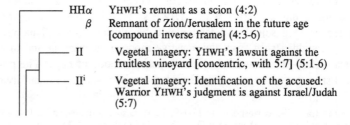

HHα   YHWH's remnant as a scion (4:2)
β   Remnant of Zion/Jerusalem in the future age [compound inverse frame] (4:3-6)
II   Vegetal imagery: YHWH's lawsuit against the fruitless vineyard [concentric, with 5:7] (5:1-6)
II^i   Vegetal imagery: Identification of the accused: Warrior YHWH's judgment is against Israel/Judah (5:7)

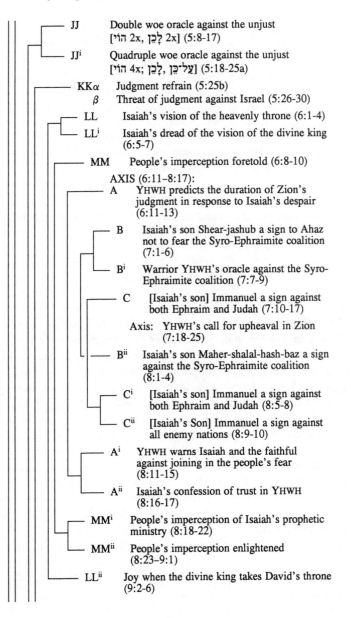

JJ	Double woe oracle against the unjust [לָכֵן 2x, הוֹי 2x] (5:8-17)
JJⁱ	Quadruple woe oracle against the unjust [עַל־כֵּן, לָכֵן ;4x הוֹי] (5:18-25a)
KKα	Judgment refrain (5:25b)
β	Threat of judgment against Israel (5:26-30)
LL	Isaiah's vision of the heavenly throne (6:1-4)
LLⁱ	Isaiah's dread of the vision of the divine king (6:5-7)
MM	People's imperception foretold (6:8-10)

AXIS (6:11–8:17):

A	YHWH predicts the duration of Zion's judgment in response to Isaiah's despair (6:11-13)
B	Isaiah's son Shear-jashub a sign to Ahaz not to fear the Syro-Ephraimite coalition (7:1-6)
Bⁱ	Warrior YHWH's oracle against the Syro-Ephraimite coalition (7:7-9)
C	[Isaiah's son] Immanuel a sign against both Ephraim and Judah (7:10-17)
Axis:	YHWH's call for upheaval in Zion (7:18-25)
Bⁱⁱ	Isaiah's son Maher-shalal-hash-baz a sign against the Syro-Ephraimite coalition (8:1-4)
Cⁱ	[Isaiah's son] Immanuel a sign against both Ephraim and Judah (8:5-8)
Cⁱⁱ	[Isaiah's Son] Immanuel a sign against all enemy nations (8:9-10)
Aⁱ	YHWH warns Isaiah and the faithful against joining in the people's fear (8:11-15)
Aⁱⁱ	Isaiah's confession of trust in YHWH (8:16-17)
MMⁱ	People's imperception of Isaiah's prophetic ministry (8:18-22)
MMⁱⁱ	People's imperception enlightened (8:23–9:1)
LLⁱⁱ	Joy when the divine king takes David's throne (9:2-6)

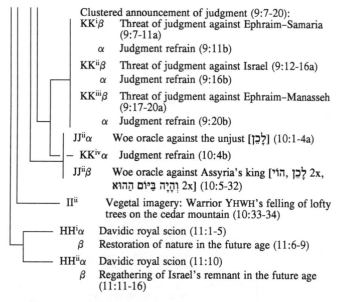

Clustered announcement of judgment (9:7-20):
KK$^i\beta$ Threat of judgment against Ephraim–Samaria (9:7-11a)
α Judgment refrain (9:11b)
KK$^{ii}\beta$ Threat of judgment against Israel (9:12-16a)
α Judgment refrain (9:16b)
KK$^{iii}\beta$ Threat of judgment against Ephraim–Manasseh (9:17-20a)
α Judgment refrain (9:20b)
JJ$^{ii}\alpha$ Woe oracle against the unjust [לָכֵן] (10:1-4a)
– KK$^{iv}\alpha$ Judgment refrain (10:4b)
JJ$^{ii}\beta$ Woe oracle against Assyria's king [הוֹי, לָכֵן 2x, וְהָיָה בַּיּוֹם הַהוּא 2x] (10:5-32)
II^{ii} Vegetal imagery: Warrior YHWH's felling of lofty trees on the cedar mountain (10:33-34)
HH$^i\alpha$ Davidic royal scion (11:1-5)
β Restoration of nature in the future age (11:6-9)
HH$^{ii}\alpha$ Davidic royal scion (11:10)
β Regathering of Israel's remnant in the future age (11:11-16)

The 'HHα' tiers (4:2; 11:1-5, 10) share the common feature of referring to a scion and, in the latter two instances, bear royal significance.[1] The juxtaposed 'HHβ' tiers all portray idealizations of the age during which the idealized royal figure will be enthroned: the HHβ-tier (4:3-6) describes a time when Zion has been thoroughly purged of its former sins and is glorified and protected by YHWH; the HH^{i}β-tier (11:6-9) depicts a time of peace and tranquility in nature precedented only in the pristine age of Eden; and the HH^{ii}β-tier (11:11-16) describes a time in which the remnant of Israel will be restored from all the nations and Ephraim and Judah will be reconciled under one ruler, as they had been when David ruled in Jerusalem.

The 'II' tiers cohere in their common function of denouncing, through the use of vegetal imagery, both Jerusalem/Judah, whom YHWH threatens to punish (5:1-6/7), and the Assyrians (10:33-34), by whom YHWH will have carried out his punishment of Jerusalem/Judah.

---

[1] The reference to a Davidic monarch is not explicit in 4:2, as in the later matching tiers, though the imagery effected by the mention of a scion nonetheless has regal connotations. The structural and thematic correlation of 4:2 to the Davidic portrayals in 11:1-5 and 10 may be helpful in understanding the more obscure reference to 'YHWH's branch' in 4:2. Cf. J.H. Hayes and S.A. Irvine, who also take 4:2 as referring to the Davidic king (*Isaiah the Eighth-century Prophet: His Times and His Preaching* [Nashville: Abingdon Press, 1987], p. 96).

The lawsuit, which incorporates a parable about YHWH's vineyard, subdivides precisely where the invitation to Jerusalem/Judah to judge the significance of the parable breaks off to identify and indict (through a rhetoric of entrapment) the real object of comparison, namely, between 5:1-6 and 7. Isaiah 5:1-7 has all the elements of a covenant lawsuit but it is in 5:7 that the parable and invitation to judge receives its 'interpretation'.[1] The denunciation of Assyria in 10:33-34 corresponds antithetically to the denunciation of Jerusalem in 5:1-6/7 and parodies the fall of Assyria (cf. 10:24), portraying it as the felling of lofty trees from the legendary cedar mountain.[2] Rightly does the reader sense the force of poetic justice when Judah's feller falls. All the 'II' tiers thus contain threats of destruction.

[1] The lawsuit of 5:1-7 comprises: (1) summons/incipit, 5:1a; (2) exoneration: description of past benefits, 5:1b-2a; (3) accusation: declaration of violation, 5:2b; (4) accusation: (rhetorical) interrogation, 5:3-4; and (5) ultimatum: threat of destruction, 5:5-6. Through a strategy of entrapment, 5:7a discloses that the judges (5:3-4) are, in fact, the accused. Isa. 5:7b specifies Jerusalem's violations with paronomastic reversals that invoke empathy for YHWH's sense of frustration, for in each case the terms used to describe YHWH's expectations are almost matched in sonority yet, ironically, are sufficiently altered to reverse the expected sense:

He hoped for justice [לְמִשְׁפָּט]
  but there was bloodshed [וְהִנֵּה מִשְׂפָּח];
for righteousness [לִצְדָקָה]
  but there was outcry [וְהִנֵּה צְעָקָה]! (5:7b)

The intervention of וְהִנֵּה conveys a sudden sense of surprise (cf. Isa. 17:14). See S. Kogut, 'On the Meaning and Syntactical Status of הִנֵּה in Biblical Hebrew', in S. Japhet (ed.), *Studies in Bible, 1986* (ScrHier, 31; Jerusalem: Magnes, 1986), pp. 133-54; and the remarks by M. Sternberg on the use of וְהִנֵּה to indicate 'free indirect discourse' in narrative (*The Poetics of Biblical Narrative* [ISBL; Bloomington: Indiana University Press, 1985], pp. 52-53).

[2] Several Assyrian monarchs boast in their annals of foreign expeditions of felling trees from the cedar mountain. For example, an annal of Ashur-nasir-pal II (883–859 BCE) reads:

> At this time I made my way to the slopes of Mount Lebanon ... I received tribute from the kings of the sea coast, from the lands of the men of Tyre, Sidon, Byblos, Mahallatu, Maizu, Kaizu, Amurru, and the city of Arvad which is (on an island) in the sea—silver, gold, tin, bronze, a bronze casserole, linen garments with multi-colored trim, a large female ape, a small female ape, ebony, box-wood, ivory ... I climbed up to Mount Amanus and cut down logs of cedar, cypress ... I transported cedar logs from Mount Amanus and brought them to Eshara for my house ... (*ARI*, II, §586)

Depictions of such timber felling are also to be found in the iconography of Mesopotamian and Egyptian monarchs. Such a feat was evidently considered a heroic exploit, befitting mighty warrior kings, since it was held that noble gods defended Lebanon's mountain garden from intruders. Hence, its timber became a veritable trophy of godlike bravery and might.

The 'JJ' and 'KK' tiers form a clustered permutation of the compound inverse framework pattern of repetitions, particularly in the latter half of the concentric structure, which comprises threats of judgment intermingled with accusations. All the 'JJ' tiers (5:8-17, 18-25a; and 10:1-4a, 5-32) present woe oracles, each comprising paired accusatory threats (beginning with הוֹי) followed by paired announcements of judgment (beginning with לָכֵן or, once, עַל־כֵּן). Among the 'KK' tiers one again finds the reverse ordering of bifid tiers about the axis of the main section so as to create a framing effect: the 'KKα' tiers (5:25b; 9:11b, 16b, 20b) all frame the 'KKβ' tiers (5:26-30; 9:7-11a, 12-16a, 17-20a) about the central axis.[1] It is worthy of note that the last three bifid 'KK' tiers form a trifid cluster.[2]

The visionary 'LL' tiers return to a theme similar to that observed among the 'HH' tiers. Among the 'LL' tiers, two tiers portray divine kingship (LL, 6:1-4; LL^i, 6:5-7) and the third describes a ruler who would exercise divine prerogatives as he reigned from David's throne over David's kingdom (LL^ii, 9:2-6). Yet, despite the glory of this prophetic vision, the temporary deafness and blindness of the prophet's audience/readers is foretold in the juxtaposed 'MM' tiers (6:8-10; 8:18-22; 8:23-9:1). Among the 'MM' tiers, images of darkness and light symbolize, alternatively, the people's imperception or insight into the meaning of the prophet's vision for a divine king's rule from David's throne in Zion. By YHWH's decree, the prophet's audience/readers were to remain unable to understand his message so as to repent (6:8-10). They would remain in that imperceptive condition because, despite the prophet's revelatory signs, they chose not to inquire of their god (8:18-22); yet, after their humiliation, the prophet foresaw that YHWH would enlighten them so that they would gain insight and understand the meaning of the prophet's vision of the divine king (8:23-9:1).

The main section's axis (6:11-8:17) is enclosed by a triadic frame comprising the 'A' tiers. Here the prophet's own apprehensions, resulting from his vision of the punishment predicted for a Zion that would reject YHWH's message (A, 6:11-13), are first assuaged by YHWH, then relayed by the prophet to his followers (A^i, 8:11-15; A^ii, 8:16-17). In the pattern formed by the 'B' and 'C' tiers one finds another

---

[1]Cf. the same framing arrangement about sectional axes effected through the reverse ordering of bifid tiers 'CCα' and 'CCβ' in Isa. 1:1-2:5, the 'DDα' and 'DDβ' tiers in 2:6-21, and the 'GGα' and 'GGβ' tiers in 3:1-4:1.

[2]In fact, wherever tiers are clustered in Isa. 4:2-11:16 and 13:1-39:8, they comprise trifid formations. Cf. the same formation among the 'PP' and 'QQ' clusters in 14:28-17:3, 18:1-20:5, 21:1-15, and 34:1-17.

example of a compound inverse frame, though in this instance the triadic frames interlock with each other. Because of its central position and interlocking pattern, the compound inverse frame formed by tiers 'B' and 'C', together with the surrounding triadic frame comprising the 'A' tiers, should probably be thought of as forming a subsection distinct from the surrounding concentric network of compound inverse frames (one of tiers 'HH' and 'II', another of tiers 'LL' and 'MM', and the intervening frame formed by the clustered tiers 'JJ' and 'KK'). All the 'B' and 'C' tiers describe situations in the prophet's ministry in which the prophetic significance of the names of Isaiah's sons played a part (cf. 8:18). The 'C' tiers (7:10-17; 8:5-8, 9-10) are the most readily isolable since they share the designation or phrase אֵל עִמָּנוּ (7:14; 8:8bβ, 10bβ); however, its use in the middle tier marks the climax of ironic reversal against the expectations of Zion's citizens as to how YHWH would be with them. The C-tier (7:10-17) predicts Judah's deliverance from the Syro-Ephraimite threat but then ironically threatens not just Ephraim but also Judah through the agent of 'deliverance', the king of Assyria.[1] In the Cⁱ-tier (8:5-8), the Assyrian threat against the region of Judah is more elaborate than it was when introduced at the end of 7:17. The Cⁱⁱ-tier then returns to the theme of

[1]This out-of-the-frying-pan-and-into-the-fire strategy of rhetoric, wherein temporary deliverance from an immediate threat serves to give just enough of a false sense of relief so as utterly to belie it at the irruption of a greater threat, is the key strategy of the narrative passages directed against Ahaz (7:1–8:10) and Hezekiah (36:1–39:8). For both of these kings of Judah there was a fear of imminent destruction, which the prophet prophetically deferred to a future cataclysm of far greater proportions. Ahaz's immediate fear of the Syro-Ephraimite threat was quelled (7:7-9a) but displaced by the greater future threat against Judah, which would come from the same Assyria in which Ahaz had sought an ally against Syria–Ephraim (though Assyria would only threaten, not conquer, Jerusalem; cf. 8:7-8a). A generation later, this Assyrian threat came to be fulfilled. Again, in 36:1–39:8, the narrative's reversed temporal order presents a similar pattern whereby Hezekiah's immediate fear, that Jerusalem would be overflowed by the Assyrians, is likewise quelled (cf. 37:35; 38:6), but only to be displaced by the greater future threat of a cataclysm at the hands of the same Babylon in which Hezekiah had sought an ally against Assyria (and Babylon would, indeed, conquer Jerusalem; cf. 39:5-7). Thus, the two narrative portrayals of Isaiah's confrontations of Judah's kings form a chainlink between the two major sections of the book of Isaiah in which they occur (i.e., the structurally twin sections of 4:2–11:16 and 13:1–39:8) and, by the pattern of deferring to a future generation the ever greater threats that would emerge from a would-be ally of the present, foreshadow the situation of Babylonian exile that forms the background of the author's rhetoric in 40:1–54:17. Hence, it is the chainlink deferral of judgment among the sections comprising 4:2–11:16, 13:1–39:8 and 40:1–54:17 that generates thematic and historical continuity among these concentric sections.

Judah's deliverance, first conveyed in the C-tier by the use of עִמָּנוּ אֵל (7:14), but it escalates this theme from an international to a universal scale. The symbolic significance of Isaiah's (other?) sons' names (שְׁאָר יָשׁוּב [7:3] and מַהֵר שָׁלָל חָשׁ בַּז [8:1, 3]) is treated among the 'B' tiers (7:1-6, 7-9; 8:1-4), whose rhetoric always operates within the context of concern for Judah's deliverance from the Syro-Ephraimite threat.

The core of the axis section is 7:18-25. Here the threat of destruction at the hands of the king of Assyria is shown to be the consummate threat posed against the king and people of Judah. Here is the vortex of the cataclysm that Ahaz should fear: that day (בַּיּוֹם הַהוּא, 7:18aα, 20aα, 21a, 23aα) which YHWH has appointed for Judah's punishment! Thus, YHWH rebukes Ahaz by measuring the present minor threat from Syria–Ephraim (from whom YHWH would deliver Judah as proof of his divine knowledge and saving power) against the greater threat posed by YHWH's decree to chastise his people at the hands of Assyria.

Complex Frameworking in Isaiah 4:2-11:16

The outer concentric structure of Isa. 4:2-11:16 is made up of three compound inverse frames recessed within one another. The axis also comprises a compound inverse frame, but it should be distinguished from the three outer compound structures by virtue of its central position, interlocking pattern, peculiar theme and separation from the others by means of a self-standing triadic frame pattern (tiers A/Aⁱ–Aⁱⁱ), which functions as an inclusio around the axis section.

The outermost compound inverse frame of the asymmetrically concentric structure that governs Isa. 4:2-11:16 is that made up of the 'HH' and 'II' tiers. They share a common feature in that both use vegetal imagery to convey either the theme of a remnant/royal scion ('HH' tiers) or some aspect of YHWH's program for the judgment and vindication of Judah ('II' tiers). The compound inverse frame made up of these tiers may be diagrammed as follows:

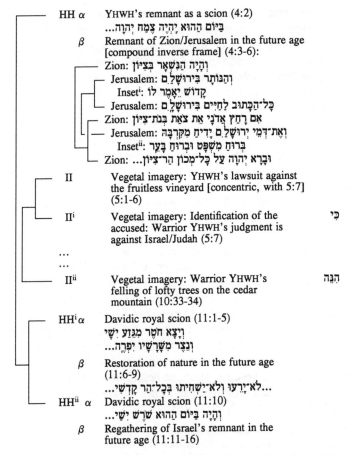

HH α   YHWH's remnant as a scion (4:2)
בַּיּוֹם הַהוּא יִהְיֶה צֶמַח יְהוָה...

β   Remnant of Zion/Jerusalem in the future age [compound inverse frame] (4:3-6):

Zion: וְהָיָה הַנִּשְׁאָר בְּצִיּוֹן
Jerusalem: וְהַנּוֹתָר בִּירוּשָׁלַ͏ִם
Inset[i]: קָדוֹשׁ יֵאָמֶר לוֹ
Jerusalem: כָּל־הַכָּתוּב לַחַיִּים בִּירוּשָׁלָ͏ִם
Zion: אִם רָחַץ אֲדֹנָי אֵת צֹאַת בְּנוֹת־צִיּוֹן
Jerusalem: וְאֶת־דְּמֵי יְרוּשָׁלַ͏ִם יָדִיחַ מִקִּרְבָּהּ
Inset[ii]: בְּרוּחַ מִשְׁפָּט וּבְרוּחַ בָּעֵר
Zion: וּבָרָא יְהוָה עַל כָּל־מְכוֹן הַר־צִיּוֹן...

II   Vegetal imagery: YHWH's lawsuit against the fruitless vineyard [concentric, with 5:7] (5:1-6)

II[i]   Vegetal imagery: Identification of the accused: Warrior YHWH's judgment is against Israel/Judah (5:7)   כִּי

...
...

II[ii]   Vegetal imagery: Warrior YHWH's felling of lofty trees on the cedar mountain (10:33-34)   הִנֵּה

HH[i] α   Davidic royal scion (11:1-5)
וְיָצָא חֹטֶר מִגֵּזַע יִשָׁי
וְנֵצֶר מִשָּׁרָשָׁיו יִפְרֶה...

β   Restoration of nature in the future age (11:6-9)
...לֹא־יָרֵעוּ וְלֹא־יַשְׁחִיתוּ בְּכָל־הַר קָדְשִׁי

HH[ii] α   Davidic royal scion (11:10)
וְהָיָה בַּיּוֹם הַהוּא שֹׁרֶשׁ יִשַׁי...

β   Regathering of Israel's remnant in the future age (11:11-16)

The opening tier (HHα, 4:2) describes the ideal agricultural conditions anticipated among the remnant of future Israel. The remnant of Zion/Jerusalem, symbolized as 'the branch of YHWH' (which may draw upon the vineyard imagery of the surrounding context [cf. 3:14b, 5:1-6, 7]), is expected to be beautiful and fruitful (in contrast to present Jerusalem/Judah, which will be described in 5:1-7 as a fruitless vineyard):

On that day [בַּיּוֹם הַהוּא] the branch of YHWH [צֶמַח יְהוָה] will be beautiful and glorious, and the fruit of the land will be the pride and glory of the survivors in Israel. (4:2)

The term צֶמַח ('branch') describes the remnant of Israel using an emblem typical of royal personages in the ancient Near East. The emblem of the scion, shoot or branch was typically associated with the king's possession of and rights to the mythical tree of life. This association probably explains the ubiquity, in ancient Near Eastern iconography, of depictions of kings holding a branch or sprig in their left hand.[1] He who symbolically held the royal scion was thought to hold the life-giving prerogatives of kingship. The corresponding 'HHα' tiers (HH^{i}α, 11:1-5; HH^{ii}α, 11:10) use similar terms (חֹטֶר מִגֶּזַע יִשַׁי, 11:1a; שֹׁרֶשׁ יִשַׁי, 11:10aβ) to symbolize the future Davidic king.[2] The structural correspondence between these tiers and Isa. 4:2 may reflect the author's ideological correlation between the emergence of a Davidic king who holds these prerogatives (11:1-5, 10) and the resurgence of Israel's remnant (4:2), among whom was the royal personage.[3]

In regard to the juxtaposition here of the HH^{i}β-tier (11:6-9), it is interesting that Kaiser commented that 'the notion of a universal peace embracing both men and animals, as expressed in 11:6-8(9), is strangely isolated in this context'.[4] However, this seeming 'erraticism' is precisely the effect one should expect of tiered architecture. In fact, the rhetorical device whereby the realm of nature anticipated in the messianic age is idealized so as to imitate the pristine conditions of Eden seems less erratic when one considers that this segment (HH^{i}β, 11:6-9) is situated between idealized descriptions of the just character (HH^{i}α, 11:1-5) and worldwide influence of the future Davidic scion (cf. HH^{ii}α, 11:10; HH^{ii}β, 11:11-16).

---

[1]Cf. G. Widengren, *The King and the Tree of Life in Ancient Near Eastern Religion* (Uppsala: Lundeqvist; Wiesbaden: Otto Harrassowitz, 1951). Widengren cites texts portraying the king as gardener (pp. 15-16), guardian (p. 11), possessor (pp. 20-35) and embodiment (pp. 42-44) of the tree of life.

[2]The royal imagery of the scion is undoubtedly also behind metonymical uses of נֵצֶר 'branch' (Isa. 14:19), צֶמַח 'shoot' (Jer. 23:5; 33:15; Zech. 3:8; 6:12) and the word pair יוֹנֵק 'sapling, scion' and שֹׁרֶשׁ 'root' (Isa. 53:2aαβ). It would not be entirely impossible that a messianic connotation was intended in Isa. 4:2 even though a first reading of the passage suggests the vegetal connotation of the resurgence of the remnant in the land of Israel (*pace* Kaiser, *Isaiah 1–12* [2d edn], pp. 85-86).

[3]In view of the multivalence of prophetic language, and by virtue of the structural correlation among the 'HHα'-tiers (of which the last two [11:1-5, 10] offer clear predictions of the Davidic remnant), perhaps it would not be outlandish to suggest that the expression צֶמַח יְהוָה 'the branch of YHWH' in 4:2 was designed to adumbrate the royal connotation of the scion motif used in the latter references.

[4]Kaiser, *Isaiah 1–12* [2d edn], p. 7.

The thematic correlation of the 'II' tiers is determined by their common use of vegetal imagery as a means to pronounce threats of disaster against Jerusalem/Judah or Assyria (cf. 5:1-6/7; 10:33-34). The implication to be drawn from a comparison of the disaster forecast for Jerusalem/Judah (characterized as a fruitless vineyard in 5:1-6/7) and that for Assyria (characterized as a haughty cedar in 10:33-34) is that, after YHWH had punished Jerusalem/Judah by means of Assyria, YHWH would return punishment upon the arrogant Assyria. A simple bifurcation of the Song of the Vineyard between a lyrical (5:1-2) and a rhetorical (5:3-7) section, of which the latter is 'a legal dispute on love', was suggested by L. Alonso-Schökel.[1] However, this bifurcation would not harmonize with the rhetorical design of a lawsuit-parable (5:1-6) if it were intended to be used here in a strategy of entrapment. In Isa. 5:1-6 the parable is set forth as the basis for inviting Jerusalem/Judah to pass judgment. Yet, it is only in 5:7 that those who were invited to judge the case become identified as those whom YHWH is accusing. Through a strategy of entrapment, the accused come to realize, but only in 5:7, that they have been made to condemn themselves.

The innermost of the three outer compound inverse frames of Isa. 4:1–11:16, comprising the 'LL' and 'MM' tiers, treats the theme of the people's imperception (through the figurative depiction of blindness and deafness) of Isaiah's prophetic vision of YHWH's rule over his people. Appropriately, these tiers immediately frame the innermost section—the axis (6:11–8:17)—where the narrative of Isaiah's confrontation with Ahaz at the aqueduct of the Upper Pool portrays the implications of Isaiah's prophetic vision for a faithless king (cf. 7:4, 9b) and people (cf. 8:6, 11-12) through a rehearsal of the symbolic names of Isaiah's sons and the events that those names portend. The following schema shows that the framing arrangement of the 'LL' and 'MM' tiers is exactly the reverse of the outermost compound inverse frame:

---

[1] L. Alonso-Schökel, 'Isaiah', in R. Alter and F. Kermode (eds.), *The Literary Guide to the Bible* (Cambridge, MA: Harvard University Press, 1987), p. 166. Cf. Kaiser, *Isaiah 1–12* [2d edn], p. 85 on the separation of v. 2 from vv. 3-6.

LL   Isaiah's vision of the heavenly throne (6:1-4)
בִּשְׁנַת־מוֹת הַמֶּלֶךְ עֻזִּיָּהוּ וָאֶרְאֶה אֶת־אֲדֹנָי יֹשֵׁב עַל־כִּסֵּא
...רָם וְנִשָּׂא
...שְׂרָפִים עֹמְדִים מִמַּעַל לוֹ שֵׁשׁ כְּנָפַיִם שֵׁשׁ כְּנָפַיִם לְאֶחָד

LLⁱ   Isaiah's dread of the vision of the divine king (6:5-7)
...[וָאֹמַר] אוֹי־לִי כִי־נִדְמֵיתִי כִּי אִישׁ טְמֵא־שְׂפָתַיִם אָנֹכִי
כִּי אֶת־הַמֶּלֶךְ יְהוָה צְבָאוֹת רָאוּ עֵינָי
...וַיָּעָף אֵלַי אֶחָד מִן־הַשְּׂרָפִים

MM   People's imperception foretold (6:8-10)
...שִׁמְעוּ שָׁמוֹעַ וְאַל־תָּבִינוּ וּרְאוּ רָאוֹ וְאַל־תֵּדָעוּ
...וְאָזְנָיו הַכְבֵּד וְעֵינָיו הָשַׁע
פֶּן־יִרְאֶה בְעֵינָיו וּבְאָזְנָיו יִשְׁמָע
וּלְבָבוֹ יָבִין וָשָׁב וְרָפָא לוֹ
...
...

MMⁱ   People's imperception of Isaiah's prophetic
      ministry (8:18-22)
...אֲשֶׁר אֵין־לוֹ שָׁחַר
...וְהִנֵּה צָרָה וַחֲשֵׁכָה מְעוּף צוּקָה וַאֲפֵלָה מְנֻדָּח

MMⁱⁱ People's imperception enlightened (8:23-9:1)
...כִּי לֹא מוּעָף לַאֲשֶׁר מוּצָק לָהּ
הָעָם הַהֹלְכִים בַּחֹשֶׁךְ רָאוּ אוֹר גָּדוֹל
יֹשְׁבֵי בְּאֶרֶץ צַלְמָוֶת אוֹר נָגַהּ עֲלֵיהֶם

LLⁱⁱ Joy when the divine king takes David's throne (9:2-6)
...כִּי־יֶלֶד יֻלַּד־לָנוּ בֵּן נִתַּן־לָנוּ
עַל־כִּסֵּא דָוִד וְעַל־מַמְלַכְתּוֹ
לְהָכִין אֹתָהּ וּלְסַעֲדָהּ
בְּמִשְׁפָּט וּבִצְדָקָה מֵעַתָּה וְעַד־עוֹלָם
קִנְאַת יְהוָה צְבָאוֹת תַּעֲשֶׂה־זֹּאת

In both MM (6:8-10) and MMⁱ (8:18-22), the prophet designates himself as one sent by YHWH to his people to convey a prophetic message that would be rejected because of their imperception. In both cases, the prophet expresses his readiness to be a messenger with הִנֵּה plus a 1 com. sg suffix or pronoun: הִנְנִי in 6:8b and הִנֵּה אָנֹכִי in 8:18aα.[1] It is perhaps no coincidence that the visions that appeared at the death of King Azariah/Uzziah, who had become diseased because of divine displeasure (LL, 6:1-4; LLⁱ, 6:5-7; cf. 2 Kgs 15:5aαβ, 2 Chron. 26:21aα, 23a), correspond structurally to the vision of the accession of an ideal king from the line of David who would bear YHWH's endorsement (LLⁱⁱ, 9:2-6).

Among the three outer compound inverse frames of Isa. 4:1–11:16, the intervening compound inverse frame is distinguished by the fact

---

[1]Cf. Gen. 37:13; 2 Sam. 15:15. See Kogut, pp. 142-43.

that it is made up of several tiers whose repetition patterns form clusters. The 'JJ' tiers comprise either doubled or quadrupled woe oracles. The 'KK' tiers are bifid in form and present, alternatively, verbatim repetitions of a judgment refrain (tiers 'KKα') or threats of judgment (tiers 'KKβ'). In one instance, three bifid 'KK' tiers combine to form a composite trifid cluster (i.e., 9:7-20):

⌐ JJ		Double woe oracle against the unjust [הוֹי 2x, לָכֵן 2x] (5:8-17):	
│		Woe against the greedy (5:8)	הוֹי
│	Insetⁱ:	Warrior YHWH's pronouncement of judgment (5:9-10)	
│		Woe against the self-indulgent (5:11-12)	הוֹי
│		Result of judgment: Exile and famine of nobility and masses (5:13)	לָכֵן
│		Result of judgment: Annihilation of nobility and masses (5:14)	לָכֵן
│	Insetⁱⁱ:	Humankind humbled before Warrior YHWH, the holy god (5:15-17)¹	
└ JJⁱ		Quadruple woe oracle against the unjust [עַל־כֵּן 4x; לָכֵן, הוֹי] (5:18-25a):	
		Woe against those who defy the holy one of Israel (5:18-19)	הוֹי
		Woe against those who pervert justice (5:20)	הוֹי
		Woe against the arrogant (5:21)	הוֹי
		Woe against the self-indulgent and unjust (5:22-23)	הוֹי
		Result of judgment: Offenders will wither like plants (5:24a)	לָכֵן
	Insetⁱⁱⁱ:	Reason for judgment: Defiance of Warrior YHWH, the Holy One of Israel (5:24b)	
		Result of judgment: YHWH strikes his people so that their bodies lie/decay in the streets (5:25a)	עַל־כֵּן
⌐ KKα		Judgment refrain (5:25b)	
│ β		Threat of judgment against Israel (5:26-30)	
│ ...			
│ ...			

---

¹Note the similarity between the phraseology of this inset (5:15-17) and that of the 'DDβ' tiers of 2:6aγ-21.

<table>
<tbody>
<tr><td></td><td>Clustered announcement of judgment (9:7-20):</td><td></td></tr>
<tr><td>KKⁱβ</td><td>Threat of judgment against Ephraim–
Samaria (9:7-11a)</td><td></td></tr>
<tr><td>α</td><td>Judgment refrain (9:11b)</td><td></td></tr>
<tr><td>KKⁱⁱβ</td><td>Threat of judgment against Israel
(9:12-16a)</td><td></td></tr>
<tr><td>α</td><td>Judgment refrain (9:16b)</td><td></td></tr>
<tr><td>KKⁱⁱⁱβ</td><td>Threat of judgment against Ephraim–
Manasseh (9:17-20a)</td><td></td></tr>
<tr><td>α</td><td>Judgment refrain (9:20b)</td><td></td></tr>
</tbody>
</table>

JJⁱⁱα Woe oracle against the unjust [הוֹי] (10:1-4a):
Woe against the unjust (10:1-2) הוֹי

Inset^{iv}: Result of judgment: No place of
escape in YHWH's day of
reckoning (10:3-4a)[1]

– KK^{iv}α Judgment refrain (10:4b)

JJⁱⁱβ Woe oracle against Assyria's king [הוֹי,
וְהָיָה בַּיּוֹם הַהוּא 2x] לָכֵן 2x] (10:5-32):
Woe against arrogance of Assyria הוֹי
(10:5-11)

Inset^v: YHWH's reversal of judgment
from Zion/Jerusalem to the king
of Assyria (10:12-15)

Result of judgment: Warrior YHWH, לָכֵן
Israel's Holy One, will waste the Assyrian
king's army like plants (10:16-19)

Inset^{vi}: Result of reversal of judgment
[from Zion/Jerusalem to the king
of Assyria]: The Holy One of Israel,
Warrior YHWH, will allow a remnant
of Israel/Jacob to return (10:20-23)

Result of judgment: Warrior YHWH לָכֵן
comforts Zion with a predicted reversal
of judgment after the Assyrian siege
of Zion (10:24-27)[2]

Inset^{vii}: Predicted advance of the Assyrian
army (10:28-32)

---

[1] Note the similarity between this inset (10:3-4a) and the result of judgment presented in the 'EEα' tiers of 2:6aγ-21.

[2] The proposal of B. Duhm that 10:27bβ be emended to עָלָה מִפְּנֵי רִמּוֹן* 'He has gone up from from Rimmon' and joined with 10:28-32 has won many adherents (*Das Buch Jesaia übersetzt und erklärt* [HKAT, 3/1; Göttingen: Vandenhoeck & Ruprecht, 2d edn, 1902], pp. 76-77; cf. RSV, NEB, *BHS*) though some view the MT as sound (so S.R. Driver, *An Introduction to the Literature of the Old Testament* [Edinburgh: T. & T. Clark, 9th edn, 1913], p. 210; NIV).

This is by far the most complex of the framing structures in Isa. 4:2–11:16. Yet, the propriety of coordinating the materials from 5:8-24 with those from 10:1-4a, 5-32, and the materials from 5:25-30 with those from 9:7-20, is amply testified by the number of interpreters who have argued that the present displacement of these oracles and judgments was occasioned by redactional processes.[1] That redactional processes are evident from the arrangement of these segments seems to be the case. However, the complex frameworking correspondence among the tiers that comprise Isa. 4:2–11:16 may undercut the inference of previous commentators that either 5:8-24, 10:1-4a and 10:5-32, on the one hand, or 5:25-30 and 9:7-20, on the other hand, were ever contiguous entities.

The axis of the asymmetrically concentric structure governing Isa. 4:2–11:16 is an interlocking compound inverse frame that is itself enclosed by a triadic frame:[2]

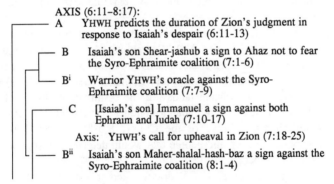

AXIS (6:11–8:17):
A   YHWH predicts the duration of Zion's judgment in response to Isaiah's despair (6:11-13)
B   Isaiah's son Shear-jashub a sign to Ahaz not to fear the Syro-Ephraimite coalition (7:1-6)
Bⁱ   Warrior YHWH's oracle against the Syro-Ephraimite coalition (7:7-9)
C   [Isaiah's son] Immanuel a sign against both Ephraim and Judah (7:10-17)
Axis: YHWH's call for upheaval in Zion (7:18-25)
Bⁱⁱ Isaiah's son Maher-shalal-hash-baz a sign against the Syro-Ephraimite coalition (8:1-4)

[1] E.g., R.E. Clements, *Isaiah 1–39* (NCB; Grand Rapids: Eerdmans, 1980), pp. 60-70, 109-120; Kaiser, *Isaiah 1–12* [2d edn], pp. 94-113, 219-251.

[2] J. Vermeylen has argued that five collections from the prophet Isaiah, of which only the first seems to have been edited by the prophet, were joined together by his disciples (*Du prophète Isaïe à l'apocalyptique: Isaïe, i–xxxv, miroir d'un demi-millénaire d'expérience religieuse en Israël* [EBib; 2 vols.; Paris: Gabalda, 1977, 1978], II, p. 656). Vermeylen presented its hypothetically reconstructed concentric structure as follows:

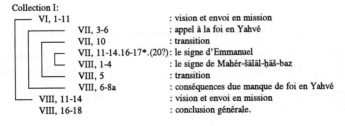

Collection I:
VI, 1-11   : vision et envoi en mission
VII, 3-6   : appel à la foi en Yahvé
VII, 10   : transition
VII, 11-14.16-17*.(20?): le signe d'Emmanuel
VIII, 1-4   : le signe de Mahér-šālāl-ḥāš-baz
VIII, 5   : transition
VIII, 6-8a   : conséquences due manque de foi en Yahvé
VIII, 11-14   : vision et envoi en mission
VIII, 16-18   : conclusion générale.

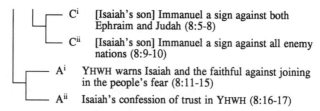

Cⁱ   [Isaiah's son] Immanuel a sign against both
        Ephraim and Judah (8:5-8)

Cⁱⁱ   [Isaiah's son] Immanuel a sign against all enemy
        nations (8:9-10)

Aⁱ   YHWH warns Isaiah and the faithful against joining
        in the people's fear (8:11-15)

Aⁱⁱ   Isaiah's confession of trust in YHWH (8:16-17)

The axis section is framed by a triadic frame (A/Aⁱ-Aⁱⁱ) so that it ends with a double closure. It is significant that the next verse (8:18), which begins tier MMⁱ and marks the transition to the latter half of the concentric section, makes explicit the main theme of the preceding axis section. Isaiah says, 'Here am I [הִנֵּה אָנֹכִי] and the children YHWH has given me as signs and symbols in Israel from Warrior YHWH [יְהוָה צְבָאוֹת], who dwells on Mount Zion'. Not by coincidence, the matching expression, 'Here am I [הִנְנִי]' appears in 6:8 and serves as the introduction to the MM-tier in the same way that הִנֵּה אָנֹכִי introduces the MMⁱ-tier.

Among the 'C' tiers, the phrase עִמָּנוּ אֵל plays the dominant role. It is the sign *par excellence* of YHWH's rebuke of Ahaz, for it equivocates between symbolizing Judah's deliverance from foreign enemies, both the feared coalition of Aram and Ephraim (tier C, 7:10-17) and any future threat from distant lands (cf. the culminating phrase of tier Cⁱⁱ, 8:9-10), and threatening Judah's conquest by the king of Assyria (cf. the culminating phrase of the Cⁱ-tier, 8:5-8). It would be the interim response of king and people that would determine just how God would be with his people.

The core of this axis (7:18-25) draws together a number of motivic threads from earlier in the book. Here the 'briars and thorns' threatened in YHWH's lawsuit against the unfruitful vineyard (5:6) find ample fulfillment (7:19, 23, 24, 25).[1] This is 'that day' (7:18, 20, 21, 23) which YHWH had threatened against the unfaithful (2:11, 17, 20) and unjust (3:7, 18; 4:1). Here, for the first time in the prophecy, the personal agent of the coming threat against Judah is explicitly disclosed to be the king of Assyria.

Selected Substructural Complexes in Isaiah 4:2–11:16

A number of the subsections that function as tiers in the concentric structure of 4:2–11:16 are themselves concentrically patterned. It will

---

[1] The 'briars and thorns' motif will recur later in 'threat' passages (9:17; 10:17) and in Isaiah's apocalypse (27:4).

have to suffice simply to mention a few of the instances in which and means by which these patterns are effected. For example, one can see that the repetitions of צִיּוֹן and יְרוּשָׁלַ͏ִם in the HHβ-tier (4:3-6) are structured according to a compound inverse framework pattern:

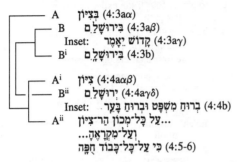

```
┌──── A      בְּצִיּוֹן (4:3aα)
│ ┌── B      בִּירוּשָׁלַ͏ִם (4:3aβ)
│ │      Inset:  קָדוֹשׁ יֵאָמֶר (4:3aγ)
└─┴── Bⁱ     בִּירוּשָׁלָ͏ִם (4:3b)

┌──── Aⁱ     צִיּוֹן (4:4aαβ)
│ ┌── Bⁱⁱ    יְרוּשָׁלַ͏ִם (4:4aγδ)
│ │      Inset:  בְּרוּחַ מִשְׁפָּט וּבְרוּחַ בָּעֵר (4:4b)
└─┴── Aⁱⁱ    ...עַל כָּל־מְכוֹן הַר־צִיּוֹן
                 ...וְעַל־מִקְרָאֶהָ
                 כִּי עַל־כָּל־כָּבוֹד חֻפָּה (4:5-6)
```

This arrangement, where the city name is the determinative structural criterion, is identical, albeit in reverse, to the pattern of repetitions found in Isa. 11:13, where the names אֶפְרַיִם and יְהוּדָה are determinative. However, Isa. 11:13 constitutes only one part (albeit the culmination) of a two-phased axis within the larger structure of the HHⁱⁱβ-tier (11:11-16). The HHⁱⁱβ-tier is asymmetrically concentric, and the operative criterion for the delineation of its structure is the sorting of the various nations from which Judah's remnant shall return according to the four main directions of geographical orientation (i.e., north, south, east, west). Of course, the assumed point of reference for this sorting of foreign nations is the land of Israel//Ephraim/Judah, the repetition of whose names forms the two-phased axis of tier HHⁱⁱβ.

Centripetal outer frame [7+1 nations] (11:11):
On that day [וְהָיָה בַּיּוֹם הַהוּא] the Lord will extend his hand
      a second time
   to reclaim the remnant of his people [אֶת־שְׁאָר עַמּוֹ] that remains
      [אֲשֶׁר יִשָּׁאֵר]

```
┌──── A    NORTH: from Assyria [מֵאַשּׁוּר],
│ ┌── B    SOUTH: from (Lower) Egypt [וּמִמִּצְרַיִם],
│ │                from (Upper) Egypt [וּמִפַּתְרוֹס],
│ │                from Cush [וּמִכּוּשׁ],
│ ┌── C    EAST:   from Elam [וּמֵעֵילָם],
│ │                from Babylon [וּמִשִּׁנְעָר],
│ │                from Hamath [וּמֵחֲמָת],
└─┴── D    WEST:   and from the Islands of the Sea
                   [וּמֵאִיֵּי הַיָּם]
```

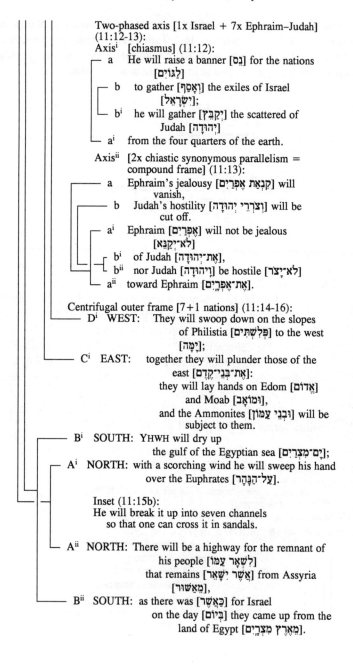

Two-phased axis [1x Israel + 7x Ephraim–Judah] (11:12-13):

Axis[i] [chiasmus] (11:12):

  a   He will raise a banner [נֵס] for the nations [לַגּוֹיִם]

    b   to gather [וְאָסַף] the exiles of Israel [יִשְׂרָאֵל];

    b[i] he will gather [יְקַבֵּץ] the scattered of Judah [יְהוּדָה]

  a[i]   from the four quarters of the earth.

Axis[ii] [2x chiastic synonymous parallelism = compound frame] (11:13):

  a   Ephraim's jealousy [קִנְאַת אֶפְרַיִם] will vanish,

   b   Judah's hostility [וְצֹרְרֵי יְהוּדָה] will be cut off.

   a[i] Ephraim [אֶפְרַיִם] will not be jealous [לֹא־יְקַנֵּא]

    b[i] of Judah [אֶת־יְהוּדָה],

    b[ii] nor Judah [וִיהוּדָה] be hostile [לֹא־יָצֹר]

  a[ii] toward Ephraim [אֶת־אֶפְרַיִם].

Centrifugal outer frame [7+1 nations] (11:14-16):

D[i] WEST: They will swoop down on the slopes of Philistia [פְלִשְׁתִּים] to the west [יָמָּה];

C[i] EAST: together they will plunder those of the east [אֶת־בְּנֵי־קֶדֶם]: they will lay hands on Edom [אֱדוֹם] and Moab [וּמוֹאָב], and the Ammonites [וּבְנֵי עַמּוֹן] will be subject to them.

B[i] SOUTH: YHWH will dry up the gulf of the Egyptian sea [יָם־מִצְרַיִם];

A[i] NORTH: with a scorching wind he will sweep his hand over the Euphrates [עַל־הַנָּהָר].

Inset (11:15b):
He will break it up into seven channels so that one can cross it in sandals.

A[ii] NORTH: There will be a highway for the remnant of his people [לִשְׁאָר עַמּוֹ] that remains [אֲשֶׁר יִשָּׁאֵר] from Assyria [מֵאַשּׁוּר],

B[ii] SOUTH: as there was [כַּאֲשֶׁר] for Israel on the day [בְּיוֹם] they came up from the land of Egypt [מֵאֶרֶץ מִצְרָיִם].

This concentric structure also has a double closure. Notice the alliterative inclusio between 11:11aγb (אֶת־שְׁאָר עַמּוֹ אֲשֶׁר יִשָּׁאֵר...) ...(מֵאַשּׁוּר) and 11:16aβγbα (...לִשְׁאָר עַמּוֹ אֲשֶׁר יִשָּׁאֵר מֵאַשּׁוּר כַּאֲשֶׁר...) that helps to delimit the structure of this poetic unit.

When, in the MM-tier (6:8-10), the divine oracle foretells the people's imperception of Isaiah's vision and prophetic ministry, the author again uses a compound frame (comprising synonymous parallelism and chiasmus) to organize this brief announcement of judgment. YHWH says (6:9-10):

'Go and say to this people:
 A "Be ever hearing, but never understand;
 B be ever seeing, but never perceive".
 Axis: Fatten the heart of this people.
A^i Make their ears dull
 B^i and close their eyes,
 B^{ii} lest they see with their eyes
A^{ii} and hear with their ears,
 Closure: understand with their hearts and turn
     and heal themselves'.

The determinative criterion for the delineation of this structure is the distinction between senses of perception (sight and hearing). Either YHWH is impelling the prophet to devise a scheme whereby his people will be incapable of making sense of his prophecy or he is decreeing himself that it shall be so. The aim, according to the axis, is to pad the people's consciences against remorse. The closure of the axis offers the most explicit and biting use of irony in the announcement. YHWH's aversion to the people's conversion is so intense that he does not even offer to say, 'and I heal them', but rather, 'and (they) heal themselves'. This implies that if they did repent—thus compelling YHWH reluctantly to forgive them out of obligation to the covenant—it would have to originate entirely from themselves.

In another divine oracle, the B^i-tier of the sectional axis (7:7-9), YHWH is quoted as pronouncing an omen against Ahaz, which is presented in a chiasmus:

 a '"It shall not stand [לֹא תָקוּם],
   nor will it happen [וְלֹא תִהְיֶה].
  b For the capital [רֹאשׁ] of Aram is Damascus,
    and the head [וְרֹאשׁ] of Damascus is Rezin.

> Axis: So within sixty-five years
>   Ephraim will be too shattered to be a people.
> b^i Now the capital [וְרֹאשׁ] of Ephraim is Samaria,
>   and the head [וְרֹאשׁ] of Samaria is the son of Remaliah.
> a^i If you do not stand firm in faith [לֹא תַאֲמִינוּ]
>   surely you will not be made to stand firm [לֹא תֵאָמֵנוּ]!"'

It is rather telling that Isaiah should be sent to pronounce this oracle against Ahaz, the head of Jerusalem, the capital of Judah, accompanied by his son Shear-jashub (7:3). The symbolic significance of Isaiah's son's name should be understood to effect the interpretation of this oracle (7:7-9) as it does that of 7:1-6 (cf. 8:18). That Ephraim is said to be too shattered to be a people (7:8bβ) implies that only a remnant would remain. That this fate is, by implication, also threatened against Ahaz, Jerusalem and Judah (cf. 7:7b with 7:9b) suggests that, if Judah was not faithful, there too only a remnant would remain (or, in the case of Jerusalem, return; cf. 10:20-23, 24).

There is, in the A^i-tier (8:11-15), another presentation of a divine oracle in an interesting frameworking arrangement. Here, the divine prohibition to/through the prophet (8:12-15) is a virtual play on antithesis:

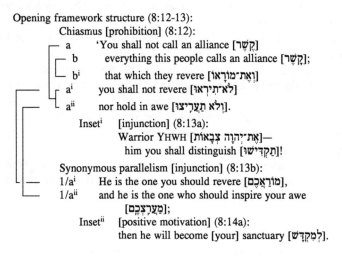

Opening framework structure (8:12-13):
  Chiasmus [prohibition] (8:12):
    a   'You shall not call an alliance [קֶשֶׁר]
      b   everything this people calls an alliance [קֶשֶׁר];
      b^i   that which they revere [וְאֶת־מוֹרָאוֹ]
    a^i   you shall not revere [לֹא־תִירְאוּ]
    a^ii   nor hold in awe [וְלֹא תַעֲרִיצוּ].
        Inset^i [injunction] (8:13a):
            Warrior YHWH [אֶת־יְהוָה צְבָאוֹת]—
            him you shall distinguish [תַקְדִּישׁוּ]!
    Synonymous parallelism [injunction] (8:13b):
    1/a^i   He is the one you should revere [מוֹרַאֲכֶם],
    1/a^ii   and he is the one who should inspire your awe
             [מַעֲרִצְכֶם];
        Inset^ii [positive motivation] (8:14a):
            then he will become [your] sanctuary [לְמִקְדָּשׁ].

Closing paneled structure [negative motivation] (8:14b-15):

```
  ┌── c      But [he will become] a stubbing stone
  │           and a stumbling rock [וּלְצוּר מִכְשׁוֹל] for the
  │           two houses of Israel,
  │─── d      a trap and a snare [וּלְמוֹקֵשׁ] for the citizens
  │           of Jerusalem.
  └── cⁱ     Thus will many of them stumble [וְכָשְׁלוּ],
  │           fall and be broken,
  └── dⁱ     be snared [וְנוֹקְשׁוּ] and caught'.
```

The chiasmus in Isa. 8:12 is antithetical along two axes: it contrasts that on which the people should not rely but do rely (8:12a) with that which they fear but should not fear (8:12b); then, this polarity is cross-cut with prohibitions that the faithful should not do (8:12aα, bβγ) what the people are doing (8:12aβ, bα). Insetⁱ (8:13a) marks the turning point in a paneled presentation of an antithesis between what the faithful are not to fear or esteem (8:12bβγ) and what the faithful are encouraged to fear and esteem (8:13b), namely, Warrior YHWH. The remainder of the oracle (8:14-15) offers motivation and, not surprisingly, presents an antithesis between the alternative fates of those who rely on or reject YHWH. Insetⁱⁱ affirms that YHWH will become a safe sanctuary for the faithful (linking the positive consequence [מִקְדָּשׁ, 8:14a] with its prerequisite condition in Insetⁱ [תַקְדִּישׁוּ, 8:13a]); however, for the people he will become an agent of sudden and surprising adversity, the paneling of 8:14b-15 alternating between showing YHWH either tripping (tiers 'c') or trapping (tiers 'd') his people.

Two levels of structural subdivision in this section are marked off by the two structural insets. Insetⁱ ('Warrior YHWH—him you shall distinguish [תַקְדִּישׁוּ]!', 8:13a) marks a subordinate turning point in the aⁱ-aⁱⁱ || 1/aⁱ-1/aⁱⁱ antithesis; however, Insetⁱⁱ ('then he will become [your] sanctuary [וְהָיָה לְמִקְדָּשׁ]', 8:14a) offers the positive motivation and marks the major turning point in the section between the opening framework (a-b-bⁱ-aⁱ-aⁱⁱ || 1/aⁱ-1/aⁱⁱ), which outlines the prohibition-injunction antithesis between the faithful and the people, and the people's negative motivation expressed in the closing paneled structure (c-d-cⁱ-dⁱ).

Persuasion as a Function of Structure in Isaiah 4:2–11:16

What is it that the author might be trying to convey to the readers through the arrangement of tiers in 4:2–11:16? To understand this one must evaluate this section's architecture against what is known about the situations that its tiers describe.

From the date given in 6:1, one may posit a *terminus a quo* of 740 BCE for the content of the tiers demarcated as 6:1-4 (LL), 6:5-7 (LL[i]), 6:8-10 (MM), and 6:11-13 (A), though it would appear from the integrated arrangement of these materials with corresponding tiers in 8:11-15 (A[i]), 8:16-17 (A[ii]), 8:18-22 (MM[i]); 8:23–9:1 (MM[ii]), and 9:2-6 (LL[ii])—tiers that were clearly designed rhetorically to regulate the intervening content of 7:1–8:10—that the final arrangement of this material did not precede Isaiah's confrontation with Ahaz described in 7:1–8:10.[1] It was only early in the overlap of Jotham's and Ahaz's reigns on the throne of Judah (i.e., 735/4–732/1 BCE) that Aram and Ephraim began, independently of each other, to harass Judah.[2] It was probably the threat of invasion from Tiglath-pileser III, who in 734/3 BCE laid siege to the coastal cities of Israel, that prompted Rezin of Damascus and Pekah of Samaria, long-standing adversaries, suddenly to collude so as to depose young Ahaz from Jerusalem's throne. Their ambition was to establish 'the son of Tabeel' in Ahaz's stead as a mutual ally in their coalition against Tiglath-pileser. That this political-military situation most likely lay behind Isa. 7:1–8:10 may be corroborated by the coincidence that the prophecy pretends to have been made known to the king some two years in advance of its fulfillment (the period from a child's birth until its weening; cf. 7:10-17) and that two Assyrian campaigns are known to have taken place in the two succeeding years. As a result of Tiglath-pileser's campaign in northern Israel (733/2 BCE), an assassin's coup in Samaria displaced Pekah with the Assyrian sympathizer Hoshea. One year later (732/1 BCE), when Tiglath-pileser conquered Damascus, Rezin was executed.[3]

The announcements of judgment in the first two of the clustered 'KK' tiers (i.e., KK[i]β, 9:7-11a; KK[ii]β, 9:12-16a), which threaten Ephraim with the onslaught of 'Rezin's enemies' (9:10) as well as

---

[1]On the dating of the year of Uzziah's death, see E.R. Thiele, *The Mysterious Numbers of the Hebrew Kings* (Grand Rapids: Zondervan, rev. edn, 1983), pp. 118-23.

[2]Cf. 2 Kgs 15:37 with 2 Chron. 28:5-8. On the coregency of Jotham and Ahaz, see Thiele, pp. 131-34. On the distinction between Aram's and Ephraim's separate and, later, joint acts of opposition to Judah, see E.J. Young, *The Book of Isaiah* (NICOT; 3 vols.; Grand Rapids: Eerdmans, 1965-1972), I, pp. 267-69; E.H. Merrill, *Kingdom of Priests: A History of Old Testament Israel* (Grand Rapids: Baker, 1987), p. 425.

[3]See 2 Kgs 15:29-30; 16:7-9. Cf. Merrill, p. 426; J. Bright, *A History of Israel* (Philadelphia: Westminster Press, 3d edn, 1981), pp. 274-75.

incursions from east and west by the Arameans and Philistines (9:11a), profess to anticipate the events of 743–742 BCE by which Tiglath-pileser III subjugated the Levant.[1] Yet, in the KK$^{iii}\beta$-tier (especially 9:19-20b), there is reference to the events of the subsequent decade, namely, to Pekah and Ephraim's opposition to Ahaz and Judah. These facts prompt me to infer a *terminus ad quem* of 743 BCE for the predictions of the KK$^{i}\beta$ and KK$^{ii}\beta$ tiers but a *terminus ad quem* of 735/4 BCE for that of the KK$^{iii}\beta$-tier.[2] In the corresponding bifid tier (KK, 5:25b-30), one sees a similar prediction of an Assyrian threat, though it is less explicit as to the national object of its threat (whether Ephraim or Judah). Typical of the first occurrences among matching tiers in Isaiah, the KK-tier is not as explicit or specific in detail as later 'KK' tiers become. However, since this passage alludes to the banner motif (5:26aα; cf. 13:2, against Judah),[3] the whistling motif (5:26aβ; cf. 7:18, against Judah), and the 'hurry and haste' motif (5:26b; cf. 5:19, against the unjust of Judah, and 8:1, 3 ['Maher-shalal-hash-baz'], against Aram and Ephraim), it would be safe to infer from its correspondence to the other 'KK' tiers that the author intended both Ephraim and Judah as objects of the threat in 5:26-30. A dual-edged denunciation of Ephraim and Judah would be in keeping with the general tenor of the section, which offers a portrayal of YHWH's program of judgment against 'the two houses of Israel' (cf. 8:14bγ) as part of an ever narrowing focus that would finally target Zion, the seat of the Davidic dynasty.

Although the 'KK' tiers were designed to threaten both Ephraim and Judah, the 'JJ' tiers (5:8-17, JJ; 5:18-25a, JJ^{i}; and 10:1-4a, JJ$^{ii}\alpha$; 10:5-32, JJ$^{ii}\beta$), with which the 'KK' tiers are interlocked (cf. 10:4b), pronounce double or quadruple woe oracles. At first, these woe oracles are unaddressed and speak generally against the unjust, but the final woe oracle reveals that a reversal will take place whereby YHWH will destroy the unjust Assyrian, the instrument of YHWH's judgment

---

[1]Cf. Bright, pp. 271-72; Merrill, p. 426. These two tiers (i.e., KK$^{i}\beta$, 9:7-11a; KK$^{ii}\beta$, 9:12-16a) are thus the earliest datable prophecies from Isaiah and the only ones in the book datable to the reign of Uzziah ([790]767–740 BCE; cf. 1:1). See, however, Hayes-Irvine (pp. 41-42, 185-88), who equate 'the oppressors of Rezin' with Rezin's own troops.

[2]Cf. Hayes-Irvine, pp. 188-90.

[3]The banner motif recurs among matched tiers that denounce Judah for relying upon Egypt as a potential ally (18:3bα; 30:17bγ) and, finally, as a symbol of military threat against Assyria itself (31:9). It takes a positive turn as a symbol for the regathering of Israel in Isa. 11:10, 12, and 62:10bγ.

against the unjust of Jerusalem.[1] This is especially clear in 10:28-32, where the portrayal of the southward advance of the Assyrian army portends disaster specifically for Jerusalem, which lies directly in its path.[2] The portrayal of the Assyrian advance in the JJ$^{ii}\beta$-tier seems to correspond to events in 701 BCE, when one branch of Sennacherib's army, under the direction of Sennacherib's prime minister (רַב־שָׁקֵה), was advancing from the north against Jerusalem.[3] Although Isa. 10:28-32 originally may have anticipated the threat against Jerusalem in 701 BCE, it is important to notice that the surrounding context (10:24-27, 33-34) foreshadows the outcome as one wherein the Assyrians would be vanquished at the perimeter of Mount Zion (cf. Isa. 14:24-25; 2 Kgs 20:35-36). Inasmuch as the 'JJ' tiers seem to develop the theme of YHWH's punishment of the unjust (cf. 1:16-17, 23; 3:1–4:1), the unjust in view are probably to be found chiefly among the citizens of Jerusalem. Only in the JJ$^{ii}\beta$-tier (10:5-32) is YHWH's wrath against the unjust aimed explicitly against the king of Assyria. Concomitantly, inasmuch as the king of Assyria is portrayed in Isa. 10:5-32 as the rod of YHWH's anger against the unjust of Jerusalem (cf. 10:5, 24), one may infer that the unaddressed threats against the unjust in the corresponding 'JJ' tiers pertain predominantly to Jerusalem. Only the clear historical reference to Samaria as a city already conquered (10:9-11) provides a *terminus a quo* of 722 BCE for the content of this segment.[4]

There has obviously been some redaction involved in the arranging of the 'KK' and 'JJ' materials into their present order. The amalgamation of earlier materials (i.e., the KK$^{i}\beta$ and KK$^{ii}\beta$ tiers from before 743 BCE, the KK$^{iii}\beta$-tier from before 735/4 BCE, and the axis section of 7:1–8:10, which portrays and interprets the event of Isaiah's confrontation of Ahaz early in the period 735/4–732/1 BCE) within the present

---

[1]Note the mention of Zion in Isa. 10:24 and of Jerusalem in the paneling of 10:10-11.

[2]Isa. 10:28-32 is not a city-by-city itinerary but portrays, through poetic parallelism, the army's advance toward Jerusalem by stages. Cf. J.M. Miller, 'Geba/Gibeah of Benjamin', *VT* 25 (1975), pp. 157-59.

[3]Cf. Y. Aharoni and M. Avi-Yonah, *The Macmillan Bible Atlas* (New York: Macmillan, rev. edn, 1977), p. 99, §154; Merrill, pp. 426-28.

[4]Clements dates the segment demarcated as 10:5-15 to a period between 722 and 705 BCE and, following H. Wildberger (*Jesaja, Kapitel 1-12* [BKAT, X/1; Neukirchen–Vluyn: Neukirchener Verlag, 1972]), A. Schoors (*Jesaja* [De Boeken van het Oude Testament; Roermond, 1972]), Kaiser (*Isaiah 1-12: A Commentary* [trans. R.A. Wilson; OTL]; Philadelphia: Westminster Press, 1972]), and W. Dietrich (*Jesaja und die Politik* [BEvT, 74; Munich: Chr. Kaiser Verlag, 1976]), prefers a situation during the period of the Philistine revolt against Sargon II, in 713-711 BCE (p. 110).

concentric arrangement need not have postdated 722 BCE by much, though the redaction may have occurred later.[1] It would appear that the JJ[ii]β-tier (10:5-32) derives from a period shortly after 722 BCE (perhaps anticipating the defeat of Sargon II at Carchemesh in 717 BCE [cf. 10:9], but especially Sennacherib's defeat of 701 BCE in Judah [10:24-32]). Since, when it is read in contiguity with the JJ[ii]α-tier (10:1-4a), it comports with the double/quadruple woe structure of the two previous 'JJ' tiers, all the 'JJ' tiers were probably compiled and integrated into their present arrangement with the 'KK' tiers at one time. This postulated process of redaction may help to account for the clustered pattern of 'JJ' and 'KK' tiers that thus melds together prophecies from different decades in the prophet's career.

The predictions in the 'HH' tiers are so idealized and the denunciations of the 'II' tiers so generalized that it would be difficult to identify their situation of origin on the basis of historical referents. However, the use of vegetal imagery in both the 'HH' and 'II' tiers as a determinative structuring criterion, when considered in combination with the pervasive use of this imagery elsewhere throughout Isa. 4:2-11:16, may imply that these tiers were adjoined and integrated with these and similar motifs as part of the final stage of redaction.[2] One might suppose that the Isaianic portions of 4:2-11:16 took on their present basic arrangement as an Isaianic compilation sometime after 722 but well before 701 BCE; however, one should recognize that the compilation may have taken place later.[3] In any case, one should probably not infer that Isa. 4:2-11:16 had yet reached its finished form, the product of its integration with later large sections of the book (especially 13:1-39:8 and 40:1-54:17), until the time of the book's final compilation.

The principal aim of the earliest forms of the Isaianic materials now contained in 4:2-11:16 was to rebuke Ahaz and the citizens of

---

[1] There are several good examples of the integration of tiers by which the author made the materials cohere, e.g., the repetitions of the 'hurry and haste' motif in the JJ[i]-tier (5:19) and the KK[b]-tier (5:26b) foreshadow Isaiah's 'Maher-shalal-hash-baz' predictions made to Ahaz (8:1, 3 in tier B[ii] of the sectional axis).

[2] Note the pervasive use of vegetal imagery to symbolize the devastation and refructification of the land in the final form of 4:2-11:16 (e.g., 4:2; 5:1-7, 10; 6:13b; 7:2, 4, 19, 23-25; 9:9b, 17; 10:15, 17-19, 33-34; 11:1, 10).

[3] Since there is no reference in Isa. 4:2-11:16 to Hezekiah's alliances with the Egyptians, made from 713-711 and 705-701 BCE, one could conceivably establish the earlier date (713 BCE) as a *terminus ad quem* for the architectural completion of those parts of this section that had been compiled by the prophet Isaiah. Yet one should be careful not to build too much of a case for dating upon arguments from silence. Cf. Clements, pp. 11, 110.

Jerusalem for seeking aid from Assyria, rather than from YHWH, against the Syro-Ephraimite threat. Accordingly, the prophet predicted that YHWH would affect the events of history so as to prove that he was capable of making good his Davidic promise to protect Zion. Hence, as an ironic reversal of Ahaz's hope for a savior in the person of the king of Assyria, YHWH himself would induce an Assyrian king to threaten Zion, only to vanquish him at its perimeter as a display of his supremacy over human power (cf. 2:22), his divine knowledge and control over Zion's destiny, and his covenant faithfulness to the Davidic promise. Then, subsequent to his vindication through combat, YHWH would bring about the promised glorious restoration of Zion under an ideal king who would come from the line of David. It is crucial to one's understanding of the continuity of Isa. 4:2–11:16 with succeeding sections of the book that one perceives the strategy by which Isaiah deflects Ahaz's concern from a present political–military threat (Syria–Ephraim) to a far greater future threat from an even more distant nation (Assyria). It is this strategy of continuity that is repeated and escalated in the next major section of the book (Isa. 13:1–39:8), culminating in Isaiah's confrontation of Ahaz's son and royal heir, Hezekiah.

The Continuity of Isaiah 4:2–12:6 with its Context

Although there is no transitional section to provide a hinge between the complex framework structure of Isa. 3:1–4:1 and the asymmetrically concentric structure of 4:2–11:16, there is a continuation into 4:3-6 of the preceding motif of defiled 'women of Zion' (cf. 3:16, 17; 4:4).[1] Moreover, the image of YHWH's ruined vineyard in Isa. 5:1-6, 7 was foreshadowed already in 3:14. It seems evident that the juxtaposition of the materials contained in Isa. 4:2, 3-6 and 5:1-6, 7 with those contained in 3:1–4:1 was judiciously arranged so as to preserve a degree of thematic continuity between the two complex framework structures, yet without disrupting the integrity of either structural pattern.

The overall rhetorical function of the section is consistent with the covenant disputation genre with which the book opened in Isa. 1:1–2:5. Moreover, the asymmetrical form and judgment–restoration scenario presented in Isa. 4:2–11:16 (i.e., that Zion's restoration would take

---

[1] The blood said to be cleansed from Jerusalem (Isa. 4:4) may allude to the accusation of Isa. 1:15, though the officials' extortion of the poor, described in 3:13-15, offers a more proximate mention of violence.

place only after punishment) align most closely with the form and function of 1:21-27, a segment that is similarly patterned into an asymmetrically concentric form and that similarly forecasts that YHWH would restore Zion only after its purgation.

It should be mentioned, in anticipation of Isa. 13:1–39:8, that 4:2–11:16 has not only thematic continuity with the following section (where YHWH's program of punishment and restoration for Zion escalates to an international scale) but structural complementarity as well. Apart from the tolerable subtlety of permutational differences, Isa. 4:2–11:16 and 13:1–39:8 are equivalent structures. Both sections present triply recessed compound inverse frames, of which the intermediary compound inverse frame comprises clustered repetitions of tiers. At the center of each section are three concentrically arranged triadic frames.

Appropriately, the intervening passage, Isa. 12:1-6, is a two-phased hymn to YHWH that forms a transition between the major sections of 4:2–11:16 and 13:1–39:8. Both phases of 12:1-6 begin with the formulaic introduction: וְאָמַרְתָּ\וַאֲמַרְתֶּם בַּיּוֹם הַהוּא ('On that day you will say'). The first phase (12:1-3) summarizes the content of Isa. 4:2–11:16, with its focus on the theme of Zion's salvation coming from YHWH only after punishment; the second phase (12:4-6) introduces the theme of Isa. 13:1–39:8, with its interest in both YHWH's vindication of Zion before the nations and his reclamation of the nations, beginning from Zion. Thus, Isa. 12:1-6 constitutes an appropriate hinge between two structurally analogous sections.

Chapter 5

ISAIAH 13:1–39:8: THE ASSYRIAN-BABYLONIAN SCHEME
FOR ZION'S JUDGMENT AND RESTORATION

AFTER PUNISHMENT YHWH WILL REMOVE
ENEMIES FROM ZION

In recent times, Isaiah 13–39 has not generally been assessed as forming a unified and coherent subdivision within the book of Isaiah.[1]
However, what has perhaps not been recognized is that this section of
Isaiah may be governed, albeit artificially, by an asymmetrically concentric pattern that proves to be analogous to the complex framework
structure observed in 4:2–11:16. This asymmetrically concentric structure enhances the argument whereby the author denounces both
Hezekiah and the Judean audience for failing to trust in YHWH as the
only one who is sufficient to avert the threat of military powers in the
present world order.

As in the previous chapter, I shall begin by delineating the major
division of Isa. 13:1–39:8 and by outlining its overarching scheme.
Following this, I shall offer evidence of complex frameworking within

[1]Most have followed the trend to assess chs. 36–39 as a separate subsection
because its framework is mainly in prose and because of its clear affinities with
2 Kgs 18:13, 17–20:19. Many therefore regard chs. 36–39 mainly as a historical
narrative transition between chs. (1–12)13–35 and 40–55(56–66), e.g., G.B. Gray,
A Critical and Exegetical Commentary on the Book of Isaiah I–XXVII (ICC;
Edinburgh: T. & T. Clark, 1912), pp. xlvii-l; R. Lack, *La symbolique du livre
d'Isaïe: Essai sur l'image littéraire comme élément de structuration* (AnBib, 59;
Rome: Biblical Institute Press, 1973), pp. 60-76; O. Kaiser, *Isaiah 13–39: A Commentary* (trans. R.A. Wilson; OTL; Philadelphia: Westminster Press, 1974),
pp. 367-68; R.E. Clements, *Isaiah 1–39* (NCB; Grand Rapids: Eerdmans, 1980),
pp. 277-80; H.M. Wolf, *Interpreting Isaiah* (Grand Rapids: Zondervan, 1985),
pp. 171-81; M.A. Sweeney, *Isaiah 1–4 and the Post-Exilic Understanding of the
Isaianic Tradition* (BZAW, 171; Berlin: de Gruyter, 1988), pp. 12-19, 27-34.
Arguing from the thematic integration of chs. 36–37, 38 and 39 with the preceding
material of Isaiah, J.H. Hayes and S.A. Irvine purported that these three units of
tradition were produced independently from one another, circulated as part of the
Isaianic traditions and were only subsequently incorporated into 2 Kings (*Isaiah the
Eighth-century Prophet: His Times and His Preaching* [Nashville: Abingdon Press,
1987], p. 372).

these chapters. Salient features of the substructures that comprise some tiers will also be illustrated. Finally, I shall summarize the implications of this literary structure in relation to the author's rhetorical task and in relation to its broader literary context.

Structural Delineation of Isaiah 13:1–39:8

I aver that Isa. 13:1–39:8 was designed to be read as a single structural subunit that coheres under the rubric of YHWH's vindication of both Zion and the Davidic king before other nations and kings. Its implied scenario, like that of 4:2–11:16, presents Zion's covenant restoration as an event that will follow her punishment for covenant violations. The section is delimited by the hymn of 12:1-6, which forms the transition from the previous section (4:2–11:16), and the dramatic shift to the rhetoric of consolation in 40:1-11.

This major section opens with the third of the book's three authorial superscriptions (13:1b; cf. 1:1; 2:1) and is characterized by the use of introductory formulae to preface many of its oracles against the nations—מַשָּׂא in the oracles of the first half of the concentric structure (13:1a; 14:28; 15:1; 17:1; 19:1; 21:1, 11, 13; 22:1; 23:1), הוֹי in the woe oracles of both the first (18:1) and latter halves of the concentric structure (28:1; 29:1; 29:15; 30:1; 31:1; [33:1]). Other terms or formulae used as delineating markers are מָשָׁל (14:3-4a), and the messenger formula כֹּה אָמַר...יְהוָה (22:15; or the like, 37:22a). In the axis of the concentric structure (24:1–27:13), the key delineating element is the sevenfold repetition of the eschatological phrase בַּיּוֹם הַהוּא (24:21; 25:9; 26:1; 27:1, 2, 12, 13).

Chapters 36–39, which close the section, are made up of the prose narrative and poetic taunt song found also in 2 Kgs 18:13, 17–20:19 (the major addition in Isaiah being Hezekiah's thanksgiving song in 38:9-20), though it is clear that the Isaiah passage was reworked so as to have a different rhetorical effect in its present context. Its interlocution of prose and poetry, a modal and rhetorical complement to the account of Isaiah's confrontation with Ahaz a generation before (7:1–8:10), serves as both the culminating frustration of the expectation of an ideal Davidic king and a structurally inverted complement to the Babylonian (13:1–14:23; ‖ 39:1-8) and Assyrian (14:3-21, 24-25; ‖ 36:1–37:38) interests with which this subdivision opens.

Asymmetrical Concentricity in Isaiah 13:1–39:8

The structural tiers of Isa. 13:1–39:8 appear to have been arranged according to a concentric pattern akin to that which was found in Isa. 4:2–11:16. Here, however, they seem to have been arranged and matched according to two main criteria: (1) a concern for the question of the national identity of those who are addressed, with several sub-categories of classification—whether Judahite or non-Judahite, whether ally or enemy, whether distant or neighboring, and (2) a concern for the question of the tone of the address—whether one of denunciation or of hope for exaltation. The concentric arrangement of nations named in this section is designed to escalate the impact of its portrayal of YHWH's vindication of Zion through world judgment and culminates in the conflagration depicted at its vortex. The asymmetrical arrangement of national oracles in this section, with oracles about Judah alternatively interlocked and juxtaposed with oracles against their near and distant enemies or allies, probably bore strong political implications for the audience/readers of Isaiah's day. A schema of this asymmetrically concentric structure might be outlined as follows:

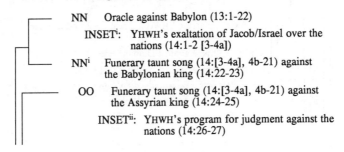

NN   Oracle against Babylon (13:1-22)

    INSET[i]:   YHWH's exaltation of Jacob/Israel over the
                nations (14:1-2 [3-4a])

NN[i]   Funerary taunt song (14:[3-4a], 4b-21) against
        the Babylonian king (14:22-23)

OO   Funerary taunt song (14:[3-4a], 4b-21) against
        the Assyrian king (14:24-25)

    INSET[ii]: YHWH's program for judgment against the
               nations (14:26-27)

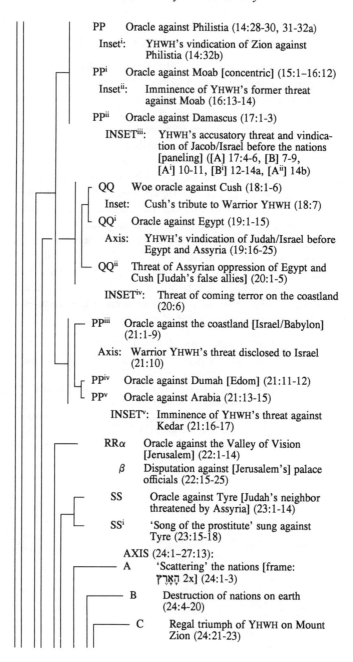

PP　　　Oracle against Philistia (14:28-30, 31-32a)

Inset[i]:　　YHWH's vindication of Zion against Philistia (14:32b)

PP[i]　　Oracle against Moab [concentric] (15:1–16:12)

Inset[ii]:　　Imminence of YHWH's former threat against Moab (16:13-14)

PP[ii]　　Oracle against Damascus (17:1-3)

INSET[iii]:　　YHWH's accusatory threat and vindication of Jacob/Israel before the nations [paneling] ([A] 17:4-6, [B] 7-9, [A[i]] 10-11, [B[i]] 12-14a, [A[ii]] 14b)

QQ　　Woe oracle against Cush (18:1-6)

Inset:　　Cush's tribute to Warrior YHWH (18:7)

QQ[i]　　Oracle against Egypt (19:1-15)

Axis:　　YHWH's vindication of Judah/Israel before Egypt and Assyria (19:16-25)

QQ[ii]　　Threat of Assyrian oppression of Egypt and Cush [Judah's false allies] (20:1-5)

INSET[iv]:　　Threat of coming terror on the coastland (20:6)

PP[iii]　　Oracle against the coastland [Israel/Babylon] (21:1-9)

Axis:　　Warrior YHWH's threat disclosed to Israel (21:10)

PP[iv]　　Oracle against Dumah [Edom] (21:11-12)

PP[v]　　Oracle against Arabia (21:13-15)

INSET[v]:　　Imminence of YHWH's threat against Kedar (21:16-17)

RRα　　Oracle against the Valley of Vision [Jerusalem] (22:1-14)

β　　Disputation against [Jerusalem's] palace officials (22:15-25)

SS　　Oracle against Tyre [Judah's neighbor threatened by Assyria] (23:1-14)

SS[i]　　'Song of the prostitute' sung against Tyre (23:15-18)

AXIS (24:1–27:13):

A　　'Scattering' the nations [frame: הָאָרֶץ 2x] (24:1-3)

B　　Destruction of nations on earth (24:4-20)

C　　Regal triumph of YHWH on Mount Zion (24:21-23)

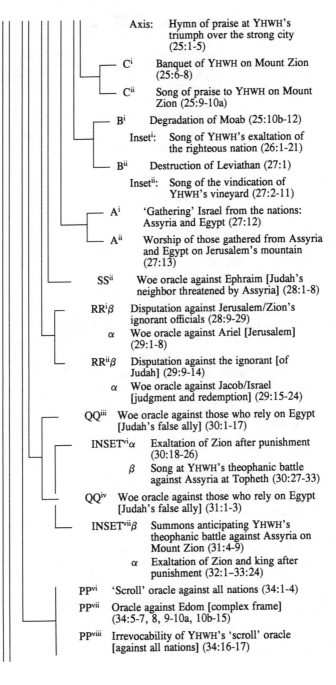

Axis: Hymn of praise at YHWH's triumph over the strong city (25:1-5)

C^i   Banquet of YHWH on Mount Zion (25:6-8)

C^ii   Song of praise to YHWH on Mount Zion (25:9-10a)

B^i   Degradation of Moab (25:10b-12)

Inset^i: Song of YHWH's exaltation of the righteous nation (26:1-21)

B^ii   Destruction of Leviathan (27:1)

Inset^ii: Song of the vindication of YHWH's vineyard (27:2-11)

A^i   'Gathering' Israel from the nations: Assyria and Egypt (27:12)

A^ii   Worship of those gathered from Assyria and Egypt on Jerusalem's mountain (27:13)

SS^ii   Woe oracle against Ephraim [Judah's neighbor threatened by Assyria] (28:1-8)

RR^iβ   Disputation against Jerusalem/Zion's ignorant officials (28:9-29)

α   Woe oracle against Ariel [Jerusalem] (29:1-8)

RR^iiβ   Disputation against the ignorant [of Judah] (29:9-14)

α   Woe oracle against Jacob/Israel [judgment and redemption] (29:15-24)

QQ^iii   Woe oracle against those who rely on Egypt [Judah's false ally] (30:1-17)

INSET^viα Exaltation of Zion after punishment (30:18-26)

β   Song at YHWH's theophanic battle against Assyria at Topheth (30:27-33)

QQ^iv   Woe oracle against those who rely on Egypt [Judah's false ally] (31:1-3)

INSET^viiβ Summons anticipating YHWH's theophanic battle against Assyria on Mount Zion (31:4-9)

α   Exaltation of Zion and king after punishment (32:1–33:24)

PP^vi   'Scroll' oracle against all nations (34:1-4)

PP^vii   Oracle against Edom [complex frame] (34:5-7, 8, 9-10a, 10b-15)

PP^viii Irrevocability of YHWH's 'scroll' oracle [against all nations] (34:16-17)

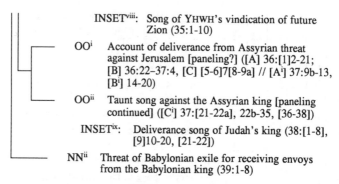

INSET^viii: Song of YHWH's vindication of future Zion (35:1-10)

OO^i   Account of deliverance from Assyrian threat against Jerusalem [paneling?] ([A] 36:[1]2-21; [B] 36:22–37:4, [C] [5-6]7[8-9a] // [A^i] 37:9b-13, [B^i] 14-20)

OO^ii   Taunt song against the Assyrian king [paneling continued] ([C^i] 37:[21-22a], 22b-35, [36-38])

INSET^ix: Deliverance song of Judah's king (38:[1-8], [9]10-20, [21-22])

NN^ii   Threat of Babylonian exile for receiving envoys from the Babylonian king (39:1-8)

Isaiah 13–39 is enclosed by two inversely paired triadic frames whose matched tiers contain both poetic and/or prose depictions of political and military affairs having to do with either Babylon (NN, 13:1-22; NN^i, 14:[3-4a]4b-23; NN^ii, 39:1-8) or Assyria (OO, 14:[3-4a]4b-21, 24-25; OO^i, 36:1–37:20; OO^ii, 37:21-38), the two nations that presented the greatest national threat to Judah and Jerusalem within the span of history during which the book of Isaiah addressed YHWH's people (i.e., the eighth to sixth centuries BCE).[1]

The innermost tiers present oracles against Tyre (SS, 23:1-14; SS^i, 23:15-18) and Ephraim (SS^ii, 28:1-8), which serve as descriptions of the devastation wrought by eighth-century BCE Assyria against these allied enemies of Judah. The bifid 'RR' tiers present disputations and woe oracles against Jerusalem. It should be noted that these bifid tiers

---

[1]For an earlier explanation of the double rhetorical function of Isa. 14:4b-21 as a taunt song directed, alternatively, against the king of Babylon (where the ending is provided by 14:22-23) or the king of Assyria (where the ending is provided by 14:24-25), see the appendix in R.H. O'Connell, 'Isaiah xiv 4b-23: Ironic Reversal through Concentric Structure and Mythic Allusion', *VT* 38 (1988), pp. 417-18. Cf. J.N. Oswalt, *The Book of Isaiah, Chapters 1–39* (NICOT; Grand Rapids: Eerdmans, 1986), pp. 7, 10, where this taunt is said to be directed chiefly against the Assyrian kings. Indeed, the correspondence of genre and addressee between this taunt song and that against the Assyrian king, Sennacherib, in Isa. 37:22b-35 might suggest a deliberate movement from a general archetypal allusion to the downfall of the one who assaults the mountain of God (in Isa. 14:4b-21, 24-25) to a specific portrayal of Sennacherib's ascent against Zion and his resultant downfall in 701 BCE (in Isa. 36–37). However, a corresponding movement from archetypal generality to historical referent in regard to the Babylonian king, described in Isa. 14:4b-23 and Isa. 39 (i.e., Merodach-baladan), is clearly not the result of an attempt to identify the specific Babylonian king who was responsible for the conquests of Jerusalem in 605, 597 or 586 BCE (i.e., Nebuchadnezzar II). It is possible, however, that the general identity of the Babylonian monarch in Isa. 14:22-23 and the specific reference to Merodach-baladan in Isa. 39 were intended to correspond as archetypal and prototypical, respectively.

appear in reverse order about the axis of the section, as did bifid tiers in previous sections.[1] The first two 'RRα' tiers outline oracles against Jerusalem, Judah's capital, using the symbolic epithets 'Valley of Vision' (RRα, 22:1-14) and 'Ariel' (RR$^i\alpha$, 29:1-8). The 'RRβ' tiers, in turn, outline disputations against the rulers of Jerusalem for usurping Davidic prerogatives (22:15-25) and against the populace of Jerusalem for ignoring the prophet's message (28:9-29; 29:9-14). Finally, the RR$^{ii}\alpha$-tier presents a culminating woe oracle against the unjust by which the oppressed, referred to by the patriarchal epithets 'Jacob/Israel', will rejoice in the Holy One (29:15-24). Taken together, these inversely paired complex frames (i.e., RRα-β—SS—SS^i $\parallel$ SS^{ii}—RR$^i\beta$-α—RR$^{ii}\beta$-α) focus YHWH's wrath upon his own people, Ephraim (with its ally Tyre) and the citizens of Judah's capital, before that wrath culminates in the cataclysmic vindication of Zion described in the intervening section of Isa. 24:1–27:13. It is the latter section, Isaiah's so-called apocalypse, that constitutes the axis of the asymmetrically concentric structure of Isa. 13:1–39:8.

The tiers designated 'PP' contain oracles against nations that play a secondary role in relation to the author's main concern with the struggle between Assyria and Tyre/Ephraim, on the one hand, and between Assyria/Babylon and Jerusalem, on the other. With the exception of the ambiguous oracle concerning/against the coastland region of Israel/Babylon (21:1-9), all the nations addressed or described were neighbors of Judah and had been either under Israelite or Judean control at the time Isaiah wrote, or later became subject to reprisals under the Assyrian–Babylonian threat. In each case, it is the middle 'PP' tier, among the trifid 'PP' clusters, that is the most significant rhetorically. The 'QQ' tiers outline either denunciations of Judah's would-be allies, Egypt and Cush (i.e., Egypt under the Cushite Dynasty [XXV]) (cf. QQ, 18:1-6; QQ^i, 19:1-15; QQ^{ii}, 20:1-5), or denunciations of those who would seek Egypt and Cush as intermediaries to rescue Judah from the Assyrian threat at the end of the eighth century BCE (cf. QQ^{iii}, 30:1-17; QQ^{iv}, 31:1-3).

The 'inset' materials that intervene between the oracular blocks serve as the structural mortar of this section, furnishing both the cohesive, thematic *Leitmotif* of YHWH's vindication of Zion and the

---

[1]Cf. the framing order of bifid tiers 'CCα' and 'CCβ' in 1:1–2:5, the 'DDα' and 'DDβ' tiers in 2:6aγ-21, the 'GGα' and 'GGβ' tiers in 3:1–4:1, and the 'KKα' and 'KKβ' tiers in 4:2–11:16. Thus, this phenomenon of reversal in the order of bifid elements that frame the axis has presented itself once in each of the main sections so far encountered in Isaiah.

structural counterpoint to the oracular blocks. In distinction from the focus on foreign nations in the oracles, these insets develop the theme of YHWH's vindication of Zion, Israel/Jacob or its king against all foreign nations and their kings. Although these insets do not always explicitly depict YHWH vindicating Zion or Israel/Jacob before the nations (as do 14:1-2 [3-4a]; 14:32b; 17:4-14; 19:16-25; [21:10]), they elsewhere always present corollary motifs, such as the certainty or imminence of YHWH's coming judgment (against all nations, 14:26-27; against Moab, 16:13-14; against Kedar, 21:16-17; against the Littoral, 20:6), the payment of vassal tribute to YHWH (by Cush, 18:7), the theophanic nature of YHWH's great battle on Mount Zion (30:27-33; 31:4-9), and the exaltation of both the city of Zion (30:18-26; 32:1–33:24; 35:1-10) and its ideal Davidic king (32:1–33:24; [38:10-20]).

Complex Frameworking in Isaiah 13:1–39:8

Having outlined the overarching asymmetrically concentric form of Isa. 13:1–39:8, I may now give consideration to Isaiah's method of linking large sections into a cohesive unity. For Isaiah 13–39, the major repetitive patterning device is, once again, that which I have called the 'triadic frame'.

Not only do the triadic framework patterns in Isaiah 13–39 alternate inversely with one another with remarkable consistency as one moves concentrically toward the core of 'Isaiah's apocalypse' (25:1-5), they are thematically paired to form compound inverse frames (i.e., the 'NN' and 'OO' triadic frames are inversely paired, as are the 'PP' and 'QQ' frames, and the 'RR' and 'SS' frames). Since Isaiah's 'apocalypse' (24:1–27:13) is set off as a unit by a triadic repetition (cf. the antipolar relationship between 24:1-3 and 27:12, 13), comes at the center of a major section (Isa. 13–39) and constitutes the only complex of triadic frames in the section that is not inversely paired, it should probably be regarded as comprising a separate subunit, the main axis of the concentric structure of chs. 13–39. There are, as a result, three concentrically paired compound inverse frames into which is set the triply recessed compound frame of Isaiah 24–27. In effect, the author builds four compound inverse frames, each one enveloping the others, like the ever receding structure of a Chinese box.[1] It is also probably not just coincidental that the nations that are joined together in each

---

[1] Observe the same general framework pattern in the previous section, Isa. 4:2–11:16.

quadruply recessed pair of compound frames had related political interests: Babylon ('NN') is associated with Assyria ('OO'), since both
were conquerors of Jerusalem/Judah deriving from the same general
distant region; the soon-to-be-conquered neighboring nations of the
coalition against Assyria ('PP')[1] are associated with Judah's soon-to-be-
conquered Egyptian allies ('QQ'); and, in contrast to the exaltation of
Jerusalem/Judah in the insets, the immediate calamitous fate of
Jerusalem/Judah ('RR') is seen to be no different from that of her
neighboring allied enemies, Tyre/Ephraim ('SS'), for all are guilty of
transgression. Indeed, it may be the latter negative association of
Jerusalem/Judah with Tyre/Ephraim that accounts for the exceptional
absence of insets among these tiers of Isaiah 13–39.

For the purposes of the present study, it will have to suffice merely
to outline in schemata and explain briefly the four main compound
framework complexes in this section. The arrangement of the outermost frame, which associates the affairs of Babylon with those of
Assyria, is in accordance with my model for the compound inverse
frame if one makes the provision that the poem of Isa. 14:4b-21 serves
double duty as a taunt song against the kings of either Babylon (where
14:22-23 ends the poem) or Assyria (if 14:24-25 functions as the
ending):

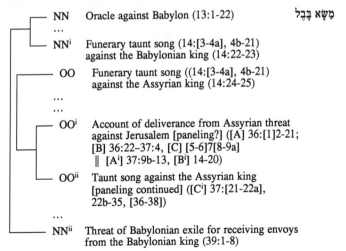

The second from the innermost compound frame—that which surrounds the central axis section and contains the oracular denunciations

---

[1]Cf. Oswalt, p. 10.

of Jerusalem/Judah and Tyre/Ephraim—appears as the reverse image of the outermost pattern except that the 'RR' tiers are bifid:

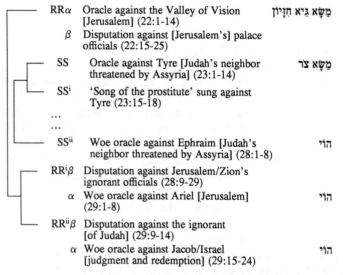

RRα   Oracle against the Valley of Vision [Jerusalem] (22:1-14)   מַשָּׂא גֵּיא חִזָּיוֹן

β   Disputation against [Jerusalem's] palace officials (22:15-25)

SS   Oracle against Tyre [Judah's neighbor threatened by Assyria] (23:1-14)   מַשָּׂא צֹר

SSⁱ   'Song of the prostitute' sung against Tyre (23:15-18)

...
...

SSⁱⁱ   Woe oracle against Ephraim [Judah's neighbor threatened by Assyria] (28:1-8)   הוֹי

RRⁱβ   Disputation against Jerusalem/Zion's ignorant officials (28:9-29)

α   Woe oracle against Ariel [Jerusalem] (29:1-8)   הוֹי

RRⁱⁱβ   Disputation against the ignorant [of Judah] (29:9-14)

α   Woe oracle against Jacob/Israel [judgment and redemption] (29:15-24)   הוֹי

The compound inverse frame that intervenes between the outer and next-to-innermost constructions just given is, unlike them, made up of clusters of tiers. Further, unlike the other two, the triadic frames of this compound inverse frame interlock with one another in what is but a permutation of compound inverse frameworking:

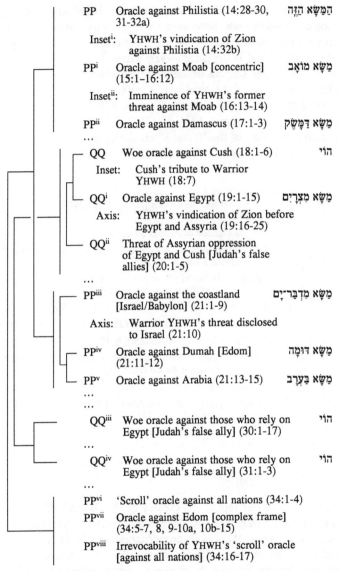

PP	Oracle against Philistia (14:28-30, 31-32a)	הַמַּשָּׂא הַזֶּה	
Inset[i]:	YHWH's vindication of Zion against Philistia (14:32b)		
PP[i]	Oracle against Moab [concentric] (15:1–16:12)	מַשָּׂא מוֹאָב	
Inset[ii]:	Imminence of YHWH's former threat against Moab (16:13-14)		
PP[ii]	Oracle against Damascus (17:1-3) ...	מַשָּׂא דַּמֶּשֶׂק	
QQ	Woe oracle against Cush (18:1-6)	הוֹי	
Inset:	Cush's tribute to Warrior YHWH (18:7)		
QQ[i]	Oracle against Egypt (19:1-15)	מַשָּׂא מִצְרַיִם	
Axis:	YHWH's vindication of Zion before Egypt and Assyria (19:16-25)		
QQ[ii]	Threat of Assyrian oppression of Egypt and Cush [Judah's false allies] (20:1-5) ...		
PP[iii]	Oracle against the coastland [Israel/Babylon] (21:1-9)	מַשָּׂא מִדְבַּר־יָם	
Axis:	Warrior YHWH's threat disclosed to Israel (21:10)		
PP[iv]	Oracle against Dumah [Edom] (21:11-12)	מַשָּׂא דּוּמָה	
PP[v]	Oracle against Arabia (21:13-15)	מַשָּׂא בַּעְרָב	
QQ[iii]	Woe oracle against those who rely on Egypt [Judah's false ally] (30:1-17) ...	הוֹי	
QQ[iv]	Woe oracle against those who rely on Egypt [Judah's false ally] (31:1-3) ...	הוֹי	
PP[vi]	'Scroll' oracle against all nations (34:1-4)		
PP[vii]	Oracle against Edom [complex frame] (34:5-7, 8, 9-10a, 10b-15)		
PP[viii]	Irrevocability of YHWH's 'scroll' oracle [against all nations] (34:16-17)		

Perhaps also significant is the fact that, among the neighboring nations of Israel and Judah, the center tier of each of the three trifid 'PP' clusters is focused, in the first instance, upon the fate of Moab, and in the last two instances, upon that of Edom. These foretold destructions

of Edom and Moab must have carried for Israel and Judah great
theological import, not only as a contemporary hope for YHWH's
vengeance but also because of the atrocities that these nations had committed against Israel in the latter's early national history.

In the following schema of Isaiah's 'apocalypse', which constitutes
the innermost core of the quadruply recessed framework pattern, one
can see that the compound (but not inverse) frame is enclosed by an
antithetical triadic frame A/A^i–A^{ii} (24:1-3; 27:12, 13). It is the
destructive modality of the 'B' tiers and the sevenfold repetition of the
introductory phrase בַּיּוֹם הַהוּא that combine to punctuate the structure
of this section:

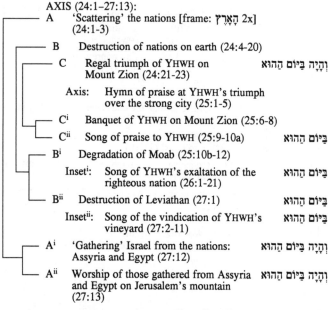

AXIS (24:1–27:13):
- A   'Scattering' the nations [frame: הָאָרֶץ 2x] (24:1-3)
- B   Destruction of nations on earth (24:4-20)
- C   Regal triumph of YHWH on Mount Zion (24:21-23)   וְהָיָה בַּיּוֹם הַהוּא
  - Axis: Hymn of praise at YHWH's triumph over the strong city (25:1-5)
- C^i Banquet of YHWH on Mount Zion (25:6-8)
- C^{ii} Song of praise to YHWH (25:9-10a)   בַּיּוֹם הַהוּא
- B^i Degradation of Moab (25:10b-12)
  - Inset^i: Song of YHWH's exaltation of the righteous nation (26:1-21)   בַּיּוֹם הַהוּא
- B^{ii} Destruction of Leviathan (27:1)   בַּיּוֹם הַהוּא
  - Inset^{ii}: Song of the vindication of YHWH's vineyard (27:2-11)   בַּיּוֹם הַהוּא
- A^i 'Gathering' Israel from the nations: Assyria and Egypt (27:12)   וְהָיָה בַּיּוֹם הַהוּא
- A^{ii} Worship of those gathered from Assyria and Egypt on Jerusalem's mountain (27:13)   וְהָיָה בַּיּוֹם הַהוּא

The pattern of tier repetitions created by the 'B' and 'C' tiers is that
of a compound frame. Because there is no inverse relationship between
the complex frames, there is disproportionate weight of emphasis upon
the closing half of the compound frame. This phenomenon is further
augmented by the fact that the structural insets, which appear between
the 'B' and 'A' tiers (i.e., 26:1-21; 27:2-11), serve to embellish and
escalate the theme of the 'C' tiers as songs concerning YHWH's exaltation of Zion. Indeed, the combined theme of YHWH's exaltation of
future Jacob/Israel//Zion and its king is developed as the consistent

interest of all the insets that appear from this axis to the end of the present main section (i.e., 30:18-26, 27-33; 31:4-9; 32:1–33:24; 35:1-10; 38:[1-8], [9]10-20, [21-22]).

Selected Substructural Complexes in Isaiah 13:1–39:8

Some of the tiers in the concentric structure of 13:1–39:8 that present complex framework patterns and symmetrically concentric configurations will be illustrated here. The following analysis of the NN-tier (Isa. 13:[1]2-22) is arranged according to a scheme of repetitions in which two thematic axes intersect. Along the axis of imagery, the alphabetical designations 'A' and 'aa' indicate images of warfare, whereas the 'B' and 'bb' letters indicate nature imagery. Intersecting this thematic contrast is another contrast between divine cause (upper case 'A' and 'B') and destructive effect (doubled lower case 'aa' and 'bb'). The grid pattern whereby these themes intersect may be diagrammed as follows:

	Divine Cause	Destructive Effect
Warfare	A	aa
Nature	B	bb

By means of these antitheses the author/compiler not only portrays Warrior YHWH (יְהוָה צְבָאוֹת) as the agent of both military and natural destruction against Babylon but contours an intricately balanced, well-integrated complex framework:

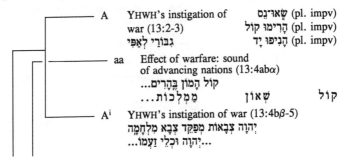

	A	YHWH's instigation of war (13:2-3) גִּבּוֹרֵי לְאַפִּי	שְׂאוּ־נֵס (pl. impv) הָרִימוּ קוֹל (pl. impv) הָנִיפוּ יָד (pl. impv)
	aa	Effect of warfare: sound of advancing nations (13:4abα) קוֹל הֲמוֹן בֶּהָרִים... מַמְלְכוֹת...	שָׁאוֹן קוֹל
	Aⁱ	YHWH's instigation of war (13:4bβ-5) יְהוָה צְבָאוֹת מְפַקֵּד צְבָא מִלְחָמָה ...יְהוָה וּכְלֵי זַעְמוֹ...	

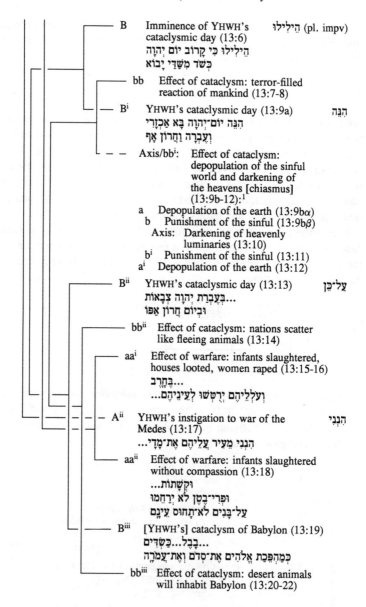

B   Imminence of YHWH's   הֵילִילוּ (pl. impv)
cataclysmic day (13:6)
הֵילִילוּ כִּי קָרוֹב יוֹם יְהוָה
כְּשֹׁד מִשַּׁדַּי יָבוֹא

bb   Effect of cataclysm: terror-filled
reaction of mankind (13:7-8)

B^i YHWH's cataclysmic day (13:9a)   הִנֵּה
הִנֵּה יוֹם־יְהוָה בָּא אַכְזָרִי
וְעֶבְרָה וַחֲרוֹן אָף

Axis/bb^i: Effect of cataclysm:
depopulation of the sinful
world and darkening of
the heavens [chiasmus]
(13:9b-12):[1]

a   Depopulation of the earth (13:9bα)
b   Punishment of the sinful (13:9bβ)
Axis: Darkening of heavenly
luminaries (13:10)
b^i Punishment of the sinful (13:11)
a^i Depopulation of the earth (13:12)

B^{ii} YHWH's cataclysmic day (13:13)   עַל־כֵּן
...בְּעֶבְרַת יְהוָה צְבָאוֹת
וּבְיוֹם חֲרוֹן אַפּוֹ

bb^{ii} Effect of cataclysm: nations scatter
like fleeing animals (13:14)

aa^i Effect of warfare: infants slaughtered,
houses looted, women raped (13:15-16)
...בֶּחָרֶב
...וְעֹלְלֵיהֶם יְרֻטְּשׁוּ לְעֵינֵיהֶם...

A^{ii} YHWH's instigation to war of the   הִנְנִי
Medes (13:17)
...הִנְנִי מֵעִיר עֲלֵיהֶם אֶת־מָדָי

aa^{ii} Effect of warfare: infants slaughtered
without compassion (13:18)
...וּקְשָׁתוֹת
וּפְרִי־בֶטֶן לֹא יְרַחֵמוּ
עַל־בָּנִים לֹא־תָחוּס עֵינָם

B^{iii} [YHWH's] cataclysm of Babylon (13:19)
...בָבֶל...כַּשְׂדִּים
כְּמַהְפֵּכַת אֱלֹהִים אֶת־סְדֹם וְאֶת־עֲמֹרָה

bb^{iii} Effect of cataclysm: desert animals
will inhabit Babylon (13:20-22)

---

[1] The broken bracket that attaches to the bb^i-tier indicates the multivalent nature of this block, which seems to serve thematically as a constituent tier, while structurally (because it is a chiasmus) and positionally (at the virtual center of the section) serving as the axis.

The 'A' and 'aa' tiers of this schema form inverse interlocking triadic frames; the 'B' and 'bb' tiers, interlocking quadruple frames. Thus, the pattern here is but a permutation of the triadic and quadruple interlocking pattern that governed Isa. 2:6aγ-21 and 3:1–4:1, except that here it is doubled. It may also be by design that the 'Day of YHWH' motif is as prominent a feature in those sections as it is in this one. From a rhetorical standpoint, it is important to notice the increase in the specificity of the author's descriptions in the final 'A' and 'B' tiers (i.e., Aii and Biii), as compared with those of the previous 'A' and 'B' tiers, and also of the effects described in the contiguous aai-, aaii- and bbiii-tiers. It is in these tiers that the author identifies the Medes and Babylonians as agent and object, respectively, of the previous generalized threats of military and natural disasters.

The literary structure of the NNii-tier (Isa. 39:1-8), which shares themes and vocabulary with ch. 13, is yet another permutation of the compound frame pattern (similar, in fact, to the structure of Isaiah 13 though, like Isaiah 24–27, it is enclosed within a triadic frame). Indeed, this repetition pattern enhances greatly the rhetorical effect of ch. 39. The following diagram represents the structure of the passage on the basis of its key word repetitions:

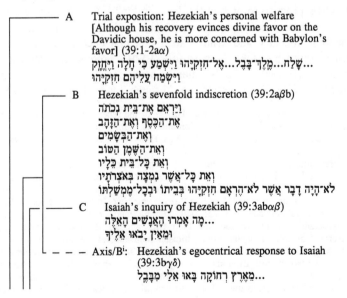

A   Trial exposition: Hezekiah's personal welfare [Although his recovery evinces divine favor on the Davidic house, he is more concerned with Babylon's favor] (39:1-2aα)

שָׁלַח...מֶלֶךְ־בָּבֶל...אֶל־חִזְקִיָּהוּ וַיִּשְׁמַע כִּי חָלָה וַיֶּחֱזָק
וַיִּשְׂמַח עֲלֵיהֶם חִזְקִיָּהוּ

B   Hezekiah's sevenfold indiscretion (39:2aβb)

וַיַּרְאֵם אֶת־בֵּית נְכֹתֹה
אֶת־הַכֶּסֶף וְאֶת־הַזָּהָב
וְאֶת־הַבְּשָׂמִים
וְאֵת הַשֶּׁמֶן הַטּוֹב
וְאֵת כָּל־בֵּית כֵּלָיו
וְאֵת כָּל־אֲשֶׁר נִמְצָא בְּאֹצְרֹתָיו
לֹא־הָיָה דָבָר אֲשֶׁר לֹא־הֶרְאָם חִזְקִיָּהוּ בְּבֵיתוֹ וּבְכָל־מֶמְשַׁלְתּוֹ

C   Isaiah's inquiry of Hezekiah (39:3abαβ)

...מָה אָמְרוּ הָאֲנָשִׁים הָאֵלֶּה
וּמֵאַיִן יָבֹאוּ אֵלֶיךָ

Axis/Bi: Hezekiah's egocentrical response to Isaiah (39:3bγδ)

...מֵאֶרֶץ רְחוֹקָה בָּאוּ אֵלַי מִבָּבֶל

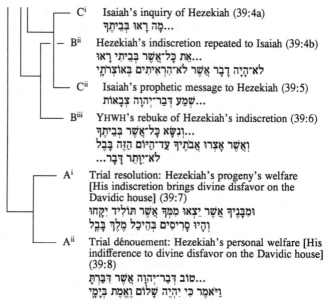

Cⁱ Isaiah's inquiry of Hezekiah (39:4a)
...מָה רָאוּ בְּבֵיתֶךָ

Bⁱⁱ Hezekiah's indiscretion repeated to Isaiah (39:4b)
...אֵת כָּל־אֲשֶׁר בְּבֵיתִי רָאוּ
לֹא־הָיָה דָבָר אֲשֶׁר לֹא־הִרְאִיתִים בְּאוֹצְרֹתָי

Cⁱⁱ Isaiah's prophetic message to Hezekiah (39:5)
...שְׁמַע דְּבַר־יְהוָה צְבָאוֹת

Bⁱⁱⁱ YHWH's rebuke of Hezekiah's indiscretion (39:6)
...וְנִשָּׂא כָּל־אֲשֶׁר בְּבֵיתֶךָ
וַאֲשֶׁר אָצְרוּ אֲבֹתֶיךָ עַד־הַיּוֹם הַזֶּה בָּבֶל
...לֹא־יִוָּתֵר דָּבָר

Aⁱ Trial resolution: Hezekiah's progeny's welfare [His indiscretion brings divine disfavor on the Davidic house] (39:7)
וּמִבָּנֶיךָ אֲשֶׁר יֵצְאוּ מִמְּךָ אֲשֶׁר תּוֹלִיד יִקָּחוּ
וְהָיוּ סָרִיסִים בְּהֵיכַל מֶלֶךְ בָּבֶל

Aⁱⁱ Trial dénouement: Hezekiah's personal welfare [His indifference to divine disfavor on the Davidic house] (39:8)
...טוֹב דְּבַר־יְהוָה אֲשֶׁר דִּבַּרְתָּ
וַיֹּאמֶר כִּי יִהְיֶה שָׁלוֹם וֶאֱמֶת בְּיָמָי

The 'A' tiers cohere in that they disclose Hezekiah's attitude toward YHWH's promise to protect the Davidic king.[1] The 'B' tiers cohere in their common focus upon Hezekiah's indiscrete exposure of the Davidide treasury and armory to a potential enemy—an indiscretion that betrayed his lack of regard for YHWH's promise to establish Zion as his royal seat.[2] The 'C' tiers portray Isaiah in his intermediary prophetic role, both setting up (through insinuating questions) and

[1]Note the strategic omission from Isa. 39 of the repetition of the divine motivation for both YHWH's defense of Zion and his healing of the Davidic king, which one finds in the parallel verses of 2 Kgs 19:34 (= Isa. 37:35) and 2 Kgs 20:6, respectively.

[2]Hezekiah's culpability for his lack of regard for YHWH's promise to establish Zion could be interpreted in two senses simultaneously. First, in regard to Hezekiah's faith, Hezekiah seems to have regarded YHWH as incapable of preserving him from the imminent Assyrian threat (which would be carried out in 701 BC) so, sometime between 703 and 701 BC, he made himself vulnerable to the Babylonians in hopes of securing their trust and an alliance with them against Assyria. Concomitantly, by allying himself with another nation, he was betraying his own lack of confidence in the divine promise that a Davidic king would emerge to rule the world from Zion and, thereby, ironically, showed his own unfitness for that 'messianic' role. Second, on the political level, Hezekiah was too naive and nearsighted to perceive the vulnerability to which he was subjecting the Davidic house by disclosing its treasury and armory to a people (i.e., the Babylonians) who were potentially as threatening as the Assyrians whom he feared.

conveying YHWH's rebuke.[1] It is probably poetic justice that Hezekiah's self-deluded egocentricism at Babylon's pretended interest in his personal welfare should provide the structural axis for the frustrated palistrophe that forms Isa. 39:1-4.[2] It may even be significant that the dialogue between Hezekiah and Isaiah (in the 'B' and 'C' tiers) has a sevenfold development that climaxes in the prophet's message that, ironically, Hezekiah's intention of ensuring safety for Jerusalem would be subverted by his display of its assets to the Babylonians.

The episode opens with a situation of testing for Hezekiah's character (39:1) and closes with a prediction of the adverse consequences that would result from his failure to exercise political discretion toward the envoys from Babylon (39:7). Between the framing tiers (A and A^i) is a compound frame whose design heightens the shock of YHWH's rebuke against Hezekiah for his political indiscretion and covenant disloyalty. In seeking to establish a treaty with the Babylonians, Hezekiah placed himself under the same divine censure that his father Ahaz had received for trying to establish a treaty with Assyria. The momentum set up by the mirrored repetition of themes among tiers A–B–C–Axis/[B^i]–C^i–B^{ii} (39:1-4) might prompt the reader to expect that the following tier should describe, perhaps, the glorious extent to which Hezekiah's influence had extended internationally (i.e., tier A^i). After all, is not such a response generated by an analogous account of David's heir at his being visited in Jerusalem by a foreign dignitary

---

[1]It is significant that Isaiah, in exercising his prophetic authority, never belies his subservience to divine or regal authority by directly rebuking Hezekiah. However, the rhetorical strategy of ch. 39 shows how deftly the prophet was able to guide Hezekiah's actions, words and thoughts so that the observer might wonder how consistent Hezekiah was being with the sentiments he had expressed in his previous prayer to YHWH for extended health and the protection of his city (cf. 38:5-6). Even after it is revealed that the consequences of Hezekiah's indiscretion would not escape his offspring (39:7), Hezekiah offers no sign of repentance and his relative disregard for the welfare of his successors is confirmed through the author's disclosure of his inner thoughts (39:8). Whether or not this brings one to question whether his prayers for YHWH's favor in the preceding chapters were sincere or not, Hezekiah's negative characterization in ch. 39 hardly befits the noble stature that one should expect from Zion's ideal king (cf. Isa. 7:15-16; 9:5-6).

[2]Although several Hebrew manuscripts, LXX, Syriac, some Targum manuscripts and the Vulgate show the presence of אֵלַי in the text of 2 Kgs 20:14, this addition appears to be a conflation to bring it into line with Isa. 39:3b. Its absence from most Hebrew manuscripts is otherwise difficult to explain, especially since the preceding question is posed using אֵלֶיךָ. Were אֵלַי originally absent from 2 Kgs 20:14, as I suggest, then its addition by the author/compiler in Isa. 39:3b is perhaps rhetorically significant as an indicator of an intended emphasis upon the egocentricism of Hezekiah.

(see 1 Kgs 10:1-13 concerning Solomon and the Queen of Sheba)? Nevertheless, just as the context following the account of the Queen of Sheba's visit is so couched in irony that it reverses the reader's initial impression of the passage, so here the concentric momentum becomes disrupted by Isaiah's unforeseen rebuke of Hezekiah, beginning with the messenger formula in 39:5.[1] In three of the 'B' tiers (excluding the B^i-tier, which may serve as the axis), the reference to Hezekiah's displaying openly everything in house and treasury sets up and then reverses his expectations as the repetition is passed from the narrator's seemingly impartial report (39:2aβb) to Hezekiah's own brash retort (39:4b) to Isaiah's ironic forecast (39:6). Indeed, the dénouement of this episode (A^{ii}, 39:8) reveals to the reader, through an inside look into Hezekiah's thoughts, an unforeseen and seemingly inexcusable laxity in his attitude toward the prophet's message of doom—the very reverse of the eagerness he showed in courting the favor of Babylon's envoys (39:2aα, וַיִּשְׂמַח עֲלֵיהֶם חִזְקִיָּהוּ). Hence, it is only in the last verse that the reader for the first time fully understands the true state of Hezekiah's devotedness to the welfare of Jerusalem: so long as YHWH's judgment for his indiscretion had no direct effect upon his personal well being, he was relatively unconcerned with the effect that it might have upon others.[2]

---

[1]The positive tone of describing Solomon's three major royal achievements, depicted in 'glowing' terms in 1 Kgs 10:14–11:8, is rhetorically reversed in the three consequent accounts of the reduction of his empire as a result of YHWH's disfavor (1 Kgs 11:9-40). The justification for this reversal derives ostensibly from Solomon's disregard for the royal prohibitions of Deut. 17:16-17. In two other places within the book of Isaiah, both in the passage immediately after the book's exordium (i.e., 2:6-8) and in that immediately before its exoneration section (i.e., 39:1-8), one may hear echoes of these deuteronomic kingly prohibitions that reverberate with the records of the first Davidic heir to epitomize their violation.

[2]This interpretation derives from the juxtaposition of YHWH's judgment against Hezekiah's progeny (39:7) and Hezekiah's affirmation that the judgment of YHWH is 'good' (i.e., acceptable) since it had no adverse effect on himself (39:8). It should be noted, by contrast, that the previous context of Isa. 38 must be brought into consideration in order to understand the significance of Hezekiah's indifference in Isa. 39:8. Isa. 39 begins with a transitional reference to Hezekiah's illness and recovery, which sets the scene (Isa. 39:1)—a recovery that was brought about by YHWH's answer to Hezekiah's prayer for personal deliverance (cf. Isa. 38:1-22 with 2 Kgs 20:1-11). Isa. 39 reveals, however, that Hezekiah was not concerned to repent of his indiscretion and covenant disloyalty (cf. his haughty attitude toward the accumulation of wealth, forbidden in Deut. 17:17b) so long as the divine displeasure took no course directly against his own person. This lessens (if not reverses) the reader's initial estimate of the purity of Hezekiah's motives in praying to and praising YHWH for his personal deliverance in Isa. 38.

The Solomonic analogy comes into play here as well, for, just like Solomon, Hezekiah is spared the judgment that he himself brings upon his lineage (cf. 1 Kgs

The NN and NN[ii] tiers (Isa. 13:[1]2-22; 39:1-8) correspond not only in their general concern with the nation of Babylon—the first section portraying Babylon as the object of YHWH's vengeance; the second, as the agent of his punishment of Zion—but on more subtle levels as well. For instance, a number of verbal, thematic and cause-effect correspondences exist between these sections:

13:1a, 19a	בָּבֶל	39:1, 3b, 6a, 7	בָּבֶל
13:2abα	raise a banner [שְׂאוּ־נֵס] ... shout [הָרִימוּ קוֹל] to them ... wave [הָנִיפוּ יָד]	39:1	sent [שָׁלַח] ... letters and a gift to Hezekiah
		7	your descendants will be taken [יִקָּחוּ] to be eunuchs in the palace of Babylon's king
13:2bβ	to enter [וְיָבֹאוּ] the gates of nobles	39:2a	was glad about them [וַיִּשְׂמַח] [עֲלֵיהֶם] ... showed them [וַיַּרְאֵם] what was in his storehouses
		4b	nothing among my treasures that I did not show them [לֹא הִרְאִיתִים]
		6b	all that your fathers have stored up ... nothing will be left
13:4b, 13b	יְהוָה צְבָאוֹת	39:5	דְּבַר־יְהוָה צְבָאוֹת
13:5a	בָּאִים מֵאֶרֶץ מֶרְחָק	39:3b	מֵאֶרֶץ רְחוֹקָה בָּאוּ
13:17	כֶּסֶף...וְזָהָב	39:2a	אֶת־הַכֶּסֶף וְאֶת־הַזָּהָב

The combined force of this collocation of expressions and themes in Isaiah 13 and 39, together with the fact that these chapters both describe the same foreign nation and hold the outermost flanking positions in the section (Isa. 13-39), suggests that their compiler intended that the reader should correlate them in reading. By Hezekiah's actions and speech, in the last chapter of the section, he unwittingly sets up the conditions for Babylon's cruelty to Jacob/Israel, which tacitly forms the foreboding background of its first chapter (i.e., the threat to future Babylon [Isa. 13], designed to vindicate Jacob/Israel [14:1-2 (3-4a)]). Ironically, and by means of allusions to ch. 13, the unsuspecting king of Judah forebodes Jerusalem's destruction in the wording of his responses to Isaiah's interrogation in ch. 39.

The NN[ii]-tier alludes also to the intervening NN[i]-tier (14:4b-23), a taunt song against the 'king of Babylon', through the use of the

11:12-13). It is also instructive to note how the deferral of divine judgment against the king of Judah is linked, in both contexts, to YHWH's covenant with David to preserve both king and city (cf. Isa. 37:35; 38:5-6; 1 Kgs 11:12-13).

expression מֶלֶךְ בָּבֶל in its framing tiers (i.e., A, 39:1; Aⁱ, 39:7). Like
the other two 'NN' tiers, the NNⁱ-tier focuses on the nation Babylon,
but its structure differs from them in that its key word repetitions form
a concentric structure that is symmetrical:[1]

A   'YHWH [יהוה]' shatters his foes (14:4b-5)   אֵיךְ

  B   Domination over the oppressed (14:6)

    C   'The whole land is at rest and peace ...' (14:7)

         נָחָה שָׁקְטָה כָּל־הָאָרֶץ...

      D   '... junipers ... cedars of Lebanon': 'No woodsman
            comes to cut us down' (14:8)

           ...בְּרוֹשִׁים...אַרְזֵי לְבָנוֹן...לֹא־יַעֲלֶה הַכֹּרֵת עָלֵינוּ

        E   The startled reaction of 'all the kings of the nations'
            [emphasis on their activity] (14:9)

             שְׁאוֹל מִתַּחַת רָגְזָה לְךָ...
             כֹּל מַלְכֵי גוֹיִם

          F   Sarcastic quotation of deceased kings
              [emphasis upon his stasis] (14:10)

            G   'Your pomp has been brought down to the grave'
                (14:11)

               ...הוּרַד שְׁאוֹל גְּאוֹנֶךָ

              Axisⁱ: Sardonic celestial pseudo-epithets   אֵיךְ
                           [2 vbs; emphasis on descent] (14:12)

              Axisⁱⁱ: Sevenfold arrogant assault upon the cosmic
                           mountain [anacrusis + 5 vbs in 7 cola;
                           emphasis on ascent] (14:13-14)

            Gⁱ   'Surely you are brought down to the grave ...'   אַךְ
                (14:15)

                אַךְ אֶל־שְׁאוֹל תּוּרָד...

          Fⁱ   Sarcastic quotation of deceased kings [emphasis
              upon his (former) activity] (14:16-17)

             ...הֲזֶה הָאִישׁ מַרְגִּיז הָאָרֶץ...

        Eⁱ   The secure state of 'all the kings of the nations'
            [emphasis on their stasis] (14:18)

            ...כָּל־מַלְכֵי גוֹיִם

      Dⁱ   'You are ... like a rejected branch'; 'covered with ...
            those pierced by the sword' (14:19ab')

           וְאַתָּה...כְּנֵצֶר נִתְעָב
           לְבוּשׁ...מְטֹעֲנֵי חָרֶב
           יוֹרְדֵי אֶל־אַבְנֵי־בוֹר

    Cⁱ   'for you have destroyed your [own] land' (14:19b''-20a)

        ...כִּי־אַרְצְךָ שִׁחַתָּ...

  Bⁱ   Domination over the oppressors (14:20b-21)

Aⁱ   'Warrior YHWH [יהוה צְבָאוֹת]' shatters his Babylonian
     foes [threefold ascription to YHWH with יהוה צְבָאוֹת as a
     frame; against the Babylonian king] (14:22-23)

---

[1] Cf. O'Connell, 'Isaiah xiv 4b-23: Ironic Reversal through Concentric Structure
and Mythic Allusion'. In Isaiah, it is usual for the author/compiler to vary the
sequential pattern of corresponding tiers in the same structure, whether for the sake
of aesthetic interest or in order to modify as little as necessary the received form of
the materials

A sudden shift occurs where the Aⁱ-tier (14:22-23), whose national referent is Babylon, is followed by another tier (14:24-25), whose national referent is Assyria. This appended alternative tier, whose correlation to the A-tier is as appropriate as that of the Aⁱ-tier, may therefore be designated tier Aⁱⁱ:

Aⁱⁱ 'Warrior YHWH [יְהוָה צְבָאוֹת]' shatters his Assyrian foes
[with יְהוָה צְבָאוֹת, opposing the Assyrian king] (14:24-25)

Thus, the addition of 14:24-25 does not merely introduce a new interest in the king of Assyria; it reorients the whole poem of 14:4b-21 so that it is made to taunt the Assyrian king as well. Consequently, its outermost inclusios can be seen to relate the poem alternatively to either the Babylonian or the Assyrian king (i.e., A:Aⁱ::A:Aⁱⁱ) as claimants to the title of universal dominion, 'King of Babylon' (14:3-4a). In fact, by extrapolating the compound inverse framing pattern of Isa. 13:1–39:8, the poem of 14:4b-21 can be seen to serve double duty—once serving as a denunciation of the Babylonian king (with 14:22-23 appended), then (with 14:24-25 appended) serving as a denunciation of the Assyrian monarch. In the second of its rhetorical functions, Isa. 14:4b-21, 24-25 may be designated the OO-tier and be regarded as parallel to the OOⁱⁱ-tier's taunt song against the Assyrian king (37:22b-35; cf. 2 Kgs 19:20-37).[1] The intervening OOⁱ-tier (Isa. 36:1–37:20), along similar lines, presents the narrative of Jerusalem's deliverance from the Assyrian king's military threat and YHWH's concomitant vindication for having been taunted by that king (cf. 2 Kgs 18:9–19:19).[2]

[1]Note the following correspondences: (1) the fivefold self-adulatory pronouncements by the Assyrian monarch in Isa. 14:13aα', aβ, b, 14a, b and 37:24aβ, bα, bβγ, 25a, b; (2) the use of vegetal imagery in both poems (e.g., Isa. 14:8, 19 and 37:24bα, bβγ, 27b, 30-31); and (3) the emphasis on the sovereign decree of YHWH in Isa. 14:24, 26-27 and 37:26.

[2]It was suggested by B. Stade ('Miscellen: Anmerkungen zu 2 Kö. 15-21', *ZAW* 6 [1886], pp. 156-89, especially pp. 172-78), and is supported in more recent studies by B.S. Childs (*Isaiah and the Assyrian Crisis* [SBT, II/3; London: SCM Press, 1967], pp. 73-103) and Clements (*Isaiah and the Deliverance of Jerusalem: A Study of the Interpretation of Prophecy in the Old Testament* [JSOTSup, 13; Sheffield: JSOT Press, 1980], pp. 52-71; idem, *Isaiah 1-39*, pp. 277-80), that two originally separate narratives, B¹ (comprising 2 Kgs 18:13, 17–19:9a, 36-37 = Isa. 36:1–37:9a, 37-38) and B² (comprising 2 Kgs 19:9b-35 = Isa. 37:9b-36), underlie the present form of Isa. 36:1–37:38. It seems evident that the arrangement of materials in 2 Kgs 18:13, 17–19:37 preceded the subtly reworked form in Isa. 36:1–37:38, though the ostensibly paneled arrangement of the former remains apparent:

The tiers designated 'PP' mark oracles against foreign nations other than Egypt and Cush (i.e., the 'QQ' tiers) and focus on nations bordering the land of Israel. The clustered 'PP' tiers of 14:28–17:3 correspond to those of 21:1-15, and these frame the oracles against Cush and Egypt (i.e., the 'QQ' tiers of 18:1–20:5). The PP^i-tier (15:1–16:12), which is the central tier of the first 'PP' cluster, contains an oracle against Moab. It is also concentric in structure, as may be seen from the following schema:

Isaiah	2 Kings			2 Kings	Isaiah
	A	α	Sennacherib's threat to Hezekiah	18:13, 17-25	36:1, 2-10
		β	Sennacherib's threat to Zion	18:26-36	36:11-21
	B		Hezekiah's solicitation of prayer for deliverance of the 'remnant'	18:37–19:4	36:22–37:4
	C		Isaiah sends message predicting YHWH's protection	19:5-6	37:5-6
		α	Report to Sennacherib	19:7aα	37:7aα
OO^i		β	Departure of Sennacherib	19:7aβ	37:7aβ
		γ	Death of Sennacherib	19:7b	37:7b
	1/C		[Protection foreshadowed:]		
		β^i	Departure of prime minister to Sennacherib	19:8	37:8
		α^i	Report to Sennacherib	19:9a	37:9a
	A^i	α	Sennacherib's threat to Hezekiah	19:9b-13	37:9b-13
	B^i		Hezekiah's prayer for deliverance	19:14-19	37:14-20
	C^i		Isaiah sends message predicting YHWH's protection	19:20-21a	37:21-22a
	1/A	α	YHWH's threat against Sennacherib	19:21b-28	37:22b-29
OO^{ii}	1/B		YHWH's sign, answering Hezekiah's prayer for deliverance of the 'remnant'	19:29-31	37:30-32
	1/A	β	YHWH's defense of Zion	19:32-34	37:33-35
	1/C^i		[Protection fulfilled:]		
		β^{ii}	Departure of Sennacherib	19:35-36	37:36-37
		γ^i	Death of Sennacherib	19:37	37:38

Tiers designated '1/X' indicate thematic inversion or the fulfillment of corresponding predictions. It would appear that the paneled structure in 2 Kings is primary and of secondary importance to the structural bifurcation of this material in Isaiah into 36:1–37:20 (OO^i) and 37:21-38 (OO^{ii}). This division seems warranted in Isaiah because of the analogous arrangement of tiers in Isa. 4:2–11:16 and 13:1–39:8, and because of the correspondence of Isa. 14:4b-21, 24-25 to 37:22b-35. As such, the most important features of differentiation between Isaiah's OO^i and OO^{ii} tiers seem to be: (1) emphasis upon prose narrative (OO^i) versus poetry (OO^{ii}); (2) emphasis upon crisis (OO^i) versus resolution (OO^{ii}); and (3) emphasis upon prayer and prediction (OO^i) versus divine response (OO^{ii}).

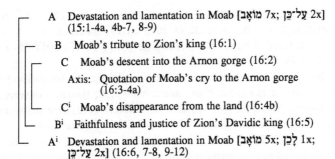

```
     ┌── A    Devastation and lamentation in Moab [מוֹאָב 7x; עַל־כֵּן 2x]
     │        (15:1-4a, 4b-7, 8-9)
     │  ┌── B    Moab's tribute to Zion's king (16:1)
     │  │  ┌── C    Moab's descent into the Arnon gorge (16:2)
     │  │  │    Axis:  Quotation of Moab's cry to the Arnon gorge
     │  │  │           (16:3-4a)
     │  │  └── Cⁱ   Moab's disappearance from the land (16:4b)
     │  └── Bⁱ   Faithfulness and justice of Zion's Davidic king (16:5)
     └── Aⁱ   Devastation and lamentation in Moab [מוֹאָב 5x; לָכֵן 1x;
              עַל־כֵּן 2x] (16:6, 7-8, 9-12)
```

If the inset that follows its final Aⁱ-tier (i.e., Insetⁱⁱ, 16:13-14) is considered in contiguity with the Aⁱ-tier, then there is a matched seven-fold repetition of the name מוֹאָב framing this concentric subunit. But even apart from this, there are obvious lexical, thematic and rhetorical similarities between the 'A' tiers of this subunit.

The oracle against Moab is the largest, and middle, among the oracles that constitute the first trifid 'PP' cluster. Its own contour is concentric. Hence, the PPⁱ-tier gives a concentric contour to the whole PP–PPⁱ–PPⁱⁱ cluster, and this symmetrically concentric pattern stands against the asymmetrically concentric formations of the PPⁱⁱⁱ–PPⁱᵛ–PPᵛ cluster (21:1-15), which forms a triadic framework, and the PPᵛⁱ–PPᵛⁱⁱ–PPᵛⁱⁱⁱ cluster (34:1-17), whose characterizing middle tier (the PPᵛⁱⁱ oracle against Edom) is, similarly, a triadic frame made up of bifid tiers:

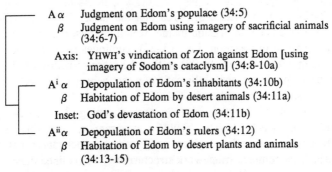

```
     ┌── A α   Judgment on Edom's populace (34:5)
     │     β   Judgment on Edom using imagery of sacrificial animals
     │         (34:6-7)
     │    Axis:  YHWH's vindication of Zion against Edom [using
     │           imagery of Sodom's cataclysm] (34:8-10a)
     │  ┌── Aⁱ α   Depopulation of Edom's inhabitants (34:10b)
     │  │     β   Habitation of Edom by desert animals (34:11a)
     │    Inset:  God's devastation of Edom (34:11b)
     └── Aⁱⁱ α   Depopulation of Edom's rulers (34:12)
           β   Habitation of Edom by desert plants and animals
               (34:13-15)
```

Just as, in the first half of the large palistrophe of Isaiah 13–39 (i.e., Isa. 13–23), the 'PP' tiers' oracles against neighboring nations are jux-taposed with the 'QQ' tiers' denunciation of Egypt and Cush as Judah's would-be allies so, in the second half (Isa. 28–39), there is a group of oracles against nations from which Egypt is differentiated. However, the 'PP'–'QQ'–'PP' pattern, which characterizes Isa. 14:28–21:15, is more truncated and intermittent in 30:1–34:17, where only the 'PP' tiers are clustered (i.e., QQ^{iii}—[INSET$^{vi}\alpha$–β—]QQ^{iv}—[INSET$^{vii}\beta$–α—] PP^{vi}—PP^{vii}—PP^{viii}).

The bifid 'RR' tiers emphasize YHWH's judgment on Judah/Zion (in contrast to the thematic motif of Zion's exaltation, which is developed by the insets). The first two 'RRα' tiers address Jerusalem indirectly, using symbolic epithets: 'Valley of Vision' (22:1, 5), and 'Ariel' (29:1, 2, 7). The third 'RRα' tier, like the second, is a woe oracle, but it identifies the addressee explicitly (or in YHWH's epithets) as 'Jacob' and 'Israel'. The 'SS' tiers portray threatening scenarios of YHWH's judgment on Judah's near neighbors, Tyre (in 23:1-14, 15-18) and Ephraim (in 28:1-8), who are about to be destroyed by the Assyrian king.

The core of the concentric structure of Isaiah 13–39 comprises the so-called 'apocalypse' of chs. 24–27, which outlines a cataclysmic upheaval of the present world order. The thematic reversal between YHWH's 'scattering' (in the A-tier) and 'gathering' (in the A^{i}- and A^{ii}-tiers) both frames and augments the intervening contrast between the nations (B/B^{i}–B^{ii}) and Zion (C/C^{i}–C^{ii}). Careful note should also be taken of the fact that the 'B tiers' disproportionate emphasis on the destruction of the nations/earth in the opening half of this asymmetrically concentric substructure (note 24:4-20, as opposed to 25:10b-12 and 27:1) is counterbalanced by an analogous emphasis on the exaltation-of-Zion theme in the 'C' tiers and insets of the closing half (cf. 24:21-23 against 25:6-8, 9-10a and the insets 26:1-21; 27:2-11). Indeed, this exaltation-of-Zion theme, which characterizes the insets of the last half of this section (i.e., 13–23), continues to recur among the remaining chapters (i.e., 28–39) so that the macrostructure of chs. 13–39 reflects the same general thematic contrast between the fates of Zion and the nations as does the axis (24–27).

A particularly lengthy inset is that spanning 32:1–33:24 (i.e., INSET$^{vii}\alpha$), which depicts YHWH's program for exalting Zion's righteous citizens under an ideal king once its wickedness has been punished. Its complex framework structure may be outlined thus:

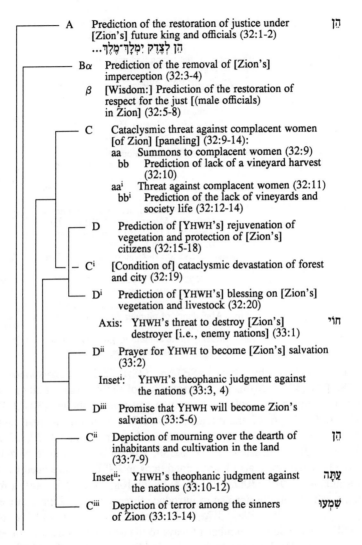

A   Prediction of the restoration of justice under [Zion's] future king and officials (32:1-2) הֵן
הֵן לְצֶדֶק יִמְלָךְ־מֶלֶךְ...

Bα   Prediction of the removal of [Zion's] imperception (32:3-4)

β   [Wisdom:] Prediction of the restoration of respect for the just [(male officials) in Zion] (32:5-8)

C   Cataclysmic threat against complacent women [of Zion] [paneling] (32:9-14):
aa   Summons to complacent women (32:9)
bb   Prediction of lack of a vineyard harvest (32:10)
aaⁱ   Threat against complacent women (32:11)
bbⁱ   Prediction of the lack of vineyards and society life (32:12-14)

D   Prediction of [YHWH's] rejuvenation of vegetation and protection of [Zion's] citizens (32:15-18)

Cⁱ   [Condition of] cataclysmic devastation of forest and city (32:19)

Dⁱ   Prediction of [YHWH's] blessing on [Zion's] vegetation and livestock (32:20)

Axis: YHWH's threat to destroy [Zion's] חוֹי
destroyer [i.e., enemy nations] (33:1)

Dⁱⁱ   Prayer for YHWH to become [Zion's] salvation (33:2)

Insetⁱ: YHWH's theophanic judgment against the nations (33:3, 4)

Dⁱⁱⁱ   Promise that YHWH will become Zion's salvation (33:5-6)

Cⁱⁱ   Depiction of mourning over the dearth of הֵן
inhabitants and cultivation in the land (33:7-9)

Insetⁱⁱ: YHWH's theophanic judgment against עַתָּה
the nations (33:10-12)

Cⁱⁱⁱ   Depiction of terror among the sinners שִׁמְעוּ
of Zion (33:13-14)

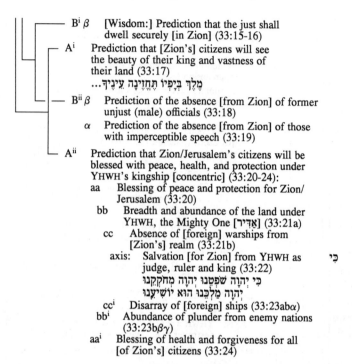

B^i β   [Wisdom:] Prediction that the just shall dwell securely [in Zion] (33:15-16)

A^i Prediction that [Zion's] citizens will see the beauty of their king and vastness of their land (33:17)

מֶלֶךְ בְּיָפְיוֹ תֶּחֱזֶינָה עֵינֶיךָ...

B^{ii} β   Prediction of the absence [from Zion] of former unjust (male) officials (33:18)

α   Prediction of the absence [from Zion] of those with imperceptible speech (33:19)

A^{ii} Prediction that Zion/Jerusalem's citizens will be blessed with peace, health, and protection under YHWH's kingship [concentric] (33:20-24):

aa   Blessing of peace and protection for Zion/Jerusalem (33:20)

bb   Breadth and abundance of the land under YHWH, the Mighty One [אַדִּיר] (33:21a)

cc   Absence of [foreign] warships from [Zion's] realm (33:21b)

axis: Salvation [for Zion] from YHWH as judge, ruler and king (33:22)   כִּי

כִּי יְהוָה שֹׁפְטֵנוּ יְהוָה מְחֹקְקֵנוּ
יְהוָה מַלְכֵּנוּ הוּא יוֹשִׁיעֵנוּ

cc^i Disarray of [foreign] ships (33:23abα)

bb^i Abundance of plunder from enemy nations (33:23bβγ)

aa^i Blessing of health and forgiveness for all [of Zion's] citizens (33:24)

It is noteworthy that INSET^{vii}α (32:1–33:24) corresponds to INSET^{vi}α (30:18-26) in its foregrounding of the reversal of siege conditions through the replenishment food and water supplies (30:20, 23, 25; [32:6]; 33:16; cf. the threats of 3:1, 6-7; 4:1) and of the restoration of just instruction and righteous rule in the very sight (30:20; 32:3a, 17, 19, 20) and hearing (30:21; 32:3b, 13a) of Zion's future citizens. Note how the reversals of siege conditions in INSET^{vi}α are cued by the formula בַּיּוֹם הַהוּא (30:23, 25; cf. 4:2a; 11:10a, 11a; 12:1a, 4a), a formula echoing its former use to introduce threats against Zion's citizens (cf. 2:11b, 17b, 20a; 3:7a, 18a; 4:1a). Indeed, INSET^{vi}α and INSET^{vii}α allude in a number of ways to the opening accusatory threats (i.e., 2:6aγ-21; 3:1–4:1) against Zion's idolaters (cf. 2:20; 30:22) and unjust officials (cf. 3:5; 32:5), women (cf. 3:16-17, 24; 32:9, 11) and male citizens (cf. 3:25-26; 33:7-8).

Persuasion as a Function of Structure in Isaiah 13:1–39:8

Once again, one must consider the rhetorical significance of the arrangement of tiers in Isa. 13:1–39:8 against the background of the ostensible situations in which they took shape. This one should do as a precursor to understanding the design of the whole section, the product of the compilation of its final author.

The clearest historical referent in the section is that of 14:28, which introduces the first of the oracles against neighboring nations, in this case, the Philistines: 'This oracle came in the year King Ahaz died'. Accordingly, the content of this oracle should probably be assigned a *terminus a quo* of 716/15 BCE.[1] This date, however, would apply only to the prediction concerning the Philistines in 14:29-32, not necessarily to its final prophetic form or to the oracles that follow (against Moab and Damascus). According to extrabiblical sources, in 712/11 BCE Assyrian troops crushed a coalition led by Ashdod (cf. Isa. 20:1), and this is probably the Philistine devastation that 14:29-32 was originally intended to predict. Thus, the *terminus ad quem* for these verses is probably 712/11 BCE. This time span of just over three years comports with the general period of delay assigned to at least two other predictions (i.e., against Moab, 16:14; against Egypt, 20:3).

Immediately following comes the prediction of Moab's devastation, the central oracle of a trifid 'PP' cluster. It contains two matching predictions of an ideal Davidic king on Zion's throne who, with righteousness and justice, would make Moab subject (16:1, 5). The author's positioning of this oracle after an oracle dated to the death of Ahaz (14:28-32) was probably with the intent that the reader should infer that this oracle, and its paired messianic predictions (16:1, 5), should refer to none other than Ahaz's successor, Hezekiah.[2]

Another dated oracle occurs where Isaiah is commissioned to begin a three-year-long symbolic act against Egypt and Cush, namely, going

---

[1]Cf. E.R. Thiele, *The Mysterious Numbers of the Hebrew Kings* (Grand Rapids: Zondervan, rev. edn, 1983), pp. 133-34. For the view that Ahaz died in 728/27 BCE, the same year in which Tiglath-pileser III died, see Hayes–Irvine, pp. 24, 43, 45, 236, and Clements, *Isaiah 1–39*, p. 148, though Clements assigns the prophecy of 14:28-32 to 722 BCE, the year in which Shalmaneser V died.

[2]Indeed, the whole of 13:1–39:8 can be seen to develop messianic expectations that, right up until the last verse, lead to the false expectation that Hezekiah might be their fulfillment. However, in the author's strategy, this buildup of messianic motifs only serves to heighten the reader's sense of disillusionment when Hezekiah shows himself to fall short of the messianic ideal.

about stripped and barefoot (20:1-2). This commission is dated to the time when the field marshal (תַּרְתָּן) of Sargon II of Assyria captured Ashdod, 712/11 BCE.[1] This would give a *terminus a quo* of 712/11 for the commencement of Isaiah's act in 20:1-2 and of ca. 709/8 for its interpretive prediction given at the end of the three years, in 20:3-6.

Only the materials of 36:1–37:37 are thereafter dated explicitly. The historical reference in 36:1 cites the fourteenth year of Hezekiah. If Hezekiah ascended the throne in 715 BCE (the year Ahaz died), this would comport with a date of 701 BCE as the date of Sennacherib's campaign against the Shephelah of Judah and his mediated threats against Jerusalem. Extrabiblical evidence indicates that the events of 37:38 occurred in 681 BCE, the accession year of Esarhaddon.[2] This is the latest datable historical reference in the entire section (13:1–39:8) and the latest in the book of Isaiah that could reasonably have fallen within the lifetime of the prophet Isaiah.

The events of Isa. 38:1–39:8 must antedate the *terminus ad quem* of 700 BCE, since this is the year in which Sennacherib installed his son Aššur-nādin-šumi as regent in Babylon, ousting Marduk-apla-iddinna (cf. מְרֹדַךְ בַּלְאֲדָן, 39:1) after the latter's third and final rebellion against Assyrian rule.[3] However, a *terminus a quo* of 703 BCE would be likely since this was the year in which Marduk-apla-iddinna recommenced his efforts to achieve independence from Sennacherib by attempting to re-establish the Sealands dynasty.[4] Since, moreover, the illness and recovery of Hezekiah anticipate Jerusalem's deliverance from the king of Assyria (38:6), and since his recovery was promised to add fifteen years to his life (which ended in 686 BCE), one would do best to date the content of 38:1–39:8 to the months that span 702/1 BCE but antedate Hezekiah's reception of Sennacherib's threats against Jerusalem (for the Assyrian threat was less imminent than his own death [38:1]). Nevertheless, the contiguity of this healing of the Davidic king and the promise of Jerusalem's deliverance in 38:5-6 suggests that the period of Hezekiah's illness would probably have been one in which Hezekiah was already aware of the approach of Assyrian forces for, far from needing elaboration on the imminence of

---

[1] Cf. Hayes–Irvine, pp. 27, 32, 48.

[2] See the annals of Ashurbanipal for an alternative account of Sennacherib's murder (*ANET*, p. 288). Cf. Clements, *Isaiah 1–39*, p. 288.

[3] L.D. Levine, 'Sennacherib's Southern Front: 704–689 B.C.', *JCS* 34 (1982), pp. 29-34; E.H. Merrill, *Kingdom of Priests: A History of Old Testament Israel* (Grand Rapids: Baker, 1987), pp. 413-14.

[4] Merrill, p. 417.

this encroaching threat, it is assumed to be a second point of concern directly contingent upon the extension of Hezekiah's lifespan.

Some of the intervening oracles against neighboring nations and false allies may be dated by inference from their prophetic descriptions.[1] However, it would appear that none of the nation oracles contained within 13:1–39:8 need be dated later than the historical reference of 37:38, which would give the final compilation of this section a *terminus a quo* of 681 BCE, though on rhetorical grounds it is more probable that its compilation was the work of a later compiler. Thus, whereas it is possible that Isaiah himself was the author of most of the nation oracles in 13:1–39:8—since their contents pertain to matters that could have fallen within his lifetime—ascribing the final compilation of Isaiah 13–39 to Isaiah is not necessarily the only valid inference.[2]

[1]For instance, the threat against Ephraim's drunken leaders in 28:1-8 (SS[ii]) must antedate a *terminus ad quem* of 722 BCE, when the siege of Shalmaneser V succeeded in subjecting Samaria to Assyrian rule. As such, this is probably the earliest prophecy in 13:1–39:8. Its incorporation into a literary framework that could have achieved its final form no earlier than 681 BCE (cf. 37:38) is evidence that it was by then in 'secondary usage'.

The condemnations against Judah (in the 'QQ' tiers) for seeking to form treaty alliances with Cushite Egypt might be dated to the period when Hezekiah was making overtures to Egypt to formulate an anti-Assyrian coalition, immediately following the death of Sargon II in 705 BCE. In line with this, Clements (*Isaiah 1–39*, p. 131) has said that the perception in the prophecies against Cush (18:1-7), Cush and Egypt (20:1-6), and those who trusted in Egypt (30:1-5; 31:1-3) is that these nations would prove worthless allies of Judah. Clements assigned 18:1-7; 19:1-15; 20:1-6 to a period prior to the Ashdod-led rebellion against Assyria in 713-711 BCE (pp. 163-64, 166-67). He has suggested that, apart from the pre-722 BCE oracle of 28:1-4, the additions of the alleged 'Josianic Redaction' (i.e., 29:5-9; 31:4-5, 8-9; 32:1-5), and some alleged post-587 BCE additions (i.e., 28:5-6, 13, etc.), the basic kernel of chs. 28–33 dates from the period of Hezekiah's revolt against Sennacherib, namely, between 705-701 BCE (pp. 223-24). Hence, Clements would assign the material in the first cluster of 'QQ' tiers (of the proposed schema) to Hezekiah's Egyptian alliance, made prior to 713 BCE, and the latter two 'QQ' tiers (i.e., the woe oracles) to a similar situation in 705-701 BCE.

Following an earlier scheme, however, Hayes–Irvine have assigned 18:1-7 to a period following Piye's (i.e., Pi-ankhi) invasion of the Nile delta in 732 BCE (specifically 728/7 BCE, pp. 253, 258), 19:1-15, 16-25 to a period following 720 BCE, when Sargon II defeated an Egyptian force at Gaza (p. 258), 20:1-6 to the Ashdod-led anti-Assyrian coalition of 715/4 BCE, which was crushed by Sargon in 712/11 (pp. 32, 268), Egypt's anguish in 23:5 to Assyria's dominance over Cypriot and Phoenician trade, beginning in 709 BCE (p. 32), but 30:1-33 and 31:1-3, 4-9 to Hoshea's appeal to So (Osorkon IV, 2 Kgs 17:4) against Shalmaneser V in 726 BCE (pp. 31, 337-38, 345)—none of these passages, which involve a denunciation of alliances with Cushite Egypt, being ascribed to Hezekiah's revolt of 705-701 BCE.

[2]The inference is possible, since: (1) the triadic framework structure of the clustered oracles and inner tiers of 4:2–11:16, a section commonly assigned to

On the basis of this set of supposed situations for the composition of the oracles of 13:1–39:8, one may attempt to make sense of its rhetorical arrangement. It is perhaps significant that the affairs of Babylon, not Assyria, hold the most strategic structural place at the outside extremities of the concentric structure that governs Isaiah 13–39. This is because it was eventually Babylon that not only threatened the security of Jerusalem, as had Assyria, but captured and razed its temple and walls. Indeed, it may have been concern to preserve the framing position held by the Babylon oracles that eventuated in the well-known chronological displacement of earlier matters, described in chs. 38–39, to follow later ones, described in 36–37.

Of course, such argumentation could suggest that the arrangement of Isaiah 36–39 preceded the insertion of its parallel account (2 Kgs 18:13, 17–20:19) into the book of Kings.[1] There is sufficient evidence for believing that the basic arrangement of materials was as it is in 2 Kgs 18:13, 17–20:19 and that this was antecedent to its subsequent adaptation to the rhetorical aims of the book of Isaiah. However, this view would not necessarily imply that the final redaction of the account in Kings antedated the final redaction of Isaiah 13–39 or even of the whole of Isaiah.[2] In addition, since Isa. 36:1–37:20 (OO^i) and 37:21-38

historical Isaiah, is a virtual replica of the structure of clustered oracles and the inner tiers of 13:1–39:8; and (2) their self-incriminating portrayals of two consecutive Davidic rulers present scenarios that are closely and ironically interrelated. However, it is not readily apparent from the book of Isaiah just how much of the impetus for its final form derived from the prophet for whom the book is named.

[1]Cf. Hayes–Irvine, pp. 372-73.

[2]There are several considerations that would support the view that the account of 2 Kgs 18:13, 17–20:19 antedated its adaptation in chs. 36–39. First, there is a series of omissions of details that may have been considered superfluous to Isaiah's aim to set up an artificially idealized portrayal of Hezekiah (e.g., 'his chief officers' [2 Kgs 18:17], 'son of Hilkiah' [18:26], 'from my hand' [18:29], 'a land of olive trees and honey. Choose life and not death!' [18:32], 'listen to' [18:32], 'Hena and Ivvah' [18:34], 'that night' [19:35a], 'the leader of my people' ... 'I will heal you. On the third day from now you will go up to the temple of YHWH' [20:5], 'on the third day from now' [20:8], 'Isaiah answered' [20:9a]). Second, the Isaiah account offers a number of idealizing substitutions for material in 2 Kings. Apart from the rather insignificant substitution of 'peoples' (Isa. 37:18) for 'nations' (2 Kgs 19:17), the prophet significantly substitutes for the assuring words, 'I have heard your prayer' (2 Kgs 19:20), the more energetic portrayal of Hezekiah in the causal clause, 'because you have prayed to me' (Isa. 37:21); for the indicative, 'they did so and applied it to the boil and he recovered' (2 Kgs 20:7b), Isaiah substitutes the imperative and result clause, 'apply it to the boil and he will recover' (38:21); for the scant depiction, 'made the shadow go back the ten steps it had gone down on the stairway/sundial of Ahaz' (2 Kgs 20:11b), Isaiah dramatizes the portrayal with, '"I will make the shadow cast by the sun go back the ten steps it has gone down on the stairway/sundial of Ahaz". So

(OO[ii]) correspond to the (probably) newly devised funerary taunt song in 14:3-21, 24-25 (OO); since 39:1-8 (NN[ii]) corresponds to the oracle against Babylon in 13:1-22 (NN) and, again, the taunt song of 14:3-21, 22-23 (NN[i]); and since the (probably) newly devised song of deliverance in 38:[1-8], [9]10-20, [21-22] corresponds to the promise of YHWH's exaltation of Zion over all nations in 14:1-2 (i.e., the first and last insets of 13–39)—all these correspondences appear to be secondary to the arrangement found in 2 Kgs 18:13, 17–20:19. However, since the tiered arrangement of both Isa. 39:1-8 and 2 Kgs 20:12-19 can be seen to conform to a triadic framework pattern that is pervasive

the sunlight went back the ten steps it had gone down' (Isa. 38:8). These embellishments lend further idealization to Hezekiah's portrayal.

Third, there are selective omissions from Isaiah of materials that might too soon betray Hezekiah's inordinate lack of personal fortitude and faith (e.g., 2 Kgs 18:14-16; or 'they called for the king' [18:18a], 'before [Isaiah] had left the middle court' [20:4a], 'for my sake and for the sake of my servant David' [20:6b; cf. 2 Kgs 19:34; Isa. 37:35], 'that YHWH will heal me and' [20:8], '"Shall the shadow go forward ten steps, or shall it go back ten steps?" "It is a simple matter for the shadow to go forward ten steps", said Hezekiah. "Rather, have it go back ten steps". Then the prophet Isaiah called upon YHWH' [20:9b-11a]). However, the war oracle consolation, 'Do not be afraid' (אַל־תִּירָא, 2 Kgs 19:6) is retained (Isa. 37:6).

Fourth, and more important, the displacement of material in 2 Kgs 20:7-8 to follow that of 20:9-11, with Hezekiah's self-motivated thanksgiving song (Isa. 38:9-20) newly interposed (cf. Isa. 38:7-8, 21-22), retards the disclosure that it was Hezekiah himself who had requested a confirming sign of YHWH's promise.

Fifth, and most important, besides Isaiah's additions in 37:9 ('when he had heard it'), 37:16 (the epithet, 'Warrior' [צְבָאוֹת]) and 37:18 ('all'), there are three additions in ch. 39 that give an inside view into Hezekiah's lack of discernment as to the Babylonian envoys' potential threat to the security of Jerusalem: 39:1b ('and had recovered' [וַיֶּחֱזָק]), 39:2 ('gladly'), and 39:3 ('to me'). To this end, it is perhaps significant to notice the transposition of כָּל from the general 'everything in his storehouses' (אֶת־כָּל־בֵּית נְכֹתֹה, 2 Kgs 20:13) to emphasize the strategic blunder of showing them 'his entire armory' (וְאֵת כָּל־בֵּית כֵּלָיו, Isa. 39:2). It is only just and fitting, therefore, that YHWH should at last respond to his indiscrete hubris with the addition of his divine epithet of warfare, יְהוָה] צְבָאוֹת] (Isa. 39:5). What assures the negative characterization of Hezekiah is the shift from his tone of self-consolation in 2 Kgs 20:19, 'Will there not be peace and security in my lifetime?', to his self-assured tone in Isa. 39:8, 'There will be peace and security in my lifetime'. Above all, this inside view into Hezekiah's lack of concern for the welfare of the Davidic house shows him to be so self-centered as to fall short of the messianic ideal. In view of the broader literary context, this realization may lessen the reader's initial impression of Hezekiah's character from that formed on the basis of his prayers and actions, described in the preceding chapters. Indeed, the contrast between Hezekiah's idealization in the preceding chapters and the disclosure of his relative dispassion for the welfare of future Jerusalem may leave the reader somewhat disillusioned with Hezekiah as a model of Davidic kingship.

in the book of Isaiah, and since there are evident deliberate rhetorical correspondences between the narrative accounts of Isaiah's confrontations with Ahaz (Isa. 7:1–8:10) and his son Hezekiah (Isa. 36:1–39:8), it may not be outlandish to suggest that the account of 2 Kgs 18:13–20:19 represents an earlier draft by the same author.[1]

The artificial idealization of the Judean king, Hezekiah, in Isa. 36:1–38:20, is deliberate and seems to have two aims: (1) to portray Hezekiah, even if only temporarily, as the fulfillment of the reader's hope for an ideal Davidic king; and (2) to heighten, through the withholding of essential information, the reader's sense of disappointment when it finally becomes evident that Hezekiah has failed to fulfill that hope. It is with the last verse of ch. 38 (v. 22) that Hezekiah's characterization begins progressively to worsen until, in the last verse of ch. 39 (v. 8), the reader discerns only a flawed model of 'messianic' expectation. Thus, Hezekiah's portrayal is not, in the end, an idealized contrast to that of his father Ahaz, but a continuation of the prophet's negative portrayal of Judah's monarchy. Even Hezekiah's song of thanksgiving (Isa. 38:10-20) is a rhetorically double-edged sword that both idealizes the Davidic king who gives thanks for YHWH's protection and, in the light of ch. 39, heightens the reader's sense of disillusionment when Hezekiah proves to lack the depth of concern for the welfare of Davidic house that would show him to be worthy of his idealized portrayal.[2]

---

[1]For a roster of correspondences between the accounts of Isaiah's confrontations with Ahaz and Hezekiah, see Sweeney, pp. 12-13.

[2]Isa. 38:10-20 is multivalent: on the surface, it is a song of thanksgiving for YHWH's deliverance and vindication of a righteous king of Judah (emitting messianic overtones that resonate with the songs of YHWH's vindicated servant in 40–66); however, in the context of Hezekiah's portrayal in ch. 39, it insinuates that Hezekiah's interest in YHWH may have been only one of self-preservation. In contrast to Hezekiah's remorse (Isa. 38:2-3), which motivates his petition and song of thanksgiving, compare his lack of remorse at God's displeasure in Isa. 39:8 simply because there the consequences have no adverse effect upon himself.

Sweeney (pp. 13-17), like others before him, seems to have been taken in by this initial idealization and to have minimized the reversal in Hezekiah's portrayal in ch. 39. While it is true that the prophet deliberately removes the negative descriptions from the account of 2 Kings (without including the idealization of Hezekiah in 2 Kgs 18:3-8), he does so that nothing should mar either the portrayal of the ideal Davidic king or one's sense of disappointment when Hezekiah incriminates himself in that regard.

This mixed characterization is completely in keeping with what may be discerned of Hezekiah's character from the more transparent original version of 2 Kings. The portrayals of Hezekiah in 2 Kgs 18:13, 17–20:19 and Isa. 36:1–39:8, while differing in detail, are essentially similar. However, the rhetorical strategy by which each portrayal affects the reader varies; the portrayal is far more dramatic and emotive in Isaiah where Hezekiah, by his own actions and words, incriminates

The outermost tiers, which treat Babylon and Assyria, have a politically antipolar correspondence to the innermost tiers of the concentric framework: the 'SS' tiers outline oracles against Tyre (SS, 23:1-14; SS^i, 23:15-18) and Ephraim (SS^{ii}, 28:1-8) as the primary nations that YHWH had targeted to be devastated by the Assyrians in the eighth century BCE; the 'RR' tiers, however, outline oracles against Jerusalem, Judah's capital, using the veiled epithets, 'Valley of Vision' (RRα, 22:1-14) and 'Ariel' (RR$^i\alpha$, 29:1-8), and the patriarchal epithets Jacob/Israel (RR$^{ii}\alpha$, 29:15-24). Yet, since Jerusalem's culpability rested mostly on their 'palace servants' and so-called 'intelligentsia', the 'RRβ' tiers, correspondingly, denounce both self-seeking usurpers and leading incompetents. It was not until the sixth century BCE that Jerusalem came to feel the ultimate effect of YHWH's judgment described in these tiers through the instrumentality of Babylonian military might, but it did experience at least a foretaste of that judgment under successive Assyrian threats. It is important, therefore, to a rhetorical understanding of the literary structure of Isaiah 13–39 that one recognizes the distinctions of nationality that the author maintained between the Assyrians and Babylonians and the specific effects that each would have, respectively, upon the Ephraim–Tyre alliance and later upon Jerusalem itself.

It is rhetorically significant that the two innermost complex frames (RRα-β—SS—SS^i//SS^{ii}—RR$^i\beta$-α—RR$^{ii}\beta$-α), which constitute the most explicit descriptions of the devastation of Ephraim and Tyre and later of Jerusalem, flank the central axis of the concentric structure (Isa. 24–27). Here, at the focal point of the concentric framework, history telescopes as the author escalates to the cosmic level the language of destruction used to describe the historical sieges of Ephraim, Tyre and Jerusalem. YHWH himself will foment the final cataclysmic upheaval of the present world order to bring about a complete revolution, namely, the inversion of the injustices worked out in history through his agents of punitive destruction, Assyria and Babylon.

All the tiers designated 'PP' contain oracles against Israel's/Judah's neighboring nations. These oracles play a supporting role to that of the

himself. Indeed, it is the very dynamic of intertextuality between Isa. 36–39, as the alluding text, and 2 Kgs 18:13, 17–20:19, as the evoked text, that highlights the rhetorical strategy of Hezekiah's characterization in the Isaiah context. Cf. also Oswalt, pp. 629-30.

main antithesis between Assyria and Ephraim–Tyre, on the one hand, and Babylon and Jerusalem, on the other. The first cluster ($PP-PP^i-PP^{ii}$, 14:28-32; 15:1–16:12; 17:1-3) outlines three consecutive oracles against such neighboring nations (i.e., Philistia, Moab, Damascus), these being devastated and annexed by Assyria from the time of Tiglath-pileser III (745–727 BCE) to that of Sargon II (722–705 BCE). Prior to Isaiah's ministry, Philistia had been governed by Judah, under Uzziah (790–739 BCE), and both Moab and Damascus were regions governed by Uzziah's Israelite contemporary, Jeroboam II (793–753 BCE). If Isaiah had written these denunciations after the death of Ahaz in 715 BCE (cf. 14:28), his Judean audience would have been readily able to discern the trend of enemy encroachment already taking place in the territories surrounding Judah. Thus, these prophetic threats may have provided the citizens of Zion with a mixed sense of fear and hope at the coming of YHWH's vindication.

The second cluster ($PP^{iii}//PP^{iv}-PP^v$, 21:1-9, 11-12, 13-15) juxtaposes an oracular denunciation of the coastland (ambivalently, the Mediterranean or Babylonian) with oracles against two regions, Edom and Arabia, that Babylon devastated in the sixth century BCE. Babylonian military campaigns in these regions are reported in the Babylonian Chronicle of Nebuchadnezzar II (605–562 BCE). Babylon is mentioned in the PP^{iii}-tier, however, not primarily as the future major threat to Jerusalem, as in the 'NN' tiers, but as the object of Judah's false hope for an ally when threatened by Assyria in the eighth century BCE. Thus, the fall of Babylon referred to in this prediction is that of 689 BCE, not that of 539 BCE.[1] The complementary third cluster ($PP^{vi}-PP^{vii}-PP^{viii}$, 34:1-4, 5-15, 16-17) presents again an oracle of Edom's devastation (5:5-15; cf. 21:11-12), but it is now flanked by descriptions of the inevitability of YHWH's destructive decree against all enemy nations under two images of an oracular 'scroll' (34:4, 16).

All the 'QQ' tiers concern denunciations of Egypt (under the last vestiges of the Saidic Dynasty XXII—especially Osorkon IV, i.e., biblical 'So', ca. 730–715 BCE; cf. 2 Kgs 17:1-6) or Cush (i.e., Egypt, under the Ethiopian Dynasty XXV, ca. 720–663 BCE, initiated by Pi-ankhi), nations that are mocked as the false hope of those who would seek in them an ally against Assyria at the end of the eighth century BCE. Isaiah 23:5, apparently referring to contemporary events, mentions that Egypt (then likely under Shebitku, 702–690 BCE, of Dyn.

---

[1]Cf. S. Erlandsson, *The Burden of Babylon: A Study of Isaiah 13:2–14:23* (trans. G.J. Houser; ConBOT, 4; Lund: Gleerup, 1970), pp. 81-92.

XXV) would be in anguish at the report of Sennacherib's destruction of Tyre in 701 BCE. The first cluster (QQ–QQ^i//QQ^{ii}, 18:1-6; 19:1-15, 20:1-5) forms a triadic frame, which contains one oracle each against Cush (QQ, 18:1-6) and Egypt (QQ^i, 19:1-15), and one against both (QQ^{ii}, 20:1-5). The axis that intervenes (19:16-25) portrays an 'apocalyptic' inversion of Egypt's denunciation. Here, Egypt's devastation turns into their becoming a people of YHWH, and this utopian vision is linked to similar expectations for both Assyria and Israel as peoples of YHWH. The cumulative effect is a complete inversion of Isaiah's present world order.

The Assyrian oppression of Egypt under its Cushite Dynasty (XXV), anticipated in Isaiah 20, took place in two phases: the first in 671 BCE when Esarhaddon drove Taharqa (690–664 BCE), brother of Shebitku, from Memphis (located at the head of the Nile delta), and the second in 667/6 BCE when Assurbanipal removed Taharqa from Thebes in Upper Egypt. Taharqa is mentioned by name in Isa. 37:9 as being 'king of Cush' at the time of Sennacherib's campaign in 701 BCE. K.A. Kitchen has cogently argued that the apparent chronological difficulty that this presents is resolved if Taharqa, as a twenty-one-year-old heir apparent (not coregent), militarily confronted Sennacherib in 701 BCE, and was only called 'king of Cush' proleptically from the vantage point of a writer who reported this event after Taharqa's royal accession.[1]

Both the second and third occurrences of 'QQ' tiers (i.e., QQ^{iii}, 30:1-17; QQ^{iv}, 31:1-3) are woe oracles against Egypt, which is denounced as the object of Judah's false hope for an ally against Assyria (cf. the QQ^{ii}-tier, 20:1-5). Neither of these, however, is clustered, as were the corresponding 'QQ' tiers in chs. 18–20, but their double statement serves to counterbalance structurally the opposing clustered grouping.

The 'RR' tiers present Zion as the object of YHWH's disfavor. This Zion is in need of purification. The last of these tiers (RR^{ii}β–α, 29:9-14, 15-24) presents a bifurcated scenario for the 'house of Jacob' that entails judgment against the willfully ignorant (29:9-14) as a prerequisite to its purification (29:15-24, especially vv. 22-24). The judgment-redemption scenario presented here is the paradigm for YHWH's program for Zion's restoration, and it epitomizes the same judgment-redemption scenario that accounts for the general thematic contrast

---

[1] K.A. Kitchen, *Ancient Orient and Old Testament* (Downers Grove: InterVarsity Press, 1966), pp. 82-84; idem, *The Third Intermediate Period in Egypt* (Warminster, England: Aris & Phillips, 1973), pp. 383-86, 387 n. 833.

between the tiers (which emphasize judgment) and insets (which emphasize redemption) of the section (chs. 13–39).

The total effect of the concentric structure of Isaiah 13–39 is one of a concentric geographical movement from those nations most remote from Jerusalem (i.e., Babylon and Assyria), through several intermediate nations (Philistia, Moab, Damascus and Edom; Cushite Egypt, serving as a vain ally), to the most proximate powers (Ephraim, Tyre and, surprisingly, Zion itself). At the center of the section, flanked by threats against all nations, comes the portrayal of YHWH's great world conflagration in Isaiah 24–27.

The Continuity of Isaiah 13:1–39:8 with its Context

In this asymmetrically concentric structure, the insets serve as an interlocking device that enhances the cohesion between the other tiers (designated 'QQ', 'PP', 'OO' and 'NN'). In addition to providing much of the material within the main axis (chs. 24–27), major structural insets appear between most outer tiers or tier clusters (i.e., between NN, NN^i–OO, PP–PP^i–PP^{ii}, QQ–QQ^i–QQ^{ii}, PP^{iii}–PP^{iv}–PP^v // QQ^{iii}, QQ^{iv}, PP^{vi}–PP^{vii}–PP^{viii}, OO^i–OO^{ii}, and NN^{ii}). These insets function as an interlocking device, the cohesive mortar for the oracular blocks of the main concentric pattern, and as a development of Judah/Zion's exaltation motif. The insets are often songs of Zion's exaltation and, taken together, show a linear development of the exaltation-of-Zion theme, which centers in the complex frame of the 'apocalypse' (C/C^i–C^{ii}) and culminates in the ultimate exaltation of both Zion (35:1-10) and its king (38:[1-8], [9]10-20, [21-22]). The thematic polarity between these recurring insets, which emphasize Zion's exaltation, and the intervening oracular denunciations of foreign nations both repeats and develops the conflagration–exaltation polarity depicted in the 'apocalypse'. That is, YHWH will exalt Zion over all nations as the seat of his worldwide rule. This repetitive developmental device gives thematic continuity to chs. 13–39. In fact, it is the interplay between structural concentricity (made up of the oracles) and the thematic continuity of the Zion motif (made up of the insets) that fuses the subunits of Isaiah 13–39 into a coherent, though implicit, argument that the citizens of Zion would not see the vindication of Zion until both Zion and the nations had undergone YHWH's judgment.

The last of the major insets (INSET[ix], 38:[1-8], [9]10-20, [21-22]) contains Hezekiah's song of deliverance. As a poem that praises YHWH for delivering Zion's king, this inset is an inversion of the downfall-of-kings theme presented in the poems of Isa. 14:4b-23, 24-25 and 37:22b-35, which taunt the downfall of Babylonian and Assyrian monarchs. However, it should also be noticed that Isaiah 38 stands in thematic antithesis to the prediction of the fall of the Davidic dynasty to the Babylonian monarchy (Isa. 39:7). The individual song of deliverance for Zion's king is an individualization of the exaltation motif that comes to its culmination in the so-called 'servant songs' of chs. 40–66.[1]

It should be noted that the pattern of complex frameworking in 13:1–39:8 is virtually the same as that in 4:2–11:16. Both sections comprise triply recessed compound inverse frames, the intermediate of which is clustered, with a triadically framed compound (inverse in the first instance) frame serving as the main axis. The two-phased hymn (12:1-3, 4-6) that serves as a structural transition between these sections both summarizes the theme of Zion's judgment turned to salvation, in this and the previous section (4:2–11:16), and introduces the theme of Zion's vindication before the nations, a distinctive of the present section (13:1–39:8).

It should also be noted that the complex frameworking pattern of 4:2–11:16 relates to that of 13:1–39:8 in the same way that the complex frameworking pattern of 2:6aγ-21 relates to that of 3:1–4:1. Apart from a permutational reordering of repetitions, the patterning between these analogous sections is the same, and their structural correspondences only serve to reinforce their thematic complementarity. Both 2:6aγ-21 and 3:1–4:1 are compound inverse frames in which triadic and quadratic frames interlock in the presentation of two covenant disputation functions: accusation and threat.[2] Analogously, both 4:2–11:16 and 13:1–39:8 are asymmetrically concentric structures in which three concentric compound inverse frames enclose a triadically framed compound frame (6:11–8:17 and 24:1–27:13, respectively), and both of these structures present three covenant disputation functions, those of accusation, threat and appeal, in a fashion analogous to that of the

---

[1]The passages that may be included as developments of the individual 'servant' motif are: 41:25 (an adumbration); 42:1-4, 6-7; 49:1b-6, 7aγb-9a; 50:4-9, [10-11]; 52:13–53:12; and, though not generally regarded as a 'servant song', 61:1-3.

[2]The main difference between them is only in the object of their denunciation: 2:6aγ-21 aiming at covenant infidelities toward YHWH; 3:1–4:1, at social injustices in Zion's official and judicial systems.

(concentric) form and (programmatic) function of 1:21-27 of the exordium.[1]

The rhetorical escalation from the two negative covenant disputation modes of accusation and threat in the paired structures of 2:6aγ-21 and 3:1–4:1 (excepting 3:10) to the three modes of accusation, threat and (positive) appeal in the paired structures of 4:2–11:16 and 13:1–39:8 sets up a pattern of accumulation from which it is only proper and justified to expect, in 40:1–54:17, the irruption of the long-awaited exoneration of YHWH that has been delayed from the very outset of the book.[2] This is, in fact, what occurs, since 40:1–54:17 will be seen to contain a rhetorical emphasis on the fourth main element of the covenant disputation: the exoneration of the offended party.

On just this point, it is noteworthy to see how the author foreshadows the recurring disputational mode of 40:1–54:17 through the threatening challenges of Sennacherib (36:[2-4a]4b-10, [11-12aα]12aβ-

---

[1]On the rhetorical level, I should also mention the strategic similarity in scenario between Isaiah's narrated denunciations of Ahaz (7:1–8:20) and Hezekiah (36:1–39:8). There is an unmistakable interrelationship ('chainlink effect') between them in their deferral of greater judgment to a future generation: in Ahaz's day, the imminent Aramean–Ephraimite threat, which prompts Ahaz's hope for an ally in the Assyrian king, provokes Isaiah to predict the even greater threat to Judah posed by the Assyrian king; in Hezekiah's day the imminent Assyrian threat (the fulfillment of Isaiah's prediction to Ahaz), which prompts Hezekiah's hope for an ally in the Babylonian king, leads Isaiah to predict the even greater threat to Jerusalem posed by the Babylonian king. Cf. the arguments of W. Roth that Isaiah is unified under its scheme of three major deliverances of Jerusalem (*Isaiah* [Knox Preaching Guides; Atlanta: John Knox, 1988]).

It should also be mentioned that these passages interrelate on the complementary scenario of their deferral of the hope for an ideal Davidic king to a future generation: in Ahaz's portrayal, the imminence of the messianic figuration of 'Immanuel' may have prompted the popular notion that the messianic hope was be found in the person of Ahaz's son, Hezekiah; indeed, in Hezekiah's idealized portrayal, one is all but convinced that the author intended that Hezekiah should be identified as fulfilling this expectation, that is, right up until the disillusioning disclosure of his mixed character (38:22–39:8). Therefore, the fulfillment of hope for an ideal Davidic monarch is, likewise, deferred to a generation beyond that of Hezekiah.

[2]While it is arguably true that 1:2bα and 5:1-2a present evidence of YHWH's past benefits to his people—an element normally contained within the exoneration segment of a covenant disputation—these verses are so disproportionately few in comparison to what would be expected of a covenant disputational work the size of the book of Isaiah that they will only remind the readers how frustrated their genre expectations have become, through the retardation of their fulfillment, by the time they see them fulfilled in chs. 40–54. In any case, 5:1-2bα is part of a parable (i.e., a subgenre) and could, therefore, hardly constitute a bona fide exoneration of YHWH at the controlling level on which Isaiah's governing covenant disputational rhetoric operates.

21; 37:[9b]10-13), the petitions of Hezekiah ([36:22–37:2]3-4; 37:[14]15-20) and the predictions of Isaiah about YHWH's self-vindication in regard to his divine power, prophetic decree and covenant loyalty to both the Davidic king and city of Zion (37:[5-6a]6b-7; 37:[21-22a]22b-35). In Hezekiah's song of thanksgiving (38:10-20), one sees the adumbration of the theme of YHWH's vindication of his royal servant, which is prominent throughout 40–66.[1] Finally, in the envoy episode of 39:1-8, the reader finds the foreboding forecast of the Babylonian deportations that provide the thematic and historical background for YHWH's great and enigmatic disputation against Zion's citizens in chs. 40–54. Thus, it is primarily on the thematic and rhetorical levels that Isa. 36:1–39:8 furnishes a transition to YHWH's self-exoneration in chs. 40–54.

---

[1] It is worth mention that the same multivalence between royal, prophetic and political-historical overtones, which one sees in the servant imagery of Isa. 40–66, is anticipated already in the divine use of 'my servant' as an epithet for David (37:35), Isaiah (20:3) and Eliakim (22:20), respectively.

Chapter 6

ISAIAH 40:1–54:17: YHWH'S EXONERATION

YHWH IS VINDICATED FROM IMPLICIT ACCUSATIONS
BY RESTORING ZION FROM BABYLON

In Isa. 40:1–54:17, the author has networked a sequence of complex
frames into a series of arguments that vindicate YHWH against Zion's
insinuations that he was either too impotent to have defended them
from the nations, too ignorant of their condition to have anticipated
their plight or too disinterested in fulfilling his covenant oath to have
taken action on their behalf.[1] This series of arguments contends for
YHWH's innocence of all allegations and, concomitantly, implies that
Zion's situation of captivity truly stems from Zion's own apostasy from
YHWH and from their practice of social injustice.

The focus of 40:1–54:17 upon the exoneration of YHWH is the special contribution that this section makes to the rhetoric of covenant disputation that governs the book of Isaiah. Consequently, it is not surprising to find here a prevalence of speech forms that are limited to this
section of the book and that comport broadly with a rhetoric of
exoneration. The latter rhetorical role is filled by the aggregate of the
various 'speech forms' of 40:1–54:17: disputation speech, trial speech
against Israel, trial speech against the nations/idols, salvation oracle,
salvation announcement and hymnic invocation to praise. Chapters 40–
54 can be seen to exonerate YHWH in such a way as to facilitate the
fulfillment of the prophet's program for Jacob/Israel//Judah/Zion, presented variously in 1:21-27, 4:2–11:16 and 13:1–39:8, a program that
combines punishment with restoration. Thus, while 40:1–54:17 rebukes
Jacob/Israel//Judah/Zion for past and present covenant failures, it also

---

[1]Cf. similarly L. Köhler (*Deuterojesaja (Jesaja 40–55) stilkritisch untersucht*
[BZAW, 37; Giessen: Töpelmann, 1923], pp. 102-42), W. Caspari (*Lieder und
Gottessprüche der Rückwanderer [Jesaja 40–55]* [BZAW, 65; Giessen:
Töpelmann, 1934], pp. 112-29), and B. Gemser ('The *Rîb*- or Controversy-Pattern
in Hebrew Mentality', in M. Noth and D.W. Thomas [eds.], *Wisdom in Israel and
in the Ancient Near East* [Festschrift H.H. Rowley; VTSup, 3; Leiden: Brill,
1955], p. 131).

furnishes the displaced citizens of Jacob/Israel//Judah/Zion (not to mention those of other nations) with proof of YHWH's power, concern and loyal love sufficient to motivate their repentance and their subsequent return to Zion once the punishment had passed.[1] This double-edged rhetorical aim, to rebuke yet conciliate, is accomplished in 40:1–54:17: (1) by means of its change of audience (i.e., the exilic generation) while ostensibly addressing the same audience (i.e., Jacob/Israel//Judah/Zion); and (2) by means of its alternating pattern of disputation and consolation. Throughout 40:1–54:17, the author presents to the new generation of Jacob/Israel//Judah/Zion such arguments and predictions as would be needed to demonstrate YHWH's infinite power, divine foreknowledge and covenant loyalty in order that this generation might be persuaded to return to their god and to his holy city. Besides the generic complementarity of this section with the overall covenant disputation rhetoric of Isaiah, the pattern of repetitions in 40:1–54:17 is also consistent with the view that the book of Isaiah employs complex frameworking as a means of achieving structural cohesion.

Structural Delineation of Isaiah 40:1–54:17

In contrast to the previous sections of the book of Isaiah, this section is characterized by a sudden and continued shift in chronological perspective (entailing a second audience for the book) and by its seemingly erratic infusion into the book of an entirely new complex of prophetic dispositions that alternate between consolations of and disputations against Jacob/Israel//Judah/Zion. The consolations are essentially affirmations of the continuance of YHWH's offer of covenant reconciliation; the disputations, protests of YHWH's innocence against implicit insinuations of his failure to uphold his covenant with Zion and the Davidic house. It is the larger complexes (i.e., 40:1–43:13; 43:16–46:13; 48:1-13; 49:1–54:17) that put into the foreground this dispositional polarity. These larger complexes are punctuated by short 'salvation predictions' (43:14-15; 47:1-7; 48:14-22) that evidence another polarity: that between YHWH's intention to save Jacob/Israel//Judah/

---

[1]There are several tiers in the preceding sections that disclose the fact that the prophet Isaiah's message would remain inscrutable to the majority of his own generation (e.g., MM, 6:8-10; 8:16-17; MM^i, 8:18-22; RR$^{ii}\beta$, 29:9-14), who would subsequently suffer the punitive destruction of their city and dissolution of their state (6:11-13a). Only then would a remnant survive to experience the illumination (6:13b; MM^{ii}, 8:23–9:1; RR$^{ii}\alpha$, especially 29:18-21) that would lead them to restoration (LL^{ii}, 9:2-6; RR$^{ii}\alpha$, especially 29:22-24).

Zion after punishing them and his intention to punish Babylon when saving Jacob/Israel//Judah/Zion. Captor Babylon's claim to have power and knowledge sufficient to save itself contrasts with YHWH's claim to have power and knowledge sufficient to save Jacob/Israel//Judah/Zion from its captor. By comparing and contrasting the three 'salvation predictions' with their neighboring contexts, one may infer a kind of trial-by-ordeal scenario in which the claims of 'YHWH, the Redeemer, the Holy One of Israel' are expected to be vindicated against those of Babylon. The axis of the section (47:8-15) seems to manifest an attempt to present a deliberately ambivalent denunciation of the unholy city. This taunt song against the unholy city equivocates between being either a taunt against Babylon, when read in contiguity with 47:1-7, or a taunt against unfaithful Zion, when read in contiguity with 48:1-13. The section ends where there is a marked shift to the mode of appeal, beginning in 55:1-3 (לְכוּ 4x), which begins the appeal section proper (55:1-66:24) within Isaiah's rhetoric of covenant disputation.

Complex Frameworking in Isaiah 40:1-54:17

The structural subunits of Isa. 40:1-54:17 are capable of alignment with other subunits so as to form a network of recognizable patterns. Although structural borders seem quite ambiguous in 40:1-54:17—and this is borne out by the plethora of alternative subdivisions presented in studies that treat their arrangement—there is throughout a fairly consistent pattern of alternation between the tone of consolation and that of disputation. A number of allusions to other parts of the book, as well as to other biblical texts that record YHWH's redemptive acts, characterize the unfolding of this defense of YHWH's innocence against allegations of his impotence, ignorance and covenant indifference. The patterns of repetition in 40:1-54:17 show not only an increased complexity but an even greater inner cohesion than those of Isa. 4:2-11:16 or 13:1-39:8. Indeed, the overall repetition pattern that governs 40:1-54:17 is but an elaborate permutation of that encountered in 2:6aγ-21 and 3:1-4:1, but its intensity, the result of its greater length and its hierarchical branching of complex framework patterns, shows it to be the structural, as well as rhetorical, climax of the book of Isaiah.

152   *Concentricity and Continuity*

In the following schema of complex frameworking in Isa. 40:1–54:17, three factors have combined to determine the structural delineations: (1) a change in designated addressee (whether Judah/Jerusalem/Zion, Jacob/Israel, YHWH's elect or the nations [especially Babylon/Chaldea]); (2) a pattern in the repetition of divine epithets; and (3) a change in prophetic disposition (i.e., whether an affirming tone of consolation or an adversarial tone of disputation):

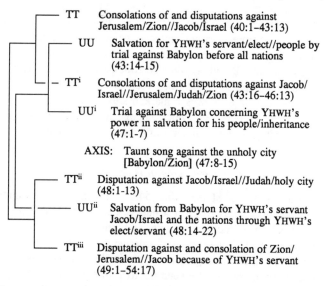

	TT	Consolations of and disputations against Jerusalem/Zion//Jacob/Israel (40:1–43:13)
	UU	Salvation for YHWH's servant/elect//people by trial against Babylon before all nations (43:14-15)
	TTⁱ	Consolations of and disputations against Jacob/Israel//Jerusalem/Judah/Zion (43:16–46:13)
	UUⁱ	Trial against Babylon concerning YHWH's power in salvation for his people/inheritance (47:1-7)
AXIS:		Taunt song against the unholy city [Babylon/Zion] (47:8-15)
	TTⁱⁱ	Disputation against Jacob/Israel//Judah/holy city (48:1-13)
	UUⁱⁱ	Salvation from Babylon for YHWH's servant Jacob/Israel and the nations through YHWH's elect/servant (48:14-22)
	TTⁱⁱⁱ	Disputation against and consolation of Zion/Jerusalem//Jacob because of YHWH's servant (49:1–54:17)

The resemblance of this complex frame pattern to the schemata for Isa. 2:6aγ-21 and 3:1–4:1 should be readily apparent. Quite noticeably, the TTⁱⁱ-tier is shorter than the other 'TT' tiers, and this seems to have been motivated by a desire to balance the proportion of tiers flanking the ambivalent taunt song against the unholy city (47:8-15). The other 'TT' tiers are themselves made up of still smaller complex frames that alternate between consolational and disputational tones, each complex frame having its own hymnic axis. The 'UU' tiers punctuate the alternating pattern of disputations and consolations with portrayals of YHWH's deliverance of Israel from the Babylonians/Chaldeans. A more detailed rendering of the structure of Isa. 40:1–54:17, including its second-level substructures, may be presented as follows:

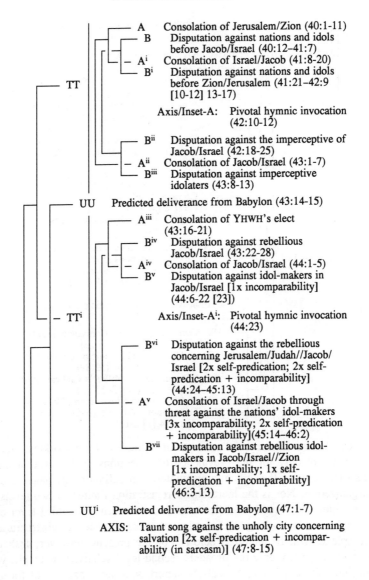

TT

A — Consolation of Jerusalem/Zion (40:1-11)
B — Disputation against nations and idols before Jacob/Israel (40:12–41:7)
A^i — Consolation of Israel/Jacob (41:8-20)
B^i — Disputation against nations and idols before Zion/Jerusalem (41:21–42:9 [10-12] 13-17)

Axis/Inset-A: Pivotal hymnic invocation (42:10-12)

B^{ii} — Disputation against the imperceptive of Jacob/Israel (42:18-25)
A^{ii} — Consolation of Jacob/Israel (43:1-7)
B^{iii} — Disputation against imperceptive idolaters (43:8-13)

UU — Predicted deliverance from Babylon (43:14-15)

A^{iii} — Consolation of YHWH's elect (43:16-21)
B^{iv} — Disputation against rebellious Jacob/Israel (43:22-28)
A^{iv} — Consolation of Jacob/Israel (44:1-5)
B^v — Disputation against idol-makers in Jacob/Israel [1x incomparability] (44:6-22 [23])

Axis/Inset-A^i: Pivotal hymnic invocation (44:23)

B^{vi} — Disputation against the rebellious concerning Jerusalem/Judah//Jacob/Israel [2x self-predication; 2x self-predication + incomparability] (44:24–45:13)
A^v — Consolation of Israel/Jacob through threat against the nations' idol-makers [3x incomparability; 2x self-predication + incomparability](45:14–46:2)
B^{vii} — Disputation against rebellious idol-makers in Jacob/Israel//Zion [1x incomparability; 1x self-predication + incomparability] (46:3-13)

TT^i

UU^i — Predicted deliverance from Babylon (47:1-7)

AXIS: Taunt song against the unholy city concerning salvation [2x self-predication + incomparability (in sarcasm)] (47:8-15)

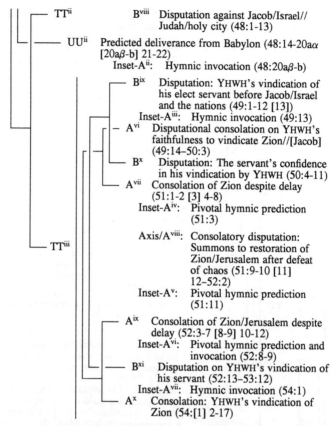

TT^{ii} B^{viii} Disputation against Jacob/Israel//
                       Judah/holy city (48:1-13)
UU^{ii} Predicted deliverance from Babylon (48:14-20aα
                   [20aβ-b] 21-22)
                   Inset-A^{ii}: Hymnic invocation (48:20aβ-b)

                        B^{ix} Disputation: YHWH's vindication of
                              his elect servant before Jacob/Israel
                              and the nations (49:1-12 [13])
                        Inset-A^{iii}: Hymnic invocation (49:13)
                        A^{vi} Disputational consolation on YHWH's
                              faithfulness to vindicate Zion//[Jacob]
                              (49:14-50:3)
                        B^{x} Disputation: The servant's confidence
                              in his vindication by YHWH (50:4-11)
                        A^{vii} Consolation of Zion despite delay
                              (51:1-2 [3] 4-8)
                        Inset-A^{iv}: Pivotal hymnic prediction
                              (51:3)

                        Axis/A^{viii}: Consolatory disputation:
                              Summons to restoration of
                              Zion/Jerusalem after defeat
                              of chaos (51:9-10 [11]
                              12-52:2)
                        Inset-A^{v}: Pivotal hymnic prediction
                              (51:11)

TT^{iii} A^{ix} Consolation of Zion/Jerusalem despite
                              delay (52:3-7 [8-9] 10-12)
                        Inset-A^{vi}: Pivotal hymnic prediction and
                              invocation (52:8-9)
                        B^{xi} Disputation on YHWH's vindication of
                              his servant (52:13-53:12)
                        Inset-A^{vii}: Hymnic invocation (54:1)
                        A^{x} Consolation: YHWH's vindication of
                              Zion (54:[1] 2-17)

These two hierarchical orders of complex frameworking may
account not only for the prevalence of repetitions in this section but
also for some of the difficulty encountered in delimiting its patterns of
organization. Nor is the hierarchical registration limited to two levels,
for within the second-level tiers there can be seen yet a third level of
complex frameworking. A selection of these third-level substructural
complexes will be analyzed below. For the present, however, I shall
attempt to justify only the broader, second-level subdivisions by showing how these subunits basically comport with the consensus of form-
critical studies of Isa. 40:1–54:17.

The three shorter 'UU' tiers are among the most structurally
definable tiers in the section because they share a common thematic
focus on the prediction of YHWH's deliverance of Israel from Babylon.
They bear the following common characteristics: (1) each 'UU' tier

comprises three subunits of which the outer two frame the middle; (2) the framing subunits always feature either the geopolitical word pair כַּשְׂדִּים ‖ בָּבֶל or the divine epithet word pair יְהוָה גֹּאַלְכֶם/ךּ or גֹּאֲלֵנוּ קְדוֹשׁ יִשְׂרָאֵל ‖ יְהוָה צְבָאוֹת; and (3) the middle subunit always features the alternative word pair of that which is repeated in the framing subunits. This triadic structure of the 'UU' tiers may be outlined as follows:

UU	43:14-15:	
	aa	(43:14a) ...יְהוָה גֹּאַלְכֶם קְדוֹשׁ יִשְׂרָאֵל
	bb	(43:14b) ...בָבֶלָה...וְכַשְׂדִּים...
	aaⁱ	(43:15) ...אֲנִי יְהוָה קְדוֹשְׁכֶם בּוֹרֵא יִשְׂרָאֵל
UUⁱ	47:1-7:	
	bbⁱ	(47:1-3) ...בַּת־בָּבֶל...בַּת־כַּשְׂדִּים
	aaⁱⁱ	(47:4) גֹּאֲלֵנוּ יְהוָה צְבָאוֹת...קְדוֹשׁ יִשְׂרָאֵל
	bbⁱⁱ	(47:5-7) ...בַּת־כַּשְׂדִּים
UUⁱⁱ	48:14-22:	
	bbⁱⁱⁱ	(48:14-16) ...בְּבָבֶל...כַּשְׂדִּים
	aaⁱⁱⁱ	(48:17-19) ...יְהוָה גֹּאַלְךָ קְדוֹשׁ יִשְׂרָאֵל
	bbⁱᵛ	(48:20-22) ...מִבָּבֶל...מִכַּשְׂדִּים

Use of the divine epithet word pairs is not limited to these tiers (cf. 41:14b, 16b, 20αβb; 43:3a; 44:6a; 45:11a; 49:7αα, bβ), but their placement into a simple framing pattern with subunits that refer to Mesopotamian nations sets these 'UU' tiers apart as structurally distinct within Isa. 40:1–54:17. The three 'UU' tiers thus serve to demarcate 40:1–54:17 into four remaining sections (i.e., 40:1–43:13; 43:16–46:13; 48:1-13; 49:1–54:17; 47:8-15 serves as the axis). It is also worth noting that the length and specificity of each succeeding 'UU' tier escalate in relation to those that precede (first two verses, then seven, then nine).

Most of the standard 'polemic genres' of form criticism (e.g. disputation speeches, trial speeches against Israel) fall within the disputational complexes designated in the large schema above as 'B' tiers. Exceptionally, since the final three 'B' tiers (within tier TTⁱⁱⁱ) portray YHWH's exoneration of his servant, who was rejected by Zion, they also implicitly function disputationally as rebuking Zion. The following table shows how the form-critical units of several form- and rhetorical-

critical studies correlate with the larger disputational complexes
suggested above:[1]

[1]In this and the following tables, proponents' names are abbreviated and listed
along the horizontal axis in the order of their studies' appearance (English transla-
tions not prevailing): H. Gressmann, 'Die literarische Analyse Deuterojesajas',
ZAW 34 (1914), pp. 254-97; Köhler, *Deuterojesaja (Jesaja 40–55) stilkritisch
untersucht*; S. Mowinckel, 'Die Komposition des deuterojesajanischen Buches',
ZAW 49 (1931), pp. 87-112, 242-60; J. Begrich, 'Das priesterliche Heilsorakel',
ZAW 52 (1934), pp. 81-92; idem, *Studien zur Deuterojesaja* (BWANT, 4; Folge
Heft 25 [77]; Stuttgart: Kohlhammer, 1938; repr., TBü, 20; Munich: Chr. Kaiser
Verlag, 1963); H.E. von Waldow, 'Anlass und Hintergrund der Verkündigung des
Deuterojesaja' (PhD diss., University of Bonn, 1953); C. Westermann, 'Sprach
und Struktur der Prophetie Deuterojesajas', in *Forschung am Alten Testament:
Gesammelte Studien, I* (TBü, 24; Munich: Chr. Kaiser Verlag, 1964), pp. 92-170;
idem, *Grundformen prophetischer Rede* (BEvT, 31; Munich: Chr. Kaiser Verlag,
1960); ET: *Basic Forms of Prophetic Speech* (trans. H.C. White; Philadelphia:
Westminster Press, 1967); idem, *Das Buch Jesaja, 40–66* (ATD, 19; Göttingen:
Vandenhoeck & Ruprecht, 1966); ET: *Isaiah 40–66: A Commentary* (trans.
D.M.G. Stalker; OTL; Philadelphia: Westminster Press, 1969); R.F. Melugin,
The Formation of Isaiah 40–55 (BZAW, 141; Berlin: de Gruyter, 1976; cf. PhD
diss., Yale University, 1968); P.-E. Bonnard, *Le Second Isaïe: Son disciple et
leurs éditeurs Isaïe 40–66* (EBib; Paris: Gabalda, 1972); A. Schoors, *I am God
Your Saviour: A Form-critical Study of the Main Genres in Is. XL–LV* (VTSup, 24;
Leiden: Brill, 1973); R.J. Clifford, *Fair Spoken and Persuading: An Interpretation
of Second Isaiah* (New York: Paulist Press, 1984); A. Wilson, *The Nations in
Deutero-Isaiah: A Study on Composition and Structure* (Ancient Near Eastern
Texts and Studies, 1; Lewiston, NY: Edwin Mellen, 1986). The delimitation of
form-critical units represents only the aggregate. For the varied delimitations of
individual scholars, their works should be consulted independently. For a con-
venient table of the delimitations of Köhler, Mowinckel, K. Elliger (*Deuterojesaja
in seinem Verhältnis zu Tritojesaja* [BWANT, IV/11; Stuttgart: Kohlhammer,
1933]), Begrich and Westermann, see Schoors, pp. 30-31. For a similar presentation of the units of Westermann, J. Muilenburg ('The Book of Isaiah: Chapters
40–66: Introduction and Exegesis', in G.A. Buttrick et al. [eds.], *The Interpreter's
Bible* [12 vols.; Nashville: Abingdon Press, 1956], V, pp. 381-773), Clifford,
C.C. Torrey (*The Second Isaiah: A New Interpretation* [Edinburgh: T. & T. Clark;
New York: Charles Scribner's Sons, 1928]), Bonnard, Y. Kaufmann (*The
Babylonian Captivity and Deutero-Isaiah* [trans. C.W. Ephroymson; New York:
Union of American Hebrew Congregations, 1970]) and Melugin, see Wilson,
pp. 17-18.
   The speech form abbreviations used in the following tables are: * = (unified
rhetorical complex), | = (vertical continuation of unit), — = (unspecified genre),
ans = *annonce de salut* ('announcement of salvation'), Anw = *kurze Anweisung*
('brief instruction'), AS = announcement of salvation, ats = *attestation de salut*
('oracle of salvation'), Bps = *Bußpsalm* ('penitential psalm'), Bs = *Botenspruch*
('messenger speech'), CLA = communal lament answer, CN = confession of the
nations, COS = commissioning oracle of the servant, d-c = *débat-contestation*
('disputation speech'), D–G = *Disputation + Gerichtsrede* ('trial speech'), DP =
disputational promise, DS = disputation speech, DSF = disputation speech fragment, Dsp = *Disputation[srede/wort]* ('disputation [speech]'), EH = eschatalogi-
cal hymn, eL = *'eschatologische' Loblied* ('"eschatological" hymn'), EoJ =

```
                  Gre  Köh MowBeg vWa Wes Mel  Bon  Sch Cli  Wil

B    40:12-41:7
     40:12-17  HymStg Stg    Dsp Dsp Dsp DSF d-c DS
     40:18-20    |    Stg  |  Dsp Dsp  |  DSF    |    |
     40:21-24    |    Stg  |  Dsp Dsp  |    |    |    |
     40:25-26    |     |   |  Dsp Dsp  |  DSF    |    |
     40:27-31   Trw    |      Dsp Dsp  |  DS     |   DS
     41:1-5     Grw Stg  Stg Grr Grr Grr TSN prn TS
     41:6-7      |   [ | ]               |        DSF
     [41:8-13]   |    |

Bᵢ   41:21-42:9,
     13-17
     41:21-24  Grw Stg Stg Grr Grr Grr TSN prn TS
     41:25-29   |   |   |   |   |   |   |   |   |
     42:1-4    Vrh               COS             VNI
     42:5-9    Vrh               COS              |
     42:13                        —
     42:14-17  Vrh        Vka    Ha CLA ans PS

Bᵢᵢ  42:18-25  Scw Stg           Grr DS pri TS

Bᵢᵢ  43:8-13   Grw Stg Stg Grr Grr Grr TSN prn TS
```

Erhörungsorakel Jahwes ('favorable-hearing oracle of Yahweh'), Exh = exhortation, Gb = *Geschichtsbetrachtung* ('historical reflection'), G–D = *Gerichtsrede* ('trial speech') + *Disputation*, G/D = *Gerichtsrede* ('trial speech') or *Disputation*, gl = gloss, Grr = *Gerichtsrede* ('trial speech'), Grw = *Gerichtswort* ('trial speech'), Ha = *Heilsankündigung* ('salvation proclamation'), Ho = *Heilsorakel* ('salvation oracle'), H–P = hymn + promise, Hym = *Hymn/hymne*/hymn, Hz = *Heilszusage* ('salvation oracle'), ICS = individual confidence of the servant, Js = *Jahwespruch* ('saying of Yahweh'), Kl = *Klagelied* ('lament'), Ko = *Königsorakel* ('royal oracle'), LF = lament fragment, LMh = *Lied einer Mehrheit* ('song of a multitude'), Mr = *Missionsrede* ('mission speech'), OS = oracle of salvation, PC = prophetic commission, pHo = *priesterliche Heilsorakel* ('priestly salvation oracle'), pri = *procès entre Yahweh et Israël* ('trial speech between YHWH and Israel'), prn = *procès entre Yahweh et les dieux des nations* ('trial speech between YHWH and the gods of the nations'), PS = proclamation of salvation, RVO = royal victory oracle, SAO = salvation-assurance oracle, SAS = salvation announcement of the servant, Scr = *Scheltrede* ('rebuke'), Scw = *Scheltwort* ('rebuke'), S–D = salvation speech + disputation, S–H = *Scheltwort* ('rebuke') + *Hymn*, Shr = *Seherspruch* ('word of prophecy'), SJY = sarcastic judgment of Yahweh, Sl = *Siegeslied* ('song of victory'), Spl = *Spottlied* ('taunt song'), SSp = salvation speech, Stg = *Streitgesprach* ('disputation'), T–D = trial speech (versus Israel) + disputation, Tnt = taunt song, Trw = *Trostwort* ('consolation speech'), TS = trial speech, TSI = trial speech versus Israel, TSN = trial speech versus nations/gods, Vdl = *Volksdanklied* ('communal song of thanksgiving'), V–H = vision + hymn, Vka = *Volksklageliedantwort* ('communal lament answer'), VNI = verdict on the nations and Israel, Vps = *Vertrauenpsalm* ('psalm of confidence'), Vrh = *Verheißung* ('promise'), V–S = song of victory + salvation speech, wGw = *Wort der Gewißheit* ('wisdom saying').

		Gre	Köh	Mow	Beg	vWa	Wes	Mel	Bon	Sch	Cli	Wil
B[iv]	43:22-28	Scw			Grr	Grr	Grr	TSI	pri	TS		
B[v]	44:6-22											
	44:6-8	Grw			Grr	Grr	Grr	TSN	prn	TS		
	44:9-20							|				
	44:21-22							Exh				
B[vi]	44:24–45:13							*			*	
	44:24-28	Hym	Bs		Dsp	Dsp	Ko	DP		DS		
	45:1-7				pHo	|		RVO				
	45:8						eL	Hym				
	45:9-10	Scw			Dsp			DS				
	45:11-13	|			|	Dsp	G/D	|	d-c	DS		
B[vii]	46:3-13							*				
	[46:1-2]		Shr					V–S				
	46:3-4		|		Ho			|				
	46:5-11				Dsp	Dsp		DS	d-c	DS		
	46:12-13	Trw			Ho			SAO		PS		
B[viii]	48:1-13											
	48:1-11	Scw		Scr	D–G	Dsp		DS	d-c	DS		
	48:12-13	Grw		Stg	Dsp	Dsp		TSN	d-c			
	[48:14-15]	|		|	|			|	|			
B[ix]	49:1-12							(*)				
	49:1-4	Kl						COS				PC
	49:5-6	Vrh						|				|
	49:7	Hym			Ho		Ha	AS		PS		
	49:8-12	Vrh			pHo		|	AS		|		
B[x]	50:4-11							*				
	50:4-9	Kl			Kl		Vps	ICS				
	50:10-11							SJY				
B[xi]	52:13–53:12							*	*	*	*	
	52:13-15	Vrh			Js			SAS				
	53:1-10	Bps			LMh			CN				
	53:11-12	|			Js			SAS				

The first 'UU' tier (43:14-15) is frequently categorized as (part of) a trial speech:

		Gre	Köh	Mow	Beg	vWa	Wes	Mel	Bon	Sch	Cli	Wil
	43:8-13					Grr						
UU	43:14-15	Vrh			Grr	Grr	|	SSp				—

Tier UU[ii] (48:14-22) presents various elements, which form critics have categorized as polemical, salvational and hymnic genres:

	Gre	Köh	Mow	Beg	vWa	Wes	Mel	Bon	Sch	Cli	Wil
UU[ii] 48:14-22											
[48:12-13]							TSN		DS		
48:14-15											
48:16							DS				
48:17-19			Ho				—				
48:20-21	Hym		Hym	Anw		eL	Hym				

The intervening 'UU' tier (UU[i], 47:1-7) is usually read in conjunction with 47:8-15 and has been categorized as follows:

	Gre	Köh	Mow	Beg	vWa	Wes	Mel	Bon	Sch	Cli	Wil
UU[i] 47:1-7	Spl						Tnt				
Axis 47:8-15											

Isaiah 47:8-15 is widely recognized as comprising elements of a taunt song against Babylon; however, because of its lack of a specific addressee (47:8), and because it is juxtaposed also with 48:1-13, it could equally well function as an taunt against the unholy city of Zion (cf. 49:14–50:3). Since, in the present study, 47:8-15 constitutes the structural axis of 40:1–54:17, the possibility of its equivocating between denouncing Babylon and denouncing Zion would be an ambivalence that enhances the polarity already explicit in Isa. 40:1–54:17 between the negative portrayal of Zion in the disputations of the 'TT' tiers and the negative characterization of Babylon in the 'UU' tiers.

Most of the 'salvation genres' of form criticism (e.g., salvation oracles, salvation announcements) fall within the consolational complexes designated above as 'A' tiers:

	Gre	Köh	Mow	Beg	vWa	Wes	Mel	Bon	Sch	Cli	Wil
A 40:1-11						*	*	*		*	
40:1-2	Trw					Ho					
40:3-5						Grr					
40:6-8	wGw					Dsp					
40:9	Sl					eL					
40:10-11											
A[i] 41:8-20											
41:8-13					Ho		Hz	SAOats	OS	VNI	
41:14-16					Ho		Hz	SAOats	OS		
41:17-20					Vka		Ha	CLAans	PS		
A[ii] 43:1-7											
43:1-4					pHo		Hz	SAOats	OS		
43:5-7							Hz	ats	OS		
A[iii] 43:16-21					Vka		Ha	SSp ans	PS		

		Gre	Köh	Mow	Beg	vWa	Wes	Mel	Bon	Sch	Cli	Wil
A^iv	44:1-5				pHo		Hz	SAO	ats	OS		
A^v	45:14–46:2											
	45:14-17	Hym		Ho			Ha	SSp	ans	PS		
	45:18-19	Hym		Dsp	Dsp		Dsp	TSN	d-c	TS		
	45:20-21	Grw					Grr					
	45:22-25	Mr						Exh				
	46:1-2	Spl		Shr				V–S				
	[46:3-4]											
A^vi	49:14–50:3											
	49:14-17	Trw	Stg	pHo	Ho		Dsp	SSp	ans	PS		
	49:18-21											
	49:22-23			Ho	Ho			SSp				
	49:24-26			Ho	Ho			SSp				DS
	50:1-3	S–H		G–D	Grr	Grr		T–D	pri	TS		
A^vii	51:1-2 [3] 4-8		*	*				*				
	51:1-2	Gb		Dsp	Dsp			S–D		PS		
	51:3	Hym					eL					
	51:4-5	Mr						AS				
	51:6			⌈pHo ⌊Vka				AS		PS		
	51:7-8	Trw						Exh		PS		
A^viii	51:9-10 [11] 12–52:2										(*)	
	51:9-11			Kl	pHo			LF	ans	PS		
	51:12-13	Trw		EoJ				SSp	ans		OS	
	51:14-16											
	51:17-23	Trw		Trw	pHo			SSp	ans	PS		
	52:1-2			Anw				Exh				
A^ix	52:3-7 [8-9] 10-12											
	52:3-6							—			gl	
	52:7-8	Sl						V–H				
	52:9-10	Hym					eL					
	52:11-12			Anw					Hym			
A^x	54:[1] 2-17							(*)	(*)		(*)	
	54:1-2	Trw		Anw			eL	H–P				
	54:3											
	54:4-6			Ho			Hz	SAO	ats	OS		
	54:7-10			pHo				DP	ans	PS		
	54:11-17			pHo	pHo			AS	ans	PS		

Isaiah 42:10-12 is the first of a series of short hymnic invocations, or predictions, that serve to delineate those literary complexes of Isa. 40:1–54:17 that comprise the 'TT' tiers. Each of these hymnic transitional units has been designated 'Inset-A':

		Gre	Köh	Mow	Beg	vWa	Wes	Mel	Bon	Sch
Inset-A	42:10-12									
	42:10-12	Hym			Hym		eL	EH	Hym	
	[42:13]													
Inset-A^i	44:23	Hym					eL	Hym	Hym	
Inset-A^ii	48:20aβ-b									
	[48:20-21]	Hym		Hym	Anw		eL	Hym	Hym	
Inset-A^iii	49:13	Hym		Vdl			eL	Hym	Hym	
Inset-A^iv	51:3	Hym								
Inset-A^v	51:11									
Inset-A^vi	52:8-9									
	[52:7]						eL			
	52:8										
	52:9	Hym							Hym	
	[52:10]											
Inset-A^vii	54:1									

These hymnic invocations and predictions are not hymns proper but
are all characterized by the use of verbal roots that convey the idea of
singing praise (e.g., שִׁיר, זָמַר and especially רָנַן):

Inset-A	42:10-12	שִׁירוּ/שִׁיר/[יִשְׂאוּ]/יָרֹנּוּ
Inset-A^i	44:23	רָנּוּ/[הָרִיעוּ]/[פִּצְחוּ]/רִנָּה
Inset-A^ii	48:20aβ-b	[בְּקוֹל] רִנָּה
Inset-A^iii	49:13	רָנּוּ/[וְגִילִי]/[וּפִצְחוּ]/רִנָּה
Inset-A^iv	51:3	[שָׂשׂוֹן וְשִׂמְחָה]/[וְקוֹל] זִמְרָה
Inset-A^v	51:11	בְּרִנָּה [וְשִׂמְחַת]/[שָׂשׂוֹן וְשִׂמְחָה]
Inset-A^vi	52:8-9	יְרַנֵּנוּ/[פִּצְחוּ] רַנְּנוּ
Inset-A^vii	54:1	רָנִּי/[פִּצְחִי] רִנָּה

Having thus compared the categorizations of the second-level substructures of Isa. 40:1–54:17 to those of modern form-critical studies,
and having found them to be in broad agreement, at least as to the
disposition of the speech forms (i.e., whether disputational or consolational in tone), I will now analyze some of the section's third-level substructures. This I do both as a means of demonstrating the pervasiveness of the author's complex frameworking pattern and as a means of
justifying the delineation of the foregoing second-level substructures.

Selected Substructural Complexes in Isaiah 40:1–54:17

It would appear that the third-level substructures in Isa. 40:1–54:17 offer confirmation both of the pervasiveness of the complex frame-working pattern within and of the hierarchical stratification among the tiers of this section. The first two tiers are paired in a relationship whereby 40:12–41:7 (tier TT-B) presents a disputation against the insinuation (cf. 40:27) that YHWH has been unable or unwilling to fulfill for Jerusalem/Zion the role ascribed to him in the consolation of 40:1-11 (tier TT-A). Isaiah 40:1-11 is the first third-level complex frame of the section. It presents YHWH's offer of consolation to Zion using the image of a prophetic herald of good news.[1] It seems that the changes of (implied) speaker serve as the determinative criterion for the structural delineation of this passage, though there are also some verbal markers that reinforce these delineations (given below in the margin):

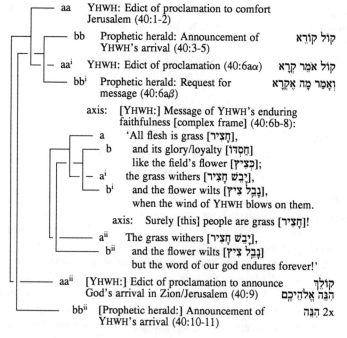

aa	YHWH: Edict of proclamation to comfort Jerusalem (40:1-2)	
bb	Prophetic herald: Announcement of YHWH's arrival (40:3-5)	קוֹל קוֹרֵא
aaⁱ	YHWH: Edict of proclamation (40:6aα)	קוֹל אֹמֵר קְרָא
bbⁱ	Prophetic herald: Request for message (40:6aβ)	וְאָמַר מָה אֶקְרָא

axis: [YHWH:] Message of YHWH's enduring faithfulness [complex frame] (40:6b-8):

a	'All flesh is grass [חָצִיר],	
b	and its glory/loyalty [חַסְדּוֹ] like the field's flower [כְּצִיץ];	
aⁱ	the grass withers [יָבֵשׁ חָצִיר],	
bⁱ	and the flower wilts [נָבֵל צִיץ], when the wind of YHWH blows on them.	

axis: Surely [this] people are grass [חָצִיר]!

aⁱⁱ	The grass withers [יָבֵשׁ חָצִיר],
bⁱⁱ	and the flower wilts [נָבֵל צִיץ] but the word of our god endures forever!'

aaⁱⁱ	[YHWH:] Edict of proclamation to announce God's arrival in Zion/Jerusalem (40:9)	קוֹלֵךְ הִנֵּה אֱלֹהֵיכֶם
bbⁱⁱ	[Prophetic herald:] Announcement of YHWH's arrival (40:10-11)	הִנֵּה 2x

[1]Cf. R.W. Fisher, 'The Herald of Good News in Second Isaiah', in J.J. Jackson and M. Kessler (eds.), *Rhetorical Criticism: Essays in Honor of James Muilenburg* (Pittsburgh: Pickwick Press, 1974), pp. 117-32.

The compound frame pattern of the axis (40:6b-8) is a microcosm of the surrounding framework structure that defines the TT-A-tier (40:1-11). The TT-A-tier both introduces the complex framework pattern of the entire TT-tier (40:1–43:13) and forms a part of it, because of the telescoping relationship that exists among its layered hierarchies. In turn, the TT-tier both introduces and forms a part of the whole section (40:1–54:17). Indeed, if the large schematic outline of the section that I have presented above is valid, all its tiers so cohere with the hierarchical branching pattern that each tier is structurally (if not also rhetorically) interdependent upon every other tier in the section.

A disposition of consolation, evident in the first tier (40:1-11), shifts suddenly to one of disputation, beginning with the cluster of insinuating rhetorical questions that introduces 40:12–41:7 (tier TT-B). In the following analysis of the TT-B-tier, two thematic axes of polarity intersect. Along the axis of potency, there is polarity between claim to divine incomparability (tiers 'aa' and 'a') and extent of political rule (tiers 'bb' and 'b'). Intersecting this polarity is another, along the axis of agency, wherein the prerogatives of YHWH (doubled letters 'aa' and 'bb') are set against those of idols/nations (single letters 'a' and 'b'). The underlying question throughout is, Who truly has control over creation and international affairs? One may diagram the relationship among these intersecting axes as follows:

	YHWH	*Idols/Nations*
Divine Incomparability	aa	*Idols* a
Political Rule	bb	*Nations* b

The following schema represents the complex frameworking of this 'disputational complex':

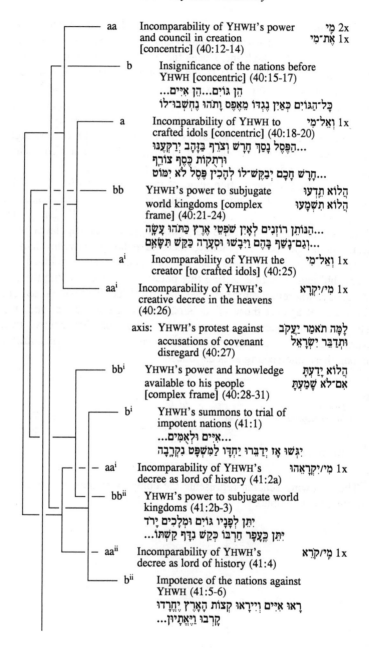

aa — Incomparability of YHWH's power and council in creation [concentric] (40:12-14)   מִי 2x   אֶת־מִי 1x

b — Insignificance of the nations before YHWH [concentric] (40:15-17)
הֵן גּוֹיִם...הֵן אִיִּים...
כָּל־הַגּוֹיִם כְּאַיִן נֶגְדּוֹ מֵאֶפֶס וָתֹהוּ נֶחְשְׁבוּ־לוֹ

a — Incomparability of YHWH to crafted idols [concentric] (40:18-20)   וְאֶל־מִי 1x
...הַפֶּסֶל נָסַךְ חָרָשׁ וְצֹרֵף בַּזָּהָב יְרַקְּעֶנּוּ
וּרְתֻקוֹת כֶּסֶף צוֹרֵף
...חָרָשׁ חָכָם יְבַקֶּשׁ־לוֹ לְהָכִין פֶּסֶל לֹא יִמּוֹט

bb — YHWH's power to subjugate world kingdoms [complex frame] (40:21-24)   הֲלוֹא תֵדְעוּ   הֲלוֹא תִשְׁמָעוּ
...הַנּוֹתֵן רוֹזְנִים לְאָיִן שֹׁפְטֵי אֶרֶץ כַּתֹּהוּ עָשָׂה
...וְגַם־נָשַׁף בָּהֶם וַיִּבָשׁוּ וּסְעָרָה כַּקַּשׁ תִּשָּׂאֵם

aⁱ — Incomparability of YHWH the creator [to crafted idols] (40:25)   וְאֶל־מִי 1x

aaⁱ — Incomparability of YHWH's creative decree in the heavens (40:26)   מִי/יִקְרָא 1x

axis: YHWH's protest against accusations of covenant disregard (40:27)   לָמָּה תֹאמַר יַעֲקֹב   וּתְדַבֵּר יִשְׂרָאֵל

bbⁱ — YHWH's power and knowledge available to his people [complex frame] (40:28-31)   הֲלוֹא יָדַעְתָּ   אִם־לֹא שָׁמַעְתָּ

bⁱ — YHWH's summons to trial of impotent nations (41:1)
...אִיִּים וּלְאֻמִּים...
יִגְּשׁוּ אָז יְדַבֵּרוּ יַחְדָּו לַמִּשְׁפָּט נִקְרָבָה

aaⁱ — Incomparability of YHWH's decree as lord of history (41:2a)   מִי/יִקְרָאֵהוּ 1x

bbⁱⁱ — YHWH's power to subjugate world kingdoms (41:2b-3)
יִתֵּן לְפָנָיו גּוֹיִם וּמְלָכִים יָרְדְּ
...יִתֵּן כֶּעָפָר חַרְבּוֹ כְּקַשׁ נִדָּף קַשְׁתּוֹ

aaⁱⁱ — Incomparability of YHWH's decree as lord of history (41:4)   מִי/קָרָא 1x

bⁱⁱ — Impotence of the nations against YHWH (41:5-6)
רָאוּ אִיִּים וְיִירָאוּ קְצוֹת הָאָרֶץ יֶחֱרָדוּ
...קָרְבוּ וַיֶּאֱתָיוּן

└────────── aⁱⁱ   Impotence of crafted idols (41:7)

וַיְחַזֵּק חָרָשׁ אֶת־צֹרֵף...

...וַיְחַזְּקֵהוּ...לֹא יִמּוֹט

In this section, rhetorical questions affirming YHWH's incomparability are posed using eight repetitions of the interrogative מִי. Four introduce repetitions of two crucial questions about the extent of YHWH's creative power and divine counsel (40:12a, 13a, 14a, 26a), and four of which introduce the four tiers that frame symmetrically the bb and bbⁱⁱ tiers (40:18a, 25a; 41:2a, 4a). In each of these 'bb' tiers (i.e., bb and bbⁱⁱ), the reader is presented with an adumbration of the answer to Jacob's/Israel's doubts as to YHWH's power and foreknowledge, and in each case the adumbration concerns the overthrow of world rulers. However, the adumbration is vague enough to apply to the actions of either Cyrus or YHWH's 'messianic' warrior. Because of an apparent division of this section into two parts—one part centering around the TT-B-bb-tier (40:21-24), the other around the TT-B-bbⁱⁱ-tier (41:2b-3)—it is not difficult to see why some rhetorical- and form-critical treatments have delimited the first part (40:12-31) as a unit to be distinguished from the second part (41:1-7).[1] Concerning the intervening TT-B-bbⁱ-tier (40:28-31), W.G.E. Watson has noted that the repetition of the word pair יגע ‖ יעף ('be weary//be faint') is the basis for a concentric pattern.[2] Indeed, there may be a complex framework pattern among these repetitions that is demarcated by the repetition of כֹּחַ:

---

[1] E.g., Y. Gitay, *Prophecy and Persuasion: A Study of Isaiah 40–48* (FTL, 14; Bonn: Linguistica Biblica, 1981), pp. 82-97. Some categorize Isa. 40:12-31 as a distinct 'disputation speech'. Isa. 41:1-7 is often taken to be a 'trial speech against the nations'. It is even possible to discern, in the matched repetitions of tiers bⁱ–aaⁱ–bbⁱⁱ–aaⁱⁱ–bⁱⁱ (41:1-6), a concentric arrangement that mimics the seemingly concentric ordering of these tiers:

bⁱ	41:1:	χ	אִיִּים (41:1a)
		ψ	יִגְּשׁוּ/נִקְרָבָה (41:1b)
aaⁱ	41:2a:	ω	מִי הֵעִיר/יִקְרָאֵהוּ (41:2aαβ')
		αα	לְרַגְלוֹ (41:2aβ")
bbⁱⁱ	41:2b-3:	ββ	יִתֵּן (41:2bα)
		ββⁱ	יִתֵּן (41:2bβγ)
		ααⁱ	בְּרַגְלָיו (41:3)
aaⁱⁱ	41:4:	ωⁱ	מִי־פָעַל וְעָשָׂה/קֹרֵא (41:4a)
bⁱⁱ	41:5-6:	χⁱ	אִיִּים (41:5aα)
		ψⁱ	קָרְבוּ וַיֶּאֱתָיוּן (41:5b)

[2] W.G.E. Watson, *Classical Hebrew Poetry: A Guide to its Techniques* (JSOTSup, 26; Sheffield: JSOT Press, 1984), p. 142.

bbⁱ   40:28-31:

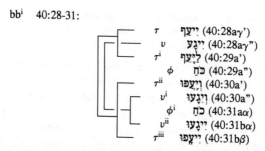

Matched repetitions within each of the first four tiers of 40:12–41:7, four tiers that together constitute an exposition of the four constituent tier groups (i.e., aa, a, b, bb), may be diagrammed as follows:

aa   40:12-14:

α   מֹאזְנַיִם (40:12bβ)
β   יוֹדִיעֶנּוּ (40:13b)
γ   וַיְלַמְּדֵהוּ (40:14aβ)
γⁱ   וַיְלַמְּדֵהוּ (40:14bα)
βⁱ   יוֹדִיעֶנּוּ (40:14bβ)

b   40:15-17:

δ   גּוֹיִם (40:15aα)
αⁱ   מֹאזְנַיִם (40:15aβ')
ε   נֶחְשָׁבוּ (40:15aβ")
ζ   אֵין דֵּי (40:16a)
ζ ⁱ   אֵין דֵּי (40:16b)
δⁱ   הַגּוֹיִם (40:17a)
εⁱ   נֶחְשָׁבוּ (40:17b)

a   40:18-20:

η   הַפֶּסֶל (40:19aα')
θ   חָרָשׁ (40:19aα")
ι   וְצֹרֵף (40:19aβ)
ιⁱ   צוֹרֵף (40:19b)
θⁱ   חָרָשׁ (40:20bα)
ηⁱ   פֶּסֶל (40:20bβ)

bb   40:21-24:

κ   הֲלוֹא, הֲלוֹא, הֲלוֹא, הֲלוֹא (40:21abα)
λ   הָאָרֶץ (40:21bβ)
μ   הַיֹּשֵׁב (40:22aα')
λⁱ   הָאָרֶץ (40:22aα")
μⁱ   וְישְׁבֶיהָ (40:22aβ)
axis: שָׁמָיִם (40:22bα)
μⁱⁱ   לָשֶׁבֶת (40:22bβ)
λⁱⁱ   אֶרֶץ (40:23b)
κⁱ   אַף בַּל, אַף בַּל, אַף בַּל (40:24aα-γ')
λⁱⁱⁱ   בָּאָרֶץ (40:24aγ")

As is evident from the last set, it is once again a 'bb' tier that presents the complex frameworking pattern. There are also examples of the rhetorical use of catchwords between subtiers that make up the TT-B-tier (e.g., the irony in the repetition of כֹּחַ יַחֲלִיפוּ between 40:31aα and 41:1aβ, which links sections contrasting YHWH's power [40:28-31] to the impotence of the nations [41:1]). While the preceding is not an exhaustive analysis of the poetic structure of 40:12–41:7, what is presented may be sufficient to suggest that it be delineated as a single unit. As a unit, it seems to center rhetorically on dispelling the insinuation of Jacob/Israel, expressed in the axis (40:27), that YHWH had disregarded his covenant.

The following paired tiers separate a consolation that assures Israel/Jacob of YHWH's covenant faithfulness (41:8-20) from a disputation that contends with Zion/Jerusalem that YHWH's incomparable foreknowledge and power to control the events of history are there on Zion's behalf (41:21–42:9 [10-12] 13-17). In the first of these paired sections (41:8-20), one sees a 'salvation oracle/announcement' arranged according to a concentric patterning of triadic frames. Its 'aa' and 'bb' tiers are bifid. Although this short section is often subdivided into two distinct 'salvation oracles' (41:8-13, 14-16) followed by a 'salvation proclamation' (41:17-20), when viewed as a whole, it focuses its concern upon affirming how YHWH has been faithful to the patriarchal covenant. Isaiah 41:8-20 (tier TT-A^i) commences with the adversative וְאַתָּה 'but as for you', which signals a disjunction from what precedes but also marks a shift from the disputational tone of YHWH's denunciation of foreign nations and idols in 40:12–41:7 to a tone of consolation.[1] The complex frameworking of tiers in Isa. 41:8-20, which rhetorically highlights YHWH's covenant loyalty to Israel/Jacob in redeeming them from adversity, may be schematized as follows:

---

[1] Reinforcing the continuity between these sections is the ironic interplay between repetitions of the catchword חזק (41:6b, 7aα, bβ and 41:9a, 13a), a root that may play on the name of the last 'righteous' Judean king under whom Isaiah wrote, Hezekiah. While it is possible, if Isaiah lived until 681 BCE (cf. Isa. 37:38), that he also lived under the reign of 'evil' Manasseh, the latter king is never mentioned in the final form of the book of Isaiah (cf. Isa. 1:1; 2 Kgs 21:1-18).

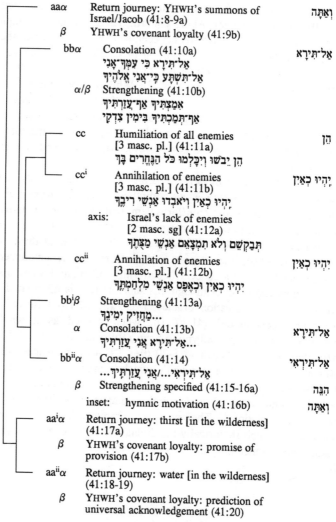

aaα	Return journey: YHWH's summons of Israel/Jacob (41:8-9a)	וְאַתָּה
β	YHWH's covenant loyalty (41:9b)	
bbα	Consolation (41:10a)	אַל־תִּירָא
	אַל־תִּירָא כִּי עִמְּךָ־אָנִי	
	אַל־תִּשְׁתָּע כִּי־אֲנִי אֱלֹהֶיךָ	
α/β	Strengthening (41:10b)	
	אִמַּצְתִּיךָ אַף־עֲזַרְתִּיךָ	
	אַף־תְּמַכְתִּיךָ בִּימִין צִדְקִי	
cc	Humiliation of all enemies [3 masc. pl.] (41:11a)	הֵן
	הֵן יֵבֹשׁוּ וְיִכָּלְמוּ כֹּל הַנֶּחֱרִים בָּךְ	
ccⁱ	Annihilation of enemies [3 masc. pl.] (41:11b)	יִהְיוּ כְאַיִן
	יִהְיוּ כְאַיִן וְיֹאבְדוּ אַנְשֵׁי רִיבֶךָ	
axis:	Israel's lack of enemies [2 masc. sg] (41:12a)	
	תְּבַקְשֵׁם וְלֹא תִמְצָאֵם אַנְשֵׁי מַצֻּתֶךָ	
ccⁱⁱ	Annihilation of enemies [3 masc. pl.] (41:12b)	יִהְיוּ כְאַיִן
	יִהְיוּ כְאַיִן וּכְאֶפֶס אַנְשֵׁי מִלְחַמְתֶּךָ	
bbⁱβ	Strengthening (41:13a)	
	...מַחֲזִיק יְמִינֶךָ	
α	Consolation (41:13b)	אַל־תִּירָא
	...אַל־תִּירָא אֲנִי עֲזַרְתִּיךָ	
bbⁱⁱα	Consolation (41:14)	אַל־תִּירְאִי
	...אַל־תִּירְאִי.../אֲנִי עֲזַרְתִּיךָ...	
β	Strengthening specified (41:15-16a)	הִגֵּה
inset:	hymnic motivation (41:16b)	וְאַתָּה
aaⁱα	Return journey: thirst [in the wilderness] (41:17a)	
β	YHWH's covenant loyalty: promise of provision (41:17b)	
aaⁱⁱα	Return journey: water [in the wilderness] (41:18-19)	
β	YHWH's covenant loyalty: prediction of universal acknowledgement (41:20)	

In this consolation poem, all the 'aa' and 'bb' tiers are essentially bifid. The 'aaα' tiers refer to YHWH's call of Israel from foreign lands and to Israel's subsequent return to their own land by means of YHWH's provision of water in the wilderness. The 'aaβ' tiers speak variously of the loyalty of YHWH, the god of Israel, to his chosen people. The triadic frame comprising the 'aa' tiers encloses the triadic frame made up of the 'bb' tiers. Tiers 'bbα' all begin with the

consoling formula אַל־תִּירָא (or the like), and all portray YHWH promis-
ing to help Israel (cf. עֲזַרְתִּיךְ 'I will help you' in 41:10bα, 13b and 14).
The 'bbβ' tiers either describe YHWH's intention to 'strengthen' his
people (41:10b, 13a) or specify the way in which he would do so (i.e.,
'I will make you a threshing sledge ...' 41:15-16a). Just as the triadic
frame comprising the 'aa' tiers encloses the triadic frame made up of
the 'bb' tiers, so the 'bb' tiers enclose the triadic frame made up of the
'cc' tiers so that the whole compound configuration forms a triply
recessed frame about the central verse, 41:12a. The 'cc' tiers describe
the humiliation (tier cc) and annihilation (יִהְיוּ כְאַיִן in tiers cc[i] and cc[ii])
of Israel's enemies, always using 3 masc. pl. verbs. The axis of the
framework, which expresses the result of YHWH's strengthening of
Israel against her enemies, shifts to 2 masc. sg verb forms: תְּבַקְשֵׁם וְלֹא
תִמְצָאֵם אַנְשֵׁי מַצֻּתֶךָ 'You will search for them/but you will not find
them—men to contend with you'. Indeed, it is the people's realization
that all their enemies were gone, uniquely portrayed in the axis, that
would allow and prompt them to return, as portrayed among the tiers
of the outermost triadic frame (tiers 'aa').

Noteworthy, too, is the increase in repetitions of clauses with divine
epithets, especially after the axis of the tier, such as: כִּי־אֲנִי אֱלֹהֶיךָ
(41:10aβ), נְאֻם־יְהוָה וְגֹאֲלֵךְ קְדוֹשׁ יִשְׂרָאֵל (41:13a), כִּי־אֲנִי יְהוָה אֱלֹהֶיךָ
(41:14b), אֲנִי יְהוָה...אֱלֹהֵי יִשְׂרָאֵל (41:16b), בְּיהוָה בִּקְדוֹשׁ יִשְׂרָאֵל
(41:17b), יְהוָה...וּקְדוֹשׁ יִשְׂרָאֵל (41:20aγb). This tier (41:8-20) testifies to
YHWH's covenant faithfulness, and it is probably not fortuitous that
Abraham is mentioned in 41:8b, since he is the fountainhead of
YHWH's faithfulness to Israel later evidenced in the Exodus and
wilderness (cf. Gen. 17:3-8). It was in Abram/Abraham that Israel was
first comforted (cf. Isa. 41:10aα, 13b, 14aα with Gen. 15:1, אַל־תִּירָא
אַבְרָם) and promised protection from all enemies (cf. Isa. 41:11-12 with
Gen. 12:3; 14:20; 15:1; 22:17), and it was in his offspring that YHWH
first evidenced the blessing of his presence (cf. Isa. 41:10aα with Gen.
26:3, 28; 31:3).

The framework pattern of Isa. 41:21–42:9 [10-12] 13-17 (tier TT-B[i])
comprises two interlocking quadratic frames. Here a trial speech
against the nations' idols interlocks with predictions of YHWH's election of the one through whom he would vindicate himself. The whole is
designed to demonstrate the incomparability of YHWH's foreknowledge
against the ignorance of idols that are unable to forecast and control the
events of history. Surrounding the first pivotal hymnic invocation of the
section (42:10-12), Isa. 41:21–42:9, 13-17 appears to form a complex
framework pattern, which may be outlined as follows:

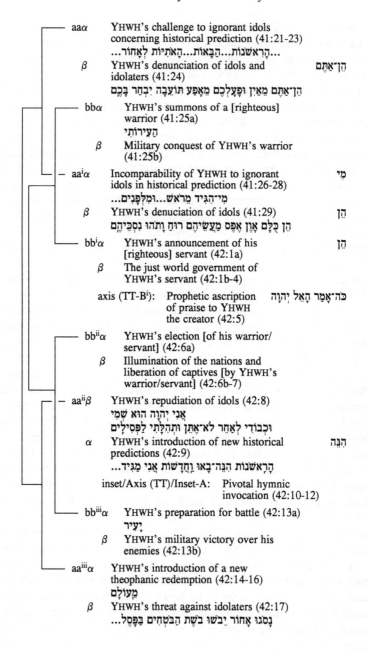

aaα   YHWH's challenge to ignorant idols
         concerning historical prediction (41:21-23)
         ...הָרִאשֹׁנוֹת...הַבָּאוֹת...הָאֹתִיּוֹת לְאָחוֹר...

β   YHWH's denunciation of idols and   הֵן־אַתֶּם
         idolaters (41:24)
         הֵן־אַתֶּם מֵאַיִן וּפָעָלְכֶם מֵאָפַע תּוֹעֵבָה יִבְחַר בָּכֶם

bbα   YHWH's summons of a [righteous]
         warrior (41:25a)
         הַעִירֹותִי

β   Military conquest of YHWH's warrior
         (41:25b)

aa^iα   Incomparability of YHWH to ignorant   מִי
         idols in historical prediction (41:26-28)
         מִי־הִגִּיד מֵרֹאשׁ...וּמִלְּפָנִים...

β   YHWH's denuciation of idols (41:29)   הֵן
         הֵן כֻּלָּם אָוֶן אֶפֶס מַעֲשֵׂיהֶם רוּחַ וָתֹהוּ נִסְכֵּיהֶם

bb^iα   YHWH's announcement of his   הֵן
         [righteous] servant (42:1a)

β   The just world government of
         YHWH's servant (42:1b-4)

axis (TT-B^i): Prophetic ascription   כֹּה־אָמַר הָאֵל יְהוָה
                of praise to YHWH
                the creator (42:5)

bb^iiα   YHWH's election [of his warrior/
         servant] (42:6a)

β   Illumination of the nations and
         liberation of captives [by YHWH's
         warrior/servant] (42:6b-7)

aa^iiβ   YHWH's repudiation of idols (42:8)
         אֲנִי יְהוָה הוּא שְׁמִי
         וּכְבוֹדִי לְאַחֵר לֹא־אֶתֵּן וּתְהִלָּתִי לַפְּסִילִים

α   YHWH's introduction of new historical   הִנֵּה
         predictions (42:9)
         הָרִאשֹׁנוֹת הִנֵּה־בָאוּ וַחֲדָשׁוֹת אֲנִי מַגִּיד...

inset/Axis (TT)/Inset-A: Pivotal hymnic
                           invocation (42:10-12)

bb^iiiα YHWH's preparation for battle (42:13a)
         יָעִיר

β   YHWH's military victory over his
         enemies (42:13b)

aa^iiiα YHWH's introduction of a new
         theophanic redemption (42:14-16)
         מֵעֹולָם

β   YHWH's threat against idolaters (42:17)
         נָסֹגוּ אָחוֹר יֵבֹשׁוּ בֹשֶׁת הַבֹּטְחִים בַּפָּסֶל...

All the tiers of this configuration are bifid. Only once, in the third 'aa' tier (42:8-9), does the order of bifid elements among the 'aa' tiers reverse about the axis. The 'aaα' tiers comprise a series of affirmations or attestations of YHWH's unique ability to predict history, whether that ability is seen as something of which foreign idols are incapable (41:21-23, 26-28) or something that YHWH discloses with eager anticipation to the citizens of Zion (42:9, 14-16). It is not idols who declared the 'former things' (41:22b) 'from the beginning' (41:26aα) or who will declare the 'things to come' (41:23a) 'beforehand' (41:26aβ), but YHWH declared the 'former things' and announces the 'new things' to Zion's citizens (42:9). Precisely what those 'new things' are, he eagerly enumerates for them (42:26-28). In the 'aaβ' tiers, YHWH passionately denounces foreign gods as capable of 'nothing' (41:24a, 29a), as mere 'molten images' (41:29b; 42:17b), 'idols' (42:8b, 17a), called 'gods' only by those who will be put to shame (42:17). The stance of YHWH in these denunciations changes, varying from direct address of the gods (41:24), to third person description (41:29), to a first person attestation of YHWH's jealousy of sharing praise with such idols (42:8), to a third person denunciation of those who trust in such molten images (42:17). In the context of the 'aa' tiers' portrayal of YHWH's jealousy for being recognized as Zion's only true god, the 'bb' tiers depict YHWH's summoning of a righteous servant who will liberate his people from captivity in order to establish a just world order. The 'bbα' tiers focus upon the portrayal of YHWH stirring up someone from the northeast (41:25a), heralding someone as his chosen servant (42:1a), someone legitimately appointed (42:6a) and for whose establishment YHWH himself will stir up his military zeal (42:13). The 'bbβ' tiers describe the effect of the rise of YHWH's servant upon the nations: though he treads upon rulers as a potter treads upon clay (41:25b), by YHWH's spirit he will establish a just government over the nations without a battle (42:1b-4); he will be protected by YHWH to become a covenant sign for the people and a light to the nations by setting free the captive citizens of Zion (42:6b-7), YHWH himself having vanquished all his enemies (42:13b).

The pivotal hymnic invocation of 42:10-12 occurs within the complex framework of 41:21–42:17 (as do Inset-A[iii], 51:3; Inset-A[iv], 51:11; and Inset-A[v], 52:8-9 within 51:1-8; 51:9–52:2 and 52:3-12, respectively). Moreover, it ostensibly serves as the structural pivot for the complex framework of the TT-tier (40:1–43:13), just as the pivotal hymnic invocation of 44:23 does for the TT[i]-tier (43:16–46:13). The insertion of Inset-A between tiers TT-B[i]-aa[ii] (42:8-9) and TT-B[i]-bb[iii]

(42:13) allows it to function both as the rhetorical climax of this disputational complex and as a demarcator between the closing pairs of its tiers (i.e. between bb^{ii}–aa^{ii} and bb^{iii}–aa^{iii}).

At this juncture it may be appropriate to present, in table form, the alternating pattern of consolational and disputational dispositions among the first four second-level tiers of this section:

		Paneling	*Chiasmus*
TT-A	40:1-11	Consolation	Jerusalem/Zion
TT-B	40:12–41:7	Disputation	Jacob/Israel
TT-A^i	41:8-20	Consolation	Israel/Jacob
TT-B^i	41:21–42:9, 13-17	Disputation	Zion/Jerusalem

This structure offers maximal variation because paneling of dispositions (consolation versus disputation) is superimposed upon a chiastic presentation of addressees (i.e., Jerusalem/Zion:Jacob/Israel:: Israel/Jacob:Zion/Jerusalem—the proper nouns appearing in their order of first mention in the tiers).[1]

The TT-B^{ii}-tier (42:18-25) appears to have the following compound frame pattern:

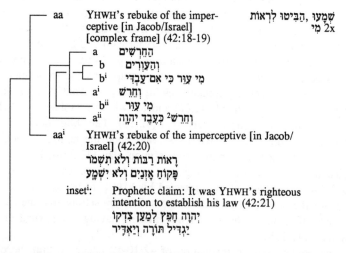

[1]Since 'Jacob' in 41:21b is part of an epithet of YHWH, it is discounted as being neither a vocative nor the addressee of a prophetic word.

[2]In Isa. 42:19bβ, two Hebrew manuscripts and Symmachus support a reading of וְחֵרֵשׁ instead of וְעִוֵּר. This is not compelling in itself, but it would suit a pattern of repetition elsewhere evident in Isaiah whereby a chiasmus is juxtaposed with a synonymous parallelism (cf. 11:13; but especially 6:9-10).

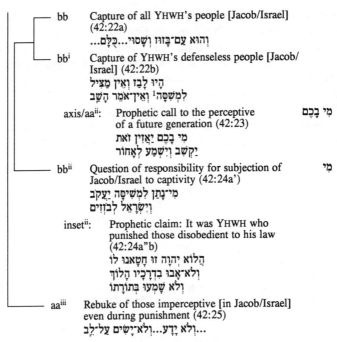

bb   Capture of all YHWH's people [Jacob/Israel]
      (42:22a)

      וְהוּא עַם־בָּזוּז וְשָׁסוּי...כֻּלָּם...

bbⁱ   Capture of YHWH's defenseless people [Jacob/
      Israel] (42:22b)

      הָיוּ לָבַז וְאֵין מַצִּיל
      לִמְשִׁסָּה¹ וְאֵין־אֹמֵר הָשַׁב

axis/aaⁱⁱ: Prophetic call to the perceptive   מִי בָכֶם
            of a future generation (42:23)

      מִי בָכֶם יַאֲזִין זֹאת
      יַקְשֵׁב וְיִשְׁמַע לְאָחוֹר

bbⁱⁱ Question of responsibility for subjection of   מִי
      Jacob/Israel to captivity (42:24a')

      מִי־נָתַן לִמְשִׁסָּה יַעֲקֹב
      וְיִשְׂרָאֵל לְבֹזְזִים

insetⁱⁱ: Prophetic claim: It was YHWH who
          punished those disobedient to his law
          (42:24a"b)

      הֲלוֹא יְהוָה זוּ חָטָאנוּ לוֹ
      וְלֹא־אָבוּ בִדְרָכָיו הָלוֹךְ
      וְלֹא שָׁמְעוּ בְּתוֹרָתוֹ

aaⁱⁱⁱ Rebuke of those imperceptive [in Jacob/Israel]
       even during punishment (42:25)

      ...וְלֹא יָדָע...וְלֹא־יָשִׂים עַל־לֵב

All the 'aa' tiers in the preceding configuration portray YHWH rebuking his servant Jacob/Israel for their willful imperception, which is figuratively depicted in 42:18-19, 20 as blindness and deafness (apparently, toward his law; cf. insetⁱ, 42:21; insetⁱⁱ 42:24a"b). This imperception continued despite YHWH's having poured out upon them his burning anger (42:25). Against the implicit inference, made by Jacob/Israel, that it was YHWH who had failed to rescue them from captivity (42:22a, 22b), the author insinuates that YHWH actually handed Jacob/Israel over to their plunderers. This he did 'for the sake of his righteousness' (42:21) because they had sinned by not obeying his law (42:24a"b).

There is an ironic reversal in the usage of עַבְדִּי 'my servant' in 42:19aα (cf. 42:19bβ), when compared to its use in 42:1a. The disloyalty of Jacob/Israel is made to seem more reprehensible, not just because their rebellion against YHWH's law is unwarranted, but also because it contrasts with the justice of YHWH's servant, whose law extends to all nations (42:1-4). The ambivalence of the aaⁱⁱ-tier (42:23),

¹In 42:22bβ, 1QIsaᵃ, a few Hebrew manuscripts, the Peshiṭta, Targum and Vulgate support the reading of לִמְשִׁסָּה instead of מְשִׁסָּה.

as perhaps either a constituent tier or the axis of the subsection, may be akin to the duality of 13:9b-12 and 39:3bγδ within their respective tiers (i.e., the outermost tiers of Isa. 13:1–39:8: NN, 13:[1]2-22; NN^ii, 39:1-8). Interpreted as the axis of 42:18-25, 42:23 poignantly calls to the perceptive of a future generation for a response to the law of which their predecessors had been incapable.

Tier TT-A^ii (43:1-7) returns to YHWH's consolation of Jacob/Israel. It commences with a disjunction (וְעַתָּה) that sets this subsection in contrast to that which precedes. Its tiered structure appears as follows:

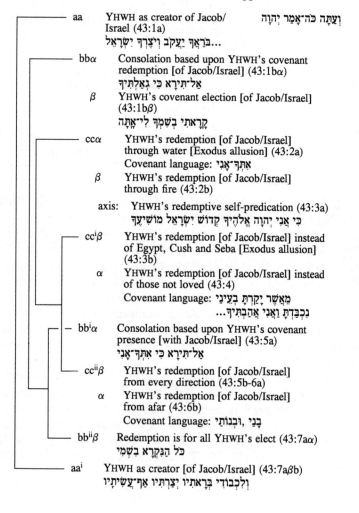

aa	YHWH as creator of Jacob/Israel (43:1a)	וְעַתָּה כֹּה־אָמַר יְהוָה
		...בֹּרַאֲךָ יַעֲקֹב וְיֹצֶרְךָ יִשְׂרָאֵל
bbα	Consolation based upon YHWH's covenant redemption [of Jacob/Israel] (43:1bα)	
		אַל־תִּירָא כִּי גְאַלְתִּיךָ
β	YHWH's covenant election [of Jacob/Israel] (43:1bβ)	
		קָרָאתִי בְשִׁמְךָ לִי־אָתָּה
ccα	YHWH's redemption [of Jacob/Israel] through water [Exodus allusion] (43:2a) Covenant language: אִתְּךָ־אָנִי	
β	YHWH's redemption [of Jacob/Israel] through fire (43:2b)	
axis:	YHWH's redemptive self-predication (43:3a)	
		כִּי אֲנִי יְהוָה אֱלֹהֶיךָ קְדוֹשׁ יִשְׂרָאֵל מוֹשִׁיעֶךָ
cc^iβ	YHWH's redemption [of Jacob/Israel] instead of Egypt, Cush and Seba [Exodus allusion] (43:3b)	
α	YHWH's redemption [of Jacob/Israel] instead of those not loved (43:4) Covenant language: מֵאֲשֶׁר יָקַרְתָּ בְעֵינַי	
		...נִכְבַּדְתָּ וַאֲנִי אֲהַבְתִּיךָ
bb^iα	Consolation based upon YHWH's covenant presence [with Jacob/Israel] (43:5a)	
		אַל־תִּירָא כִּי אִתְּךָ־אָנִי
cc^iiβ	YHWH's redemption [of Jacob/Israel] from every direction (43:5b-6a)	
α	YHWH's redemption [of Jacob/Israel] from afar (43:6b) Covenant language: בָּנַי, וּבְנוֹתַי	
bb^iiβ	Redemption is for all YHWH's elect (43:7aα)	
		כֹּל הַנִּקְרָא בִשְׁמִי
aa^i	YHWH as creator [of Jacob/Israel] (43:7aβb)	
		וְלִכְבוֹדִי בְּרָאתִיו יְצַרְתִּיו אַף־עֲשִׂיתִיו

The outer inclusio, comprising the 'aa' tiers, clearly delimits this tier as addressed to Jacob/Israel, whom YHWH himself 'created' (43:1a, 7aβ) and 'formed' (43:1a, 7b). The 'bb' and 'cc' tiers appear to be bifid. Both 'bbα' tiers present the consolational assurance of salvation, אַל־תִּירָא 'fear not', followed by a substantiation clause, 'for I have redeemed you' (43:1bα) or 'for I am with you' (43:5a). Both 'bbβ' tiers describe Jacob/Israel as a people either 'called by name' (קָרָאתִי בְשִׁמְךָ, 43:1bβ) or 'called by the name' of YHWH (הַנִּקְרָא בִשְׁמִי, 43:7aα). In order to specify the ways in which YHWH is with Jacob/Israel (43:5a) as their redeemer (43:1bα), the apparently bifid 'cc' tiers alternatively depict YHWH with his people redeeming them: (1) through water (43:2a) and fire (43:2b); (2) instead of Egypt, Cush and Seba, specifically (43:3b), and all other people, generally (43:4); and (3) as Jacob/Israel's children to be brought from the four points of the compass (43:5b-6a) or as YHWH's sons and daughters to be brought from afar (43:6b). If the use of covenant language were taken to be the basis for distinguishing the 'α' from the 'β' halves of the bifid 'cc' tiers, it might be worth noticing that the order of 'α' and 'β' halves of these bifid tiers reverses about the central axis, which enhances the concentricity of the repetition pattern. In view of the emphasis upon redemption in this tier, it is appropriate that the axis portrays YHWH making the epithetic self-predication: 'I am YHWH, your god, the Holy One of Israel, your savior' (43:3a).

The imagery that began the disputation against Israel in 42:18-25 (especially vv. 18-19) is repeated in Isa. 43:8-13 (tier TT-B[iii]), another disputational complex. However, in this case it remains ambiguous as to whether YHWH is calling Israel or all nations to trial. This tier has a pattern of triadic frames similar to that of the preceding tier:

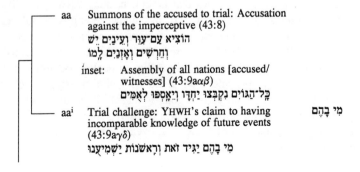

aa Summons of the accused to trial: Accusation against the imperceptive (43:8)
הוֹצִיא עַם־עִוֵּר וְעֵינַיִם יֵשׁ
וְחֵרְשִׁים וְאָזְנַיִם לָמוֹ

inset: Assembly of all nations [accused/witnesses] (43:9aαβ)
כָּל־הַגּוֹיִם נִקְבְּצוּ יַחְדָּו וְיֵאָסְפוּ לְאֻמִּים

aa[i] Trial challenge: YHWH's claim to having incomparable knowledge of future events (43:9aγδ)
מִי בָהֶם
מִי בָהֶם יַגִּיד זֹאת וְרִאשֹׁנוֹת יַשְׁמִיעֻנוּ

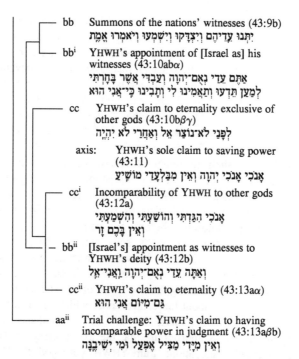

bb Summons of the nations' witnesses (43:9b)
יִתְּנוּ עֵדֵיהֶם וְיִצְדָּקוּ וְיִשְׁמְעוּ וְיֹאמְרוּ אֱמֶת

bb^i YHWH's appointment of [Israel as] his witnesses (43:10abα)
אַתֶּם עֵדַי נְאֻם־יְהוָה וְעַבְדִּי אֲשֶׁר בָּחָרְתִּי
לְמַעַן תֵּדְעוּ וְתַאֲמִינוּ לִי וְתָבִינוּ כִּי־אֲנִי הוּא

cc YHWH's claim to eternality exclusive of other gods (43:10bβγ)
לְפָנַי לֹא־נוֹצַר אֵל וְאַחֲרַי לֹא יִהְיֶה

axis: YHWH's sole claim to saving power (43:11)
אָנֹכִי אָנֹכִי יְהוָה וְאֵין מִבַּלְעָדַי מוֹשִׁיעַ

cc^i Incomparability of YHWH to other gods (43:12a)
אָנֹכִי הִגַּדְתִּי וְהוֹשַׁעְתִּי וְהִשְׁמַעְתִּי
וְאֵין בָּכֶם זָר

bb^ii [Israel's] appointment as witnesses to YHWH's deity (43:12b)
וְאַתֶּם עֵדַי נְאֻם־יְהוָה וַאֲנִי־אֵל

cc^ii YHWH's claim to eternality (43:13aα)
גַּם־מִיּוֹם אֲנִי הוּא

aa^ii Trial challenge: YHWH's claim to having incomparable power in judgment (43:13aβb)
וְאֵין מִיָּדִי מַצִּיל אֶפְעַל וּמִי יְשִׁיבֶנָּה

וּמִי

The 'aa' tiers of the preceding schema use the language of the summons to trial (43:8) and of the challenge to trial of potential rivals (מִי 'Who?', in 43:9aγδ, 13aβb). Specifically, YHWH claims to have incomparable knowledge and power, and his rivals are challenged to identify themselves. All the 'bb' tiers describe 'witnesses' to the facts relating to the question of YHWH's claim to deity: the bb-tier calls for the nations to present witnesses that others, besides YHWH, predicted the 'former things' (43:9b; cf. v. 9a); in the succeeding two 'bb' tiers, YHWH identifies his own people as witnesses to the fact that he is God (43:10abα, 12b). In the 'cc' tiers, YHWH declares his exclusive eternality (43:10bβγ, 13aα) and sole ability to declare beforehand that he will save his people and then to do it. Quite clearly, his claims exclude those of potentially rival gods (43:12a). Once again, the axis appropriately epitomizes the theme of the subsection in a self-predicating proclamation of YHWH: 'I, even I, am YHWH, and besides me there is no one who can save' (43:11).

Isaiah 43:16-21 (tier TT^i-A^{iii}) commences the second 'TT' tier with a consolational complex. It comprises quadratic and simple frames whose pattern of repetitions surrounds a central axis in 43:18-19a:

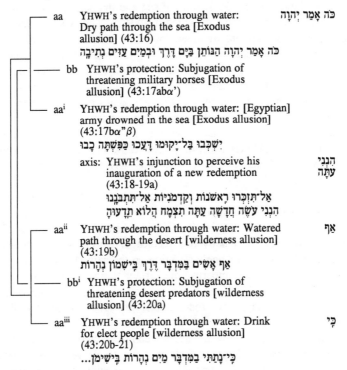

aa	YHWH's redemption through water: Dry path through the sea [Exodus allusion] (43:16)	כֹּה אָמַר יְהוָה
		כֹּה אָמַר יְהוָה הַנּוֹתֵן בַּיָּם דָּרֶךְ וּבְמַיִם עַזִּים נְתִיבָה
bb	YHWH's protection: Subjugation of threatening military horses [Exodus allusion] (43:17abα')	
aa^i	YHWH's redemption through water: [Egyptian] army drowned in the sea [Exodus allusion] (43:17bα"β)	
		יִשְׁכְּבוּ בַּל־יָקוּמוּ דָּעֲכוּ כַּפִּשְׁתָּה כָבוּ
axis:	YHWH's injunction to perceive his inauguration of a new redemption (43:18-19a)	הִנְנִי עֹתָּה
		אַל־תִּזְכְּרוּ רִאשֹׁנוֹת וְקַדְמֹנִיּוֹת אַל־תִּתְבֹּנָנוּ
		הִנְנִי עֹשֶׂה חֲדָשָׁה עַתָּה תִצְמָח הֲלוֹא תֵדָעוּהָ
aa^{ii}	YHWH's redemption through water: Watered path through the desert [wilderness allusion] (43:19b)	אַף
		אַף אָשִׂים בַּמִּדְבָּר דָּרֶךְ בִּישִׁמוֹן נְהָרוֹת
bb^i	YHWH's protection: Subjugation of threatening desert predators [wilderness allusion] (43:20a)	
aa^{iii}	YHWH's redemption through water: Drink for elect people [wilderness allusion] (43:20b-21)	כִּי
		כִּי־נָתַתִּי בַמִּדְבָּר מַיִם נְהָרוֹת בִּישִׁימֹן...

In this subsection, YHWH promises to protect his people during their desert pilgrimage by means of a redemption that will surpass even that of the Exodus from Egypt. YHWH is here portrayed as the ruler both of nature and the nations. The axis of the framework structure begins with a consoling prohibition against considering former things because YHWH is now doing something new (43:18-19a). Correspondingly, it is framed by descriptions of the Exodus from Egypt (43:16-17) and of YHWH's new redemptive pilgrimage through the wilderness (43:19b-21). The description of YHWH's suppression of the 'animal threat' of military horses (tier bb, 43:17abα') is framed by a corresponding contrast between a description of his forming dry land in the sea as a means of salvation (tier aa, 43:16aβb) and his making the sea a means of destruction for the Egyptian army (tier aa^i, 43:17bα"β). Similarly, YHWH's suppression of the 'animal threat' of desert predators (tier bb^i,

43:20a) is framed by corresponding references to streams in the desert (tiers aa^{ii} and aa^{iii}, 43:19b, 20b-21), streams that would both pacify the wild beasts and provide for YHWH's people. Indeed, in the 'aa' tiers of this consolation poem, the realms of sea and dry land are used to describe the contrasting ways in which YHWH did and would achieve the old and new redemptions by means of water: the image of the dry land in the midst of the sea (tiers aa and aa^{i}, 43:16aβb, 17bα"β) contrasts with that of the emergence of streams in the desert (tiers aa^{ii} and aa^{iii}, 43:19b, 20b). Among the 'bb' tiers, whereas the suppression of threatening animals in tier bb (43:17abα') comes by using water as the means of their death, the subjugation of threatening animals in tier bb^{i} (43:20a) comes about by the provision of water as a means to ending their predatory behavior (i.e., they seem to become herbivores with an abundance of plants to eat in what was formerly a desert; cf. Isa. 11:6-7; 65:25).

In this example, complex frameworking accounts mainly for the patterns of semantic parallelism among the 'aa' tiers, whose quadratic frame interlocks with the simple inclusio formed by the two 'bb' tiers. The concentricity formed by this pattern of parallelisms is unusually symmetrical and focuses one's attention on the axis (43:18-19a), whose prohibition against remembering the former things in view of the new things that YHWH is about to do epitomizes succinctly the contrast between the old and new redemptions of YHWH described in the surrounding framework.

If taken in contiguity with the preceding prediction of Babylonian deliverance, Isa. 43:16-21 could be seen to serve as a salvation announcement, the proclamation of a redemptive pilgrimage of YHWH's elect from Babylon. The whole announcement is a plea for YHWH's right to be recognized (43:21) for what he truly is—Israel's redemptive creator and king (cf. 43:14a, 15).

In form, tier TT^{i}-B^{iv} (43:22-28) presents a permutation of the framework pattern of the preceding tier. However, inasmuch as it is disputational, it contrasts in mood with the preceding and succeeding consolatory tiers. The focus of its denunciation is the rebellion of Jacob/Israel in regard to the cult:

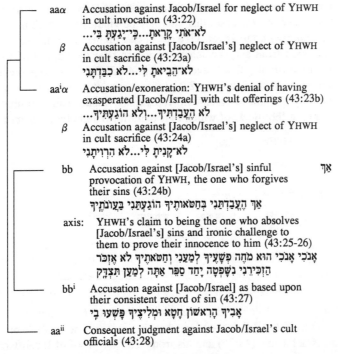

aaα   Accusation against Jacob/Israel for neglect of YHWH in cult invocation (43:22)

לֹא־אֹתִי קָרָאתָ...כִּי־יָגַעְתָּ בִּי...

β   Accusation against [Jacob/Israel's] neglect of YHWH in cult sacrifice (43:23a)

לֹא־הֵבֵיאתָ לִי...לֹא כִבַּדְתָּנִי

aaⁱα   Accusation/exoneration: YHWH's denial of having exasperated [Jacob/Israel] with cult offerings (43:23b)

לֹא הֶעֱבַדְתִּיךָ...וְלֹא הוֹגַעְתִּיךָ...

β   Accusation against [Jacob/Israel's] neglect of YHWH in cult sacrifice (43:24a)

לֹא־קָנִיתָ לִי...לֹא הִרְוִיתָנִי

bb   Accusation against [Jacob/Israel's] sinful   אַךְ
provocation of YHWH, the one who forgives their sins (43:24b)

אַךְ הֶעֱבַדְתַּנִי בְּחַטֹּאותֶיךָ הוֹגַעְתַּנִי בַּעֲוֹנֹתֶיךָ

axis: YHWH's claim to being the one who absolves [Jacob/Israel's] sins and ironic challenge to them to prove their innocence to him (43:25-26)

אָנֹכִי אָנֹכִי הוּא מֹחֶה פְשָׁעֶיךָ לְמַעֲנִי וְחַטֹּאתֶיךָ לֹא אֶזְכֹּר
הַזְכִּירֵנִי נִשָּׁפְטָה יָחַד סַפֵּר אַתָּה לְמַעַן תִּצְדָּק

bbⁱ   Accusation against [Jacob/Israel] as based upon their consistent record of sin (43:27)

אָבִיךָ הָרִאשׁוֹן חָטָא וּמְלִיצֶיךָ פָּשְׁעוּ בִי

aaⁱⁱ   Consequent judgment against Jacob/Israel's cult officials (43:28)

The 'aa' tiers of the preceding schema make accusations (43:22-23a, 23b-24a) and a pronouncement of judgment (43:28) against 'Jacob/Israel', a pair whose double mention frames the subunit. In this instance, the relation between the former accusations and latter judgment is one of cause and effect. In addition, each of the first two 'aa' tiers presents the same two themes in a pattern that suggests a bifid structure. That is, the 'aaα' halves focus upon how Jacob/Israel has 'not grown weary' (43:22), nor has YHWH 'burdened [them] or made [them] weary' with cult obligations (43:23b); the 'aaβ' halves focus upon what Jacob/Israel has neglected to bring to YHWH in sacrifice ('you have not brought me sheep ... nor honored me with your sacrifices' [43:23a], 'you have not acquired for me calamus nor sated me with the fat of your sacrifices' [43:24a]). In contrast, both 'bb' tiers explicitly accuse Jacob/Israel of having burdened and wearied YHWH with 'sins' (43:24bα, 27a), 'iniquities' (43:24bβ), and 'transgressions' (43:27b). Yet for all this, at the axis of this subunit, YHWH first proclaims his innocence: 'I, even I, am he who blots out your transgressions ... and does not remember your sins' (43:25). Only then, does he challenge his people: 'Make me remember; let us arbitrate together; recount [the case] that you may be vindicated' (43:26).

Beginning with the adversative אַךְ of tier bb (43:24b), there is a discernible shift from an expression of concern over the neglect of YHWH in the cultic ritual (cf. לֹא seven times in 43:22-24a) to outright denunciation of sins (43:24b, 25, 27). In addition, this complex is linked together by a chain of catchword repetitions, found mainly in the axis and flanking 'bb' tiers, of which four pairs form a double chiasmus:

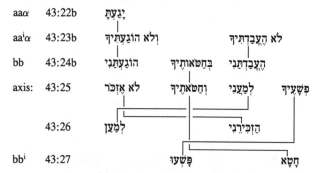

aaα	43:22b	יָגַעְתָּ
aaiα	43:23b	וְלֹא הוֹגַעְתִּיךָ לֹא הֶעֱבַדְתִּיךָ
bb	43:24b	הוֹגַעְתַּנִי בְּחַטֹּאותֶיךָ הֶעֱבַדְתַּנִי
axis:	43:25	לֹא אֶזְכֹּר וְחַטֹּאתֶיךָ לְמַעֲנִי פְּשָׁעֶיךָ
	43:26	לְמַעַן הַזְכִּירֵנִי
bbi	43:27	פָּשְׁעוּ חָטָא

The structural center and rhetorical climax of this complex comes only with YHWH's declaration that he is the one who blots out Jacob/Israel's sins (43:25) and his ironic call for proof of Jacob/Israel's covenant innocence (43:26). This rhetorical request was probably designed to invoke in them a realization that it was, as always (cf. 43:27), they who were at fault, while YHWH remained innocent (cf. 43:23b).

Tier TTi-Aiv (44:1-5) offers a brief resumption of the consolatory disposition last evident in tier TTi-Aiii. Its repetitions form a triadic frame surrounding a simple frame and axis:

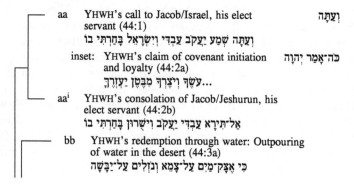

	aa	YHWH's call to Jacob/Israel, his elect servant (44:1)	וְעַתָּה
		וְעַתָּה שְׁמַע יַעֲקֹב עַבְדִּי וְיִשְׂרָאֵל בָּחַרְתִּי בוֹ	
	inset:	YHWH's claim of covenant initiation and loyalty (44:2a)	כֹּה־אָמַר יְהוָה
		...עֹשֶׂךָ וְיֹצֶרְךָ מִבֶּטֶן יַעְזְרֶךָ	
	aai	YHWH's consolation of Jacob/Jeshurun, his elect servant (44:2b)	
		אַל־תִּירָא עַבְדִּי יַעֲקֹב וִישֻׁרוּן בָּחַרְתִּי בוֹ	
	bb	YHWH's redemption through water: Outpouring of water in the desert (44:3a)	
		כִּי אֶצָּק־מַיִם עַל־צָמֵא וְנֹזְלִים עַל־יַבָּשָׁה	

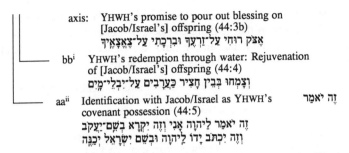

axis: YHWH's promise to pour out blessing on
[Jacob/Israel's] offspring (44:3b)

אֶצֹּק רוּחִי עַל־זַרְעֶךָ וּבִרְכָתִי עַל־צֶאֱצָאֶיךָ

bb[i] YHWH's redemption through water: Rejuvenation
of [Jacob/Israel's] offspring (44:4)

וְצָמְחוּ בְּבֵין חָצִיר כַּעֲרָבִים עַל־יִבְלֵי־מָיִם

aa[ii] Identification with Jacob/Israel as YHWH's   זֶה יֹאמַר
covenant possession (44:5)

זֶה יֹאמַר לַיהוָה אָנִי וְזֶה יִקְרָא בְשֵׁם־יַעֲקֹב
וְזֶה יִכְתֹּב יָדוֹ לַיהוָה וּבְשֵׁם יִשְׂרָאֵל יְכַנֶּה

The 'aa' tiers of this configuration correspond to one another in their
parallelism of 'Jacob' and 'Israel' (44:1, 2b, 5) and in their shared
portrayal of Jacob/Israel as YHWH's chosen possession: 'my servant
Jacob' (44:1a, 2bα), 'Israel/Jeshurun whom I have chosen' (44:1b,
2bβ). Indeed, Jacob/Israel are so much the possession of YHWH that,
in order to become YHWH's possession, others will have to take the
name of Jacob/Israel (44:5). The 'bb' tiers correspond in their
portrayal of YHWH's blessing upon nature through the outpouring of
water in springs and streams (44:3a, 4). The axis, correspondingly,
portrays YHWH's blessing upon society through the outpouring of his
spirit upon Jacob/Israel's descendants (44:3b). This consolation speech,
therefore, presents an eschatological vision of the rejuvenation of
nature and society, whose focal point YHWH will make his chosen
servant, Jacob/Israel.

As should be apparent, the reference to YHWH's redemptive outpouring of water in the desert (44:3a) alludes to the previous passage,
where similar consolatory imagery was used (i.e., 43:16-21, tier TT[i]-
A[iii]). Perhaps the reuse of imagery among these consolatory tiers attests
the author's concern to maintain some degree of thematic continuity
among tiers of similar disposition that make up the larger complex
(i.e., tier TT[i]). A similar thematic continuity also links the intervening
'B' tiers.

Isaiah 44:6-22 (the TT[i]-B[v]-tier) presents counterpoint to the foregoing consolation by means of a disputation against the idol-makers of
Jacob/Israel. This is one of the more complicated framework structures
in Isa. 40:1–54:17. The pattern that appears among the tiers designated
with double letters (i.e., 'aa', 'bb' and 'cc') is a permutation of the triadic pattern of repetitions that occurred in 43:8-13. In this tier,
however, there is no axis. Rather, the axis is virtual and may be
deduced as occurring between 44:14 and 44:15, because this is the
point where the axis should come within the triadic framework (i.e.,

between aa–aa^i—bb—cc and cc^i–bb^i–bb^ii—cc^ii—aa^ii), and because this point lies between the flanking compound frames made up of tiers 'a' and 'b', on the one hand, and 'c' and 'd', on the other. The schematic form of Isa. 44:6-22 may be diagrammed as follows:

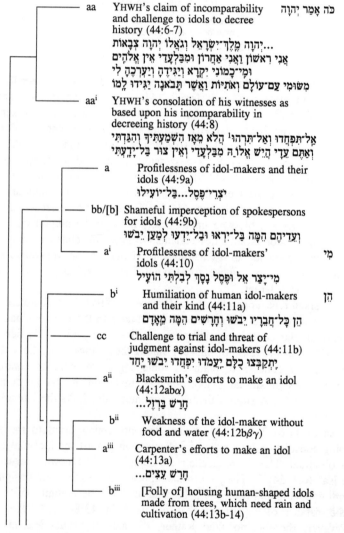

aa	YHWH's claim of incomparability and challenge to idols to decree history (44:6-7)		כֹּה אָמַר יְהוָה
	יְהוָה מֶלֶךְ־יִשְׂרָאֵל וְגֹאֲלוֹ יְהוָה צְבָאוֹת...		
	אֲנִי רִאשׁוֹן וַאֲנִי אַחֲרוֹן וּמִבַּלְעָדַי אֵין אֱלֹהִים		
	וּמִי־כָמוֹנִי יִקְרָא וְיַגִּידֶהָ וְיַעְרְכֶהָ לִי		
	מִשּׂוּמִי עַם־עוֹלָם וְאֹתִיּוֹת וַאֲשֶׁר תָּבֹאנָה יַגִּידוּ לָמוֹ		
aa^i	YHWH's consolation of his witnesses as based upon his incomparability in decreeing history (44:8)		
	אַל־תִּפְחֲדוּ וְאַל־תִּרְהוּ[1] הֲלֹא מֵאָז הִשְׁמַעְתִּיךָ וְהִגַּדְתִּי		
	וְאַתֶּם עֵדָי הֲיֵשׁ אֱלוֹהַּ מִבַּלְעָדַי וְאֵין צוּר בַּל־יָדָעְתִּי		
a	Profitlessness of idol-makers and their idols (44:9a)		
	יֹצְרֵי־פֶסֶל...בַּל־יוֹעִילוּ		
bb/[b]	Shameful imperception of spokespersons for idols (44:9b)		
	וְעֵדֵיהֶם הֵמָּה בַּל־יִרְאוּ וּבַל־יֵדְעוּ לְמַעַן יֵבֹשׁוּ		
a^i	Profitlessness of idol-makers' idols (44:10)		מִי
	מִי־יָצַר אֵל וּפֶסֶל נָסָךְ לְבִלְתִּי הוֹעִיל		
b^i	Humiliation of human idol-makers and their kind (44:11a)		הֵן
	הֵן כָּל־חֲבֵרָיו יֵבֹשׁוּ וְחָרָשִׁים הֵמָּה מֵאָדָם		
cc	Challenge to trial and threat of judgment against idol-makers (44:11b)		
	יִתְקַבְּצוּ כֻלָּם יַעֲמֹדוּ יִפְחֲדוּ יֵבֹשׁוּ יָחַד		
a^ii	Blacksmith's efforts to make an idol (44:12abα)		
	חָרַשׁ בַּרְזֶל...		
b^ii	Weakness of the idol-maker without food and water (44:12bβγ)		
a^iii	Carpenter's efforts to make an idol (44:13a)		
	חָרַשׁ עֵצִים...		
b^iii	[Folly of] housing human-shaped idols made from trees, which need rain and cultivation (44:13b-14)		

[1] 1QIsa^a witnesses תיראו (i.e., תִּירָאוּ) instead of the *hapax legomenon* תִּרְהוּ in the MT. On the authenticity of the *hapax legomenon* רהה 'to fear', see F.E. Greenspahn, *Hapax Legomena in Biblical Hebrew: A Study of the Phenomenon and Its Treatment Since Antiquity with Special Reference to Verbal Forms* (SBLDS, 74;

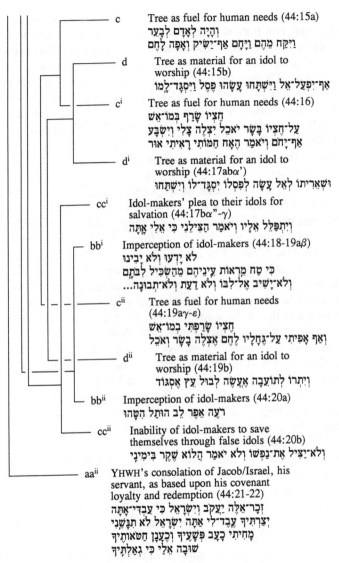

c	Tree as fuel for human needs (44:15a)

וְהָיָה לְאָדָם לְבָעֵר
וַיִּקַּח מֵהֶם וַיָּחָם אַף־יַשִּׂיק וְאָפָה לָחֶם

| d | Tree as material for an idol to worship (44:15b) |

אַף־יִפְעַל־אֵל וַיִּשְׁתָּחוּ עָשָׂהוּ פֶסֶל וַיִּסְגָּד־לָמוֹ

| cⁱ | Tree as fuel for human needs (44:16) |

חֶצְיוֹ שָׂרַף בְּמוֹ־אֵשׁ
עַל־חֶצְיוֹ בָּשָׂר יֹאכֵל יִצְלֶה צָלִי וְיִשְׂבָּע
אַף־יָחֹם וְיֹאמַר הֶאָח חַמּוֹתִי רָאִיתִי אוּר

| dⁱ | Tree as material for an idol to worship (44:17abα') |

וּשְׁאֵרִיתוֹ לְאֵל עָשָׂה לְפִסְלוֹ יִסְגָּד־לוֹ וְיִשְׁתַּחוּ

| ccⁱ | Idol-makers' plea to their idols for salvation (44:17bα"-γ) |

וְיִתְפַּלֵּל אֵלָיו וְיֹאמַר הַצִּילֵנִי כִּי אֵלִי אָתָּה

| bbⁱ | Imperception of idol-makers (44:18-19aβ) |

לֹא יָדְעוּ וְלֹא יָבִינוּ
כִּי טַח מֵרְאוֹת עֵינֵיהֶם מֵהַשְׂכִּיל לִבֹּתָם
וְלֹא־יָשִׁיב אֶל־לִבּוֹ וְלֹא דַעַת וְלֹא־תְבוּנָה...

| cⁱⁱ | Tree as fuel for human needs (44:19aγ-ε) |

חֶצְיוֹ שָׂרַפְתִּי בְמוֹ־אֵשׁ
וְאַף אָפִיתִי עַל־גֶּחָלָיו לֶחֶם אֶצְלֶה בָשָׂר וְאֹכֵל

| dⁱⁱ | Tree as material for an idol to worship (44:19b) |

וְיִתְרוֹ לְתוֹעֵבָה אֶעֱשֶׂה לְבוּל עֵץ אֶסְגּוֹד

| bbⁱⁱ | Imperception of idol-makers (44:20a) |

רֹעֶה אֵפֶר לֵב הוּתַל הִטָּהוּ

| ccⁱⁱ | Inability of idol-makers to save themselves through false idols (44:20b) |

וְלֹא־יַצִּיל אֶת־נַפְשׁוֹ וְלֹא יֹאמַר הֲלוֹא שֶׁקֶר בִּימִינִי

| aaⁱⁱ | YHWH's consolation of Jacob/Israel, his servant, as based upon his covenant loyalty and redemption (44:21-22) |

זְכָר־אֵלֶּה יַעֲקֹב וְיִשְׂרָאֵל כִּי עַבְדִּי־אָתָּה
יְצַרְתִּיךָ עֶבֶד־לִי אַתָּה יִשְׂרָאֵל לֹא תִנָּשֵׁנִי
מָחִיתִי כָעָב פְּשָׁעֶיךָ וְכֶעָנָן חַטֹּאותֶיךָ
שׁוּבָה אֵלַי כִּי גְאַלְתִּיךָ

The outer 'aa' tiers of the foregoing schema depict YHWH as Israel's 'redeemer' (44:6a, 22b). Although these tiers are consolational in disposition, they enclose a configuration of tiers that is quite disputational

Chico, CA: Scholars Press, 1984), pp. 5, 52, 55, 81, 90, 97, 100, 156, 174, 175, 179.

in tone. Hence, the overall character of Isa. 44:6-22 is disputational, though the fact that its denunciation of idolatry is framed within an affirmation of YHWH's commitment to Israel makes the disputation more poignant. The 'bb' and 'cc' tiers constitute a compound frame in which the 'bb' tiers denounce as imperceptive those who defend or make idols (44:9b, 18-19aβ, 20a) and the 'cc' tiers portray these idol-makers as summoned to trial and threatened to be put to shame (44:11b), yet unable to discern that their idols are impotent to 'save' (44:17bα"-γ, 20b).

Two further compound frames flank the virtual axis of Isa. 44:6-22. That comprising tiers 'a' and 'b' mocks the folly of mere humans who make idols in their own frail image: tiers 'a' mock the futility of effort lavished on iron and wood to form a worthless god (44:9a, 10, 12abα, 13a), and tiers 'b' heap shame upon hungry and thirsty artisans who make idols in their own frail image from trees that need rain to grow (44:[9b], 11a, 12bβγ, 13b-14). Tiers 'c' and 'd' combine to form a compound frame that mocks the folly of worshiping wood that might otherwise have been burned to meet human needs. The 'c' tiers portray the use of wood as fuel for the fire that warms or bakes (44:15a, 16, 19aγ-ε), and the 'd' tiers contrastively mock those who worship wood that has been made into an idol (44:15b, 17abα', 19b).

One finds the second pivotal hymnic invocation (Inset-A^i, 44:23) at the close of this disputational complex. Indeed, the invocation may furnish the fulcrum of the compound frame comprising tier TT^i.

Tier TT^i-B^vi (44:24–45:13) again takes up a disputation against the rebellious, except that here there is no explicit identification of the rebels who protest YHWH's benevolence toward Jerusalem/Judah//Jacob/Israel. In the bifid 'aa' tiers, YHWH affirms to himself and functions in the role of creator (subtiers 'aaα': 44:24b; 45:7, 12) and lord of salvation history (subtiers 'aaβ': 44:25-26a; 45:8, 11b). In the bifid 'bb' tiers, he promises to rebuild the ruins of Judah, Jerusalem and its temple (subtiers 'bbα': 44:26b, 28b; 45:13b), this promise being related to his appointment of Cyrus as his royal elect (subtiers 'bbβ': 44:28a; 45:1, 13a). Of the bifid 'cc' tiers, the 'ccα' halves make predictions of how YHWH would grant military victory, divine recognition and divine strengthening to his royal elect (45:2-3a, 4b, 5b), while the 'ccβ' halves state the purposes of YHWH's granting these things to his royal elect, namely, to authenticate YHWH's divine self-predications (45:3b, 6) and to redeem his servant [Jacob/Israel] (45:4a). The axis of the section is yet another divine self-predication, but it may be distinguished from the others in the section inasmuch as only here does YHWH identify himself as the only true 'god' (זוּלָתִי אֵין אֱלֹהִים, 45:5a). The section may have the following contour:

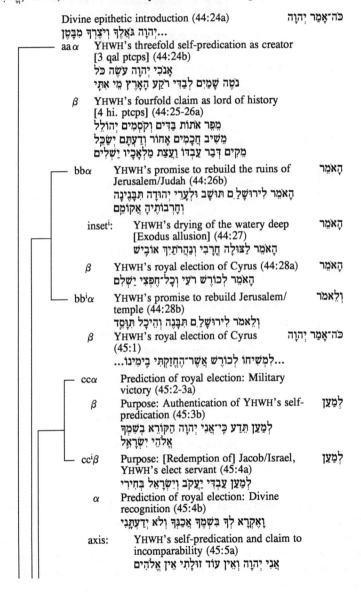

	Divine epithetic introduction (44:24a)		כֹּה־אָמַר יְהוָה
	יְהוָה גֹּאֲלֶךָ וְיֹצֶרְךָ מִבָּטֶן...		
aa α	YHWH's threefold self-predication as creator [3 qal ptcps] (44:24b)		
	אָנֹכִי יְהוָה עֹשֶׂה כֹּל		
	נֹטֶה שָׁמַיִם לְבַדִּי רֹקַע הָאָרֶץ מֵי אִתִּי		
β	YHWH's fourfold claim as lord of history [4 hi. ptcps] (44:25-26a)		
	מֵפֵר אֹתוֹת בַּדִּים וְקֹסְמִים יְהוֹלֵל		
	מֵשִׁיב חֲכָמִים אָחוֹר וְדַעְתָּם יְשַׂכֵּל		
	מֵקִים דְּבַר עַבְדּוֹ וַעֲצַת מַלְאָכָיו יַשְׁלִים		
bb α	YHWH's promise to rebuild the ruins of Jerusalem/Judah (44:26b)		הָאֹמֵר
	הָאֹמֵר לִירוּשָׁלַ ִם תּוּשָׁב וּלְעָרֵי יְהוּדָה תִּבָּנֶינָה		
	וְחָרְבוֹתֶיהָ אֲקוֹמֵם		
inset[i]:	YHWH's drying of the watery deep [Exodus allusion] (44:27)		הָאֹמֵר
	הָאֹמֵר לַצּוּלָה חֳרָבִי וְנַהֲרֹתַיִךְ אוֹבִישׁ		
β	YHWH's royal election of Cyrus (44:28a)		הָאֹמֵר
	הָאֹמֵר לְכוֹרֶשׁ רֹעִי וְכָל־חֶפְצִי יַשְׁלִם		
bb[i] α	YHWH's promise to rebuild Jerusalem/ temple (44:28b)		וְלֵאמֹר
	וְלֵאמֹר לִירוּשָׁלַ ִם תִּבָּנֶה וְהֵיכָל תִּוָּסֵד		
β	YHWH's royal election of Cyrus (45:1)		כֹּה־אָמַר יְהוָה
	לִמְשִׁיחוֹ לְכוֹרֶשׁ אֲשֶׁר־הֶחֱזַקְתִּי בִימִינוֹ...		
cc α	Prediction of royal election: Military victory (45:2-3a)		
β	Purpose: Authentication of YHWH's self-predication (45:3b)		לְמַעַן
	לְמַעַן תֵּדַע כִּי־אֲנִי יְהוָה הַקּוֹרֵא בְשִׁמְךָ		
	אֱלֹהֵי יִשְׂרָאֵל		
cc[i] β	Purpose: [Redemption of] Jacob/Israel, YHWH's elect servant (45:4a)		לְמַעַן
	לְמַעַן עַבְדִּי יַעֲקֹב וְיִשְׂרָאֵל בְּחִירִי		
α	Prediction of royal election: Divine recognition (45:4b)		
	וָאֶקְרָא לְךָ בִּשְׁמֶךָ אֲכַנְּךָ וְלֹא יְדַעְתָּנִי		
axis:	YHWH's self-predication and claim to incomparability (45:5a)		
	אֲנִי יְהוָה וְאֵין עוֹד זוּלָתִי אֵין אֱלֹהִים		

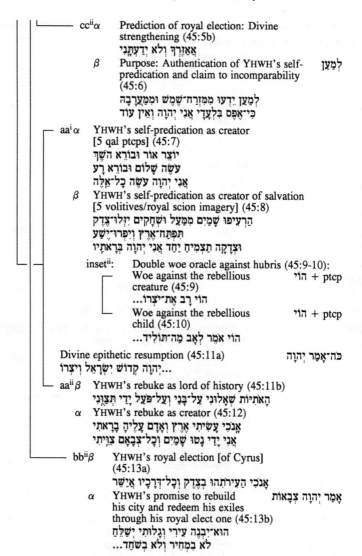

ccⁱⁱα   Prediction of royal election: Divine strengthening (45:5b)

אֲאַזֶּרְךָ וְלֹא יְדַעְתָּנִי

β   Purpose: Authentication of YHWH's self-predication and claim to incomparability (45:6)   לְמַעַן

לְמַעַן יֵדְעוּ מִמִּזְרַח־שֶׁמֶשׁ וּמִמַּעֲרָבָה
כִּי־אֶפֶס בִּלְעָדָי אֲנִי יְהוָה וְאֵין עוֹד

aaⁱα   YHWH's self-predication as creator [5 qal ptcps] (45:7)

יוֹצֵר אוֹר וּבוֹרֵא חֹשֶׁךְ
עֹשֶׂה שָׁלוֹם וּבוֹרֵא רָע
אֲנִי יְהוָה עֹשֶׂה כָל־אֵלֶּה

β   YHWH's self-predication as creator of salvation [5 volitives/royal scion imagery] (45:8)

הַרְעִיפוּ שָׁמַיִם מִמַּעַל וּשְׁחָקִים יִזְּלוּ־צֶדֶק
תִּפְתַּח־אֶרֶץ וְיִפְרוּ־יֶשַׁע
וּצְדָקָה תַצְמִיחַ יַחַד אֲנִי יְהוָה בְּרָאתִיו

insetⁱⁱ: Double woe oracle against hubris (45:9-10):
Woe against the rebellious creature (45:9)   הוֹי + ptcp

הוֹי רָב אֶת־יֹצְרוֹ...

Woe against the rebellious child (45:10)   הוֹי + ptcp

הוֹי אֹמֵר לְאָב מַה־תּוֹלִיד...

Divine epithetic resumption (45:11a)   כֹּה־אָמַר יְהוָה

...יְהוָה קְדוֹשׁ יִשְׂרָאֵל וְיֹצְרוֹ

aaⁱⁱβ   YHWH's rebuke as lord of history (45:11b)

הָאֹתִיּוֹת שְׁאָלוּנִי עַל־בָּנַי וְעַל־פֹּעַל יָדַי תְּצַוֻּנִי

α   YHWH's rebuke as creator (45:12)

אָנֹכִי עָשִׂיתִי אֶרֶץ וְאָדָם עָלֶיהָ בָרָאתִי
אֲנִי יָדַי נָטוּ שָׁמַיִם וְכָל־צְבָאָם צִוֵּיתִי

bbⁱⁱβ   YHWH's royal election [of Cyrus] (45:13a)

אָנֹכִי הַעִירֹתִהוּ בְצֶדֶק וְכָל־דְּרָכָיו אֲיַשֵּׁר

α   YHWH's promise to rebuild his city and redeem his exiles through his royal elect one (45:13b)   אָמַר יְהוָה צְבָאוֹת

הוּא־יִבְנֶה עִירִי וְגָלוּתִי יְשַׁלֵּחַ
לֹא בִמְחִיר וְלֹא בְשֹׁחַד...

The order of bifid halves of several tiers in this complex framework varies—once for each set of tier designations, whether 'aa', 'bb' or 'cc' (i.e., aaⁱⁱ, bbⁱⁱ and ccⁱ). In two instances, this reverse ordering centers about the axis (tiers aaⁱⁱ and bbⁱⁱ), which heightens the sense of concentricity in the section, but in each case the variation in order serves to heighten interest.

In Isa. 45:14–46:2 (tier TTⁱ-Aᵛ) is a threat against foreign idols and
nations that functions as a consolation of Israel/Jacob since it promises
them vindication. For this reason, it is designated an 'A' tier, along
with other tiers that aim at consoling YHWH's people. In the succeeding schema, the 'aa' tiers depict YHWH's subjugation of foreign nations
and idols, in the first instance the nation of Egypt (45:14abα), in the
latter instances the idols and idolaters of Babylon (46:1a, 1b-2). In the
bifid 'bb' tiers, the 'bbα' halves present Egypt, then YHWH, then all
the earth (cf. 45:22) confessing YHWH's incomparable deity (45:14bβ,
18b, 24a), while the 'bbβ' halves present insinuations of YHWH's hid-
denness (45:15, 19), which are then refuted by a sure prediction that all
will one day acknowledge that YHWH is God (45:23). To that end, the
'ccα' halves of the bifid 'cc' tiers present predictions of the humiliation
of idol-makers (45:16), a summons to trial of the nations who carry and
pray to idols that cannot save (45:20-21a) and an invitation of the same
to YHWH's salvation (45:22a). The 'ccβ' halves, concomitantly,
portray YHWH as Israel's only god of salvation (45:17, 21b, 22b, 25).
The axis sets forth three pairs of epithetic ascriptions of praise to
YHWH, creator of a world that he made to be inhabited (45:18a),
presumably by those whom he will save. The patterning of triadic
frames in this subsection may be outlined in the following manner:

aa	YHWH's subjugation of Egypt (45:14abα)	כֹּה אָמַר יְהוָה
	...יְגִיעַ מִצְרַיִם וּסְחַר־כּוּשׁ וּסְבָאִים אַנְשֵׁי מִדָּה	
	עָלַיִךְ יַעֲבֹרוּ וְלָךְ יִהְיוּ אַחֲרַיִךְ יֵלֵכוּ בַּזִּקִּים יַעֲבֹרוּ	
	וְאֵלַיִךְ יִשְׁתַּחֲווּ אֵלַיִךְ יִתְפַּלָּלוּ	
bbα	Egypt's confession of YHWH's incomparability (45:14bβ)	אַךְ
	אַךְ בָּךְ אֵל וְאֵין עוֹד אֶפֶס אֱלֹהִים	
β	Insinuation of YHWH's hiddenness (45:15)	אָכֵן
	אָכֵן אַתָּה אֵל מִסְתַּתֵּר אֱלֹהֵי יִשְׂרָאֵל מוֹשִׁיעַ	
ccα	Humiliation of idol-makers (45:16)	
	בּוֹשׁוּ וְגַם־נִכְלְמוּ כֻּלָּם יַחְדָּו	
	הָלְכוּ בַכְּלִמָּה חָרָשֵׁי צִירִים	
β	Eternal salvation of Israel (45:17)	
	יִשְׂרָאֵל נוֹשַׁע בַּיהוָה תְּשׁוּעַת עוֹלָמִים	
	לֹא־תֵבֹשׁוּ וְלֹא־תִכָּלְמוּ עַד־עוֹלְמֵי עַד	
axis:	Prophetic ascription of praise to YHWH the creator (45:18a)	כִּי כֹה אָמַר־יְהוָה
	...יְהוָה בּוֹרֵא הַשָּׁמַיִם הוּא הָאֱלֹהִים	
	יֹצֵר הָאָרֶץ וְעֹשָׂהּ הוּא כוֹנְנָהּ	
	לֹא־תֹהוּ בְרָאָהּ לָשֶׁבֶת יְצָרָהּ	

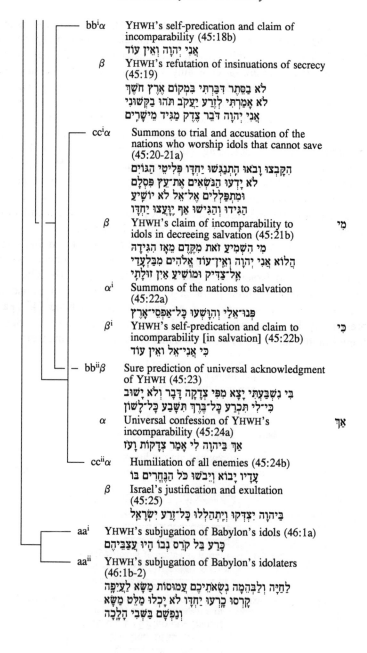

bbⁱα   YHWH's self-predication and claim of incomparability (45:18b)

אֲנִי יְהוָה וְאֵין עוֹד

β   YHWH's refutation of insinuations of secrecy (45:19)

לֹא בַסֵּתֶר דִּבַּרְתִּי בִּמְקוֹם אֶרֶץ חֹשֶׁךְ
לֹא אָמַרְתִּי לְזֶרַע יַעֲקֹב תֹּהוּ בַקְּשׁוּנִי
אֲנִי יְהוָה דֹּבֵר צֶדֶק מַגִּיד מֵישָׁרִים

ccⁱα   Summons to trial and accusation of the nations who worship idols that cannot save (45:20-21a)

הִקָּבְצוּ וָבֹאוּ הִתְנַגְּשׁוּ יַחְדָּו פְּלִיטֵי הַגּוֹיִם
לֹא יָדְעוּ הַנֹּשְׂאִים אֶת־עֵץ פִּסְלָם
וּמִתְפַּלְלִים אֶל־אֵל לֹא יוֹשִׁיעַ
הַגִּידוּ וְהַגִּישׁוּ אַף יִוָּעֲצוּ יַחְדָּו

β   YHWH's claim of incomparability to idols in decreeing salvation (45:21b)   מִי

מִי הִשְׁמִיעַ זֹאת מִקֶּדֶם מֵאָז הִגִּידָהּ
הֲלוֹא אֲנִי יְהוָה וְאֵין־עוֹד אֱלֹהִים מִבַּלְעָדַי
אֵל־צַדִּיק וּמוֹשִׁיעַ אַיִן זוּלָתִי

αⁱ   Summons of the nations to salvation (45:22a)

פְּנוּ־אֵלַי וְהִוָּשְׁעוּ כָּל־אַפְסֵי־אָרֶץ

βⁱ   YHWH's self-predication and claim to incomparability [in salvation] (45:22b)   כִּי

כִּי אֲנִי־אֵל וְאֵין עוֹד

bbⁱⁱβ   Sure prediction of universal acknowledgment of YHWH (45:23)

בִּי נִשְׁבַּעְתִּי יָצָא מִפִּי צְדָקָה דָּבָר וְלֹא יָשׁוּב
כִּי־לִי תִּכְרַע כָּל־בֶּרֶךְ תִּשָּׁבַע כָּל־לָשׁוֹן

α   Universal confession of YHWH's incomparability (45:24a)   אַךְ

אַךְ בַּיהוָה לִי אָמַר צְדָקוֹת וָעֹז

ccⁱⁱα   Humiliation of all enemies (45:24b)

עָדָיו יָבוֹא וְיֵבֹשׁוּ כֹל הַנֶּחֱרִים בּוֹ

β   Israel's justification and exultation (45:25)

בַּיהוָה יִצְדְּקוּ וְיִתְהַלְלוּ כָּל־זֶרַע יִשְׂרָאֵל

aaⁱ   YHWH's subjugation of Babylon's idols (46:1a)

כָּרַע בֵּל קֹרֵס נְבוֹ הָיוּ עֲצַבֵּיהֶם

aaⁱⁱ   YHWH's subjugation of Babylon's idolaters (46:1b-2)

לַחַיָּה וְלַבְּהֵמָה נְשֻׂאֹתֵיכֶם עֲמוּסוֹת מַשָּׂא לַעֲיֵפָה
קָרְסוּ כָרְעוּ יַחְדָּו לֹא יָכְלוּ מַלֵּט מַשָּׂא
וְנַפְשָׁם בַּשְּׁבִי הָלָכָה

The final tier of the TT[i] complex appears in 46:3-13 (tier TT[i]-B[vii]). Its complex framework structure may be outlined as follows:

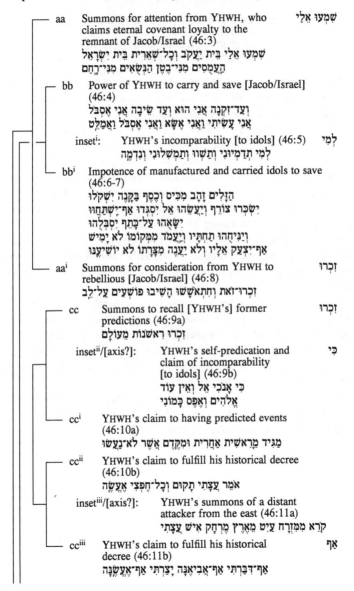

aa	Summons for attention from YHWH, who claims eternal covenant loyalty to the remnant of Jacob/Israel (46:3)		שִׁמְעוּ אֵלַי

שִׁמְעוּ אֵלַי בֵּית יַעֲקֹב וְכָל־שְׁאֵרִית בֵּית יִשְׂרָאֵל
הַעֲמֻסִים מִנִּי־בֶטֶן הַנְּשֻׂאִים מִנִּי־רָחַם

| bb | Power of YHWH to carry and save [Jacob/Israel] (46:4) |

וְעַד־זִקְנָה אֲנִי הוּא וְעַד־שֵׂיבָה אֲנִי אֶסְבֹּל
אֲנִי עָשִׂיתִי וַאֲנִי אֶשָּׂא וַאֲנִי אֶסְבֹּל וַאֲמַלֵּט

| inset[i]: | YHWH's incomparability [to idols] (46:5) | | לְמִי |

לְמִי תְדַמְיוּנִי וְתַשְׁווּ וְתַמְשִׁלוּנִי וְנִדְמֶה

| bb[i] | Impotence of manufactured and carried idols to save (46:6-7) |

הַזָּלִים זָהָב מִכִּיס וְכֶסֶף בַּקָּנֶה יִשְׁקֹלוּ
יִשְׂכְּרוּ צוֹרֵף וְיַעֲשֵׂהוּ אֵל יִסְגְּדוּ אַף־יִשְׁתַּחֲווּ
יִשָּׂאֻהוּ עַל־כָּתֵף יִסְבְּלֻהוּ
וְיַנִּיחֻהוּ תַחְתָּיו וְיַעֲמֹד מִמְּקוֹמוֹ לֹא יָמִישׁ
אַף־יִצְעַק אֵלָיו וְלֹא יַעֲנֶה מִצָּרָתוֹ לֹא יוֹשִׁיעֶנּוּ

| aa[i] | Summons for consideration from YHWH to rebellious [Jacob/Israel] (46:8) | | זִכְרוּ |

זִכְרוּ־זֹאת וְהִתְאֹשָׁשׁוּ הָשִׁיבוּ פוֹשְׁעִים עַל־לֵב

| cc | Summons to recall [YHWH's] former predictions (46:9a) | | זִכְרוּ |

זִכְרוּ רִאשֹׁנוֹת מֵעוֹלָם

| inset[ii]/[axis?]: | YHWH's self-predication and claim of incomparability [to idols] (46:9b) | | כִּי |

כִּי אָנֹכִי אֵל וְאֵין עוֹד
אֱלֹהִים וְאֶפֶס כָּמוֹנִי

| cc[i] | YHWH's claim to having predicted events (46:10a) |

מַגִּיד מֵרֵאשִׁית אַחֲרִית וּמִקֶּדֶם אֲשֶׁר לֹא־נַעֲשׂוּ

| cc[ii] | YHWH's claim to fulfill his historical decree (46:10b) |

אֹמֵר עֲצָתִי תָקוּם וְכָל־חֶפְצִי אֶעֱשֶׂה

| inset[iii]/[axis?]: | YHWH's summons of a distant attacker from the east (46:11a) |

קֹרֵא מִמִּזְרָח עַיִט מֵאֶרֶץ מֶרְחָק אִישׁ עֲצָתִי

| cc[iii] | YHWH's claim to fulfill his historical decree (46:11b) | | אַף |

אַף־דִּבַּרְתִּי אַף־אֲבִיאֶנָּה יָצַרְתִּי אַף־אֶעֱשֶׂנָּה

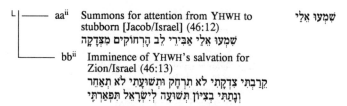

aaⁱⁱ Summons for attention from YHWH to stubborn [Jacob/Israel] (46:12)

שִׁמְעוּ אֵלַי

שִׁמְעוּ אֵלַי אַבִּירֵי לֵב הָרְחוֹקִים מִצְּדָקָה

bbⁱⁱ Imminence of YHWH's salvation for Zion/Israel (46:13)

קֵרַבְתִּי צִדְקָתִי לֹא תִרְחָק וּתְשׁוּעָתִי לֹא תְאַחֵר

וְנָתַתִּי בְצִיּוֹן תְּשׁוּעָה לְיִשְׂרָאֵל תִּפְאַרְתִּי

The 'aa' tiers of the foregoing schema correspond in their function as YHWH's summons of the rebellious remnant of Jacob/Israel to attention, each beginning with a command: שִׁמְעוּ 'hear' (46:3, 8, 12) or זִכְרוּ...הָשִׁיבוּ...עַל־לֵב 'remember ... take ... to heart' (46:8). The 'bb' tiers contrast the power of YHWH to that of idols in regard to their ability to save Zion//Jacob/Israel (46:4, 6-7, 13). To the 'cc' tiers belong a general summons to consider YHWH's predictions in regard to salvation history (46:9a) and his claims to have fulfilled them (46:10a, 10b, 11b). The insets here punctuate and separate the repetitions of similar tiers (i.e., separating bb from bbⁱ, cc from ccⁱ, and ccⁱⁱ from ccⁱⁱⁱ) by repeating the motif of YHWH's incomparability to idols (46:5, 9b) and by giving one example of YHWH's control of history, that of his summoning a distant attacker from the east (46:11a [rhetorical axis?]).

This disputational complex presents a quadratic frame (tiers 'cc') within a compound frame made up of tiers 'aa' and 'bb'. This is another example of frameworking where the formal axis is virtual, unless, for rhetorical reasons, one views either insetⁱⁱ (46:9b) or insetⁱⁱⁱ (46:11a) as functioning in that capacity, despite its not occurring where expected, between tiers ccⁱ and ccⁱⁱ.

The TTⁱⁱ-Bᵛⁱⁱⁱ-tier (48:1-13) stands isolated between the sectional axis (47:8-15) and the final 'UU' tier (48:14-22). It bears throughout a disputational tone and may take the following form:

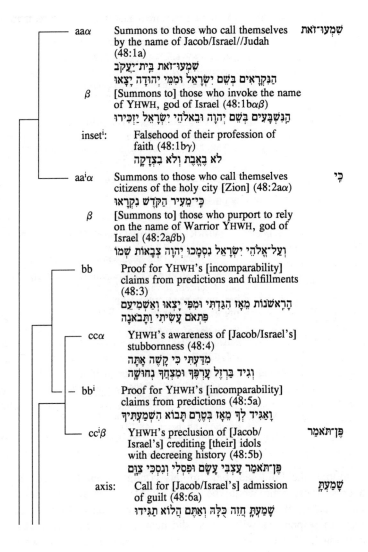

aaα   Summons to those who call themselves   שִׁמְעוּ־זֹאת
by the name of Jacob/Israel//Judah
(48:1a)

שִׁמְעוּ־זֹאת בֵּית־יַעֲקֹב
הַנִּקְרָאִים בְּשֵׁם יִשְׂרָאֵל וּמִמֵּי יְהוּדָה יָצָאוּ

β   [Summons to] those who invoke the name
of YHWH, god of Israel (48:1bαβ)

הַנִּשְׁבָּעִים בְּשֵׁם יְהוָה וּבֵאלֹהֵי יִשְׂרָאֵל יַזְכִּירוּ

inset[i]:   Falsehood of their profession of
faith (48:1bγ)

לֹא בֶאֱמֶת וְלֹא בִצְדָקָה

aa[i]α   Summons to those who call themselves   כִּי
citizens of the holy city [Zion] (48:2aα)

כִּי־מֵעִיר הַקֹּדֶשׁ נִקְרָאוּ

β   [Summons to] those who purport to rely
on the name of Warrior YHWH, god of
Israel (48:2aβb)

וְעַל־אֱלֹהֵי יִשְׂרָאֵל נִסְמָכוּ יְהוָה צְבָאוֹת שְׁמוֹ

bb   Proof for YHWH's [incomparability]
claims from predictions and fulfillments
(48:3)

הָרִאשֹׁנוֹת מֵאָז הִגַּדְתִּי וּמִפִּי יָצְאוּ וְאַשְׁמִיעֵם
פִּתְאֹם עָשִׂיתִי וַתָּבֹאנָה

ccα   YHWH's awareness of [Jacob/Israel's]
stubbornness (48:4)

מִדַּעְתִּי כִּי קָשֶׁה אָתָּה
וְגִיד בַּרְזֶל עָרְפֶּךָ וּמִצְחֲךָ נְחוּשָׁה

bb[i]   Proof for YHWH's [incomparability]
claims from predictions (48:5a)

וָאַגִּיד לְךָ מֵאָז בְּטֶרֶם תָּבוֹא הִשְׁמַעְתִּיךָ

cc[i]β   YHWH's preclusion of [Jacob/   פֶּן־תֹּאמַר
Israel's] crediting [their] idols
with decreeing history (48:5b)

פֶּן־תֹּאמַר עָצְבִּי עָשָׂם וּפִסְלִי וְנִסְכִּי צִוָּם

axis: Call for [Jacob/Israel's] admission   שָׁמַעְתָּ
of guilt (48:6a)

שָׁמַעְתָּ חֲזֵה כֻּלָּה וְאַתֶּם הֲלוֹא תַגִּידוּ

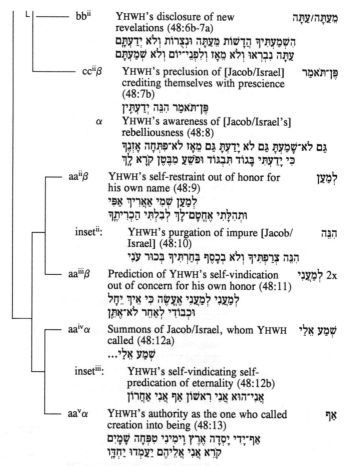

L — bbⁱⁱ YHWH's disclosure of new revelations (48:6b-7a) מֵעַתָּה/עַתָּה

הִשְׁמַעְתִּיךָ הֲדָשׁוֹת מֵעַתָּה וּנְצֻרוֹת וְלֹא יְדַעְתָּם
עַתָּה נִבְרְאוּ וְלֹא מֵאָז וְלִפְנֵי־יוֹם וְלֹא שְׁמַעְתָּם

ccⁱⁱβ YHWH's preclusion of [Jacob/Israel] crediting themselves with prescience (48:7b) פֶּן־תֹּאמַר

פֶּן־תֹּאמַר הִנֵּה יְדַעְתִּין

α YHWH's awareness of [Jacob/Israel's] rebelliousness (48:8)

גַּם לֹא־שָׁמַעְתָּ גַּם לֹא יָדַעְתָּ גַּם מֵאָז לֹא־פִּתְּחָה אָזְנֶךָ
כִּי יָדַעְתִּי בָּגוֹד תִּבְגּוֹד וּפֹשֵׁעַ מִבֶּטֶן קֹרָא לָךְ

aaⁱⁱβ YHWH's self-restraint out of honor for his own name (48:9) לְמַעַן

לְמַעַן שְׁמִי אַאֲרִיךְ אַפִּי
וּתְהִלָּתִי אֶחֱטָם־לָךְ לְבִלְתִּי הַכְרִיתֶךָ

insetⁱⁱ: YHWH's purgation of impure [Jacob/Israel] (48:10) הִנֵּה

הִנֵּה צְרַפְתִּיךָ וְלֹא בְכָסֶף בְּחַרְתִּיךָ בְּכוּר עֹנִי

aaⁱⁱⁱβ Prediction of YHWH's self-vindication out of concern for his own honor (48:11) לְמַעֲנִי 2x

לְמַעֲנִי לְמַעֲנִי אֶעֱשֶׂה כִּי אֵיךְ יֵחָל
וּכְבוֹדִי לְאַחֵר לֹא־אֶתֵּן

aaⁱᵛα Summons of Jacob/Israel, whom YHWH called (48:12a) שְׁמַע אֵלַי

שְׁמַע אֵלַי...

insetⁱⁱⁱ: YHWH's self-vindicating self-predication of eternality (48:12b)

אֲנִי־הוּא אֲנִי רִאשׁוֹן אַף אֲנִי אַחֲרוֹן

aaᵛα YHWH's authority as the one who called creation into being (48:13) אַף

אַף־יָדִי יָסְדָה אֶרֶץ וִימִינִי טִפְּחָה שָׁמָיִם
קֹרֵא אֲנִי אֲלֵיהֶם יַעַמְדוּ יַחְדָּו

Among the bifid 'aa' tiers of this configuration, the 'aaα' halves address those who would be called (נִקְרָא) either Jacob/Israel (aaα, 48:1a; aaⁱᵛα, 48:12a) or citizens of the holy city (aaⁱα, 48:2aα), calling them to respond as willingly as did heaven and earth when called at creation (קֹרֵא, aaᵛα, 48:13). The 'aaβ' halves concern those who purport to venerate YHWH/God's name (שֵׁם), whether by invoking or claiming to rely upon (aaβ, 48:1bαβ; aaⁱβ, 48:2aβb) the name that YHWH holds in honor (aaⁱⁱβ, 48:9; aaⁱⁱⁱβ, 48:11). The 'bb' tiers portray YHWH demonstrating his incomparability to other gods in revealing to his people in advance what is to come. The 'cc' tiers serve to rebuff Jacob/Israel for their arrogance and rebelliousness in failing to respond appropriately to YHWH's exclusive claims upon their loyalty. The incongruity between a revealing god and an obstinate people is illustrated in the way that the first two 'bb' tiers, which claim that YHWH's forecasts had been previously 'declared' (הִגַּדְתִּי, bb, 48:3; וָאַגִּיד, bbⁱ, 48:5a), find paronomastic and ironic contrast to the intervening characterization of Israel as having responded with iron-tendoned necks (וְגִיד בַּרְזֶל עָרְפֶּךָ, ccα, 48:4). The axis (48:6a) presses the issue of the incongruity among the themes of the 'aa', 'bb' and 'cc' tiers by summoning from Jacob/Israel an admission of guilt in regard to their claim to having been a people who honor YHWH's name. Correspondingly, the insets of this section variously accuse Jacob/Israel of making an impure profession of loyalty to YHWH's name (48:1bγ), justify YHWH's purgation of that impurity through affliction (48:10) and reaffirm for Jacob/Israel that YHWH alone is God (48:12b).

The first tier of the TTⁱⁱⁱ complex, designated TTⁱⁱⁱ-Bⁱˣ (49:1-12), is the first of three songs of the servant's vindication before Israel/Zion or the nations. Each of the songs of vindication functions as a prophetic disputation against Israel/Zion for having rejected or mistreated YHWH's servant. The complex framework structure of 49:1-12 may be outlined as follows:

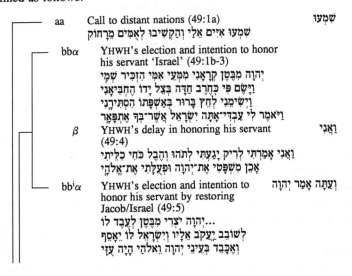

aa	Call to distant nations (49:1a)		שִׁמְעוּ
	שִׁמְעוּ אִיִּים אֵלַי וְהַקְשִׁיבוּ לְאֻמִּים מֵרָחוֹק		
bbα	YHWH's election and intention to honor his servant 'Israel' (49:1b-3)		
	יְהוָה מִבֶּטֶן קְרָאָנִי מִמְּעֵי אִמִּי הִזְכִּיר שְׁמִי		
	וַיָּשֶׂם פִּי כְּחֶרֶב חַדָּה בְּצֵל יָדוֹ הֶחְבִּיאָנִי		
	וַיְשִׂימֵנִי לְחֵץ בָּרוּר בְּאַשְׁפָּתוֹ הִסְתִּירָנִי		
	וַיֹּאמֶר לִי עַבְדִּי־אָתָּה יִשְׂרָאֵל אֲשֶׁר־בְּךָ אֶתְפָּאָר		
β	YHWH's delay in honoring his servant (49:4)		וַאֲנִי
	וַאֲנִי אָמַרְתִּי לְרִיק יָגַעְתִּי לְתֹהוּ וְהֶבֶל כֹּחִי כִלֵּיתִי		
	אָכֵן מִשְׁפָּטִי אֶת־יְהוָה וּפְעֻלָּתִי אֶת־אֱלֹהָי		
bbⁱα	YHWH's election and intention to honor his servant by restoring Jacob/Israel (49:5)		וְעַתָּה אָמַר יְהוָה
	...יְהוָה יֹצְרִי מִבֶּטֶן לְעֶבֶד לוֹ		
	לְשׁוֹבֵב יַעֲקֹב אֵלָיו וְיִשְׂרָאֵל לוֹ יֵאָסֵף		
	וְאֶכָּבֵד בְּעֵינֵי יְהוָה וֵאלֹהַי הָיָה עֻזִּי		

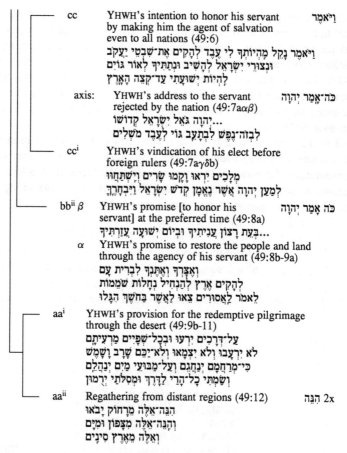

cc YHWH's intention to honor his servant by making him the agent of salvation even to all nations (49:6)   וַיֹּאמֶר

וַיֹּאמֶר נָקֵל מִהְיוֹתְךָ לִי עֶבֶד לְהָקִים אֶת־שִׁבְטֵי יַעֲקֹב
וּנְצוּרֵי יִשְׂרָאֵל לְהָשִׁיב וּנְתַתִּיךָ לְאוֹר גּוֹיִם
לִהְיוֹת יְשׁוּעָתִי עַד־קְצֵה הָאָרֶץ

axis: YHWH's address to the servant rejected by the nation (49:7aαβ)   כֹּה־אָמַר יְהוָה

...יְהוָה גֹּאֵל יִשְׂרָאֵל קְדוֹשׁוֹ
לִבְזֹה־נֶפֶשׁ לִמְתָעֵב גּוֹי לְעֶבֶד מֹשְׁלִים

cc[i] YHWH's vindication of his elect before foreign rulers (49:7aγδb)

מְלָכִים יִרְאוּ וָקָמוּ שָׂרִים וְיִשְׁתַּחֲווּ
לְמַעַן יְהוָה אֲשֶׁר נֶאֱמָן קְדֹשׁ יִשְׂרָאֵל וַיִּבְחָרֶךָ

bb[ii] β YHWH's promise [to honor his servant] at the preferred time (49:8a)   כֹּה אָמַר יְהוָה

...בְּעֵת רָצוֹן עֲנִיתִיךָ וּבְיוֹם יְשׁוּעָה עֲזַרְתִּיךָ

α YHWH's promise to restore the people and land through the agency of his servant (49:8b-9a)

וְאֶצָּרְךָ וְאֶתֶּנְךָ לִבְרִית עָם
לְהָקִים אֶרֶץ לְהַנְחִיל נְחָלוֹת שְׁמֵמוֹת
לֵאמֹר לַאֲסוּרִים צֵאוּ לַאֲשֶׁר בַּחֹשֶׁךְ הִגָּלוּ

aa[i] YHWH's provision for the redemptive pilgrimage through the desert (49:9b-11)

עַל־דְּרָכִים יִרְעוּ וּבְכָל־שְׁפָיִים מַרְעִיתָם
לֹא יִרְעָבוּ וְלֹא יִצְמָאוּ וְלֹא־יַכֵּם שָׁרָב וָשָׁמֶשׁ
כִּי־מְרַחֲמָם יְנַהֲגֵם וְעַל־מַבּוּעֵי מַיִם יְנַהֲלֵם
וְשַׂמְתִּי כָל־הָרַי לַדָּרֶךְ וּמְסִלֹּתַי יְרֻמוּן

aa[ii] Regathering from distant regions (49:12)   הִנֵּה 2x

הִנֵּה־אֵלֶּה מֵרָחוֹק יָבֹאוּ
וְהִנֵּה־אֵלֶּה מִצָּפוֹן וּמִיָּם
וְאֵלֶּה מֵאֶרֶץ סִינִים

The tiers of the preceding schema have been arranged according to the following criteria. The 'aa' tiers correspond inasmuch as together they portray YHWH summoning his people to return from distant nations: there is a call to the distant nations (49:1a), a promise to make provision for the redemptive pilgrimage of his people through the desert (49:9b-11) and a prediction that they will come from all the distant regions of the world (49:12). The 'bbα' elements of the bifid 'bb' tiers depict YHWH's intention to honor his servant 'Israel' by making his (prophetic) servant the agent of Jacob/Israel's restoration from captivity (49:1b-3, 5, 8b-9a). The 'bbβ' elements, however, express both the servant's confidence in YHWH despite his delay in honoring him (49:4) and YHWH's assurance of his servant that the deferral will last only until the preferred time, the 'day of salvation' (49:8a). The paired 'cc' tiers match in their mutual portrayal of YHWH's intention to make his servant the agent of salvation not only for Jacob/Israel but for all nations and thus to honor him even before foreign kings and princes (49:6, 7aγδb). The axis affirms that YHWH has addressed these promises, made in the surrounding context, to his servant, 'to him who was despised and abhorred by the nation [Jacob/Israel], to the servant of rulers' (49:7aαβ).

Tier TT[iii]-A[vi] (49:14–50:3) is a rhetorically ambiguous complex that is seemingly both consolatory and disputational. It is designated a '(disputational) consolation', however, under the force of its position in relation to the servant songs of tier TT[iii]. In what follows, I offer a model of how its framework structure may be outlined:

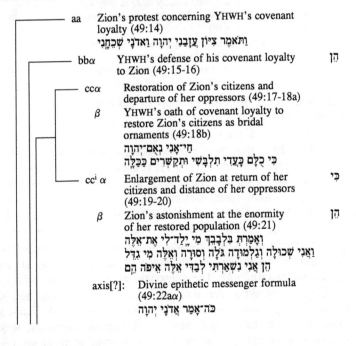

aa	Zion's protest concerning YHWH's covenant loyalty (49:14)	
	וַתֹּאמֶר צִיּוֹן עֲזָבַנִי יְהוָה וַאדֹנָי שְׁכֵחָנִי	
bbα	YHWH's defense of his covenant loyalty to Zion (49:15-16)	הֵן
ccα	Restoration of Zion's citizens and departure of her oppressors (49:17-18a)	
β	YHWH's oath of covenant loyalty to restore Zion's citizens as bridal ornaments (49:18b)	
	חַי־אָנִי נְאֻם־יְהוָה	
	כִּי כֻלָּם כָּעֲדִי תִלְבָּשִׁי וּתְקַשְּׁרִים כַּכַּלָּה	
cc[i] α	Enlargement of Zion at return of her citizens and distance of her oppressors (49:19-20)	כִּי
β	Zion's astonishment at the enormity of her restored population (49:21)	הֵן
	וְאָמַרְתְּ בִּלְבָבֵךְ מִי יָלַד־לִי אֶת־אֵלֶּה	
	וַאֲנִי שְׁכוּלָה וְגַלְמוּדָה גֹּלָה וְסוּרָה וְאֵלֶּה מִי גִדֵּל	
	הֵן אֲנִי נִשְׁאַרְתִּי לְבַדִּי אֵלֶּה אֵיפֹה הֵם	
axis[?]:	Divine epithetic messenger formula (49:22aα)	
	כֹּה־אָמַר אֲדֹנָי יְהוָה	

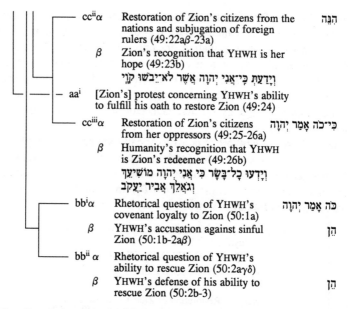

ccⁱⁱα		Restoration of Zion's citizens from the nations and subjugation of foreign rulers (49:22aβ-23a)	הִנֵּה
	β	Zion's recognition that YHWH is her hope (49:23b)	
		וְיָדַעַתְּ כִּי־אֲנִי יְהוָה אֲשֶׁר לֹא־יֵבֹשׁוּ קֹוָי	
aaⁱ		[Zion's] protest concerning YHWH's ability to fulfill his oath to restore Zion (49:24)	
ccⁱⁱⁱα		Restoration of Zion's citizens from her oppressors (49:25-26a)	כִּי־כֹה אָמַר יְהוָה
	β	Humanity's recognition that YHWH is Zion's redeemer (49:26b)	
		וְיָדְעוּ כָל־בָּשָׂר כִּי אֲנִי יְהוָה מוֹשִׁיעֵךְ	
		וְגֹאֲלֵךְ אֲבִיר יַעֲקֹב	
bbⁱα		Rhetorical question of YHWH's covenant loyalty to Zion (50:1a)	כֹּה אָמַר יְהוָה
	β	YHWH's accusation against sinful Zion (50:1b-2aβ)	הֵן
bbⁱⁱ α		Rhetorical question of YHWH's ability to rescue Zion (50:2aγδ)	
	β	YHWH's defense of his ability to rescue Zion (50:2b-3)	הֵן

The disputational 'aa' and 'bb' tiers of this configuration ostensibly frame the consolational language of the 'cc' tiers, which results in a poignant mixture of their contrasting dispositions toward YHWH's people. Both the 'aa' tiers of the foregoing diagram present protests from Zion, once concerning YHWH's alleged covenant disloyalty (49:14) and once regarding his ability to fulfill his oath to restore Zion's citizens from their captors (49:24). Against these implicit accusations, the 'bbα' tiers answer that YHWH has been loyal to Zion (49:15-16; 50:1a, 2aγδ), while the 'bbβ' tiers respond with a counteraccusation that it is Zion who has been sinful (50:1b-2aβ) and an attestation of YHWH's power to rescue as demonstrated by his control over nature (50:2b-3). The consolational 'cc' tiers are bifid, the 'ccα' halves portraying the restoration of Zion's citizens and the simultaneous expulsion of her oppressors (49:17-18a, 19-20, 22aβ-23a, 25-26a), the 'ccβ' halves depicting Zion's various responses, which include putting on her restored citizens like a bridal garment (49:18b), reacting with astonishment at the enormity of her restored population (49:21) and recognizing that it is YHWH who has fulfilled her hope (49:23b), a recognition that will eventually be shared by all humankind (49:26b).

The third tier of the TT[iii] complex (TT[iii]-B[x], 50:4-11) is, like its first tier, disputational by virtue of its rhetorical function as a vindication of YHWH's servant against Zion's rejection of his message. Its structure appears as follows:

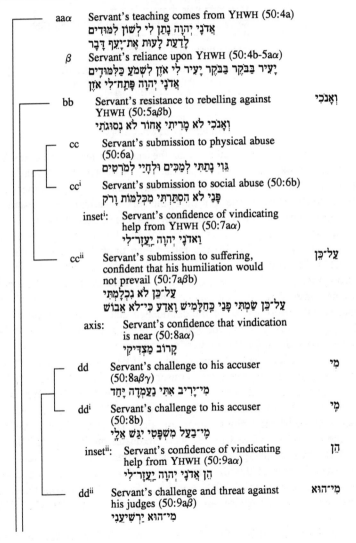

aaα	Servant's teaching comes from YHWH (50:4a)	
	אֲדֹנָי יְהוָה נָתַן לִי לְשׁוֹן לִמּוּדִים	
	לָדַעַת לָעוּת אֶת־יָעֵף דָּבָר	
β	Servant's reliance upon YHWH (50:4b-5aα)	
	יָעִיר בַּבֹּקֶר בַּבֹּקֶר יָעִיר לִי אֹזֶן לִשְׁמֹעַ כַּלִּמּוּדִים	
	אֲדֹנָי יְהוָה פָּתַח־לִי אֹזֶן	
bb	Servant's resistance to rebelling against YHWH (50:5aβb)	וְאָנֹכִי
	וְאָנֹכִי לֹא מָרִיתִי אָחוֹר לֹא נְסוּגֹתִי	
cc	Servant's submission to physical abuse (50:6a)	
	גֵּוִי נָתַתִּי לְמַכִּים וּלְחָיַי לְמֹרְטִים	
cc[i]	Servant's submission to social abuse (50:6b)	
	פָּנַי לֹא הִסְתַּרְתִּי מִכְּלִמּוֹת וָרֹק	
inset[i]:	Servant's confidence of vindicating help from YHWH (50:7aα)	
	וַאדֹנָי יְהוָה יַעֲזָר־לִי	
cc[ii]	Servant's submission to suffering, confident that his humiliation would not prevail (50:7aβb)	עַל־כֵּן
	עַל־כֵּן לֹא נִכְלָמְתִּי	
	עַל־כֵּן שַׂמְתִּי פָנַי כַּחַלָּמִישׁ וָאֵדַע כִּי־לֹא אֵבוֹשׁ	
axis:	Servant's confidence that vindication is near (50:8aα)	
	קָרוֹב מַצְדִּיקִי	
dd	Servant's challenge to his accuser (50:8aβγ)	מִי
	מִי־יָרִיב אִתִּי נַעַמְדָה יָּחַד	
dd[i]	Servant's challenge to his accuser (50:8b)	מִי
	מִי־בַעַל מִשְׁפָּטִי יִגַּשׁ אֵלָי	
inset[ii]:	Servant's confidence of vindicating help from YHWH (50:9aα)	הֵן
	הֵן אֲדֹנָי יְהוָה יַעֲזָר־לִי	
dd[ii]	Servant's challenge and threat against his judges (50:9aβ)	מִי־הוּא
	מִי־הוּא יַרְשִׁיעֵנִי	

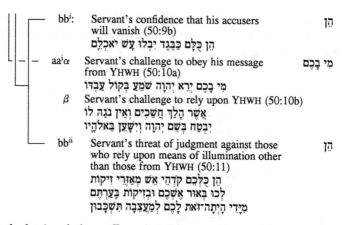

bbⁱ: Servant's confidence that his accusers הֵן
will vanish (50:9b)

הֵן כֻּלָּם כַּבֶּגֶד יִבְלוּ עָשׁ יֹאכְלֵם

aaⁱα Servant's challenge to obey his message מִי בָכֶם
from YHWH (50:10a)

מִי בָכֶם יְרֵא יְהוָה שֹׁמֵעַ בְּקוֹל עַבְדּוֹ

β Servant's challenge to rely upon YHWH (50:10b)

אֲשֶׁר הָלַךְ חֲשֵׁכִים וְאֵין נֹגַהּ לוֹ
יִבְטַח בְּשֵׁם יְהוָה וְיִשָּׁעֵן בֵּאלֹהָיו

bbⁱⁱ Servant's threat of judgment against those הֵן
who rely upon means of illumination other
than those from YHWH (50:11)

הֵן כֻּלְּכֶם קֹדְחֵי אֵשׁ מְאַזְּרֵי זִיקוֹת
לְכוּ בְּאוּר אֶשְׁכֶם וּבְזִיקוֹת בִּעַרְתֶּם
מִיָּדִי הָיְתָה־זֹּאת לָכֶם לְמַעֲצֵבָה תִּשְׁכָּבוּן

Both the 'aaα' tiers affirm that the servant's teaching comes from
YHWH (50:4a, 10a), while the 'aaβ' tiers depict the servant's continuous reliance upon YHWH (50:4b-5aα) and his urging of others to do
likewise (50:10b). In the 'bb' tiers, the servant affirms his resistance to
rebelling against YHWH (50:5aβb), his confidence that he will be
exonerated before his accusers (50:9b) and his threat against all who
rely upon rites of illumination rather than upon YHWH's illumination
(50:11). Enclosed within the framework of the 'aa' and 'bb' tiers are
two discrete triadic frames, each with an inset as its axis. The triadic
frame comprising tiers 'cc' depicts the servant's submission to physical
and social sufferings out of the confidence that, in the end, he will not
be put to shame (50:6a, 6b, 7aβb). Its ostensible axis, insetⁱ (50:7aα),
states the reason for the servant's confidence: 'The Lord YHWH will
help me'. In the triadic frame made up of tiers 'dd', the servant turns
to challenge and threaten his accusers/judges (50:8aβγ, 8b, 9aβ). Its
ostensible axis, insetⁱⁱ (50:9aα), reiterates his confidence: 'Watch, the
Lord YHWH will help me'. The axis of the TTⁱⁱⁱ complex, positioned
between the triadic frames comprising tiers 'cc' and 'dd', is a statement
of the servant's confidence: 'He who vindicates me is near' (50:8aα).

With its two juxtaposed internal triadic frames (tiers 'cc' and 'dd'),
the overall form of this disputational complex bears some resemblance
to its more complicated relative in Isa. 44:6-22. Its flanking tiers, tiers
'aa' and 'bb', comprise an interlocking simple and triadic frame,
respectively.

The structure of Isa. 51:1-8 (tier TTⁱⁱⁱ-Aᵛⁱⁱ) is demarcated by injunctions whose structural function is, generally, to create a pattern of
alternation between the sense of hearing and the sense of vision,

senses used elsewhere in Isaiah 40–54 to convey in a figurative manner Israel/Zion's spiritual imperception. This third-level compound inverse frame appears as follows:

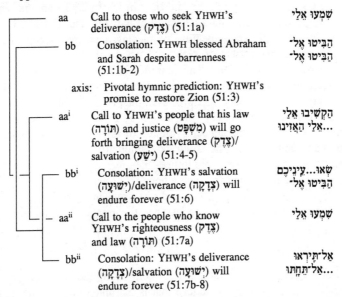

	aa	Call to those who seek YHWH's deliverance (צֶדֶק) (51:1a)	שִׁמְעוּ אֵלַי
	bb	Consolation: YHWH blessed Abraham and Sarah despite barrenness (51:1b-2)	הַבִּיטוּ אֶל־ הַבִּיטוּ אֶל־
	axis:	Pivotal hymnic prediction: YHWH's promise to restore Zion (51:3)	
	aaⁱ	Call to YHWH's people that his law (תּוֹרָה) and justice (מִשְׁפָּט) will go forth bringing deliverance (צֶדֶק)/salvation (יֶשַׁע) (51:4-5)	הַקְשִׁיבוּ אֵלַי ...אֵלַי הַאֲזִינוּ
	bbⁱ	Consolation: YHWH's salvation (יְשׁוּעָה)/deliverance (צְדָקָה) will endure forever (51:6)	שְׂאוּ...עֵינֵיכֶם הַבִּיטוּ אֶל־
	aaⁱⁱ	Call to the people who know YHWH's righteousness (צֶדֶק) and law (תּוֹרָה) (51:7a)	שִׁמְעוּ אֵלַי
	bbⁱⁱ	Consolation: YHWH's deliverance (צְדָקָה)/salvation (יְשׁוּעָה) will endure forever (51:7b-8)	אַל־תִּירְאוּ ...אַל־תֵּחַתּוּ

The 'aa' tiers of this consolation poem all begin with a 3 com. pl. imperative of a verb of hearing followed by אֵלַי: the command שִׁמְעוּ אֵלַי, 'Listen to me', introduces the outermost 'aa' tiers; הַקְשִׁיבוּ אֵלַי, 'Incline/attend to me' (with the connotation of hearing) introduces the middle 'aa' tier. In the aggregate, the 'aa' tiers speak of YHWH's justice (מִשְׁפָּט), law (תּוֹרָה), deliverance or righteousness (always using the shorter, masculine form צֶדֶק) and salvation (using only the shorter, masculine form יֶשַׁע).

The three 'bb' tiers present words of consolation to those who hope in YHWH. Like the 'aa' tiers, all the 'bb' tiers begin with 3 com. pl. imperatives. The first two 'bb' tiers use imperatives of verbs of seeing: הַבִּיטוּ אֶל־, 'Look at', appears in tiers bb and bbⁱ, though the idiom שְׂאוּ...עֵינֵיכֶם, 'Lift up your eyes', introduces the latter. The third and final 'bb' tier begins likewise with a 3 com. pl. imperative, but it departs from the pattern of using verbs of seeing by issuing in the formulaic consolation אַל־תִּירְאוּ, 'Be not afraid', which is paralleled by אַל־תֵּחַתּוּ, 'Be not shattered'. Tier bbⁱⁱ thereafter closely parallels the language of tier bbⁱ by speaking of the everlasting character of YHWH's 'salvation' (both times using only the longer, feminine form יְשׁוּעָה) and 'deliverance' (both times using only the longer, feminine form צְדָקָה). Thus, these feminine forms in the 'bb' tiers alternate with their masculine counterparts used in the 'aa' tiers in what may be another example of gender-matched parallelism in Isaiah (cf. Isa. 3:18b-23). The first 'bb' tier (51:1b-2) begins by placing into the foreground the unpretentious beginnings of Zion as the bedrock from which the later city would be quarried. The parallel lines in 51:2 portray the unpretentious beginnings of incipient Israel in their parents, Abraham and Sarah, to whom God had promised offspring. When Isa. 51:1b and 51:2 are read in contiguity, the image of a rock nearly becomes an emblem of genetic impotence, symbolic of Israel/Zion's beginnings in Abraham and Sarah. The assurance implicitly offered here is that YHWH is able to bring multiplied blessing where otherwise there appears to be no ground for such a hope. If necessary, YHWH is able to bring forth a flourishing people and city from mere rock. The second 'bb' tier (51:6) argues from the lesser to the greater. Heaven and earth, normally emblems of permanence, are considered impermanent in comparison to the lasting comfort that YHWH will bring upon future Zion.

For all this, the two triadic frames comprising the 'aa' and 'bb' tiers interlock in an alternating pattern that is disrupted only by the hymnic prediction of 51:3. This verse, which seems to serve as the axis of the complex frameworking pattern, is one of only eight such hymnic invocations or predictions in Second Isaiah. In this verse, the heart of the consolation speech, the prophet predicts that YHWH will comfort Zion, that joy and gladness, thanksgiving and the sound of singing, will again be found in her.

The next tier is another ambiguous tier, a consolatory disputation addressed to Zion/Jerusalem. It functions as the structural axis of the TT[iii] complex. Its three 'aa' tiers arouse the power of YHWH for redemption (51:9a), arouse Jerusalem from her ruin and abandonment (51:17aαβ) and arouse Zion/Jerusalem to her redemption (51:1-2). The two outer 'aa' tiers enclose the poem, while the middle one subdivides it into two subunits, each with its own compound frame and axis (inset[ii] and inset[iii], respectively). This makes it difficult to decide which of these two axes may have been intended to function as the main axis of the triadic frame comprising the 'aa' tiers. The pattern of repetitions in Isa. 51:9–52:2 (tier TT[iii]-Axis/A[viii]) may take the following shape:

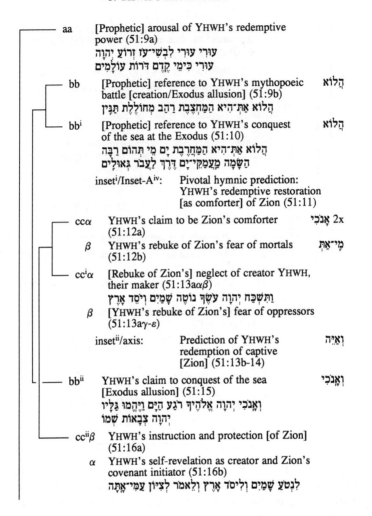

aa   [Prophetic] arousal of YHWH's redemptive
      power (51:9a)
      עוּרִי עוּרִי לִבְשִׁי־עֹז זְרוֹעַ יְהוָה
      עוּרִי כִּימֵי קֶדֶם דֹּרוֹת עוֹלָמִים

bb   [Prophetic] reference to YHWH's mythopoeic   הֲלוֹא
      battle [creation/Exodus allusion] (51:9b)
      הֲלוֹא אַתְּ־הִיא הַמַּחְצֶבֶת רַהַב מְחוֹלֶלֶת תַּנִּין

bbⁱ   [Prophetic] reference to YHWH's conquest   הֲלוֹא
      of the sea at the Exodus (51:10)
      הֲלוֹא אַתְּ־הִיא הַמַּחֲרֶבֶת יָם מֵי תְּהוֹם רַבָּה
      הַשָּׂמָה מַעֲמַקֵּי־יָם דֶּרֶךְ לַעֲבֹר גְּאוּלִים

      insetⁱ/Inset-Aⁱᵛ: Pivotal hymnic prediction:
                             YHWH's redemptive restoration
                             [as comforter] of Zion (51:11)

ccα   YHWH's claim to be Zion's comforter   2x אָנֹכִי
      (51:12a)

 β   YHWH's rebuke of Zion's fear of mortals   מִי־אַתְּ
      (51:12b)

ccⁱα [Rebuke of Zion's] neglect of creator YHWH,
      their maker (51:13aαβ)
      וַתִּשְׁכַּח יְהוָה עֹשֶׂךָ נוֹטֶה שָׁמַיִם וְיֹסֵד אָרֶץ

 β   [YHWH's rebuke of Zion's] fear of oppressors
      (51:13aγ-ε)

      insetⁱⁱ/axis: Prediction of YHWH's   וְאַיֵּה
                             redemption of captive
                             [Zion] (51:13b-14)

bbⁱⁱ YHWH's claim to conquest of the sea   וְאָנֹכִי
      [Exodus allusion] (51:15)
      וְאָנֹכִי יְהוָה אֱלֹהֶיךָ רֹגַע הַיָּם וַיֶּהֱמוּ גַּלָּיו
      יְהוָה צְבָאוֹת שְׁמוֹ

ccⁱⁱβ YHWH's instruction and protection [of Zion]
      (51:16a)

 α   YHWH's self-revelation as creator and Zion's
      covenant initiator (51:16b)
      לִנְטֹעַ שָׁמַיִם וְלִיסֹד אָרֶץ וְלֵאמֹר לְצִיּוֹן עַמִּי־אָתָּה

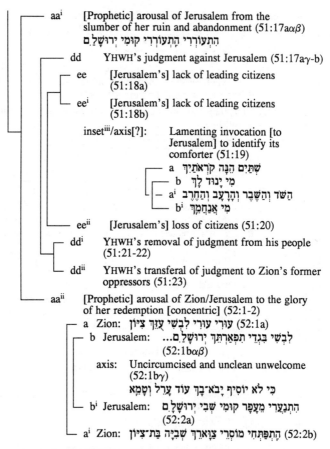

Together, the 'bb' tiers and the bifid 'cc' tiers form one compound
frame. The 'bb' tiers correspond in making allusions to YHWH's great
redemptive acts, his mythopoeic battle at creation or the Exodus
(51:9b) and his conquest of the sea at the Exodus (51:10, 15). The
'ccα' tiers portray YHWH comforting Zion in his role as Zion's
creator/covenant initiator (51:12a, 13aαβ, 16b). The 'ccβ' tiers, for
their part, portray YHWH rebuking Zion for fearing mortal oppressors
(51:12b, 13aγ-ε) and instructing her people as to his protection
(51:16a). Note again the reverse order of the bifid elements in these
'cc' tiers as they flank their axis at 51:13b-14. At the center of this
compound frame is a prediction that YHWH's redemption of captive
Zion is imminent (51:13b-14).

The 'dd' and 'ee' tiers, likewise, form an additional compound frame. The 'dd' tiers trace the transferal of YHWH's judgment: initially it is directed against Jerusalem (51:17aγ-b), then it is removed from his people (51:21-22), and finally it is transferred to Zion's former oppressors (51:23). The 'ee' tiers depict the loss of Zion's leading citizens during the period of her judgment (51:18a, 18b, 20). Functioning as the axis of this compound frame, Isa. 51:19 invokes Jerusalem to lament the calamities that befell her.

Whether inset[ii] or inset[iii] is understood to function as the main axis of the section, tier TT[iii]-Axis/A[viii], which comprises three triadic frames, resembles a frameworking pattern often found in 40:1–54:17 (cf. TT-A[i], 41:8-20; TT-B[iii], 43:8-13; TT[i]-B[vi], 44:24–45:13; TT[i]-A[v], 45:14–46:2). Its uniqueness lies in its having two compound frames, one (comprising tiers 'bb' and 'cc') positioned between its opening tiers (aa and aa[i]), the other (comprising tiers 'dd' and 'ee') positioned between its closing tiers (aa[i] and aa[ii]). For practical reasons, owing to the additional presence of inset[i]/Inset-A[iv] (51:11) between the opening 'aa' tiers, one may regard inset[ii] as the main axis of Isa. 51:9–52:2.

The TT[iii]-A[ix]-tier (52:3-12) consoles Zion/Jerusalem with the assurance that redemption will come despite its apparent delay. It may evidence the following compound frame pattern:

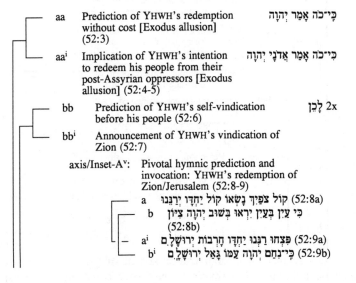

aa   Prediction of YHWH's redemption without cost [Exodus allusion] (52:3)   כִּי־כֹה אָמַר יְהוָה

aa[i]   Implication of YHWH's intention to redeem his people from their post-Assyrian oppressors [Exodus allusion] (52:4-5)   כִּי־כֹה אָמַר אֲדֹנָי יְהוָה

bb   Prediction of YHWH's self-vindication before his people (52:6)   לָכֵן 2x

bb[i]   Announcement of YHWH's vindication of Zion (52:7)

axis/Inset-A[v]:   Pivotal hymnic prediction and invocation: YHWH's redemption of Zion/Jerusalem (52:8-9)

a   (52:8a) קוֹל צֹפַיִךְ נָשְׂאוּ קוֹל יַחְדָּו יְרַנֵּנוּ

b   כִּי עַיִן בְּעַיִן יִרְאוּ בְּשׁוּב יְהוָה צִיּוֹן (52:8b)

a[i]   (52:9a) פִּצְחוּ רַנְּנוּ יַחְדָּו חָרְבוֹת יְרוּשָׁלָ ִם

b[i]   (52:9b) כִּי־נִחַם יְהוָה עַמּוֹ גָּאַל יְרוּשָׁלָ ִם

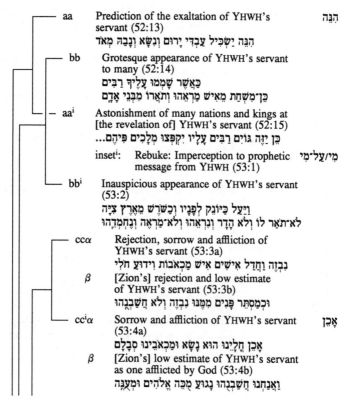

bb^ii   Prediction of YHWH's self-vindication before all nations (52:10)

aa^ii   Injunction and prediction concerning YHWH's new redemption without haste [Exodus allusion] (52:11-12)

In the preceding schema, the 'aa' tiers correspond in their prediction of YHWH's new redemption of his people from their foreign oppressors (52:3, 4-5, 11-12). The 'bb' tiers predict that, by fulfilling this predicted redemption of his people (the subject of the 'aa' tiers), YHWH will vindicate himself before the people of Zion (52:6, 7), and before all the nations of the earth (52:10). A hymnic invocation (Inset-A^v) serves as the axis of this compound frame (52:8-9).

Tier TT^iii-B^xi (52:13–53:12) is the third song of the servant's vindication directed against Zion and, as such, constitutes the third and final disputation of the TT^iii complex. Here, in outline, is what appears to be its complex framework structure:

aa   Prediction of the exaltation of YHWH's servant (52:13)   הִנֵּה

הִנֵּה יַשְׂכִּיל עַבְדִּי יָרוּם וְנִשָּׂא וְגָבַהּ מְאֹד

bb   Grotesque appearance of YHWH's servant to many (52:14)

כַּאֲשֶׁר שָׁמְמוּ עָלֶיךָ רַבִּים

כֵּן־מִשְׁחַת מֵאִישׁ מַרְאֵהוּ וְתֹאֲרוֹ מִבְּנֵי אָדָם

aa^i   Astonishment of many nations and kings at [the revelation of] YHWH's servant (52:15)

כֵּן יַזֶּה גוֹיִם רַבִּים עָלָיו יִקְפְּצוּ מְלָכִים פִּיהֶם...

inset^i: Rebuke: Imperception to prophetic message from YHWH (53:1)   מִי/עַל־מִי

bb^i   Inauspicious appearance of YHWH's servant (53:2)

וַיַּעַל כַּיּוֹנֵק לְפָנָיו וְכַשֹּׁרֶשׁ מֵאֶרֶץ צִיָּה

לֹא־תֹאַר לוֹ וְלֹא הָדָר וְנִרְאֵהוּ וְלֹא־מַרְאֶה וְנֶחְמְדֵהוּ

cc⍺   Rejection, sorrow and affliction of YHWH's servant (53:3a)

נִבְזֶה וַחֲדַל אִישִׁים אִישׁ מַכְאֹבוֹת וִידוּעַ חֹלִי

β   [Zion's] rejection and low estimate of YHWH's servant (53:3b)

וּכְמַסְתֵּר פָּנִים מִמֶּנּוּ נִבְזֶה וְלֹא חֲשַׁבְנֻהוּ

cc^i⍺   Sorrow and affliction of YHWH's servant (53:4a)   אָכֵן

אָכֵן חֳלָיֵנוּ הוּא נָשָׂא וּמַכְאֹבֵינוּ סְבָלָם

β   [Zion's] low estimate of YHWH's servant as one afflicted by God (53:4b)

וַאֲנַחְנוּ חֲשַׁבְנֻהוּ נָגוּעַ מֻכֵּה אֱלֹהִים וּמְעֻנֶּה

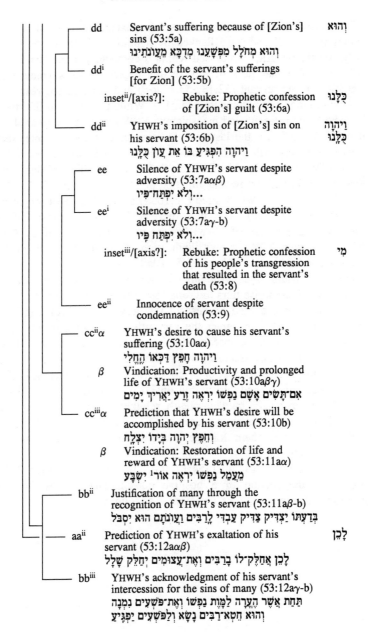

dd	Servant's suffering because of [Zion's] sins (53:5a)	וְהוּא מְחֹלָל מִפְּשָׁעֵנוּ מְדֻכָּא מֵעֲוֹנֹתֵינוּ	וְהוּא
dd[i]	Benefit of the servant's sufferings [for Zion] (53:5b)		
inset[ii]/[axis?]:	Rebuke: Prophetic confession of [Zion's] guilt (53:6a)		כֻּלָּנוּ
dd[ii]	YHWH's imposition of [Zion's] sin on his servant (53:6b)	וַיהוָה הִפְגִּיעַ בּוֹ אֵת עֲוֹן כֻּלָּנוּ	וַיהוָה כֻּלָּנוּ
ee	Silence of YHWH's servant despite adversity (53:7aαβ)	וְלֹא יִפְתַּח־פִּיו...	
ee[i]	Silence of YHWH's servant despite adversity (53:7aγ-b)	וְלֹא יִפְתַּח פִּיו...	
inset[iii]/[axis?]:	Rebuke: Prophetic confession of his people's transgression that resulted in the servant's death (53:8)		מִי
ee[ii]	Innocence of servant despite condemnation (53:9)		
cc[ii]α	YHWH's desire to cause his servant's suffering (53:10aα)	וַיהוָה חָפֵץ דַּכְּאוֹ הֶחֱלִי	
β	Vindication: Productivity and prolonged life of YHWH's servant (53:10aβγ)	אִם־תָּשִׂים אָשָׁם נַפְשׁוֹ יִרְאֶה זֶרַע יַאֲרִיךְ יָמִים	
cc[iii]α	Prediction that YHWH's desire will be accomplished by his servant (53:10b)	וְחֵפֶץ יְהוָה בְּיָדוֹ יִצְלָח	
β	Vindication: Restoration of life and reward of YHWH's servant (53:11aα)	מֵעֲמַל נַפְשׁוֹ יִרְאֶה אוֹר[1] יִשְׂבָּע	
bb[ii]	Justification of many through the recognition of YHWH's servant (53:11aβ-b)	בְּדַעְתּוֹ יַצְדִּיק צַדִּיק עַבְדִּי לָרַבִּים וַעֲוֹנֹתָם הוּא יִסְבֹּל	
aa[ii]	Prediction of YHWH's exaltation of his servant (53:12aαβ)	לָכֵן אֲחַלֶּק־לוֹ בָרַבִּים וְאֶת־עֲצוּמִים יְחַלֵּק שָׁלָל	לָכֵן
bb[iii]	YHWH's acknowledgment of his servant's intercession for the sins of many (53:12aγ-b)	תַּחַת אֲשֶׁר הֶעֱרָה לַמָּוֶת נַפְשׁוֹ וְאֶת־פֹּשְׁעִים נִמְנָה וְהוּא חֵטְא־רַבִּים נָשָׂא וְלַפֹּשְׁעִים יַפְגִּיעַ	

[1]1QIsa[a,b] and the LXX attest the addition of אוֹר.

This disputational complex offers two juxtaposed internal triadic frames (tiers 'dd' and 'ee') flanked by a bifid quadratic frame (tiers 'cc'), which, in turn, is recessed within a compound frame (tiers 'aa' and 'bb'). The 'aa' tiers of this section depict YHWH's vindicating exaltation of his servant (52:13; 53:12a$\alpha\beta$) and describe the response of foreign kings and nations to it (52:15). While the first two 'bb' tiers describe how grotesque and inauspicious YHWH's servant appeared 'to many' (52:14; 53:2), the last two 'bb' tiers nevertheless counter that YHWH's servant will justify 'many' and intercede for the sins 'of many' (53:11aβ-b, 12aγ-b). The 'ccα' halves of the bifid 'cc' tiers describe the rejection, sorrow and affliction of YHWH's servant (53:3a, 4a) as something that YHWH desired (53:10aα) so that his desire might be accomplished (53:10b). The first two 'ccβ' halves contrast Zion's rejection and estimate of YHWH's servant as one afflicted by God (53:3b, 4b) with YHWH's own vindication of his servant through the prolongation/restoration of his life (53:10a$\beta\gamma$, 11aα).

Enclosed within the preceding frames are two separate triadic frames, which comprise tiers 'dd' and 'ee', respectively. The 'dd' tiers show how Zion benefited because of the servant's sufferings (53:5a, 5b, 6b). The 'ee' tiers depict the servant's silence despite adversity (53:7a$\alpha\beta$, 7aγ-b) and innocence despite condemnation (53:9). These frame the axis of the structure, which is virtual, unless, for rhetorical reasons, either inset[ii] (53:6a) or inset[iii] (53:8) is seen to function in that capacity (cf. 46:9b, and 11a within 46:3-13). Otherwise, each triadic frame has its own axis, inset[ii] implicitly rebuking Zion's people through the prophet's communal confession of guilt (53:6a), and inset[iii] explicitly rebuking them for the transgression that resulted in the servant's demise (53:8).

The final tier of Isa. 40:1–54:17 (i.e., tier TT[iii]-A[x], 54:[1] 2-17) closes out the section in a positive consolational disposition. Its architectural contour may be represented as follows:

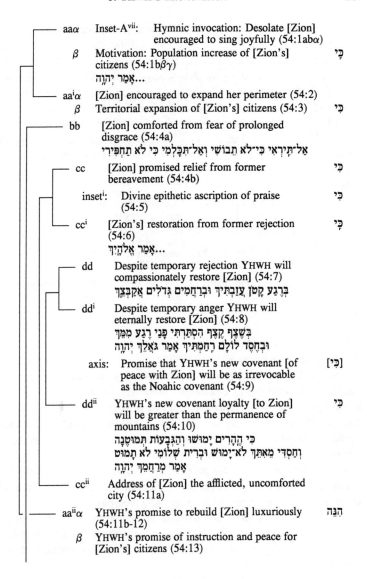

aaα   Inset-A[vii]:   Hymnic invocation: Desolate [Zion] encouraged to sing joyfully (54:1abα)

β   Motivation: Population increase of [Zion's] citizens (54:1bβγ)   כִּי

...אָמַר יְהוָה

aa[i]α   [Zion] encouraged to expand her perimeter (54:2)

β   Territorial expansion of [Zion's] citizens (54:3)   כִּי

bb   [Zion] comforted from fear of prolonged disgrace (54:4a)

אַל־תִּירְאִי כִּי־לֹא תֵבוֹשִׁי וְאַל־תִּכָּלְמִי כִּי לֹא תַחְפִּירִי

cc   [Zion] promised relief from former bereavement (54:4b)   כִּי

inset[i]:   Divine epithetic ascription of praise (54:5)   כִּי

cc[i]   [Zion's] restoration from former rejection (54:6)   כִּי

...אָמַר אֱלֹהָיִךְ

dd   Despite temporary rejection YHWH will compassionately restore [Zion] (54:7)

בְּרֶגַע קָטֹן עֲזַבְתִּיךְ וּבְרַחֲמִים גְּדֹלִים אֲקַבְּצֵךְ

dd[i]   Despite temporary anger YHWH will eternally restore [Zion] (54:8)

בְּשֶׁצֶף קֶצֶף הִסְתַּרְתִּי פָנַי רֶגַע מִמֵּךְ
וּבְחֶסֶד עוֹלָם רִחַמְתִּיךְ אָמַר גֹּאֲלֵךְ יְהוָה

axis: Promise that YHWH's new covenant [of peace with Zion] will be as irrevocable as the Noahic covenant (54:9)   [כִּי]

dd[ii]   YHWH's new covenant loyalty [to Zion] will be greater than the permanence of mountains (54:10)   כִּי

כִּי הֶהָרִים יָמוּשׁוּ וְהַגְּבָעוֹת תְּמוּטֶנָה
וְחַסְדִּי מֵאִתֵּךְ לֹא־יָמוּשׁ וּבְרִית שְׁלוֹמִי לֹא תָמוּט
אָמַר מְרַחֲמֵךְ יְהוָה

cc[ii]   Address of [Zion] the afflicted, uncomforted city (54:11a)

aa[ii]α   YHWH's promise to rebuild [Zion] luxuriously (54:11b-12)   הִנֵּה

β   YHWH's promise of instruction and peace for [Zion's] citizens (54:13)

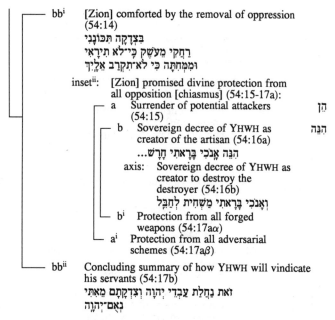

bb[i] [Zion] comforted by the removal of oppression (54:14)

בְּצְדָקָה תִּכּוֹנָנִי
רַחֲקִי מֵעֹשֶׁק כִּי־לֹא תִירָאִי
וּמִמְּחִתָּה כִּי לֹא־תִקְרַב אֵלָיִךְ

    inset[ii]: [Zion] promised divine protection from all opposition [chiasmus] (54:15-17a):

      a   Surrender of potential attackers (54:15)   הֵן

      b   Sovereign decree of YHWH as creator of the artisan (54:16a)   הִנֵּה

          הִנֵּה אָנֹכִי בָּרָאתִי חָרָשׁ...

      axis: Sovereign decree of YHWH as creator to destroy the destroyer (54:16b)

          וְאָנֹכִי בָּרָאתִי מַשְׁחִית לְחַבֵּל

      b[i] Protection from all forged weapons (54:17aα)

      a[i] Protection from all adversarial schemes (54:17aβ)

bb[ii] Concluding summary of how YHWH will vindicate his servants (54:17b)

זֹאת נַחֲלַת עַבְדֵי יְהוָה וְצִדְקָתָם מֵאִתִּי
נְאֻם־יְהוָה

In the foregoing schema, the bifid 'aa' tiers give encouragements regarding the expansion of the dwelling place/city of Zion (tiers 'aaα') because of YHWH's increase of and blessing upon her children (tiers 'aaβ'). In the 'bb' tiers, Zion and YHWH's servants who dwell there are comforted by his vindicating removal of their disgrace and oppression (54:4a, 14, 17b). In the 'cc' tiers, YHWH addresses Zion with words of empathy for her bereavement, rejection and uncomforted affliction (54:4b, 6, 11a). The 'dd' tiers again depict YHWH consoling Zion's citizens at the turning point in their relationship, each time contrasting the brevity of his anger and judgment with the eternality of his intentions to favor them with peace and compassion (54:7, 8, 10). Appropriately, at the axis, one finds an affirmation of the irrevocability of the new and everlasting covenant of peace that YHWH intends to make with his people, with allusion to the irrevocable covenant that he made with Noah (54:9).

Although some of the foregoing structural analyses may require revision or refinement in the light of further study, its seems safe to say that there are demonstrable and recurring patterns of repetition within these third-level tiers of Isa. 40:1–54:17. Moreover, the patterns of repetition reflect a strategy in keeping with that of the organizational patterns encountered in the previous chapters of the book. Here also the repetition patterns include combinations of simple and, more often, complex (triadic and quadratic) frames. Despite their asymmetry, all the foregoing third-level complexes of 40:1–54:17 are basically concentric. Some lack, but most feature, an explicit structural axis.

Admittedly, one's confidence about many tier divisions within these complexes may be lessened by the observation that not all word repetitions should be construed as contributing to the framework design. Some formulaic repetitions serve merely as delineators, and some word repetitions serve as catchwords between successive tiers to lend coherence and continuity to the reading of a subsection. Moreover, at times, it is only the thematic content of a tier that justifies identifying it as belonging to a similar set of tiers that develop the same theme or motif. Although the present study cannot present a full rhetorical analysis of each third-level tier in Isa. 40:1–54:17, it may be possible to make some observations regarding the implications of their broader arrangement according to the pattern of the second- and first-level tiers.

Persuasion as a Function of Structure in Isaiah 40:1–54:17

Perhaps because of its peculiar rhetorical strategy within the book of Isaiah, the section comprising chs. 40–54 makes fewer specific references to the historical situation of its composition than does any of the previous sections comprising chs. 1–39. Indeed, the first confrontation with the present section seems to be a flight into situational ambiguity, for the reader is unprepared for the suddenness of the shift from the chronological point of view of chs. 1–39, a perspective mostly at home in the late eighth to early seventh centuries BCE, to one of the mid-sixth century BCE. Yet, while the (implied) author of Isa. 40:1–54:17 is obviously addressing a new audience, the citizens of Jacob/Israel//Judah/Zion in Babylonian exile, the author is also ostensibly (analeptically) rebuking Isaiah's eighth- and early seventh-century BCE contemporaries, with whom the generation of the Exile are reckoned to be one people.

It is important to note, in support of the hypothesis that Isa. 40:1–54:17 constitutes the exoneration section of Isaiah's covenant disputation rhetoric, that the 'TT' tiers often allude to YHWH's voluntary initiation of the covenant (e.g., 41:8-9a; [44:24a]; 51:1b-2) and his past benefits to Jacob/Israel//Judah/Zion (e.g., 41:18-19; 43:16-17) and often reiterate injunctions to comfort Zion (e.g., 40:1-2, 9; 51:3, 12a;

52:7-8, 9), reminding her of YHWH's standing offer of reinstatement. The 'TT' tiers center on YHWH's exoneration with respect to his power (e.g., 40:10, 12, 26, 29-31; 43:13aβb; cf. 49:24 with 50:2aγ-3; 52:10; [cf. 59:1]) and knowledge (e.g., 40:13-14, 28; 41:22-23, 26-28; 42:9; 43:9aγδ; 44:6-7, 8; 45:21b; 46:9-10, 11b; 48:3, 5a, 6b-7a; 52:6), especially as these relate to his loyalty to his covenant with Israel and Zion (e.g., 40:6b-8; cf. 40:27 with 41:9b, 17b; 42:16bγδ; 43:2-3; [43:26]; 44:21-22; cf. 49:14 with 49:15-16 and 50:1a; 54:7-10).

The 'UU' tiers, for their part, present YHWH's ostensible trial by combat with Babylon (and its gods) as proof of his supreme power and decree to bring about salvation for Jacob/Israel//Judah/Zion. Hence, the 'UU' tiers focus on YHWH's right to vindication against allegations, from both Israel and the nations, that he has been either too impotent, too ignorant or too indifferent to Zion's welfare to save them from Babylon and its gods.

There is a notable division of thematic emphasis in 40:1–54:17, a division that turns on the axis of 47:8-15. The first half, 40:1–47:15, focuses preeminently upon YHWH's vindication against accusations that question his ability to save Israel/[Zion] by his divine power and knowledge and presents his vindication in the form of challenges to contest with the nations and their idols. The second half, 47:8–54:17, focuses preeminently upon YHWH's vindication from accusations that question his willingness to save Zion/[Israel]—a willingness to remain faithful to his covenant to preserve Zion—and presents his own vindication in conjunction with the vindication of his righteous servant (historically, the prophet Isaiah of the eighth to seventh century BCE).

The primary audience throughout chs. 40:1–54:17 is the community of Jacob/Israel//Judah/Zion in exile.[1] Even the 'trial speeches' against the idols of other nations are rhetorically designed to be overheard by Jacob/Israel//Judah/Zion so that they function as either consolations (when YHWH vindicates Jacob/Israel//Judah/Zion by threatening their enemies) or disputations (when YHWH rebukes his people for worshiping impotent or ignorant foreign gods). The structural continuity and rhetorical function of Isa. 40:1–54:17 within the overall covenant disputation rhetoric that makes up the book of Isaiah make it clear that these 'trial speeches' were not designed to be read by the nations whom they ostensibly address. Hence, subsections that are 'trial speeches' in

[1]This remains consistent throughout the book of Isaiah despite Jacob/Israel//Judah/Zion's change of geographical locale and the shift from the period of Isaiah the prophet, to that of the Babylonian exile, and finally to that of the restoration under the returned remnant.

form actually function, within the controlling strategy of the book, as either consolations of or disputations against Jacob/Israel//Judah/Zion. This may help to account for some differences among scholars as to the particular intention of these confrontational or 'polemic' sections. Unfortunately, however, much of the discussion has been based upon the forms of the individual subunits in isolation rather than upon an appreciation of the role that they play within the broader patterns of their context. For example, of the 'trial speech' in Isa. 41:1-7, Melugin has argued:

> ... Isaiah 41:1-7, which Begrich calls an appeal-to-trial speech of the accuser, lacks a typical accusing question like, "Why have you done this thing?" Nor is there a hint of the accuser's indication of the punishment which he believes should be assigned. The questions in Isaiah 41:1ff. are disputational rather than questions for the purpose of making accusation ... It is better to consider the form as Deutero-Isaiah's own creation. The form is as follows: 1) a summons to trial added to 2) the disputation-speech style common throughout Deutero-Isaiah.[1]

Melugin's assessment of the form seems correct, but perhaps his argument would have been more compelling had he viewed 41:1-7 as the culmination of a disputational complex spanning 40:12–41:7. Instead, he has categorized 41:1-7 as a 'trial speech against the nations' and reckoned it as forming a unit with what follows in the context (i.e., 41:1–42:13).[2]

Throughout 40:1–54:17, repeated allusion to the 'first Exodus', the unmerited deliverance that inaugurated Israel's eternal covenant obligation to YHWH, reinforces the consciousness that the exiled citizens of Zion are now in exile because they had violated their covenant obligations but simultaneously renews their hope with YHWH's proposal of inaugurating a 'second Exodus'.[3] Not only does this defend YHWH's standing as one who has remained loyal to the covenant instituted by the first Exodus—since he would, eventually, recall Zion from Babylon—but it shows the unlimited extent of his unmerited favor toward Zion. Indeed, the 'everlasting covenant' that the second Exodus would inaugurate would be no more, perhaps even less, merited than

---

[1]R.F. Melugin, 'The Typical Versus the Unique among the Hebrew Prophets', in L.C. McGaughy (ed.), *The Society of Biblical Literature, 1972 Proceedings* (2 vols.; Missoula, MT: SBL, 1972), II, pp. 339-40.

[2]Melugin, *The Formation of Isaiah 40–55*, pp. 54-55, 93-94.

[3]Allusions to the first Exodus [and wilderness wandering] may be found in 43:2a, 3b, 16aβ-17, [19b-21]; 44:27; 50:2b-3; 51:9b-10, 15; and 52:3-5, 11-12. Cf. K. Kiesow, *Exodustexte im Jesajabuch: Literarkritische und motivgeschichtliche Analysen* (OBO, 24; Freiburg, Seitzerland: Universitätsverlag, 1979).

the covenant instituted under Moses. In addition, the prophetic servant referred to in 40:1–54:17, whose message formerly had been a matter of scorn in Zion, is portrayed as one who would be vindicated by YHWH when YHWH came to fulfill his prophecy to deliver Jacob/Israel//Judah/Zion from Babylon. Indeed, when considered together with the predictions of a new Exodus from Babylon, the servant's portrayals seem intended to serve as further motivations for the exiles to repent and return to Zion. In this way the prophet becomes, albeit posthumously, a second Moses.

The 'return from Babylon' motif recurs throughout Isa. 40:1–54:17 since it is, rhetorically speaking, both the proof of YHWH's power, foreknowledge and good intentions toward Jacob/Israel//Judah/Zion and the evidence of YHWH's (and his servant's) innocence of allegations to the contrary. In the so-called 'servant songs', one sees the full force of verbal amphibology and double entendre. Perhaps the servant songs are best interpreted as idealized descriptions of the experience of Isaiah the prophet as a divine messenger. They are, in short, descriptions that suit a messenger formerly rejected by his people and, therefore, not descriptions of their author, who apparently survived the Babylonian captivity. It is the messenger of YHWH whose words, long since rejected by his contemporaries in Zion, are now being fulfilled by YHWH in the presence of the descendants of those who rejected them. The only historical figure referred to in the book of Isaiah for whom such a portrayal could hold true is that of the eighth- to seventh-century BCE prophet Isaiah. Thus, it would appear that the intended readers were expected to surmise that it was through the fulfillment of the predictions of historical Isaiah that YHWH was vindicating this prophetic servant. This seems to be what the book as a whole claims through its implied equation of the prophet Isaiah with the rejected servant. On the other hand, however, one must be careful not always to identify the prophet Isaiah with the book's own prophetic persona.

The Continuity of Isaiah 40:1–54:17 with its Context

It is not without warrant that this section of Isaiah (40:1–54:17) has commonly been regarded as a compilation secondary to that of the materials that make up the corpus of Isaiah's writings contained within chs. 1–39. Neither its shift of chronological perspective from that which precedes, its hierarchical organization of framing repetitions, nor its focus upon the defense of YHWH's innocence against implied accusations of divine impotence (e.g., 40:18-20, 25; 41:7, 10; 59:1), ignorance (e.g., 40:28; 41:21-29) or covenant indifference (cf. 40:27 with 41:9b, 17b; cf. 49:14 with 49:15-16 and 50:1a) are anticipated in either the prologue or thematic emphases of the preceding chapters.[1] Even if Zion were to offer a disclaimer of ignorance (i.e., that she had not been aware of her guilt since YHWH had failed to inform her and warn her of his plans to punish her), this too is refuted (cf. 45:15 with 45:19). Establishing YHWH's innocence in consigning Zion to chastisement is essential to the success of the author's rhetorical strategy, which operates within the context of a covenant relationship between YHWH as suzerain and Zion's citizens as his earthly vassals. This is perhaps why such a point is made of refuting Zion's claim to covenant innocence through the denunciation of the idolatrous hypocrisies of the people and their temple dignitaries (43:22-28; especially v. 26). If Zion had been truly innocent, then YHWH would have been in the wrong, whether for failing (through ignorance or covenant neglect) to defend her from her enemies or, worse, for deliberately consigning her (by sovereign caprice) to needless judgment.

The only way that YHWH could be excused morally from the indictments of covenant disloyalty or misjudgment is on the ground that, though willing to defend Zion, he had simply been too impotent against the gods of foreign nations to have defended them. And it is this, together with Zion's other misconceptions, that YHWH would dismiss once and for all when he finally recalled Zion from Babylon. By one emancipation, he would establish his covenant loyalty to Zion, his divine power over the gods of foreign nations and, since he had decreed this event to be the conclusion of the punishment appropriate to her guilt, his divine right not only to punish but also to restore Zion.

In this regard, 40:1-54:17 should not be regarded as primarily a polemical case against the idols of Babylon, but as a case against the Judean exiles' notion that YHWH was no greater than the idols of that nation that had subjected Zion to capture. This is why the force of YHWH's rebuttal against his people's false assumptions takes the double thrust of demonstrating both the impotence and ignorance of idols in general.

In keeping with the spirit of its emphasis on the exoneration of YHWH, there is evident, in 40:1-54:17, a continuation of the earlier hymnic mode of the songs of Zion's exaltation (i.e., the 'insets' of

[1] YHWH's denunciation of the rebellious (nations) for questioning his sovereign right over his children (45:9-10, 11) is ostensibly a defense of his innocence against charges that he disregarded his covenant obligation to chastise, then embrace, Zion.

13:1–39:8). This continuation is manifested in the hymnic genre of the 'Insets-A' of the present section (i.e., 42:10-12; 44:23; [48:20aβ-b]; 49:13; 51:3, 11; 52:8-9; 54:1; cf. 61:10). From a rhetorical standpoint, it is also appropriate that the section that is to come (i.e., 55:1–66:24) constitutes the strongest and longest covenant appeal of the book of Isaiah. Such an appeal to be reconciled to YHWH could hardly find better ground for motivation than in the defense of YHWH's covenant faithfulness to Jacob/Israel//Judah/Zion presented in chs. 40–54.

Chapter 7

ISAIAH 55:1–66:24: FINAL ULTIMATUM

YHWH WILL ADMIT INTO FUTURE ZION
ONLY THE FAITHFUL AND JUST

The final segment of the book of Isaiah, comprising 55:1–66:24, is the
rhetorical culmination of the whole. It is not the climax of emotional
tension, which one finds in chs. 40–54, but the point of crisis from
which the intended readers would have to determine what response to
make to its message. It is here that the intended readers would discern
most clearly the author's aim for the prophecy as a whole, namely, that
YHWH's people should confess their sins of apostasy and injustice and
be reconciled to him both so as to escape the punishment due those who
remain at enmity with YHWH and so as to enjoy the covenant benefits
promised to future citizens of Zion.

The appeal to be reconciled that is being made in this section is consistent with the covenant disputation rhetoric of the book of Isaiah as a
whole. The new and 'everlasting covenant' being offered (55:3b; 61:8;
cf. 24:5bβ) was to be none other than a fulfillment of the ideals of that
covenant that had been promised to David (55:3b) and that the former
citizens of Zion (including its Davidic rulers) had forsaken. Yet this
new offer of covenant reconciliation is escalated to such proportions
that the faithful and just of other nations are also invited to partake of
YHWH's coming vindication and blessing of future Zion (55:4-5; 56:3-
8). The chronological perspective of the previous section (chs. 40–54)
advances somewhat in this section in the portrayal of the inner view of
the penitent (63:7–65:7) and in the portrayal of Zion's redemption after
punishment (58:1–59:15a, 60:1-20 and 60:21–61:11).[1]

---

[1]From the vantage point of the supplicant, the temple is portrayed as still lying
in ruins (63:18; 64:10) and Jerusalem and its environs as still devastated (64:9).
Elsewhere, the appeal to covenant restoration is motivated by the promise to
rebuild Jerusalem's ruined walls (58:12; 60:10) and those of its environs (61:4). In
chs. 55–66, one meets the reiteration of accusations and injunctions that were once
also germane to Isaiah's eighth- to seventh-century contemporaries (e.g., 56:1-2
[cf. 1:17]; 56:9-12; 57:3-13a; 58:2-5 [6-7, 9b-10a, 13]; 59:2-8, [12-13]; [63:10a;
64:4b-6; 65:2-5]). Interestingly, the accusations, which pertain to Zion's postexilic

Structural Delineation of Isaiah 55:1–66:24

The section commences in 55:1-3 with an invitation (לְכוּ 4x) that marks the beginning of the appeal section of Isaiah's covenant disputation (i.e., 55:1–66:24).[1] As previously mentioned, this appeal was foreshadowed in the prologue of the book (cf. repetitions of לְכוּ in 1:18a; 2:3a, 5). The closure of the section is also the peroration of the book (65:8–66:24) and it, too, repeats themes and key words reminiscent of those used in the prologue (1:1–2:5). Thus, through an inclusio created by the collocation of key words and themes in the opening and closing chapters, the prophecy as a whole subscribes to the same principle of closure that has governed each of its constituent sections.

Asymmetrical Concentricity in Isaiah 55:1–66:24

It was E. Charpentier who first suggested that Isa. 56:1–66:24 was concentric in structure.[2] Following Charpentier's suggestion,

community, reiterate the implied author's main concern in the prophecy with the dual problem of religious apostasy and social injustice.

[1] Recently, M.A. Sweeney has summarized the arguments for grouping ch. 55 with the section that follows (i.e., 55:1–66:24) ('Isaiah 1-4 and the Post-Exilic Understanding of the Isaianic Tradition', [PhD diss., Claremont Graduate School, 1983], pp. 216-31, 232, 237; idem, *Isaiah 1-4 and the Post-Exilic Understanding of the Isaianic Tradition* [BZAW, 171; Berlin: de Gruyter, 1988], pp. 87-92, 95). See especially his arguments on pp. 87-89 of the published work (= PhD diss., pp. 216-19).

[2] E. Charpentier, *Jeunesse du Vieux Testament* (Paris: Fayard, 1963), pp. 79-80. Cf. R. Tournay's asymmetrical version of the concentric outline of chs. 56–66 ('Bulletin: Livres prophétiques', *RB* 74 [1967], pp. 120-21), which appeared as follows:

```
A    56:1-9
  B    57:5ff
    C    57:15
      D    57:18-19
        E    59[:1-15a]   lamentation nationale
          F    59:15bff
            G    60:1-22
              Axis:  61:1-11   l'oracle messianique
            G'   62:1-12
          F'   63:1-6
        E'   63:7ff        lamentation nationale
  B'   65:11
    C'   66:1
  B"   66:3
      D'   66:10-13
  B"'  66:17
A'   66:18, 24
```

P.-E. Bonnard proposed a five-tiered asymmetrical palistrophe for Isaiah 56–66, which may be schematized as follows:

A   56:1-8   Respect du sabbat; Les étrangers venant à la Sainte
                   Montagne
 B   56:9–57:21   Reproches. Promesses aux fidèles
  C   58   Reproches: jeûne in authentique, sabbat frelaté
  C'   59:1-15a   Reproches. Aveu des péchés
   D   59:15b-20   Fureur du Dieu juste, vengeur et rédempteur,
                   apportant le salut
    E   60:1-22   Jérusalem: la gloire de la ville
    Axis: 61:1-11 Mission du prophète et son écho
    E' 62:1-12   Jérusalem: la gloire de la ville
   D'   63:1-6   Fureur du Dieu juste, vengeur et rédempteur,
                   apportant le salut
  C"   63:7–64:11 Implorations. Aveu des péchés
 B'   65:1–66:17   Reproches. Promesses aux fidèles
A'   66:18-24   Respect du sabbat; Les nations venant à la Sainte
                   Montagne[1]

R. Lack devised a three-tiered concentric schema for chs. 56–66 on the basis of collocations of vocabulary and changes in 'disposition' among various sections:

```
                        60–62
            59:15-21            63:1-6
      59:1-14                         63:7–64:11
56–58                                       65–66[2]
```

More recently, G.J. Polan, following Charpentier's earlier model, offered a similar symmetrical five-tiered analysis:

(A) 56:1-8 — Conditions for the entrance to the People of God
 (B) 56:9–58:14 — Reproaches to the wicked; promises to the faithful
  (C) 59:1-14 — Two psalms and confession of sin
   (D) 59:15-20[21] — Divine Vengeance
    (E) 60:1-22 — The New Jerusalem; financée of God
     (F) 61:1-11 — The announcement of messianic times.
                    The Spirit of the Lord is upon me.
    (E') 62:1-12 — The New Jerusalem; financée of God
   (D') 63:1-6 — Divine Vengeance
  (C') 63:7–64:11 — Two psalms and confession of sin

This model suffers from the fact that it leaves a number of intervening gaps (i.e., 56:10–57:4; 57:16-17; 57:20–58:14; 64:1–65:10; 65:12-25; 66:2, 4-9, 14-16, 19-23) though, admittedly, it does not appear that Tournay was attempting to present an exhaustive analysis.

[1]P.-E. Bonnard, *Le Second Isaïe: Son disciple et leurs éditeurs Isaïe 40–66* (EBib; Paris: Gabalda, 1972), p. 318.
[2]R. Lack, *La symbolique du livre d'Isaïe: Essai sur l'image littéraire comme élément de structuration* (AnBib, 59; Rome: Biblical Institute Press, 1973), pp. 125-34.

(B') 65:1–66:17 — Reproaches to the wicked; promises to the faithful
(A') 66:18-24 — Conditions for the entrance to the People of God[1]

However, Charpentier's most recent version of a palistrophic model for Isaiah 56–66 has grown to a six-tiered structure, which may be presented as follows:

(A) 56:1-8 — Strangers can belong to the people of God
 (B) 56:9–57:21 — The prophet laments those who think they are the people of God
  (C) 58:1-14 — True fasting is to do away with injustice
   (D) 59:1-14 — The prophet's accusation bears fruit: the people confess their sins
    (E) 59:15-20[21] — God will trample on his enemies
     (F) 60:1-22 — Zion rejoices
      Axis: 61:1-11 — Climax: the spirit of the Lord is upon me
     (F') 62:1-12 — Zion rejoices
    (E') 63:1-6 — God will trample on his enemies
   (D') 63:7–64:11 — Psalm of supplication: an appeal to God
  (C') 65:1-25 — Blessings and Curses
 (B') 66:1-16 — God gives Zion power to bring forth the new people
(A') 66:17-24 — God will gather all the nations[2]

These schemata present alternative symmetrical, and asymmetrical, concentric analyses of Isaiah 56–66 and, as far as they delimit the section, basically concur with the pattern of repetition that I shall propose in what follows. However, the prefixing of ch. 55, as a necessary component of the appeal section within Isaiah's rhetoric of covenant disputation, and the recognition of some alternative correspondences among its tiers, results in a concentric structure whose pattern, in conformity with that of previous concentric structures in Isaiah, is asymmetrical. An asymmetrically concentric model of repetitions in chs. 55–66 may be outlined in this way:

---

[1] G.J. Polan, *In the Ways of Justice toward Salvation: A Rhetorical Analysis of Isaiah 56–59* (American University Studies, Series VII: Theology and Religion, 13; New York: Peter Lang, 1986), p. 15; cf. idem, 'Salvation in the Midst of Struggle', *TBT* 23 (1985), p. 94.

[2] Charpentier, *How to Read the Old Testament* (trans. J. Bowden; New York: Crossroad, 1981), p. 77.

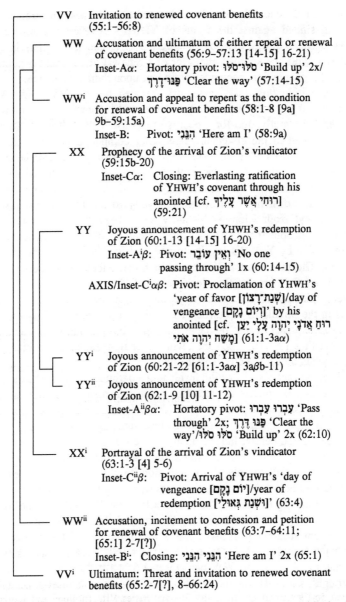

VV Invitation to renewed covenant benefits
(55:1–56:8)

WW Accusation and ultimatum of either repeal or renewal
of covenant benefits (56:9–57:13 [14-15] 16-21)
Inset-Aα: Hortatory pivot: סֹלּוּ־סֹלּוּ 'Build up' 2x/
פַּנּוּ־דָרֶךְ 'Clear the way' (57:14-15)

WWⁱ Accusation and appeal to repent as the condition
for renewal of covenant benefits (58:1-8 [9a]
9b–59:15a)
Inset-B: Pivot: הִנֵּנִי 'Here am I' (58:9a)

XX Prophecy of the arrival of Zion's vindicator
(59:15b-20)
Inset-Cα: Closing: Everlasting ratification
of YHWH's covenant through his
anointed [cf. רוּחִי אֲשֶׁר עָלֶיךָ]
(59:21)

YY Joyous announcement of YHWH's redemption
of Zion (60:1-13 [14-15] 16-20)
Inset-Aⁱβ: Pivot: וְאֵין עוֹבֵר 'No one
passing through' 1x (60:14-15)

AXIS/Inset-Cⁱαβ: Pivot: Proclamation of YHWH's
'year of favor [שְׁנַת־רָצוֹן]/day of
vengeance [וְיוֹם נָקָם]' by his
anointed [cf. רוּחַ אֲדֹנָי יְהוָה עָלַי יַעַן
[מָשַׁח יְהוָה אֹתִי] (61:1-3aα)

YYⁱ Joyous announcement of YHWH's redemption
of Zion (60:21-22 [61:1-3aα] 3aβb-11)

YYⁱⁱ Joyous announcement of YHWH's redemption
of Zion (62:1-9 [10] 11-12)
Inset-Aⁱⁱβα: Hortatory pivot: עִבְרוּ עָבְרוּ 'Pass
through' 2x; פַּנּוּ דֶּרֶךְ 'Clear the
way'/סֹלּוּ סֹלּוּ 'Build up' 2x (62:10)

XXⁱ Portrayal of the arrival of Zion's vindicator
(63:1-3 [4] 5-6)
Inset-Cⁱⁱβ: Pivot: Arrival of YHWH's 'day of
vengeance [יוֹם נָקָם]/year of
redemption [וּשְׁנַת גְּאוּלַי]' (63:4)

WWⁱⁱ Accusation, incitement to confession and petition
for renewal of covenant benefits (63:7–64:11;
[65:1] 2-7[?])
Inset-Bⁱ: Closing: הִנֵּנִי הִנֵּנִי 'Here am I' 2x (65:1)

VVⁱ Ultimatum: Threat and invitation to renewed covenant
benefits (65:2-7[?], 8–66:24)

The outer 'VV' tiers highlight the mode of invitation, which is the
offer of covenant reconciliation to prospective worshipers of YHWH
and citizens of future Zion. The 'WW' tiers set forth the conditions on

which such reconciliation depends, namely, an acknowledgment of having sinned against the terms of YHWH's covenant. It appears to have been by design that, by reading the 'VV' and 'WW' tiers in conjunction with one another, the offer of a renewal of covenant benefits to YHWH's people thus becomes contingent upon their repentance.

It is within this dual framework, created by the 'VV' and 'WW' frames, that another similarly contoured, compound framework presents the motivation for a positive response to YHWH's invitation to be reinstated to the covenant. This inner compound frame comprises the 'XX' and 'YY' tiers. The 'XX' tiers portray the imminence of YHWH's arrival in Zion, the zealous desire with which he will vindicate Zion before all the nations of the world and the manner in which he will manifest his own covenant loyalty to the Davidic promise to protect and exalt Zion as his holy seat. They function to reassure YHWH's people that there is still present an offer of reconciliation, exemplified by YHWH's loyalty to and zeal for his covenant of grant to David. The innermost 'YY' tiers, which ostensibly frame the sectional axis (61:1-3a), present the glorification of YHWH through his redemptive vindication of Zion and the joyous restoration of her citizens. But it is in the middle of the three 'YY' tiers that the motivational rhetoric of appeal reaches its pinnacle through the prediction of unmixed 'everlasting joy' (61:7bβ) that will be shared among the citizens of Zion when at last the city is redeemed.

The various insets, while furnishing continuity among the tiers of this section by means of verbatim repetition, also demarcate the patterns of repetition within each tier. The latter demarcating function may become more apparent through a closer analysis of each tier, which will be offered below. Indeed, many of the insets serve as the structural axes of the complexes in which they are found. For the present, however, I will simply draw attention to the correspondences and differences between the repetition pattern among the tiers of this section and that among its insets. The two motifs of the 'Insets-A' do not occur in symmetry yet there seems to be some rhetorical strategy to their placement at ideological pivot points within the tiers. That is, Inset-Aα (סֹלּוּ־סֹלּוּ 'Build up' 2x/פַּנּוּ־דָרֶךְ 'Clear the way', 57:14-15) serves as the hortatory pivot of the WW-tier, Inset-A$^i\beta$ (וְאֵין עוֹבֵר 'No one passing through', 60:14-15) as the pivot of the YY-tier, and Inset-A$^{ii}\beta\alpha$ (עָבְרוּ עִבְרוּ 'Pass through' 2x; [הָעָם] [בַּשְּׁעָרִים] פַּנּוּ דֶרֶךְ [הָעָם] 'Clear the way'/סֹלּוּ סֹלּוּ 'Build up' 2x, [הַמְסִלָּה] 62:10) as the hortatory pivot of the YY^{ii}-tier. There is also a noticeable increase in referential specificity in the third 'Inset-A' (62:10), where both the 'α' and 'β' motifs of the inset occur in juxtaposition. The 'Insets-B', while positioned differently within their respective tiers, each occur in contiguity with 'WW' tiers: tier WW[i] contains Inset-B (Pivot: הִנֵּנִי [וַיֹּאמֶר] 'Here am I', 58:9a), and tier WW[ii] presents Inset-B[i] (הִנֵּנִי הִנֵּנִי [אָמַרְתִּי] 'Here am I' 2x, 65:1) in a multivalent verse near its conclusion. Finally, one may observe that the three 'Insets-C', while positioned in a balanced arrangement within the section, develop a theme that links the promise of vindication for YHWH's anointed with a portrayal of YHWH's own great day of vindication/redemption. The framing instances of these insets occur in contiguity with the matching 'XX' tiers, XX with Inset-Cα (Closing: YHWH's promise of vindication for his anointed, 59:21), and XX[i] with Inset-C[ii]β (Pivot: Arrival of YHWH's 'day of vengeance/year of redemption', 63:4). The middle occurrence, Inset-C[i]αβ (Pivot: Proclamation of YHWH's 'year of favor/day of vengeance' by his anointed, 61:1-3a), which alone juxtaposes the two motifs of these C-insets, serves also as the main axis of the section comprising chs. 55–66. The interrelation between the triadic repetition patterns of the A-, and C-insets, together with the simple framing repetition of the B-insets, offers structural counterpoint to the alternative concentric patterning of repetitions exhibited among the main tiers of the section. The variation between the repetition pattern of insets and that of the tiers only serves to heighten aesthetic interest, especially since by this means the correspondence between insets and their host tiers fluctuates (e.g., the A-insets are twice hosted by matching 'YY' tiers, but once by the WW-tier; the B-insets are both hosted by the other two of the three 'WW' tiers; the C-insets are twice hosted by the matching 'XX' tiers, but also by the remaining central 'YY' tier). This results in a general conformity to a pattern of concentricity, but with asymmetrical variation.

Substructural Complexes in Isaiah 55:1–66:24

In what follows, I offer an expanded outline of each tier that appears in the foregoing diagram of Isa. 55:1–66:24. By and large, the patterns of repetition that emerge are similar to those previously encountered in every major section of the book of Isaiah. For instance, the VV-tier (55:1–56:8), which commences the appeal section of Isaiah, seems to manifest the following pattern of triadic repetitions:

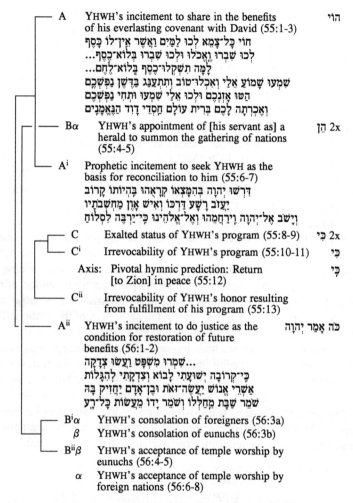

A   YHWH's incitement to share in the benefits
of his everlasting covenant with David (55:1-3)   הוֹי

חוֹי כָּל־צָמֵא לְכוּ לַמַּיִם וַאֲשֶׁר אֵין־לוֹ כָּסֶף
לְכוּ שִׁבְרוּ וֶאֱכֹלוּ וּלְכוּ שִׁבְרוּ בְּלוֹא־כֶסֶף...
לָמָּה תִשְׁקְלוּ־כֶסֶף בְּלוֹא־לֶחֶם...
שִׁמְעוּ שָׁמוֹעַ אֵלַי וְאִכְלוּ־טוֹב וְתִתְעַנַּג בַּדֶּשֶׁן נַפְשְׁכֶם
הַטּוּ אָזְנְכֶם וּלְכוּ אֵלַי שִׁמְעוּ וּתְחִי נַפְשְׁכֶם
וְאֶכְרְתָה לָכֶם בְּרִית עוֹלָם חַסְדֵי דָוִד הַנֶּאֱמָנִים

Bα   YHWH's appointment of [his servant as] a
herald to summon the gathering of nations
(55:4-5)   הֵן 2x

A^i   Prophetic incitement to seek YHWH as the
basis for reconciliation to him (55:6-7)

דִּרְשׁוּ יְהוָה בְּהִמָּצְאוֹ קְרָאֻהוּ בִּהְיוֹתוֹ קָרוֹב
יַעֲזֹב רָשָׁע דַּרְכּוֹ וְאִישׁ אָוֶן מַחְשְׁבֹתָיו
וְיָשֹׁב אֶל־יְהוָה וִירַחֲמֵהוּ וְאֶל־אֱלֹהֵינוּ כִּי־יַרְבֶּה לִסְלוֹחַ

C   Exalted status of YHWH's program (55:8-9)   כִּי 2x
C^i   Irrevocability of YHWH's program (55:10-11)   כִּי

Axis: Pivotal hymnic prediction: Return   כִּי
[to Zion] in peace (55:12)

C^ii   Irrevocability of YHWH's honor resulting
from fulfillment of his program (55:13)

A^ii   YHWH's incitement to do justice as the   כֹּה אָמַר יְהוָה
condition for restoration of future
benefits (56:1-2)

שִׁמְרוּ מִשְׁפָּט וַעֲשׂוּ צְדָקָה...
כִּי־קְרוֹבָה יְשׁוּעָתִי לָבוֹא וְצִדְקָתִי לְהִגָּלוֹת
אַשְׁרֵי אֱנוֹשׁ יַעֲשֶׂה־זֹּאת וּבֶן־אָדָם יַחֲזִיק בָּהּ
שֹׁמֵר שַׁבָּת מֵחַלְּלוֹ וְשֹׁמֵר יָדוֹ מֵעֲשׂוֹת כָּל־רָע

B^iα   YHWH's consolation of foreigners (56:3a)
β   YHWH's consolation of eunuchs (56:3b)
B^iiβ   YHWH's acceptance of temple worship by
eunuchs (56:4-5)
α   YHWH's acceptance of temple worship by
foreign nations (56:6-8)

The next tier is the first of the three accusatory 'WW' tiers (i.e., tier
WW, 56:9–57:21) and seems to take the following form:

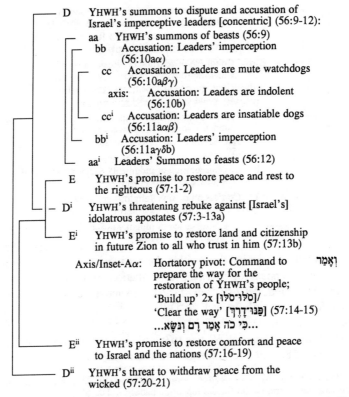

D   YHWH's summons to dispute and accusation of Israel's imperceptive leaders [concentric] (56:9-12):

   aa   YHWH's summons of beasts (56:9)

    bb   Accusation: Leaders' imperception (56:10aα)

     cc   Accusation: Leaders are mute watchdogs (56:10aβγ)

      axis: Accusation: Leaders are indolent (56:10b)

     cc^i   Accusation: Leaders are insatiable dogs (56:11aαβ)

    bb^i   Accusation: Leaders' imperception (56:11aγδb)

   aa^i   Leaders' Summons to feasts (56:12)

E   YHWH's promise to restore peace and rest to the righteous (57:1-2)

D^i   YHWH's threatening rebuke against [Israel's] idolatrous apostates (57:3-13a)

E^i   YHWH's promise to restore land and citizenship in future Zion to all who trust in him (57:13b)

Axis/Inset-Aα: Hortatory pivot: Command to   וְאָמַר
prepare the way for the restoration of YHWH's people;
'Build up' 2x [סֹלּוּ־סֹלּוּ]/
'Clear the way' [פַּנּוּ־דָרֶךְ] (57:14-15)
...כִּי כֹה אָמַר רָם וְנִשָּׂא...

E^ii   YHWH's promise to restore comfort and peace to Israel and the nations (57:16-19)

D^ii   YHWH's threat to withdraw peace from the wicked (57:20-21)

The second 'WW-tier' (i.e., tier WW^i, 58:1–59:15a) shares a similar accusatory–appeal function and seems to bear the following pattern of repetitions:

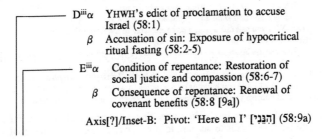

D^iii α   YHWH's edict of proclamation to accuse Israel (58:1)

   β   Accusation of sin: Exposure of hypocritical ritual fasting (58:2-5)

E^iii α   Condition of repentance: Restoration of social justice and compassion (58:6-7)

   β   Consequence of repentance: Renewal of covenant benefits (58:8 [9a])

Axis[?]/Inset-B: Pivot: 'Here am I' [הִנֵּנִי] (58:9a)

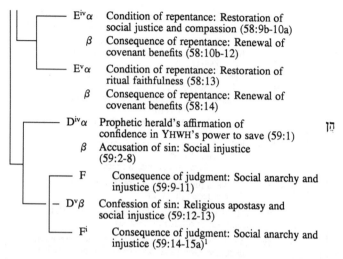

$E^{iv}\alpha$ — Condition of repentance: Restoration of social justice and compassion (58:9b-10a)

β — Consequence of repentance: Renewal of covenant benefits (58:10b-12)

$E^v\alpha$ — Condition of repentance: Restoration of ritual faithfulness (58:13)

β — Consequence of repentance: Renewal of covenant benefits (58:14)

$D^{iv}\alpha$ — Prophetic herald's affirmation of confidence in Y<small>HWH</small>'s power to save (59:1)

הַ

β — Accusation of sin: Social injustice (59:2-8)

F — Consequence of judgment: Social anarchy and injustice (59:9-11)

$D^v\beta$ — Confession of sin: Religious apostasy and social injustice (59:12-13)

F^i — Consequence of judgment: Social anarchy and injustice (59:14-15a)[1]

It is worth mentioning that, within the broader rhetorical concerns of chs. 55–66 to appeal for covenant reconciliation the formal 'accusations of sin' (i.e., $D^{iii}\beta$, 58:2-5; $D^{iv}\beta$, 59:2-8) are functionally elicitations of a 'confession of sin'. Indeed, a '$D\beta$' subtier once becomes explicitly confessional (i.e., $D^v\beta$, 59:12-13).

The third and final 'WW' tier (63:7–65:7) bears closest affinities to tier WW^i (58:1–59:15a), though the rhetorical function of all three

---

[1]Polan (*In the Ways of Justice toward Salvation*, p. 233) has proposed the following concentric model for the repetition pattern in Isa. 58:1-14:

  (A) Declare to the *house of Jacob* their transgressions (58:1b)

    (B) Yet me *day after day* they seek, a knowledge of *my ways they take pleasure in*, like a nation which *has acted* in righteousness [...] (58:2)

      (C) Why [...] do *we humble ourselves* and you do not know it (58:3a)

        (D) Behold, you fast [...] to strike with a *wicked* fist (58:4a)

          (E) Is *this* the *fast I choose* [...] (58:5a)

            (F) Will you call this a *fast*, a *day* acceptable to the *Lord* (58:5bγδ)

          (E) Is not *this* the *fast I choose*? (58:6aα)

        (D) To loose the bonds of *wickedness* (58:6aβ)

      (C) And the *self* of the *humbled one* you satisfy (58:10a)

    (B) If you turn back your foot from the sabbath, from *doing* your own *pleasures* on my holy *day* [...] If you honor it by not *acting* in *your own ways* [...] (58:13)

  (A) And I shall nourish you with the *inheritance of Jacob* your father (58:14bα).

However, this model seems less than compelling as a structural schema for 58:1-14, partly because it fails to account for over sixty percent of the material that it purports to diagram, and partly because it runs askew of the rhetorical shift from accusation (58:2-5) to an alternation between three protases (58:6-7, 9b-10a, 13) and their respective apodoses (58:8[-9a], 10b-12, 14) on the issue of the renewal of covenant benefits. Polan elsewhere does acknowledge the shift between 58:1-5 and 58:6-14 (cf. p. 325).

'WW' tiers remains predominantly accusatory. The framework pattern
of repetitions in the WW[ii]-tier may be as follows:

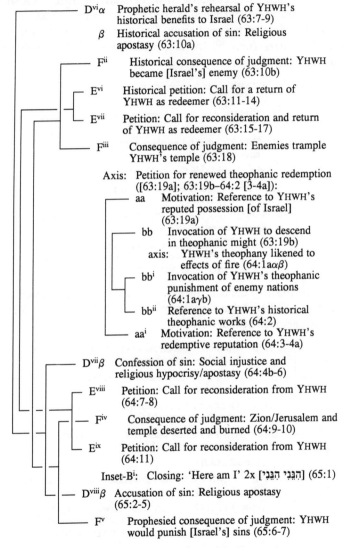

D[vi]α Prophetic herald's rehearsal of YHWH's
historical benefits to Israel (63:7-9)

β Historical accusation of sin: Religious
apostasy (63:10a)

F[ii] Historical consequence of judgment: YHWH
became [Israel's] enemy (63:10b)

E[vi] Historical petition: Call for a return of
YHWH as redeemer (63:11-14)

E[vii] Petition: Call for reconsideration and return
of YHWH as redeemer (63:15-17)

F[iii] Consequence of judgment: Enemies trample
YHWH's temple (63:18)

Axis: Petition for renewed theophanic redemption
([63:19a]; 63:19b–64:2 [3-4a]):

aa Motivation: Reference to YHWH's
reputed possession [of Israel]
(63:19a)

bb Invocation of YHWH to descend
in theophanic might (63:19b)

axis: YHWH's theophany likened to
effects of fire (64:1aαβ)

bb[i] Invocation of YHWH's theophanic
punishment of enemy nations
(64:1aγb)

bb[ii] Reference to YHWH's historical
theophanic works (64:2)

aa[i] Motivation: Reference to YHWH's
redemptive reputation (64:3-4a)

D[vii]β Confession of sin: Social injustice and
religious hypocrisy/apostasy (64:4b-6)

E[viii] Petition: Call for reconsideration from YHWH
(64:7-8)

F[iv] Consequence of judgment: Zion/Jerusalem and
temple deserted and burned (64:9-10)

E[ix] Petition: Call for reconsideration from YHWH
(64:11)

Inset-B[i]: Closing: 'Here am I' 2x [הִנֵּנִי הִנֵּנִי] (65:1)

D[viii]β Accusation of sin: Religious apostasy
(65:2-5)

F[v] Prophesied consequence of judgment: YHWH
would punish [Israel's] sins (65:6-7)

Once again, in a 'WW' tier, there is functional (and structural)
correlation between those 'Dβ' subtiers that are formally 'accusations

of sin' (e.g., D^viβ, 63:10a; D^viiiβ, 65:2-5) and that which is a 'confession of sin' (D^viiβ, 64:4b-6).

Enclosed within the accusatory 'WW' tiers are the paired 'XX' tiers, whose primary rhetorical function seems to be to predict and portray the arrival in Zion of her vindicator. The structure of the first of these paired 'XX' tiers (i.e., 59:15b-20), with Inset-C (59:21) appended, appears as follows:

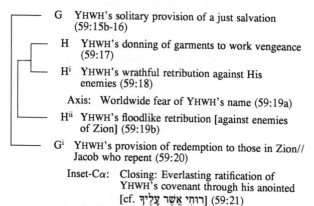

    G   YHWH's solitary provision of a just salvation
          (59:15b-16)

      H   YHWH's donning of garments to work vengeance
          (59:17)

      H^i YHWH's wrathful retribution against His
           enemies (59:18)

      Axis: Worldwide fear of YHWH's name (59:19a)

      H^ii YHWH's floodlike retribution [against enemies
            of Zion] (59:19b)

    G^i   YHWH's provision of redemption to those in Zion//
           Jacob who repent (59:20)

      Inset-Cα: Closing: Everlasting ratification of
                 YHWH's covenant through his anointed
                 [cf. רוּחִי אֲשֶׁר עָלֶיךָ] (59:21)

Tier XX^i (63:1-6) contains themes and motifs similar to those of the foregoing 'XX' tier. It has a pattern of repetition that seems to form the following compound framework:

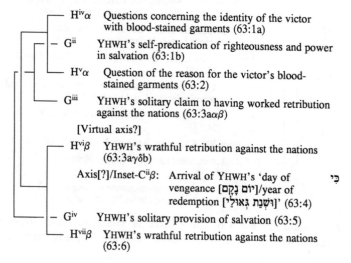

      H^ivα   Questions concerning the identity of the victor
              with blood-stained garments (63:1a)

    G^ii   YHWH's self-predication of righteousness and power
             in salvation (63:1b)

      H^vα   Question of the reason for the victor's blood-
              stained garments (63:2)

    G^iii   YHWH's solitary claim to having worked retribution
             against the nations (63:3aαβ)

      [Virtual axis?]

      H^viβ   YHWH's wrathful retribution against the nations
              (63:3aγδb)

      Axis[?]/Inset-C^iiβ: Arrival of YHWH's 'day of   כִּי
                            vengeance [יוֹם נָקָם]/year of
                            redemption [וּשְׁנַת גְּאוּלַי]' (63:4)

    G^iv   YHWH's solitary provision of salvation (63:5)

      H^viiβ YHWH's wrathful retribution against the nations
              (63:6)

Complementing the 'WW' tiers, and in inverse rhetorical and structural relation to them, are the 'YY' tiers. These comprise the innermost triadic framework of tiers within Isaiah 55–66. They share a common focus on themes associated with Zion's redemption. The first 'YY' tier (60:1-20) seems to have the following asymmetrically concentric framework structure:

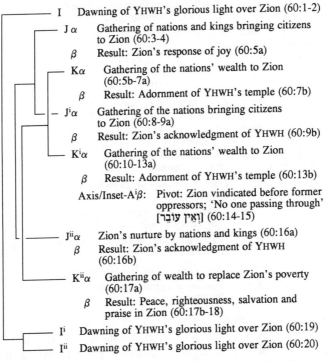

I   Dawning of YHWH's glorious light over Zion (60:1-2)

J α   Gathering of nations and kings bringing citizens to Zion (60:3-4)

β   Result: Zion's response of joy (60:5a)

K α   Gathering of the nations' wealth to Zion (60:5b-7a)

β   Result: Adornment of YHWH's temple (60:7b)

Jⁱ α   Gathering of the nations bringing citizens to Zion (60:8-9a)

β   Result: Zion's acknowledgment of YHWH (60:9b)

Kⁱ α   Gathering of the nations' wealth to Zion (60:10-13a)

β   Result: Adornment of YHWH's temple (60:13b)

Axis/Inset-Aⁱβ: Pivot: Zion vindicated before former oppressors; 'No one passing through' [וְאֵין עוֹבֵר] (60:14-15)

Jⁱⁱ α   Zion's nurture by nations and kings (60:16a)

β   Result: Zion's acknowledgment of YHWH (60:16b)

Kⁱⁱ α   Gathering of wealth to replace Zion's poverty (60:17a)

β   Result: Peace, righteousness, salvation and praise in Zion (60:17b-18)

Iⁱ   Dawning of YHWH's glorious light over Zion (60:19)

Iⁱⁱ   Dawning of YHWH's glorious light over Zion (60:20)

The triadic outer frame, comprising the 'I' subtiers, is unique to the first 'YY' tier. So also is the balanced representation of both 'α' and 'β' elements in each of the bifid 'J' and 'K' subtiers of this segment. Thus, the YY-tier is distinguished from the succeeding two 'YY' tiers by being the only complete 'YY' tier. Correspondingly, tiers YYⁱ and YYⁱⁱ will tend to fragment the bifid 'J' and 'K' subtiers and emphasize the 'β' and 'α' halves, respectively.

The main axis of chs. 55–66 (i.e., 61:1-3aα) appears to be contained within the second 'YY' tier (60:21–61:11), though its placement at the beginning of this tier gives it a demarcating force that ostensibly separates tier YY from tiers YYⁱ and YYⁱⁱ. The YYⁱ-tier (60:21–61:11), in association with the main axis of the section, thus becomes the rhetorical high point of chs. 55–66, with Zion's everlasting joy at YHWH's redemption being its thematic focus. The compound framework structure of this central tier appears to be as follows:

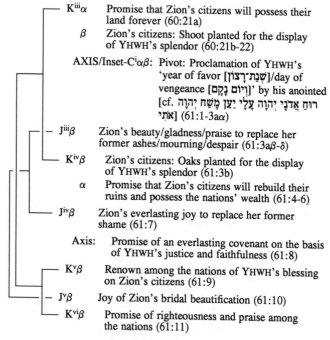

K^{iii}α Promise that Zion's citizens will possess their land forever (60:21a)

β Zion's citizens: Shoot planted for the display of YHWH's splendor (60:21b-22)

AXIS/Inset-C^{i}αβ: Pivot: Proclamation of YHWH's 'year of favor [שְׁנַת־רָצוֹן]/day of vengeance [וְיוֹם נָקָם]' by his anointed [cf. רוּחַ אֲדֹנָי יְהוָה עָלָי יַעַן מָשַׁח יְהוָה אֹתִי] (61:1-3aα)

J^{iii}β Zion's beauty/gladness/praise to replace her former ashes/mourning/despair (61:3aβ-δ)

K^{iv}β Zion's citizens: Oaks planted for the display of YHWH's splendor (61:3b)

α Promise that Zion's citizens will rebuild their ruins and possess the nations' wealth (61:4-6)

J^{iv}β Zion's everlasting joy to replace her former shame (61:7)

Axis: Promise of an everlasting covenant on the basis of YHWH's justice and faithfulness (61:8)

K^{v}β Renown among the nations of YHWH's blessing on Zion's citizens (61:9)

J^{v}β Joy of Zion's bridal beautification (61:10)

K^{vi}β Promise of righteousness and praise among the nations (61:11)

Of the formerly bifid 'J' subtiers (in tier YY, 60:1-20), only the 'β' element is now represented in tier YY^i. Similarly, only the 'β' element of the bifid 'K' subtiers is consistently present. An analogous imbalance in the YY^{ii}-tier that follows fairly compensates for this imbalance in the presentation of the bifid elements.

The final 'YY' tier (62:1-12) has the following structure, which comprises paired triadic frames:

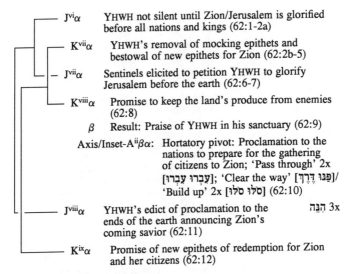

$J^{vi}\alpha$ — YHWH not silent until Zion/Jerusalem is glorified before all nations and kings (62:1-2a)

$K^{vii}\alpha$ — YHWH's removal of mocking epithets and bestowal of new epithets for Zion (62:2b-5)

$J^{vii}\alpha$ — Sentinels elicited to petition YHWH to glorify Jerusalem before the earth (62:6-7)

$K^{viii}\alpha$ — Promise to keep the land's produce from enemies (62:8)

β — Result: Praise of YHWH in his sanctuary (62:9)

Axis/Inset-$A^{ii}\beta\alpha$: Hortatory pivot: Proclamation to the nations to prepare for the gathering of citizens to Zion; 'Pass through' 2x [עִבְרוּ עִבְרוּ]; 'Clear the way' [פַּנּוּ דֶרֶךְ]/ 'Build up' 2x [סֹלּוּ סֹלּוּ] (62:10)

$J^{viii}\alpha$ — YHWH's edict of proclamation to the ends of the earth announcing Zion's coming savior (62:11)   הִנֵּה 3x

$K^{ix}\alpha$ — Promise of new epithets of redemption for Zion and her citizens (62:12)

As previously noted, the YY^{ii}-tier represents only the 'α' elements of the bifid 'J' subtiers, and similarly, of the bifid 'K' subtiers, only the 'α' element is consistently present. This structural complementarity between the bifid elements of the YY^{i} and YY^{ii} tiers, which brings only their aggregate into conformity with the prototypical form given in the YY-tier can hardly be fortuitous. Once again, the principle of repetition with variation serves to elevate interest and intensifies the rhetorical force of these complementary and highly motivating 'YY' tiers.

The final tier of the appeal section (i.e., VV^{i}, 65:2-7[?], 8–66:24) is also the final tier of the book of Isaiah. Accordingly, the author/compiler incorporated into this closing appeal section something of a peroration of key themes and motifs taken from the whole book and especially from the exordium, with which it forms an inclusio about the book as a whole. Owing to the regularity of the triadic repetition pattern in both this and the matching VV-tier (55:1–56:8), one should expect to find three repetitions of threats against idolaters in this tier, and one may, but only if the first 'A' subtier (65:2-7) is judged to serve double duty as a hinge linking tier WW^{ii} with tier VV^{i}. The pattern of repetitions in this final tier may be diagrammed as follows:

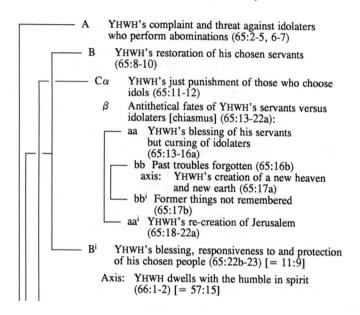

A   YHWH's complaint and threat against idolaters
     who perform abominations (65:2-5, 6-7)

B   YHWH's restoration of his chosen servants
     (65:8-10)

Cα   YHWH's just punishment of those who choose
     idols (65:11-12)

 β   Antithetical fates of YHWH's servants versus
     idolaters [chiasmus] (65:13-22a):

     aa YHWH's blessing of his servants
         but cursing of idolaters
         (65:13-16a)

       bb Past troubles forgotten (65:16b)
           axis: YHWH's creation of a new heaven
                  and new earth (65:17a)
       bbⁱ Former things not remembered
           (65:17b)

     aaⁱ YHWH's re-creation of Jerusalem
          (65:18-22a)

Bⁱ   YHWH's blessing, responsiveness to and protection
     of his chosen people (65:22b-23) [= 11:9]

Axis: YHWH dwells with the humble in spirit
       (66:1-2) [= 57:15]

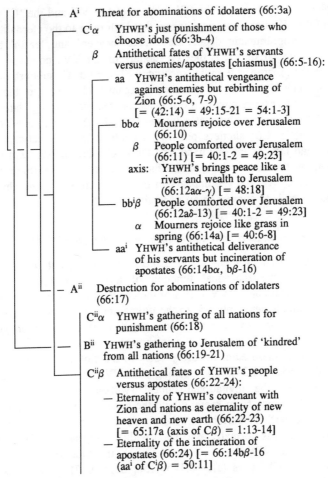

A^i Threat for abominations of idolaters (66:3a)

$C^i\alpha$ YHWH's just punishment of those who choose idols (66:3b-4)

β Antithetical fates of YHWH's servants versus enemies/apostates [chiasmus] (66:5-16):

aa   YHWH's antithetical vengeance against enemies but rebirthing of Zion (66:5-6, 7-9) [= (42:14) = 49:15-21 = 54:1-3]

bbα Mourners rejoice over Jerusalem (66:10)

β People comforted over Jerusalem (66:11) [= 40:1-2 = 49:23]

axis: YHWH's brings peace like a river and wealth to Jerusalem (66:12aα-γ) [= 48:18]

bb$^i\beta$ People comforted over Jerusalem (66:12aδ-13) [= 40:1-2 = 49:23]

α Mourners rejoice like grass in spring (66:14a) [= 40:6-8]

aa^i YHWH's antithetical deliverance of his servants but incineration of apostates (66:14bα, bβ-16)

A^{ii} Destruction for abominations of idolaters (66:17)

$C^{ii}\alpha$ YHWH's gathering of all nations for punishment (66:18)

B^{ii} YHWH's gathering to Jerusalem of 'kindred' from all nations (66:19-21)

$C^{ii}\beta$ Antithetical fates of YHWH's people versus apostates (66:22-24):

— Eternality of YHWH's covenant with Zion and nations as eternality of new heaven and new earth (66:22-23) [= 65:17a (axis of Cβ) = 1:13-14]

— Eternality of the incineration of apostates (66:24) [= 66:14bβ-16 (aa^i of C$^i\beta$) = 50:11]

This closing 'VV' tier complements, positionally and thematically, the 'VV' tier that opened chs. 55–66. For instance, the 'A' subtiers of tier VV^i, which portray the punishment threatened against idolaters who neglect YHWH's covenant appeals, contrast with the 'A' subtiers of tier VV (55:1–56:8), where such appeals were more positive in tone and offered a restoration of covenant benefits. The 'B' subtiers of tier VV^i, which portray the gathering to the elect of Jerusalem of 'kindred' from all nations, complement the 'B' subtiers of tier VV, where faithful foreigners and eunuchs were portrayed as comforted by being allowed to enter the temple of future Zion. There seems to be no thematic

complementarity between the 'C' subtiers of tier VV and the 'C' subtiers of the VV^i-tier, however, except that both refer to the eternality of
YHWH's programmatic decree and make 'heaven' and 'earth' their
object of comparison. It is the 'C' subtiers of tier VV^i, however, that
achieve the greatest referential specificity. The bifid 'C' subtiers of the
VV^i-tier match threats of punishment against idolaters (in the 'α'
halves) with programmatic portrayals of the contrasting fates of
YHWH's servants and apostates (in the 'β' halves). Thus, each of the
programmatic 'Cβ' subtiers portrays a contrast in fates between the
faithful and just, on the one hand, and those who have apostasized from
YHWH, on the other. Each of the final statements of the three main
subtiers (i.e., A^{ii}, B^{ii}, C^{ii}) appears in prose, which is a fitting shift of
discourse mode to convey an air of finality.

Persuasion as a Function of Structure in Isaiah 55:1–66:24

The organization of themes and dispositions throughout this section
conforms to the rhetorical function of a covenant appeal to be
reconciled. The outer ('VV') tiers of the concentric structure presented
here contain elements intrinsic to the ultimatum expected of a covenant
disputation. Normally, the ultimatum segment of a disputation genre
would include either a threat of punishment or an appeal to be reconciled; both of these elements are present in the closing tier of the section (VV^i, 65:8–66:24). The opening tier (VV, 55:1–56:8), however,
presents only the invitational appeal (without any accompanying
threat), which may be in keeping with the generally positive disposition
of the section.[1] Nevertheless, the threat of a repeal of covenant
benefits, which is normally associated with the appeal, may be seen in
the contiguous WW-tier (i.e., 56:9–57:21), the first of the generally
accusatory 'WW' tiers (cf. 58:1–59:15a; 63:7–65:7). In any case, it
would appear that the 'VV' and 'WW' tiers share the closest rhetorical
affinities since they both focus on conditions necessary to the renewal
of covenant benefits.

In contrast, the affiliated inner tiers ('XX' and 'YY') offer positive
motivation for this section's overall appeal to be reinstated to the terms
of YHWH's covenant. There is both the portrayal of the imminence of
the fulfillment of YHWH's promise to vindicate Zion before her

---

[1] In any event, motivation for covenant reconciliation would always remain the
main rhetorical aim for a covenant ultimatum, whether represented in the form of
threat or appeal, since otherwise there would be little reason for writing a work
under the rhetoric of covenant disputation.

enemies, in the 'XX' tiers (59:15b-20; 63:1-6), and, in the 'YY' tiers, the promise of redemption and jubilation for all who would be citizens of future Zion.

The Continuity of Isaiah 55:1–66:24 with its Context

This section's development of the motif of light (e.g., 58:8a, 10b; 59:9-10; 60:1-3, 5, 19-20; 62:1) and of the exaltation of YHWH's (holy) mountain (e.g., 56:7; 57:13; 64:1, 3; 65:7, 9, 11, 25; 66:20) was anticipated already in the closing appeals of Isaiah's exordium (cf. 'Come, O house of Jacob, let us walk in the light of YHWH' [2:5] and the interest in YHWH's mountain, in 2:2-3a). Indeed, the evident motivic affinities between chs. 55–66 and the 'CC' tiers of Isaiah's exordium is in keeping with my proposal that the exordium was intended to serve as a cameo of the rhetorical elements of the covenant disputation pattern that governs the book as a whole (excepting, of course, the strategic omission of any foreshadowing of its exoneration section).

The asymmetrically concentric structure of this section bears closest affinities with the similar arrangement of 4:2–11:16 and 13:1–39:8. This correlation, in concert with structural correspondences among the other main sections of the book, furnishes the last needed indication that a pattern of complex frameworking pervades the book as a whole. I shall discuss the implications of the pervasiveness of this pattern in the conclusion to this study.

CONCLUSION

A number of inferences may be drawn from the findings of the foregoing chapters of this study. Initially, a structural summation that presents together the patterns of all the main sections of Isaiah would be in order. Then, on the basis of this summation, it should be ascertained how best to read the book's contributing sections and their constituents in the light of its comprehensive structure. How does the author make structural cohesion serve rhetorical development? Related to the foregoing question, one should also attempt to form some set of genre criteria whereby to make sense of the totality of the book. What are the most legitimate methods by which to read Isaiah competently? What are its enabling conventions? Finally, as a means of synthesizing one's reading, one should ask, What was the (implied) author's message to the original (intended) readers? This last question may sharpen one's focus in regard to those issues of central concern to Isaiah's (implied) author and may lay the ground for developing a biblical theology of the book that also takes account of its literary interests. In what follows, I shall briefly address, in succession, each of these four concerns.

The Literary Structure of Isaiah

In retrospect, one can see that the book of Isaiah comprises a series of asymmetrically concentric structures arranged into an implicit line of argumentation that seems to have been designed to evoke from its readers a response of remorse for sin and a desire to be reconciled with YHWH. Including the exordium, there are seven sections in all, and, apart from the exordium, the sections offer permutations of essentially two complex framework patterns of repetition. The following is an arrangement of the schemata of Isaiah's main sections, which, despite their varying proportions, can be seen to share quite analogous architectural designs:

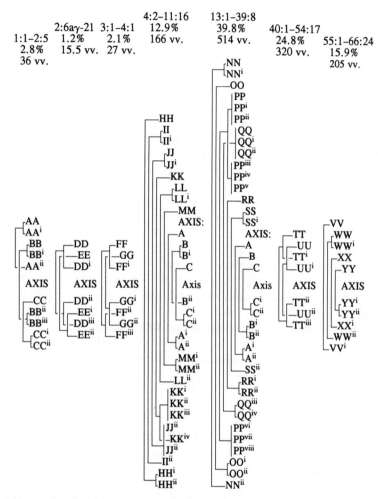

It is difficult to imagine how such order could have occurred apart from deliberate adherence to a single structural design during the process of the compilation of each of the book's main sections as well as of its final form. This is not necessarily proof of a single author for every subsection or speech form now contained in the book of Isaiah, but it does imply that the book came into its present arrangement largely as the work of a single compiler. At the remotest extent, it might be reasonable to contend that the book was compiled in stages by a series of authors executing an agreed upon strategy for its overall tiered architectural arrangement and its asymmetrically concentric ordering of tier repetitions. More to my own way of thinking, however, is the proposition that the book as a whole was the creation of a sixth-century author/compiler who integrated the written prophecies of eighth-century Isaiah, together with that author/compiler's own writings, into a prophetic exemplar of covenant disputation. This would account not only for the pervasiveness of its pattern of tier repetitions but for the coherent rhetorical strategy of the book as a whole under the rubric of covenant disputation.[1]

[1]The arrangement (if not composition) of certain portions of chs. 1–39 readily emerges as the work of the sixth-century author/compiler, even if many of the materials contained there had been composed originally by the eighth-century author. The transitional materials between the large concentric sections (i.e., 2:6aαβ, 22; 12:1-6) clearly reflect the hand of a compiler. In the exordium of 1:1–2:5, the 'CC' tiers seem newly added, insofar as they are clearly linked with the invitation motif in the opening section of chs. 55–66, and insofar as this might explain the unusual grouping of the three complex frames in 1:1–2:5. It is doubtful whether tiers 'AA' and 'BB' were arranged into their present order by the eighth-century prophet, even though they appear to have been composed by him, yet their arrangement (with interlocking triadic and quadruple frames) resembles the complex frameworking of both the 'DD' and 'EE' tiers in 2:6aγ-21 and the 'FF' and 'GG' tiers in 3:1–4:1, two sections whose materials (if not arrangement) may likewise be attributable to the eighth-century prophet. The positioning (if not composition) of 1:21-27, which appears at the climactic position (two thirds into the section), may likewise derive from the sixth-century author/compiler.

Further, the placement of the 'HH' and 'II' tiers may be the sixth-century author's/compiler's work. The themes reflected in the 'HH' tiers (4:2-6; 11:1-9, 10-16) are themes that recur and predominate in chs. 40–54 and 55–66. Although the vegetal 'II' tiers may have been separately composed by eighth-century Isaiah, their structural coordination here is more likely the result of the sixth-century author's architectural engineering. Analogously, although ch. 13 of the Babylonian 'NN' tiers is explicitly attributed to the prophet Isaiah, and ch. 39 borrowed from 2 Kgs 20:1-19, their positioning in concert with the poem of 14:4b-23 (itself perhaps newly composed by the final author) probably stems from the sixth-century milieu. If this were so, the same would apply to the addendum of 14:24-25, which reorients the poem of 14:4b-21 to taunt the Assyrian king in accord with the borrowed materials from 2 Kgs 18:13, 17–19:37.

The positioning and, perhaps, composition of the major insets contained in chs. 13–39 may likewise stem from the sixth-century author/compiler. Most of these insets reflect concern to establish continuity between this section (i.e., chs. 13–39) and the contiguous major sections of Isaiah (e.g., 27:2-11 develops the theme of YHWH's vineyard, contained in 5:1-6, 7; 35:1-10 develops the glorious second Exodus theme of 11:11-16 and anticipates the same throughout chs. 40–54 and 55–66). Overall, since the major insets of chs. 13–39 develop the theme of YHWH's exaltation of Zion before the nations, they reflect concern to set up a rhetorical context for the exoneration and appeals of chs. 40–54 and 55–66, respectively, and therefore seem most in line with the rhetorical strategy of the sixth-century author.

No doubt, some of the structural schemata presented in this treatise will require refinement in the light of further study, but in their present condition they offer a number of intriguing correlations. Both the exordium (1:1–2:5) and the final section (55:1–66:24) present a total of ten tiers that, despite their asymmetrical arrangements, are bifurcated by their axes into halves of five tiers each. Of the seven main sections in Isaiah (which, incidentally, differ widely in relative size), this ten-fold arrangement remains unique to these two sections that enclose the book as a whole. It may also be worth observing that the three triadic frames of 1:1–2:5 (those comprising tiers 'AA', 'BB', and 'CC') complement the four frames of 55:1–66:24 (comprising tiers 'VV', 'WW', 'XX', and 'YY') so as to produce an aggregate sum of seven different frames between them. This in itself would not be of much significance were it not for the fact that the number seven otherwise figures so predominantly in the book's overall architecture.

Each of the main sections 2:6aγ-21, 3:1–4:1 and 40:1–54:17 offers a total of seven tiers. Each of these sevenfold structures is bifurcated by its axis into uneven halves, containing 3 + 4, 3 + 4, and 4 + 3 tiers, respectively. However, unlike the outer sections of the book, each of these sections presents only two tier variants (i.e., tiers 'DD' and 'EE', 'FF' and 'GG', and 'TT' and 'UU') so that their aggregate sum is six.

The two remaining main sections (i.e., 4:2–11:16 and 13:1–39:8), while more difficult to number with precision, seem to present a total of twenty-one and twenty-six tiers, respectively, which are bifurcated by their complex axes into uneven halves of 9 + 12 and 15 + 11 tiers, respectively. What is more intriguing, however, is the fact that each of these main sections presents what appear to be six concentric triadic frames (i.e., 4:2–11:16 has frames comprising tiers 'HH', 'II', 'JJ', 'KK', 'LL', and 'MM'; 13:1–39:8 has frames comprising tiers 'NN', 'OO', 'PP', 'QQ', 'RR', and 'SS'), which, with the addition of their complex axes (i.e., 6:11–8:17 and 24:1–27:13), may also comprise sevenfold arrangements.

The correlation between analogous main sections may place added emphasis on the importance of the transitions that come between. This factor may heighten the importance of the transitional role played by Isa. 2:22, which intervenes between 2:6aγ-21 and 3:1–4:1, and by the

Concomitantly, however, since many of the accusations contained within chs. 55–66 were germane to the idolatrous and socially unjust contemporaries of eighth-century Isaiah, perhaps some of the materials in this section (particularly in the 'WW' tiers) were borrowed from Isaiah by the sixth-century author.

hymnic invocation predicted in 12:1-6, which intervenes between 4:2–11:16 and 13:1–39:8. As it turns out, the latter is, rhetorically speaking, a significant hymnic invocation because of its salvific echoes of the Song of YHWH's Victory in Exodus 15.[1]

Literary Networking in the Light of the Literary Structure of Isaiah

By literary networking, I refer to the means by which patterns of structural organization serve the interests of rhetorical development. In the light of the pervasive patterns among the tier repetitions of the book of Isaiah, and the essentially concentric contour of those patterns, how

---

[1]The phraseology of Isa. 12:2b seems to derive from Exod. 15:2, 'YHWH is my strength and my song; he has become my salvation' (cf. also C.A. Evans, 'On the Unity and Parallel Structure of Isaiah', *VT* 38 (1988), p. 139 n.39). The repetition 'YHWH, YHWH' (Isa. 12:2bα) may allude to a similar hymnic passage in Exod. 34:6-7a, where YHWH names himself as the covenant-loyal god: 'YHWH, YHWH, the compassionate and gracious god, slow to anger, abounding in love and faithfulness, maintaining love to thousands and forgiving wickedness, rebellion and sin'. Thus, within Isaiah, there is anticipation that future Zion will experience her deliverance from Assyria (and later enemies) with the same sentiment that Israel had expressed in regard to deliverance from the armies of Egypt.

Given the prevalence of allusion to the Exodus in this context, one may infer that the well imagery of 12:3 derives from Exod. 15:22-27, which describes the situation that followed immediately upon the crossing of the sea. There the turning of bitter water into sweet, followed by reference to the wells of Elim (with the eschatologically symbolic figures, twelve wells and seventy date palms) was conditioned upon the nation obeying YHWH. It was also linked to the deliverance from Egypt: 'If you listen carefully to the voice of YHWH your god and do what is right in his eyes, if you pay attention to his commands and keep all his decrees, I will not bring upon you any of the diseases that I brought upon the Egyptians, for I am YHWH who heals you'.

Further in keeping with the theme of YHWH's victory hymn in Exod. 15 is the fact that the verses of Isa. 12:1-6 seem to incorporate a number of incipits from psalms written in praise of Israel's national deliverance:

Isaiah	Psalms
12:1	9:1?
12:2	26:1?; 18:1?
12:4	105:1
12:5	98:1 [cf. Exod. 15:21]
12:6	48:1; 98:4

There is a strong probability that these were such well-known hymns of national deliverance in the author's day that this concatenated allusion to the incipits of these psalms would have evoked in its hearers a sense of exhilaration not unlike that of the jubilants portrayed in Exod. 15.

does one go about reading and interpreting the book? Perhaps I should make a few suggestions as to how one might discern Isaiah's rhetorical strategy from its repetition patterns, though the limited scope of this study prevents me from elaborating this aspect of the reading process beyond citing just a few examples. First, in all sections where matching tiers (i.e., tiers with the same letter designation) correspond because of shared or antithetical themes or vocabulary, these tiers should be read and interpreted in the context of one another and should be read in succession as thematically developmental. Usually, referential specificity increases with the successive unfolding of these coordinated tiers, making the interpretation of their interrelationship more readily accessible. For example, the 'HHa' tiers, which share the imagery of the royal scion, should probably be interpreted so as to coordinate ideas associated with the royal scion of YHWH (4:2) with those associated with the royal scion of Jesse (11:1-5, 10). Similarly, the ideal natural conditions described in the 'HHb' tiers should probably be interpreted as beginning in Zion (4:3-6), emanating to the whole natural realm (11:6-9), and culminating in the regathering of the remnant (11:11-16).

Second, a prominent place should be given to the ideas conveyed by the axes of concentric forms. When present (i.e., not virtual), such axes will usually yield information that is crucial to the interpretation of the concentric segments in which they occur. It is no coincidence that the cosmic cataclysm of 'Isaiah's apocalypse' (chs. 24–27) finds itself at the center of a palistrophe featuring YHWH's punishment of all nations (chs. 13–39) nor that its own core (25:1-5) celebrates YHWH's triumph over all the ruthless citizens of foreign cities throughout the world.

Third, because certain segments of Isaiah were deliberately juxtaposed, these should be read and interpreted as serving a close rhetorical relationship to each other and, for an interpretation of that relationship, should be read in successive pairs. This is especially the case between all the bifid tiers in the book. For instance, the juxtaposition of the 'HHa' and 'HHb' halves in the bifid 'HH' tiers may be taken to convey a causal relation between the glorification of the royal scion ('HHa' tiers) and the refructification and pacification of the earth ('HHb' tiers). Moreover, even the larger juxtaposed sections of Isaiah that are structurally analogous (i.e., 2:6aγ-21 being analogous to 3:1–4:1; 4:2–11:16 being analogous to 13:1–39:8) should be interpreted as parallel pairs. Isaiah 2:6aγ-21 describes YHWH's judgment against the religiously unfaithful, and 3:1–4:1 delineates his judgment against the socially unjust. Together they decree a dual-edged punishment for humanity's rejection of YHWH's religious and social standards.

Fourth, where there are clustered tiers, such as one finds in the intermediate compound inverse frames of both 4:2–11:16 (i.e., the 'JJ' and 'KK' tiers) and 13:1–39:8 (i.e., tiers 'PP' and 'QQ'), these should be read in contiguity. Nowhere is this better exemplified than among the 'QQ' tiers' that unite Cush and Egypt (symbolic of Egypt's Cushite Dyn. XXV) under the domination of Assyria in 18:1–20:5.

Fifth, it would appear that, when combinations of two or more complex frames make up a compound frame, one should interpret the former as forming a part of the wider context of the latter since compound frames ostensibly comprise superimposed complex frames. In some sections (e.g., 2:6aγ-21 and 3:1–4:1), this is a matter of default since the entire section presents but a single compound frame. In the larger sections (e.g., 4:2–11:16 and 13:1–39:8), this principle becomes more a matter of practice. For example, the 'JJ' and 'KK' tiers of 4:2–11:16 similarly present woe oracles and threats, respectively, that are aimed at the enemies of YHWH (whether the unjust of Israel or Assyria). Likewise, the notion that the roles of Assyria and Babylon should be coordinated in the interpretation of 13:1–39:8 seems corroborated by the fact that the pattern of repetitions among references to these nations in that section forms a unified compound inverse frame (comprising tiers 'NN' and 'OO').

Sixth, the insets of a concentric section should not necessarily be regarded as mere filler (despite my describing them as furnishing structural mortar between the oracular blocks) but should be read in succession so as to determine whether they may be interpreted as thematically developmental. The insets of 13:1–39:8 are particularly important for the development of the theme of YHWH's exaltation of Zion and its Davidic ruler over enemy nations. Indeed, the full import of this section would be missed if YHWH's intervening oracles against the nations were not read in the light of the intermittent development of this theme. It is only through a recognition of YHWH's ongoing intention to exalt Zion through the rulership of her Davidic king that Isaiah 13–39 sets up the expectation that Hezekiah might be the one to fulfill this hope. And this, in turn, is an expectation that is set up in chainlink sequence with the preceding section, in which Isaiah confronts Ahaz for his failure to fulfill the Davidic ideal, namely, that the king should trust YHWH to defend him and his city.

Finally, stress should be laid upon the fact that the three-leveled hierarchy of tiers in Isa. 40:1–54:17 should be interpreted according to its branching pattern. For example, the second-level tiers that make up the section 43:16–46:13 should be interpreted in relation to one another as comprising a unified and coherent structure under one first-level branch (i.e., tier TT^i) before this complex is read in relation to other equal ranking complexes (i.e., tiers TT, TT^{ii} or TT^{iii}). The same principle should hold true for all third-level tiers, where they cohere structurally under the single branch of a second-level tier. For instance, the fact that the complex comprising tier TT^{iii} (49:1–54:17) is so emotionally wringing has everything to do with its juxtaposing of contrasts into a coherent design. The poignancy effected by contrasting YHWH's words of comfort to Zion (in the 'A' tiers), which culminate in his summoning her from dormancy (51:9–52:2), with the stark pathos-filled descriptions of the suffering of his rejected messenger and the resultant vindication that YHWH intends to bring about on his servant's behalf (in the 'B' tiers), is unparalleled in Hebrew literature.

Genre Competence in the Light of Isaiah's Literary Form

One may conclude that the book of Isaiah presents the structural unity, logical coherence and rhetorical emphasis that one should expect of a literary entity composed under the controlling conventions of a single literary genre. Its structural unity is particularly evident in the pervasive use of closely analogous asymmetrical, concentric patterns of tier repetitions. The matching tiers within these asymmetrical palistrophes correspond to one another in such a way that they are mutually interpretative and focus rhetorical emphasis upon the axes of each of the main sections of the book. In addition, there is evidence that the main sections have been arranged according to a strategy whereby they present progressively rhetorical elements that are germane to and cohere under the rubric of a biblical covenant disputation.

On the strength of Isaiah's conformity to the set of rhetorical conventions found to be typical of covenant disputations, there may be sufficient ground for asserting that the book of Isaiah as a whole was thus ordered as a means whereby its author/compiler might evoke in the reader a desire for covenant reconciliation to YHWH. It would appear that this controlling hypothesis (that Isaiah is controlled by a rhetoric of covenant disputation) may better enable the reader to generate maximal relevance in interrelating and interpreting the parts of the book of Isaiah in relation to the whole.

The patterns of collocation and thematic registration recognized in this study need not be seen to stray from the patterns of compilation proposed under the various source- and redaction-critical treatments of Isaiah that have been offered to date. Nevertheless, one is not likely to find an accounting for the structural model proposed in this study in the standard models of the formation of Isaiah. By recognizing that the coherence that exists among the major sections of Isaiah derives from their analogous patterns and from their aggregate conformity to a rhetoric of covenant disputation, one may be in a better position to account for the design of the whole book than one would be if limited to the proposals for Isaiah's formation that have thus far appeared. In view of the structural cohesion afforded the book of Isaiah by the concentric and complex framing patterns within each of its main sections, as well as the structural analogy among the sections 2:6aγ-21, 3:1–4:1 and 40:1–54:17, or between 4:2–11:16 and 13:1–39:8, it is difficult to imagine that, apart from possible minor adjustments, all the various parts of these sections came to be compiled into their present arrangement apart from the control of a single rhetorical-structural design.

In view of the introductory role that Isaiah's exordium (1:1–2:5) has in relation to the book as a whole, one should perhaps count it significant that this exordium has sometimes been recognized as displaying a set of elements that is typical of covenant disputation. This alone may have prompted its genre-competent readers to suspect that a rhetoric of covenant disputation controls the book of Isaiah. But what seems more significant to the rhetorical strategy of the prophecy is the omission from the exordium of any statement of the innocence of the offended party (namely, YHWH). It is this omission that, while frustrating one's genre sensitivities, sets up a delay of genre expectations, through a strategy of retardation, that continues until the climactic arrival of YHWH's (and his servant's) exoneration in chs. 40–54. Furthermore, this pattern of delay becomes a literary emblem of the delay in history of YHWH's long-awaited vindication of Zion before her Babylonian captors.

The Message of Isaiah in the Light of its Literary Form

One's view of the referential significance of the book of Isaiah is crucial to one's understanding of the message of the book and how it was intended to function as a persuasive device when received by its intended readers. It seems that the rhetoric of Isaiah is complicated by the fact that it aims at two, or possibly three, groups of intended readers separated in time and locale: the unrepentant eighth- to seventh-century BCE contemporaries of Isaiah in Zion, their yet-to-be-repentant descendants in exile in Babylon and ostensibly the same community, after they had returned to Jerusalem, who needed to be reminded to repent as the prerequisite for rebuilding the temple and walls of Jerusalem. In fact, it is this very temporal and geographical multivalence of the book's prophecy–fulfillment scenario that constitutes the proof for YHWH's claims of incomparability in chs. 40–54. Who else but the true god could accurately have portrayed an event such as that of Cyrus' deliverance of Zion from Babylon and have used this as means to vindicate himself and his prophetic servant from Zion's previous rejection? Although YHWH had fully intended to rebuke and punish the Zion of Isaiah's day, he had also predicted in Isaiah's day that, after punishment, he would restore a remnant to future Zion. The means by which this rhetorical task would be accomplished in history mirrors the strategy of delay and the transference from blindness to perception that are portrayed in the book of Isaiah.

The prophetic scenario by which YHWH's message was effected in history developed in the following manner: First, the prophet was commissioned to relate YHWH's message to his evil contemporaries in such a way that it would remain inscrutable to them (cf. 6:8-10), and this so that they should suffer the effects of having rejected YHWH's message (cf. 6:11-13). The prophet twice conveyed this message of coming punishment through historical confrontations with Zion's kings, Ahaz (7:1–8:10) and Hezekiah (36:1–39:8). The terms for reconciliation, as set forth in his prophecies, required both a confession of guilt for religious apostasy (cf. 2:6aγ-21) and social injustices (cf. 3:1–4:1) and a consequent return to covenant loyalty to YHWH and his standards of justice. However, the citizens of Zion utterly rejected both YHWH's message and his prophetic messenger.[1] Next, the prophecy's chainlink pattern of the deferral of punishment (evident in both literary form and historical fulfillment), whereby Isaiah had twice predicted to a Davidic monarch that an imminent military threat against Zion would be delayed until that nation in whom they had sought an ally had later become an even greater threat to Zion (i.e., 7:1–8:10; 36:1–39:8), is further linked with a delay of fulfillment for YHWH's promise to

---

[1] According to Jewish tradition, the prophet Isaiah was martyred by being sawn in half during Manasseh's reign. Cf. the testimony of the uncorroborated Jewish tradition in *The Martyrdom of Isaiah* with Heb. 11:37.

vindicate his rejected messenger (again, evident in both literary form
and historical fulfillment). Just as the delay of the genre's exoneration
section, omitted from the exordium, is retarded until chs. 40–54, so
there would be a prolonged delay in history between the time of
Isaiah's rejection by Zion, the intervening devastation of the generation
that had rejected him and Isaiah's final vindication (albeit
posthumously) through the fulfillment of his predictions concerning
Zion's exile to and deliverance from Babylon (cf. 13:1-22; 39:5-7).
Thus, and finally, the deliverance of Zion's expatriated citizens from
their captivity in Babylon would come to be fulfilled according to the
prediction of YHWH's rejected prophetic messenger. By allowing his
prediction to be fulfilled through Cyrus' edict of emancipation, YHWH
would not only fulfill his promise to vindicate Zion from her national
enemies but also vindicate his prophetic servant (whose prediction had
now been fulfilled). It is also essential to realize that, by acting according to Isaiah's prophetic decree, YHWH was likewise vindicating himself against Zion's former allegations as to his divine impotence to
save, ignorance of world affairs and covenant disloyalty to David's
house (cf. chs. 40–54). Thus, it would come to be seen that YHWH had
fully endorsed the mission and person of his servant since he thus made
his own exoneration directly dependent upon the vindication of his
prophet and his prophecy.

It is unnecessary to conclude that all biblical books that present
themselves as unified, coherent and thematically focused are necessarily the product of a single author or compiler. For example, J.H.
Tigay has, it seems, sufficiently demonstrated the composite nature and
long historical development of the Gilgamesh Epic, despite the
apparent literary unity, coherence and emphasis of that work discernible in an interpretation such as that of T. Jacobsen.[1] Nevertheless, the
patterning of literary subunits within Isaiah's overall design makes it
difficult to imagine that its overall design should be accounted for as the

---

[1]J.H. Tigay, *The Evolution of the Gilgamesh Epic* (Philadelphia: University of
Pennsylvania Press, 1982); T. Jacobsen, 'Second Millennium Metaphors. "And
Death the Journey's End": The Gilgamesh Epic', in *The Treasures of Darkness: A
History of Mesopotamian Religion* (New Haven: Yale University Press, 1976),
pp. 193-219. Cf. however, A. Berlin, *Poetics and Interpretation of Biblical
Narrative* (BLS, 9; Sheffield: Almond Press, 1983), pp. 129-34, where she says:

> The study of *Gilgamesh*'s literary history makes clear that even though it incorporated
> other sources, occasionally with little modification of them, it was not the result of the
> kind of cut and paste operation that source critics describe, nor was it the product of a
> slow, natural accretion of materials, as form critics assume. Rather it was the result of
> creative authors and editors working within their literary tradition, drawing on existing
> sources but reshaping them for their own purposes (p. 132).

product of accretion under (three or more) separate hands. Indeed, preferring to choose that set of interpretative criteria that grants maximal relevance to the existence and arrangement of the book prompts me to postulate that the compilation of Isaiah took place under a single rhetorical program and, probably, a single hand in the late sixth century BCE. The pervasiveness of the triadic and quadratic framing patterns is such that it virtually precludes the likelihood that prophetic materials were admitted to the book except under the development of such a structural patterning. Thus, while the eighth-century prophet may have composed some portion of the oracles normally ascribed to him, their positioning into the complex framing patterns that characterize the final architecture of the book of Isaiah and their general subservience to a rhetorical strategy of covenant disputation are most probably the work of a single sixth-century author/compiler who wrote for the benefit of that author/compiler's exilic and postexilic contemporaries.

BIBLIOGRAPHY

Ackroyd, P.R., 'Isaiah i–xii: Presentation of a Prophet', in *Congress Volume, Göttingen, 1977* (VTSup, 29; Leiden: Brill, 1978), pp. 16-48.
—'A Note on Isaiah 2:1', *ZAW* 75 (1963), pp. 320-21.
Aharoni, Y., and M. Avi-Yonah, *The Macmillan Bible Atlas* (New York: Macmillan, 1968; rev. edn, 1977).
Alonso-Schökel, L., *Estudios de Poética Hebrea* (Barcelona: Juan Flors, Editor, 1963).
—'Isaiah', in R. Alter and F. Kermode (eds.), *The Literary Guide to the Bible* (Cambridge, MA: Harvard University Press, 1987), pp. 165-83.
Alter, R., *The Art of Biblical Poetry* (New York: Basic Books, 1985).
Baird, J.A., 'Genre Analysis as a Method of Historical Criticism', in L.C. McGaughy (ed.), *The Society of Biblical Literature, 1972 Proceedings* (2 vols.; Missoula, MT: SBL, 1972), II, pp. 385-411.
Barr, J., *Holy Scripture: Canon, Authority, Criticism* (Philadelphia: Westminster Press, 1983).
Begrich, J., 'Das priesterliche Heilsorakel', *ZAW* 52 (1934), pp. 81-92.
—*Studien zur Deuterojesaja* (BWANT, 4; Folge Heft 25 [77]; Stuttgart: Kohlhammer, 1938; repr., TBü, 20; Munich: Chr. Kaiser Verlag, 1963).
Bentzen, A., *Introduction to the Old Testament* (2 vols.; Copenhagen: Gad, 1948, 1949).
Berlin, A., *Poetics and Interpretation of Biblical Narrative* (BLS, 9; Sheffield: Almond Press, 1983).
Birks, T.R., *Commentary on the Book of Isaiah: Critical, Historical and Prophetical* (Cambridge: Rivingtons, 1871).
Blenkinsopp, J., 'Fragments of Ancient Exegesis in an Isaian Poem (Isa 2:6-22)', *ZAW* 93 (1981), pp. 51-62.
Boecker, H.J., *Redeformen des Rechtslebens im Alten Testament* (WMANT, 14; Neukirchen-Vluyn: Neukirchener Verlag, 1964; 2d edn, 1970).
Bonnard, P.-E., *Le Second Isaïe: Son disciple et leurs éditeurs Isaïe 40–66* (EBib; Paris: Gabalda, 1972).
Bright, J., *A History of Israel* (Philadelphia: Westminster Press, 1959; 3d edn, 1981).
Brownlee, W.H., *The Meaning of the Qumrân Scrolls for the Bible* (New York: Oxford University Press, 1964).
Bullinger, E.W., *The Companion Bible* (N.p., 1900; repr., Grand Rapids: Zondervan, 1964).
Callaway, J.A., 'Isaiah in Modern Scholarship', *RevExp* 65 (1968), pp. 397-407.
Caspari, W., *Lieder und Gottessprüche der Rückwanderer [Jesaja 40–55]* (BZAW, 65; Giessen: Töpelmann, 1934).
Cathcart, K.J., 'Kingship and the "Day of YHWH" in Isaiah 2:6-22', *Hermathena* 125 (1978), pp. 48-59.
Charpentier, E., *How to Read the Old Testament* (trans. J. Bowden; New York: Crossroad, 1981).
—*Jeunesse du Vieux Testament* (Paris: Fayard, 1963).
Childs, B.S., 'Childs Versus Barr: *Holy Scripture: Canon, Authority, Criticism*, by James Barr. The Westminster Press, Philadelphia, 1983.', *Int* 38 (1984), pp. 66-70.
—*Introduction to the Old Testament as Scripture* (Philadelphia: Fortress Press, 1979).

—*Isaiah and the Assyrian Crisis* (SBT, II/3; London: SCM Press, 1967).

Christensen, D.L., *Transformations of the War Oracle in Old Testament Prophecy* (HDR, 3; Missoula, MT: Scholars Press, 1975).

Clements, R.E., 'Beyond Tradition History: Deutero-Isaianic Development of First Isaiah's Themes', *JSOT* 31 (1985), pp. 95-113.

—*Isaiah 1–39* (NCB; Grand Rapids: Eerdmans, 1980).

—*Isaiah and the Deliverance of Jerusalem: A Study of the Interpretation of Prophecy in the Old Testament* (JSOTSup, 13; Sheffield: JSOT Press, 1980).

—*Prophecy and Tradition* (Oxford: Basil Blackwell, 1975).

—'The Unity of the Book of Isaiah', *Int* 36 (1982), pp. 117-29 (reprinted in J.L. Mays and P.J. Achtemeier [eds.], *Interpreting the Prophets* [Philadelphia: Fortress Press, 1987], pp. 50-61).

Clifford, R.J., *Fair Spoken and Persuading: An Interpretation of Second Isaiah* (New York: Paulist Press, 1984).

Condamin, A., 'Les chapitres I et II du livre d'Isaïe', *RB* 13 (1904), pp. 7-26.

Cross, F.M., 'The Council of Yahweh in Second Isaiah', *JNES* 12 (1953), pp. 274-77.

Culler, J., *Structuralist Poetics: Structuralism, Linguistics and the Study of Literature* (Ithaca, NY: Cornell University Press, 1975).

Daniels, D.R., 'Is There a "Prophetic Lawsuit" Genre?', *ZAW* 99 (1987), pp. 339-60.

Davidson, R., 'The Interpretation of Isaiah ii 6ff', *VT* 16 (1966), pp. 1-7.

Delcor, M., 'Les attaches littéraires, l'origine et la signification de l'expression biblique "prendre à témoin le ciel et la terre"', *VT* 16 (1966), pp. 8-25.

Delitzsch, Franz, *Biblical Commentary on the Prophecies of Isaiah* (trans. from 3d German edn by J. Martin; 2 vols.; Edinburgh: T. & T. Clark, 1873).

Dietrich, W., *Jesaja und die Politik* (BEvT, 74; Munich: Chr. Kaiser Verlag, 1976).

Dillmann, A., *Der Prophet Jesaja* (KEHAT, 5; Leipzig: S. Hirzel, 5th edn, 1898).

Doty, W.G., 'The Concept of Genre in Literary Analysis', in L.C. McGaughy (ed.), *The Society of Biblical Literature, 1972 Proceedings* (2 vols.; Missoula, MT: SBL, 1972), II, pp. 413-48.

Duhm, B., *Das Buch Jesaia übersetzt und erklärt* (HKAT, 3/1; Göttingen: Vandenhoeck & Ruprecht, 1892; 2d edn, 1902; 4th [repr.] edn, 1922).

Dumbrell, W.J., 'The Purpose of the Book of Isaiah', *TynBul* 36 (1985), pp. 111-28.

Eaton, J.H., 'The Isaiah Tradition', in R. Coggins, A. Phillips, and M. Knibb (eds.), *Israel's Prophetic Tradition: Essays in Honour of Peter R. Ackroyd* (Cambridge: Cambridge University Press, 1982), pp. 58-76.

Eissfeldt, O., *Einleitung in das Alte Testament unter Einschluss der Apokryphen und Pseudepigraphen* (Neue theologische Grundrisse; Tübingen: Mohr, 1934; 3d edn, 1964; ET of 3d German edn: *The Old Testament: An Introduction including the Apocrypha and Pseudepigrapha, and also the Works of Similar Type from Qumran* (trans. P.R. Ackroyd; Oxford: Basil Blackwell; New York: Harper & Row, 1965).

Elliger, K., *Deuterojesaja in seinem Verhältnis zu Tritojesaja* (BWANT, IV/11; Stuttgart: Kohlhammer, 1933).

Erlandsson, S., *The Burden of Babylon: A Study of Isaiah 13:2–14:23* (trans. G.J. Houser; ConBOT, 4; Lund: Gleerup, 1970).

Evans, C.A., 'On the Unity and Parallel Structure of Isaiah', *VT* 38 (1988), pp. 129-47.

Everson, A.J., 'The Days of Yahweh', *JBL* 93 (1974), pp. 329-37.

Fisher, R.W., 'The Herald of Good News in Second Isaiah', in J.J. Jackson and M. Kessler (eds.), *Rhetorical Criticism: Essays in Honor of James Muilenburg* (Pittsburgh: Pickwick Press, 1974), pp. 117-32.

Fohrer, G., *Das Buch Jesaja* (Zürcher Bibelkommentare; 3 vols.; Zürich: Zwingli-Verlag, 1964–1966).

—*History of Israelite Religion* (trans. D.E. Green; Nashville: Abingdon Press, 1972; London: SPCK, 1973); originally *Geschichte der Israelitischen Religion* (De Gruyter Lehrbuch; Berlin: de Gruyter, 1969).

—'Jesaja 1 als Zusammenfassung der Verkündigung Jesajas', *ZAW* 74 (1962), pp. 251-68 (reprinted in *Studien zur alttestamentlichen Prophetie [1949-1965]* [BZAW, 99; Berlin: Töpelmann, 1967], pp. 148-66).

—'The Origin, Composition and Tradition of Isaiah i-xxxix', ALUOS, 3 (1961-1962), pp. 3-38; German Translation: 'Entstehung, Komposition und Überlieferung von Jesaja 1-39', in *Studien zur alttestamentlichen Prophetie (1949-1965)* (BZAW, 99; Berlin: Töpelmann, 1967), pp. 113-47.

Fullerton, K., 'The Original Form of the Refrains in Is. 2:6-21', *JBL* 38 (1919), pp. 64-76.

Gemser, B., 'The *Rîb*- or Controversy-Pattern in Hebrew Mentality', in M. Noth and D.W. Thomas (eds.), *Wisdom in Israel and in the Ancient Near East* (Festschrift H.H. Rowley; VTSup, 3; Leiden: Brill, 1955), pp. 120-137.

Gileadi, A., 'A Holistic Structure of the Book of Isaiah' (PhD diss., Brigham Young University, 1981).

Gitay, Y., 'Isaiah and His Audience', *Prooftexts* 3 (1983), pp. 223-30.

—*Prophecy and Persuasion: A Study of Isaiah 40-48* (FTL, 14; Bonn: Linguistica Biblica, 1981).

—'Rhetorical Analysis of Isaiah 40-48' (PhD diss., Emory University, 1978).

Graffy, A., *A Prophet Confronts His People: The Disputation Speech in the Prophets* (AnBib, 104; Rome: Biblical Institute Press, 1984).

Gray, G.B., *A Critical and Exegetical Commentary on the Book of Isaiah I-XXVII* (ICC; Edinburgh: T. & T. Clark, 1912).

Gray, J., 'The Day of Yahweh in Cultic Experience and Eschatological Prospect', *SEÅ* 39 (1974), pp. 12-16.

Grayson, A.K., *Assyrian Royal Inscriptions* (2 vols.; Wiesbaden: Otto Harrassowitz, 1972, 1976).

Greenspahn, F.E., *Hapax Legomena in Biblical Hebrew: A Study of the Phenomenon and Its Treatment Since Antiquity with Special Reference to Verbal Forms* (SBLDS, 74; Chico, CA: Scholars Press, 1984).

Gressmann, H., 'Die literarische Analyse Deuterojesajas', *ZAW* 34 (1914), pp. 254-97.

Gunkel, H., 'Die Propheten als Scriftsteller und Dichter', in H. Schmidt (ed.), *Die grossen Propheten übersetzt und erklärt* (Die Schriften des Alten Testaments, II/2; Göttingen: Vandenhoeck & Ruprecht, 1915), pp. xxxvi-lxxii.

Gunkel, H., and J. Begrich, *Einleitung in die Psalmen: Die Gattungen der religiösen Lyrik Israels* (Göttingen: Vandenhoeck & Ruprecht, 1933).

Hahn, H.F., *The Old Testament in Modern Research* (Philadelphia: Fortress Press, 1954).

Haran, M., 'The Literary Structure and Chronological Framework of the Prophecies of Is. xl-xlviii', in *Congress Volume, Bonn* (VTSup, 9; Leiden: Brill, 1963), pp. 127-55.

Harrison, R.K., *Introduction to the Old Testament* (Grand Rapids: Eerdmans, 1969).

Harvey, J., *Le plaidoyer prophétique contre Israël après la rupture de l'alliance: Etude d'une formule littéraire de l'Ancien Testament* (Studia, 22; Paris: Desclée de Brouwer; Montreal: Les Editions Bellarmin, 1967).

—'Le "Rîb-Pattern", réquisitoire prophétique sur la rupture de l'alliance', *Bib* 43 (1962), pp. 172-96.

Hayes, J.H., and S.A. Irvine, *Isaiah the Eighth-century Prophet: His Times and His Preaching* (Nashville: Abingdon Press, 1987).

Herbert, A.S., *The Book of the Prophet Isaiah: Chapters 1-39* (CBC; Cambridge: Cambridge University Press, 1973).

Hesse, F., 'Wurzelt die prophetische Gerichtsrede im israelitischen Kult?', *ZAW* 65 (1953), pp. 45-53.

Hessler, E., 'Gott der Schöpfer: Ein Beitrag zur Komposition und Theologie Deuterojesajas' (PhD diss., Greifswald, 1961).

—'Die Struktur der Bilder bei Deuterojesaja', *EvT* 25 (1965), pp. 349-69.

Hoffmann, H.W., *Die Intention der Verkündigung Jesajas* (BZAW, 136; Berlin: de Gruyter, 1974).

Hoffmann, Y., 'The Day of the Lord as a Concept and a Term in the Prophetic Literature', *ZAW* 93 (1981), pp. 37-50.

Holladay, W.L., 'Isa iii 10-11: An Archaic Wisdom Passage', *VT* 18 (1968), pp. 481-87.

—*Isaiah: Scroll of a Prophetic Heritage* (Grand Rapids: Eerdmans, 1978).

Huffmon, H.B., 'The Covenant Lawsuit in the Prophets', *JBL* 78 (1959), pp. 285-95.

Jacobsen, T., *The Treasures of Darkness: A History of Mesopotamian Religion* (New Haven: Yale University Press, 1976).

Jensen, J., *Isaiah 1–39* (Old Testament Message, 8; Wilmington, DE: Michael Glazier, 1984).

Kaiser, O., *Isaiah 1–12: A Commentary* (trans. R.A. Wilson; OTL; Philadelphia: Westminster Press, 1972); ET of 5th German edn: *Isaiah 1–12: A Commentary* (trans. J. Bowden; OTL; Philadelphia: Westminster Press, 2d edn, 1983); originally *Das Buch des Propheten Jesaja, Kapitel 1–12* (ATD, 17; Göttingen: Vandenhoeck & Ruprecht, 1960; 5th edn, 1981).

—*Isaiah 13–39: A Commentary* (trans. R.A. Wilson; OTL; Philadelphia: Westminster Press, 1974); originally *Der Prophet Jesaja, Kapitel 13–39* (ATD, 18; Göttingen: Vandenhoeck & Ruprecht, 1973).

Kaufmann, Y., *The Babylonian Captivity and Deutero-Isaiah* (trans. C.W. Ephroymson; New York: Union of American Hebrew Congregations, 1970).

Kiesow, K., *Exodustexte im Jesajabuch: Literarkritische und motivgeschichtliche Analysen* (OBO, 24; Freiburg, Switzerland: Universitätsverlag, 1979).

Kissane, E.J., *The Book of Isaiah: Translated from a Critically Revised Hebrew Text with Commentary* (2 vols.; Dublin: Browne and Nolan, 1941, 1943; rev. edn, 1960).

Kitchen, K.A., *Ancient Orient and Old Testament* (Downers Grove: InterVarsity Press, 1966).

—*The Third Intermediate Period in Egypt* (Warminster, England: Aris & Phillips, 1973).

Knierim, R., 'Old Testament Form Criticism Reconsidered', *Int* 27 (1973), pp. 435-68.

Koch, K., *The Growth of the Biblical Tradition: The Form-Critical Method* (trans. S.M. Cupitt; New York: Charles Scribner's Sons, 1969).

Kogut, S., 'On the Meaning and Syntactical Status of הִנֵּה in Biblical Hebrew', in S. Japhet (ed.), *Studies in Bible, 1986* (ScrHier, 31; Jerusalem: Magnes, 1986), pp. 133-54.

Köhler, L., *Deuterojesaja (Jesaja 40–55) stilkritisch untersucht* (BZAW, 37; Giessen: Töpelmann, 1923).

Lack, R., *La symbolique du livre d'Isaïe: Essai sur l'image littéraire comme élément de structuration* (AnBib, 59; Rome: Biblical Institute Press, 1973).

Levine, L.D., 'Sennacherib's Southern Front: 704–689 B.C.', *JCS* 34 (1982), pp. 29-34.

Limburg, J., 'The Root ריב and the Prophetic Lawsuit Speeches', *JBL* 88 (1969), pp. 291-304.

Lindblom, J., *Die literarische Gattung der prophetischen Literatur: Eine literargeschichtliche Untersuchung zum Alten Testament*, in *Uppsala Universitets Arsskrift (1924)* (2 vols.; Uppsala: Lundeqvist, 1924), I, pp. 1-122.

Long, B.O., 'Framing Repetitions in Biblical Historiography', *JBL* 106 (1987), pp. 385-99.

Loretz, O., *Der Prolog des Jesaja Buches (1,1-2,5)* (Ugaritologische und kolometrische Studien zum Jesaja-Buch, 1; Altenberg: CIS-Verlag, 1984).

Lovering, E.H. Jr (ed.), *SBL 1991 Seminar Papers* (Atlanta: Scholars Press, 1991).

—(ed.), *SBL 1992 Seminar Papers* (Atlanta: Scholars Press, 1992).

—(ed.), *SBL 1993 Seminar Papers* (Atlanta: Scholars Press, 1993).

Lucas, E.C., 'Covenant, Treaty and Prophecy', *Themelios* 8/1 (1982), pp. 19-23.

Lund, N.W., *Chiasmus in the New Testament* (Chapel Hill: University of North Carolina, 1942).

Machinist, P.B., 'The Epic of Tukulti-Ninurta I: A Study in Middle Assyrian Literature' (PhD diss., Yale University, 1978).

Marti, K., *Das Buch Jesaja* (KHAT, 10; Tübingen: Mohr, 1900).

Mattioli, A., 'Due schemi letterari negli oracoli d'introduzione al libro di Isaia', *RivB* 14 (1966), pp. 345-64.

McCarthy, D.J., *Old Testament Covenant: A Survey of Current Opinions* (Richmond, VA: John Knox, 1972).

—*Treaty and Covenant: A Study in Form in the Ancient Oriental Documents and in the Old Testament* (AnBib, 21; Rome: Biblical Institute Press, 1963; rev. edn, 1978).

McGaughy, L.C. (ed.), *The Society of Biblical Literature, 1972 Proceedings* (2 vols.; Missoula, MT: SBL, 1972).

Melugin, R.F., *The Formation of Isaiah 40-55* (BZAW, 141; Berlin: de Gruyter, 1976; revision of his PhD diss., Yale University, 1968).

—'The Typical Versus the Unique among the Hebrew Prophets', in L.C. McGaughy (ed.), *The Society of Biblical Literature, 1972 Proceedings* (2 vols.; Missoula, MT: SBL, 1972), II, pp. 331-41.

Mendenhall, G.E., 'Covenant Forms in Israelite Tradition', *BA* 17 (1954), pp. 50-76.

—'Law and Covenant in Israel and the Ancient Near East', *BA* 17 (1954), pp. 26-46.

—*Law and Covenant in Israel and the Ancient Near East* (Pittsburgh: Biblical Colloquium, 1955).

Merrill, E.H., *Kingdom of Priests: A History of Old Testament Israel* (Grand Rapids: Baker, 1987).

Miller, J.M., 'Geba/Gibeah of Benjamin', *VT* 25 (1975), pp. 145-66.

Moran, W., 'The Ancient Near Eastern Background of the Love of God in Deuteronomy', *CBQ* 25 (1963), pp. 77-87.

Mowinckel, S., 'Die Komposition des deuterojesajanischen Buches', *ZAW* 49 (1931), pp. 87-112, 242-60.

—'Neuere Forschungen zu Deuterojesaja, Tritojesaja und den Äbäd-Jahwä-Problem', *AcOr* 16 (1938), pp. 1-40.

Muilenburg, J., 'The Book of Isaiah: Chapters 40-66: Introduction and Exegesis', in G.A. Buttrick et al. (eds.), *The Interpreter's Bible* (12 vols.; Nashville: Abingdon Press, 1956), V, pp. 381-773.

—'Form Criticism and Beyond', *JBL* 88 (1969), pp. 1-18.

Nicholson, E.W., *Exodus and Sinai in History and Tradition* (Oxford: Basil Blackwell, 1973).

Niditch, S., 'The Composition of Isaiah 1', *Bib* 61 (1980), pp. 509-29.

Nielsen, K., 'Das Bild des Gerichts (RIB-Pattern) in Jes. i-xii: Eine Analyse der Beziehungen zwischen Bildsprache und dem Anliegen der Verkündigung', *VT* 29 (1979), pp. 309-24.

—*Yahweh as Prosecutor and Judge: An Investigation of the Prophetic Lawsuit (Rîb-Pattern)* (trans. F. Cryer; JSOTSup, 9; Sheffield: JSOT Press, 1978).

O'Connell, R.H., 'Deuteronomy vii 1-26: Asymmetrical Concentricity and the Rhetoric of Conquest', *VT* 42 (1992), pp. 248-65.

—'Deuteronomy ix 7–x 7, 10-11: Panelled Structure, Double Rehearsal and the Rhetoric of Covenant Rebuke', *VT* 42 (1992), pp. 492-509.

—'Isaiah xiv 4b-23: Ironic Reversal through Concentric Structure and Mythic Allusion', *VT* 38 (1988), pp. 407-18.

Orelli, C. von, *The Prophecies of Isaiah* (trans. J.S. Banks; Edinburgh: T. & T. Clark, 1889); originally *Die Propheten Jesaja und Jeremia* (Kurzgefaßter Kommentar zu den heiligen Schriften Alten und Neuen Testamentes sowie zu den Apocryphen, A. Altes Testament, IV; Munich: Beck, 2d edn, 1891).

Oswalt, J.N., *The Book of Isaiah, Chapters 1–39* (NICOT; Grand Rapids: Eerdmans, 1986).

Platt, E.E., 'Jewelry of Bible Times and the Catalog of Isa 3:18-23', *AUSS* 17 (1979), pp. 71-81, 189-201.

Polan, G.J., *In the Ways of Justice toward Salvation: A Rhetorical Analysis of Isaiah 56–59* (American University Studies, Series VII: Theology and Religion, 13; New York: Peter Lang, 1986).

—'Salvation in the Midst of Struggle', *TBT* 23 (1985), pp. 90-97.

Pritchard, J.B. (ed.), *Ancient Near Eastern Texts Relating to the Old Testament* (Princeton, NJ: Princeton University Press, 3d edn, 1969).

Procksch, O., *Jesaia I* (KAT, IX/1; Leipzig: Deichert, 1930).

Rad, G. von, 'The Origin of the Concept of the Day of Yahweh', *JSS* 4 (1959), pp. 97-108.

Rendtorff, R., 'Zur Komposition des Buches Jesaja', *VT* 34 (1984), pp. 295-320.

Richter, W., *Exegese als Literaturwissenschaft* (Göttingen: Vandenhoeck & Ruprecht, 1971).

Ricoeur, P., *Time and Narrative* (trans. K. [McLaughlin] Blamey and D. Pellauer; 3 vols.; Chicago: Chicago University Press, 1984–1988).

Rignell, L.G., 'Isaiah Chapter I', *ST* 11 (1957), pp. 140-58.

Robinson, H.W., 'The Council of Yahweh', *JTS* 45 (1944), pp. 151-55.

Robinson, T.H., *Prophecy and the Prophets in Ancient Israel* (Studies in Theology; New York: Charles Scribner's Sons, 1923).

Roche, M. de, 'Yahweh's *Rîb* against Israel: A Reassessment of the So-called "Prophetic Lawsuit" in the Preexilic Prophets', *JBL* 102 (1983), pp. 563-74.

Rogerson, J.W., 'Recent Literary Structuralist Approaches to Biblical Interpretation', *The Churchman* 90 (1976), pp. 165-77.

Roth, W., *Isaiah* (Knox Preaching Guides; Atlanta: John Knox, 1988).

Sawyer, J.F.A., *Isaiah* (Philadelphia: Westminster Press, 1984).

Schoors, A., *I am God Your Saviour: A Form-critical Study of the Main Genres in Is. XL–LV* (VTSup, 24; Leiden: Brill, 1973).

—*Jesaja* (De Boeken van het Oude Testament; Roermond, 1972).

Scott, R.B.Y., 'The Book of Isaiah, Chapters 1–39: Introduction and Exegesis', in G.A. Buttrick et al. (eds.), *The Interpreter's Bible* (12 vols.; Nashville: Abingdon Press, 1956), V, pp. 149-381.

Seitz, C.R. (ed.), *Reading and Preaching the Book of Isaiah* (Philadelphia: Fortress Press, 1988).

Skinner, J., *The Book of the Prophet Isaiah, Chapters I–XXXIX* (CBSC; Cambridge: Cambridge University Press, 1896; rev. edn, 1905).

Sloan, T.O., and C. Perelman, 'Rhetoric', in M.J. Adler et al. (eds.), *The New Encyclopaedia Britannica* (30 vols.; Chicago: Encyclopaedia Britannica, 1982), XV, pp. 798-805.

Slotki, I.W., *Isaiah* (Soncino Books of the Bible; London: Soncino Press, 1949).

Stade, B., 'Miscellen: Anmerkungen zu 2 Kö. 15–21', *ZAW* 6 (1886), pp. 156-89.

Sternberg, M., *The Poetics of Biblical Narrative* (ISBL; Bloomington: Indiana University Press, 1985).

Sweeney, M.A., *Isaiah 1–4 and the Post-Exilic Understanding of the Isaianic Tradition* (BZAW, 171; Berlin: de Gruyter, 1988); a revision of 'Isaiah 1–4 and the Post-Exilic Understanding of the Isaianic Tradition' (PhD diss., Claremont Graduate School, 1983).

Talmon, S., 'The Presentation of Synchroneity and Simultaneity in Biblical Narrative', in J. Heinemann and S. Werses (eds.), *Studies in Hebrew Narrative Art through the Ages* (ScrHier, 27; Jerusalem: Magnes, 1978), pp. 9-26.

Thiele, E.R., *The Mysterious Numbers of the Hebrew Kings* (Grand Rapids: Zondervan, rev. edn, 1983).

Thompson, J.A., 'The Significance of the Ancient Near Eastern Treaty Pattern', *TynBul* 13 (1963), pp. 1-6.

Tigay, J.H., *The Evolution of the Gilgamesh Epic* (Philadelphia: University of Pennsylvania Press, 1982).

Torrey, C.C., *The Second Isaiah: A New Interpretation* (Edinburgh: T. & T. Clark; New York: Charles Scribner's Sons, 1928).

Tournay, R., 'Bulletin: Livres prophétiques', *RB* 74 (1967), pp. 119-21.

Tucker, G.M., 'Prophetic Superscriptions and the Growth of a Canon', in G.W. Coats and B.O. Long (eds.), *Canon and Authority: Essays in Old Testament Religion and Theology* (Philadelphia: Fortress Press, 1977), pp. 56-70.

Vermeylen, J., *Du prophète Isaïe à l'apocalyptique: Isaïe, i–xxxv, miroir d'un demi-millénaire d'expérience religieuse en Israël* (EBib; 2 vols.; Paris: Gabalda, 1977, 1978).

Volz, P., *Jesaia, Zweite Hälfte: Kapitel 40–66 übersetzt und erklärt* (KAT, IX/2; Leipzig: Deichert, 1932).

Wade, G.W., *The Book of the Prophet Isaiah with Introduction and Notes* (Westminster Commentaries; London: Methuen, 2d edn, 1911).

Waldow, H.E. von, 'Anlass und Hintergrund der Verkündigung des Deuterojesaja' (PhD diss., University of Bonn, 1953).

—*Der traditionsgeschichtliche Hintergrund der prophetischen Gerichtsreden* (BZAW, 85; Berlin: Töpelmann, 1963).

Watson, W.G.E., *Classical Hebrew Poetry: A Guide to its Techniques* (JSOTSup, 26; Sheffield: JSOT Press, 1984).

Watts, J.D.W., *Isaiah 1–33* (WBC, 24; Waco, TX: Word Books, 1985).

Weiss, M., 'The Origin of the "Day of the Lord"—Reconsidered', *HUCA* 37 (1966), pp. 29-72.

Welch, J.W. (ed.), *Chiasmus in Antiquity: Structures, Analysis, Exegesis* (Hildesheim: Gerstenberg, 1981).

Westermann, C., *Isaiah 40–66: A Commentary* (trans. D.M.G. Stalker; OTL; Philadelphia: Westminster Press, 1969); originally *Das Buch Jesaja, 40–66* (ATD, 19; Göttingen: Vandenhoeck & Ruprecht, 1966).

—*Basic Forms of Prophetic Speech* (trans. H.C. White; Philadelphia: Westminster Press, 1967); originally *Grundformen prophetischer Rede* (BEvT, 31; Munich: Chr. Kaiser Verlag, 1960).

—'Sprach und Struktur der Prophetie Deuterojesajas', in *Forschung am Alten Testament: Gesammelte Studien, I* (TBü, 24; Munich: Chr. Kaiser Verlag, 1964), pp. 92-170 (reprinted as *Sprache und Struktur der Prophetie Deuterojesajas* [Calwer Theologische Monographien, Reihe A (Bibelwissenschaft), 11; Stuttgart: Calwer Verlag, 1981]).

Widengren, G., *The King and the Tree of Life in Ancient Near Eastern Religion* (Uppsala: Lundeqvist; Wiesbaden: Otto Harrassowitz, 1951).

Wiklander, B., *Prophecy as Literature: A Text-Linguistic And Rhetorical Approach to Isaiah 2–4* (ConBOT, 22; Stockholm: Gleerup, 1984).

Wildberger, H., *Jesaja, Kapitel 1–12* (BKAT, X/1; Neukirchen–Vluyn: Neukirchener Verlag, 1972; 2d edn, 1980); ET of 2d German edn: *Isaiah 1–12: A Commentary* (trans. T.H. Trapp; Continental Commentaries; Minneapolis, MN: Augsburg–Fortress, 1991).

—*Jesaja, Kapitel 28–39* (BKAT, X/3; Neukirchen–Vluyn: Neukirchener Verlag, 1982).

Willis, J.T., 'The First Pericope in the Book of Isaiah', *VT* 34 (1984), pp. 63-77.

Wilson, A., *The Nations in Deutero-Isaiah: A Study on Composition and Structure* (Ancient Near Eastern Texts and Studies, 1; Lewiston, NY: Edwin Mellen, 1986).

Wolf, H.M., *Interpreting Isaiah* (Grand Rapids: Zondervan, 1985).

Wright, G.E., 'The Lawsuit of God: A Form-critical Study of Deuteronomy 32', in B.W. Anderson and W. Harrelson (eds.), *Israel's Prophetic Heritage: Essays in Honor of James Muilenburg* (New York: Harper & Row, 1962), pp. 26-67.

Würthwein, E., 'Der Ursprung der prophetischen Gerichtsrede', *ZTK* 49 (1952), pp. 1-16 (reprinted in *Wort und Existenz: Studien zum Alten Testament* [Göttingen: Vandenhoeck & Ruprecht, 1970], pp. 111-26).

Young, E.J., *The Book of Isaiah* (NICOT; 3 vols.; Grand Rapids: Eerdmans, 1965–1972).

INDEXES

INDEX OF REFERENCES

Genesis
12:3   169
14:20   169
15:1   169
17:3-8   169
22:17   169
26:3   169
26:28   169
31:3   169
37:13   92

Exodus
15   239
15:2   239
15:21   239
15:22-27   239
34:6-7a   239

Deuteronomy
7   28
9:7-10:11   28
17:16-17   58, 66, 126
17:17b   126
28   32
29:22   45
30:19   42
31:28   42
32   32, 33, 39,
              40
32:1-2   40
32:1   42
32:3-5   40
32:6   40
32:7-14   40
32:15-18   40
32:16-17   40
32:19-25   40
32:26-43   40

2 Samuel
15:15   92

1 Kings
10:1-13   126
10:14-11:8   126
10:14-25   59
10:26-29   59
11:1-13   59
11:4   59
11:6   59
11:9-40   126
11:12-13   126, 127

2 Kings
15:5a   92
15:29-30   102
15:37   102
16:7-9   102
17:1-6   142
17:4   137
18:9-19:19   129
18:13-20:19   140
18:13   109, 110,
              129, 130,
              138, 139,
              140, 141, 237
18:14-16   139
18:17-20:19   109, 110,
              138, 139,
              140, 141
18:17-19:37   129, 237
18:17-19:9a   129
18:17-25   130
18:17   138
18:18a   139
18:26-36   130
18:26   138
18:29   138
18:32   138
18:34   138
18:37-19:4   130
19:5-6   130
19:6   139

19:7a   130
19:7b   130
19:8   130
19:9a   130
19:9b-35   129
19:9b-13   130
19:14-19   130
19:17   138
19:20-37   129
19:20-21a   130
19:20   138
19:21b-28   130
19:29-31   130
19:32-34   130
19:34   124, 139
19:35-36   130
19:35a   138
19:36-37   129
19:37   130
20:1-19   237
20:1-11   126
20:4a   139
20:5   138
20:6   124
20:6b   139
20:7-8   139
20:7b   138
20:8   138, 139
20:9-11   139
20:9a   138
20:9b-11a   139
20:11b   138
20:12-19   139
20:13   139
20:14   125
20:19   139
20:35-36   104
21:1-18   167

2 Chronicles
26:21a   92

26:23a	92	1:2-17	36	1:15b-17	48
28:5-8	102	1:2-15	53	1:15b	31
		1:2-9	52	1:16-20	40
Psalms		1:2-3	31, 39, 69	1:16-19	54
9:1	239	1:2	36, 48	1:16-17	42, 43, 46,
18:1	239	1:2a	31, 40, 42,		49, 50, 52,
26:1	239		43, 44, 48,		53, 77, 78,
48:1	239		49		104
50	39, 40	1:2b-9	49	1:16b	77
50:1-7a	40	1:2b-4	37	1:17	215
50:7b	40	1:2b-3	31, 33, 37,	1:18-2:5	37, 53
50:8-13	40		38, 40, 42,	1:18-20	31, 36, 37,
50:14-15	40		43, 44, 49,		39, 48, 53
50:16a	40		51, 53, 67	1:18-19	31, 49, 54,
50:16b	40	1:2b	51, 54, 146		67, 81
50:17-20	40	1:4-9	31, 32	1:18	33, 37, 52
50:21	40	1:4-5	48	1:18a	42, 43, 44,
50:22-23	40	1:4	31, 35, 37,		46, 50, 52,
98:1	239		38, 40, 42,		53, 216
98:4	239		43, 45, 49,	1:18b-19	42, 44, 46,
105:1	239		51, 53, 67,		50, 53, 58
			69	1:18b	37
Isaiah		1:4b	33	1:19-20	37
1-39	17, 19, 34,	1:5-6	49, 51	1:19	37
	35, 36, 53,	1:5a	40, 42, 43,	1:19a	37
	209, 212, 237		45, 49	1:19b	37
1-12	34, 53, 109	1:5b-6	40, 42, 43,	1:20-31	52
1-9	19		45, 49, 53	1:20-25	54
1-5	18	1:6-7a	48	1:20	37, 42, 43,
1:1-2:5	20, 21, 31,	1:7-9	40, 42, 43,		44, 46, 49,
	32, 33, 34,		45, 49, 51,		52, 53, 67
	37, 38, 42,		53	1:20a	37
	43, 50, 51,	1:7b-9	48	1:20b	37
	52, 53, 54,	1:8	51	1:21-2:5	37
	55, 57, 58,	1:9b	45, 51	1:21-27	40, 43, 44,
	67, 69, 77,	1:10-17	31, 32, 37		46, 50, 51,
	86, 106, 115,	1:10-15	52		52, 53, 78,
	216, 236,	1:10-15a	48		107, 146,
	237, 238, 243	1:10	40, 42, 43,		149, 237
1	32, 33, 35,		45, 48, 49	1:21-23	31, 38, 42,
	38, 39, 52,	1:10a	78		44, 48, 51,
	53	1:11-2:5	49		67, 69, 78
1:1-17	37, 52	1:11-15[16-17]	69	1:21	46
1:1-15	54	1:11-15	37, 38, 42,	1:22	46
1:1	34, 35, 36,		43, 46, 49,	1:23	104
	43, 44, 49,		51, 53, 67	1:23a	46
	54, 103, 110,	1:11-12	40	1:23b	47
	167	1:13-15a	40	1:24-26	31
1:2-66:24	35	1:13-14	231	1:24-25	44, 51, 78
1:2-31	36, 54	1:15	106	1:24a	47, 78
1:2-23	48	1:15a	40	1:24b	47

1:25	47	2:6-21[22]	58, 69, 75, 77, 78, 79	2:19	28, 60, 62, 66, 67
1:25b	78	2:6-21	20, 27, 31, 38, 58, 59, 61, 65, 66, 67, 68, 70, 77, 81, 86, 93, 94, 115, 123, 134, 145, 146, 151, 152, 236, 237, 238, 240, 241, 243, 244	2:19a	64, 67
1:26-27	42, 44, 51, 54, 78			2:19b	28, 60, 62, 64
1:26a	47			2:20-21	60
1:26b	47			2:20	28, 60, 62, 63, 64, 67, 96, 134
1:27	47			2:20a	62, 63, 64, 66, 134
1:28-31	40, 42, 43, 44, 47, 49, 53, 54, 67			2:20b	62, 64
1:28	47			2:21	28, 60, 62, 66
1:29a	47			2:21a	64
1:29b	47			2:21b	28, 60, 62, 64
1:30a	47	2:6-8	28, 38, 58, 59, 60, 61, 65, 66, 67, 77, 126	2:22	20, 59, 60, 61, 68, 70, 77, 81, 106, 237, 238
1:30b	47	2:6-7	61	3:1-4:1	20, 27, 31, 38, 58, 64, 65, 67, 68, 69, 70, 75, 76, 77, 78, 79, 81, 86, 104, 106, 115, 123, 134, 145, 146, 151, 152, 236, 237, 238, 240, 241, 243, 244
2-4	35	2:6	69		
2:1-4:6	60, 71, 75, 77	2:6a	20, 37, 38, 58, 61, 237		
2:1-4:1	70	2:7	61		
2:1-5	33	2:7a	63		
2:1-4	53, 60, 77	2:8	61		
2:1	34, 35, 36, 43, 44, 47, 49, 54, 110	2:8a	63		
2:2-5	31, 36, 49, 54, 58, 67	2:8b	63		
2:2-4	35, 77	2:9-21	58, 59, 66, 67, 69		
2:2-3a	81, 233	2:9-10	60, 61		
2:2	40, 42, 44, 48, 50, 52, 53, 58, 67	2:9	28, 59, 61, 63, 64	3:1-26	60, 61
2:3a	37, 40, 42, 43, 44, 48, 50, 52, 53, 216	2:10	28, 59, 61, 67	3:1-15	77
2:3b-5	81	2:10a	64	3:1-7	70, 77
2:3b-4	40, 42, 44, 48, 50, 52, 53, 58	2:10b	64	3:1	70, 72, 76, 134
2:4	22	2:11-21	60, 61, 77	3:1a	70, 78
2:5	37, 40, 42, 43, 44, 48, 50, 52, 53, 60, 77, 216, 233	2:11	28, 59, 60, 66, 96	3:2-3	70, 72, 75, 76, 78
		2:11a	61, 63, 64	3:4-5	70, 72, 76, 78
2:6-66:24	58	2:11b	61, 64, 134	3:5	134
2:6-39:8	54	2:12-16	59, 60, 62, 66, 67	3:6-7	70, 72, 76, 78, 134
2:6-4:6	77	2:17	28, 60, 66, 96	3:6a	78
2:6-4:1	60	2:17a	62, 63, 64	3:7	96
2:6-3:26	60	2:17b	62, 64, 134	3:7a	134
2:6-22	57, 77	2:18-19	60		
		2:18	28, 60, 62, 67		
		2:18a	63		

3:8-11   71, 72, 76
3:8-9a   70, 76
3:9b-11   70
3:9b   76
3:10   70, 76, 77,
            78, 146
3:11   76
3:12-17   74
3:12-16   70
3:12-15   39
3:12a   71, 73, 74,
            76
3:12b   71, 73, 74,
            76, 78
3:13-15   71, 74, 76,
            78, 106
3:13-15a   73
3:13-14a   21, 77
3:14   106
3:14b   89
3:15b   73
3:16–4:1   70
3:16-17   71, 73, 74,
            76, 77, 134
3:16   106
3:17–4:1   70
3:17   106
3:18–4:6   77
3:18-23   71, 73, 75,
            76, 78
3:18   70, 73, 75,
            78, 96
3:18a   134
3:18b-23   200
3:19   75
3:20-21   75
3:22-23   75
3:22   75
3:24   71, 73, 76,
            134
3:25-26   71, 73, 76,
            78, 134
4:1-6   77
4:1   60, 61, 71,
            74, 76, 96,
            134
4:1a   134
4:1b   70, 78
4:2–11:16   20, 25, 71,
            79, 81, 82,
            86, 87, 88,

            91, 92, 95,
            96, 101, 105,
            106, 107,
            109, 110,
            111, 115,
            116, 130,
            137, 145,
            146, 149,
            151, 233,
            236, 238,
            239, 240,
            241, 243
4:2-6   60, 70, 71,
            81, 237
4:2   81, 82, 84,
            89, 90, 105,
            106, 240
4:2a   134
4:3-6   82, 84, 89,
            97, 106, 240
4:3a   97
4:3b   97
4:4   106
4:4a   97
4:4b   97
4:5-6   97
5:1-7   33, 85, 89,
            105
5:1-6/7   84, 85, 91
5:1-6   82, 85, 89,
            91, 106, 237
5:1-2   91, 146
5:1-2a   146
5:1a   85
5:1b-2a   85
5:2   91
5:2b   85
5:3-7   91
5:3-6   91
5:3-4   85
5:5-15   142
5:5-6   85
5:6   96
5:7   82, 85, 89,
            91, 106, 237
5:7a   85
5:7b   85
5:8-24   95
5:8-17   83, 86, 93,
            103
5:8   93

5:9-10   93
5:10   105
5:11-12   93
5:13   93
5:14   93
5:15-17   93
5:18-25a   83, 86, 93,
            103
5:18-19   93
5:19   103, 105
5:20   93
5:21   93
5:22-23   93
5:24a   93
5:24b   93
5:25-30   95
5:25a   93
5:25b-30   103
5:25b   83, 86, 93
5:26-30   83, 86, 93,
            103
5:26a   103
5:26b   103, 105
6:1–9:6   23
6–8   18
6:1-11   95
6:1-4   34, 83, 86,
            92, 102
6:1   35, 102
6:5-7   34, 83, 86,
            92, 102
6:8-10   34, 83, 86,
            92, 99, 102,
            150, 244
6:8   96
6:8b   92
6:9-10   99, 172
6:11–8:17   83, 86, 91,
            95, 145, 238
6:11-13   83, 86, 95,
            102, 244
6:11-13a   150
6:11   34
6:13b   105, 150
7:1–8:20   146
7:1–8:10   87, 102, 104,
            110, 140, 244
7   34
7:1-6   83, 88, 95,
            100
7:1   35

7:2	35, 105	8:13a	100, 101	10:16-19	94
7:3-6	95	8:13b	100, 101	10:17-19	105
7:3	35, 88, 100	8:14-15	101	10:17	96
7:4	91, 105	8:14a	100, 101	10:20-23	94, 100
7:7-9	83, 88, 95,	8:14b-15	101	10:24-32	105
	99, 100	8:14b	103	10:24-27	94, 104
7:7-9a	87	8:16-18	95	10:24	85, 100, 104
7:7b	100	8:16-17	34, 83, 86,	10:27b	94
7:8b	100		96, 102, 150	10:28-32	94, 104
7:9b	91, 100	8:18-22	83, 86, 92,	10:33-34	84, 85, 89,
7:10-17	83, 87, 95,		102, 150		91, 104, 105
	96, 102	8:18	34, 87, 96,	11:1-9	71, 81, 237
7:10	35, 95		100	11:1-5	82, 84, 89,
7:11-14	95	8:18a	92		90, 240
7:12	35	8:23–9:1	83, 86, 92,	11:1	105
7:14	87, 88		102, 150	11:1a	90
7:15-16	125	9–12	18	11:6-9	82, 84, 89,
7:16-17	95	9:2-6	83, 86, 92,		90, 240
7:17	87		102, 150	11:6-8[9]	90
7:18-25	83, 88, 95,	9:5-6	125	11:6-7	178
	96	9:7-20	84, 93, 94,	11:9	230
7:18	96, 103		95	11:10-16	71, 81, 237
7:18a	88	9:7-11a	84, 86, 94,	11:10	82, 84, 89,
7:19	96, 105		102, 103		90, 103, 105,
7:20	95, 96	9:9b	105		240
7:21	96	9:10	102	11:10a	90, 134
7:23-25	105	9:11a	103	11:11-16	82, 84, 89,
7:23	96	9:11b	84, 86, 94		90, 97, 237,
7:24	96	9:12-16a	84, 86, 94,		240
7:25	96		102, 103	11:11	97, 99
8:1-4	83, 88, 95	9:16b	84, 86, 94	11:11a	134
8:1	88, 103, 105	9:17-20a	84, 86, 94	11:12-13	98
8:3	88, 103, 105	9:17	96, 105	11:12	98, 103
8:5-8	83, 87, 96	9:19-20b	103	11:13	97, 98, 172
8:5	95	9:20b	84, 86, 94	11:14-16	98
8:6-8	51	10:1-4a	84, 86, 94,	11:15b	98
8:6-8a	95		95, 103, 105	11:16	99
8:6	91	10:1-2	94	12:1-6	20, 82, 107,
8:7-8a	87	10:3-4a	94		110, 237, 239
8:8b	87	10:4b	84, 94, 103	12:1-3	107, 145
8:9-10	83, 87, 96	10:5-32	84, 86, 94,	12:1	239
8:10b	87		95, 103, 104,	12:1a	134
8:11-15	34, 83, 86,		105	12:2	239
	96, 100, 102	10:5-15	104	12:2b	239
8:11-14	95	10:5-11	94	12:3	239
8:11-12	91	10:5	104	12:4-6	107, 145
8:12-15	100	10:9-11	104	12:4	239
8:12-13	100	10:9	105	12:4a	134
8:12	100, 101	10:10-11	104	12:5	239
8:12a	101	10:12-15	94	12:6	239
8:12b	101	10:15	105	13–39	35, 36, 109,

	114, 116, 117, 127, 131, 132, 137, 138, 139, 141, 144, 237, 240, 241
13:1–39:8	20, 25, 27, 79, 82, 86, 87, 105, 106, 107, 109, 110, 111, 115, 116, 121, 129, 130, 135, 136, 137, 138, 145, 146, 149, 151, 174, 214, 233, 236, 238, 239, 240, 241, 243
13–35	109
13–23	18, 35, 132
13–14	35
13:1–14:23	110
13	35, 48, 123, 127, 237
13:1-22	26, 111, 114, 117, 139, 245
13:1	34, 35, 36, 47, 121, 127, 174
13:1a	110, 127
13:1b	110
13:2-22	121, 127, 174
13:2-3	121, 131
13:2	103, 127
13:2b	127
13:4	121
13:4b-5	121
13:4b	127
13:5a	127
13:6	122
13:7-8	122
13:9a	122
13:9b-12	122, 174
13:9b	122
13:10	122
13:11	122

13:12	122
13:13	122
13:13b	127
13:14	122
13:15-16	122
13:17	122, 127
13:18	122
13:19	45, 122
13:19a	127
13:20-22	122
14:1-2	111, 116, 127, 128, 139
14:3-21	110, 139
14:3-4a	110, 111, 114, 116, 117, 127, 129
14:4b-23	114, 127, 145, 237
14:4b-21	23, 26, 111, 114, 117, 129, 130, 237
14:4b-5	128
14:6	128
14:7	128
14:8	128, 129
14:9	128
14:10	128
14:11	128
14:13-14	128
14:13a	129
14:13b	129
14:14a	129
14:14b	129
14:15	128
14:16-17	128
14:18	128
14:19	90, 128, 129
14:19b-20a	128
14:20b-21	128
14:22-23	26, 111, 114, 117, 128, 129, 139
14:24-25	26, 104, 110, 111, 114, 117, 129, 130, 139, 145, 237
14:24	129
14:26-27	111, 116, 129
14:28-21:15	132
14:28-17:3	86, 130

14:28-32	135, 142
14:28-30	112, 119
14:28	35, 110, 135, 142
14:29-32	135
14:31-32a	112
14:32b	112, 116, 119
15:1–16:12	112, 119, 130, 142
15:1-4a	131
15:1	110
15:4b-7	131
15:8-9	131
16:1	131, 135
16:2	131
16:3-4a	131
16:4b	131
16:5	131, 135
16:6	131
16:7-8	131
16:9-12	131
16:13-14	112, 116, 119, 131
16:14	135
17:1-3	112, 119, 142
17:1	110
17:4-14	116
17:4-6	112
17:7-9	112
17:10-11	112
17:12-14a	112
17:14	85
17:14b	112
18–20	143
18:1–20:5	86, 130, 241
18:1-7	137
18:1-6	112, 115, 119, 143
18:1	110
18:3b	103
18:7	112, 116, 119
19:1-15	112, 115, 119, 137, 143
19:1	110
19:16-25	112, 116, 119, 137, 143
20	34, 143
20:1-6	137
20:1-5	112, 115, 119, 143
20:1-2	136

20:1	135
20:3-6	136
20:3	135, 147
20:6	112, 116
21:1-15	86, 130, 131
21:1-9	112, 115, 119, 142
21:1	110
21:10	112, 116, 119
21:11-12	112, 119, 142
21:11	110
21:13-15	112, 119, 142
21:13	110
21:16-17	112, 116
22:1-14	112, 115, 118, 141
22:1	110, 132
22:5	132
22:14	34
22:15-25	112, 115, 118
22:15	110
22:20	147
23:1-14	112, 114, 118, 132, 141
23:1	110
23:5	137, 142
23:15-18	112, 114, 118, 132, 141
24–27	18, 116, 123, 132, 141, 144, 240
24:1–27:13	110, 112, 115, 116, 120, 145, 238
24:1-3	112, 116, 120
24:4-20	112, 120, 132
24:5b	215
24:16a	34
24:21-23	36, 112, 120, 132
24:21	110
25:1-5	113, 116, 120, 240
25:6-8	36, 113, 120, 132
25:9-10a	113, 120, 132
25:9	110
25:10b-12	113, 120, 132
26:1-21	113, 120, 132
26	36
26:1	110
27:1	110, 113, 120, 132
27:2-11	36, 113, 120, 132, 237
27:2	110
27:4	96
27:8	21
27:12	110, 113, 116, 120
27:13	110, 113, 116, 120
28–39	131, 132
28–35	35
28–33	137
28–31	18
28:1-8	113, 114, 118, 132, 137, 141
28:1-4	137
28:1	110
28:5-6	137
28:9-29	113, 115, 118
28:13	137
29:1-8	113, 115, 118, 141
29:1	110, 132
29:2	132
29:5-9	137
29:7	132
29:9-14	113, 115, 118, 143, 150
29:15-24	113, 115, 118, 141, 143
29:15	110
29:18-21	150
29:22-24	143, 150
30:1–34:17	132
30:1-33	137
30:1-17	113, 115, 119, 143
30:1-5	137
30:1	110
30:17b	103
30:18-26	113, 116, 121, 134
30:19-26	36
30:20	134
30:21	134
30:22	134
30:23	134
30:25	134
30:27-33	113, 116, 121
31:1-3	113, 115, 119, 137, 143
31:1	110
31:4-9	113, 116, 121, 137
31:4-5	137
31:8-9	137
31:9	103
32–33	18, 36
32:1–33:24	113, 116, 121, 132, 134
32:1-5	137
32:1-2	133
32:3-4	133
32:3a	134
32:3b	134
32:5-8	133
32:5	134
32:6	134
32:9-14	133
32:9	133, 134
32:10	133
32:11	133, 134
32:12-14	133
32:13a	134
32:15-18	133
32:17	134
32:19	133, 134
32:20	133, 134
33	18
33:1	110, 133
33:2	133
33:3	133
33:4	133
33:5-6	133
33:7-9	133
33:7-8	134
33:10-12	133
33:13-14	133
33:15-16	134
33:16	134
33:17	134
33:18	134
33:19	134
33:20-24	134
33:20	134
33:21a	134
33:21b	134
33:22	134
33:23	134

33:23b 134
33:24 134
34–35 18
34 18
34:1-17 86, 131
34:1-4 113, 119, 142
34:4 142
34:5-15 142
34:5-7 113, 119
34:5 131
34:6-7 131
34:8-10a 131
34:8 113, 119
34:9-10a 113, 119
34:10b-15 113, 119
34:10b 131
34:11a 131
34:11b 131
34:12 131
34:13-15 131
34:16-17 113, 119, 142
34:16 142
35 36
35:1-10 114, 116, 121, 144, 237
36–40 18
36–39 35, 109, 110, 138, 141
36:1–39:8 87, 140, 146, 147, 244
36:1–38:20 140
36–37 109, 114, 138
36:1–37:38 23, 110, 129
36:1–37:37 136
36:1–37:20 26, 114, 129, 130, 138
36:1–37:9a 129
36:1 114, 117, 130, 136
36:2-21 114, 117
36:2-10 130
36:2-4a 146
36:4b-10 146
36:5-6 117
36:7 117
36:8-9a 117
36:11-21 130
36:11-12a 146
36:12-21 147
36:22–37:4 114, 117, 130
36:22–37:2 147

37–39 34
37:3-4 147
37:5-6 114, 130
37:5-6a 147
37:6 139
37:6b-7 147
37:7 114
37:7a 130
37:7b 130
37:8-9a 114
37:8 130
37:9 139, 143
37:9a 130
37:9b-36 129
37:9b-13 114, 117, 130
37:9b 147
37:10-13 147
37:14-20 117, 130
37:14 147
37:15-20 147
37:16 139
37:18 138, 139
37:21-38 114, 130, 138
37:21-22a 114, 117, 130, 147
37:21 138
37:22a 110
37:22b-35 114, 117, 129, 130, 145, 147
37:22b-29 130
37:24a 129
37:24b 129
37:25a 129
37:25b 129
37:26 129
37:27b 129
37:30-32 130
37:30-31 129
37:33-35 130
37:35 87, 124, 127, 139, 147
37:36-38 114, 117
37:36-37 130
37:37-38 129
37:38 130, 136, 137, 167

38–39 138
38:1–39:8 136
38 109, 126, 145
38:1-22 126

38:1-8 114, 121, 139, 144, 145
38:1 136
38:2-3 140
38:5-6 125, 127, 136
38:6 87, 136
38:7-8 139
38:8 139
38:9-20 110, 139
38:9 114, 121, 139, 144, 145
38:10-20 114, 116, 121, 139, 140, 144, 145, 147
38:21-22 114, 121, 139, 144, 145
38:21 138
38:22–39:8 146
38:22 140
39 35, 109, 114, 123, 124, 125, 126, 127, 139, 140, 237
39:1-8 26, 110, 114, 117, 123, 126, 127, 139, 147, 174
39:1-4 125
39:1-2a 123
39:1 125, 126, 127, 128, 136
39:1b 139
39:2 123, 126, 139
39:2a 126, 127
39:3 123, 139
39:3b 123, 125, 127, 174
39:4a 124
39:4b 124, 126, 127
39:5-7 87, 245
39:5 124, 126, 127, 139
39:6 124, 126
39:6a 127
39:6b 127
39:7 124, 125, 126, 127, 128, 145
39:8 124, 125,

	126, 139, 140	40:13b	166	41:2b-3	164, 165
40-66	19, 35, 53,	40:14a	165, 166	41:2b	165
	140, 145, 147	40:14b	166	41:3	165
40-55	17, 19, 109	40:15-17	164, 166	41:4	164, 165
40-54	27, 33, 146,	40:15a	166	41:4a	165
	147, 149,	40:16a	166	41:5-6	164, 165
	199, 209,	40:16b	166	41:5a	165
	214, 215,	40:17a	166	41:5b	165
	237, 243,	40:17b	166	41:6-7	157
	244, 245	40:18-20	157, 164,	41:6b	167
40:1-54:17	20, 54, 55,		166, 212	41:7	165, 212
	87, 105, 146,			41:7a	167
	149, 150,	40:18a	165	41:7b	167
	151, 152,	40:19a	166	41:8-20	153, 159,
	154, 155,	40:19b	166		167, 169,
	159, 160,	40:20b	166		172, 203, 167
	161, 162,	40:21-24	157, 164,	41:8-13	157, 159, 167
	163, 181,		165, 166	41:8-9a	168, 209
	203, 206,	40:21	166	41:8b	169
	208, 209,	40:21b	166	41:9a	167
	210, 211,	40:22a	166	41:9b	168, 210, 213
	212, 213,	40:22b	166	41:10	212
	236, 238,	40:23b	166	41:10a	168, 169
	241, 243	40:24a	166	41:10b	168, 169
40:1-47:15	210	40:25-26	157	41:11-12	169
40:1-43:13	150, 152,	40:25	164, 212	41:11	22
	155, 163, 171	40:25a	165	41:11a	168
40:1-11	24, 110, 153,	40:26	164, 210	41:11b	168
	159, 162,	40:26a	165	41:12a	168, 169
	163, 172	40:27-31	157	41:12b	168
40:1-2	24, 159, 162,	40:27	162, 164,	41:13a	167, 168, 169
	209, 210, 231		167, 210, 213	41:13b	168, 169
40:3-5	159, 162	40:28-31	164, 165,	41:14-16	159, 167
40:6-8	159, 231		166, 167	41:14	168, 169
40:6a	24, 34, 162	40:28	210, 213	41:14a	169
40:6b-8	162, 163, 210	40:28a	166	41:14b	155, 169
40:9	24, 159, 162,	40:29-31	210	41:15-16a	168, 169
	209	40:29a	166	41:16b	155, 168, 169
40:10-11	159, 162	40:30a	166	41:17-20	159, 167
40:10	210	40:31a	166, 167	41:17a	168
40:12-41:7	153, 157,	40:31b	166	41:17b	168, 169,
	162, 163,	41-46	18		210, 213
	166, 167,	41-45	18	41:18-19	168, 209
	172, 211	41:1-42:13	211	41:20	155, 168, 169
40:12-31	165	41:1-7	165, 211	41:21-42:17	26, 171
40:12-17	157	41:1-6	165	41:21-42:9	33, 153, 157,
40:12-14	164, 166	41:1-5	157		167, 169, 172
40:12a	165	41:1	164, 165, 167	41:21-29	213
40:12b	166	41:1a	165, 167	41:21-24	157
40:13-14	210	41:1b	165	41:21-23	26, 170, 171
40:13a	165	41:1ff	211	41:21b	172
		41:2a	164, 165		

41:22-23	210	42:19b	172, 173	43:16	25, 177, 178
41:22b	171	42:20	172, 173	43:17b	25, 177, 178
41:23a	171	42:21	172, 173	43:18-19a	177, 178
41:24	26, 170, 171	42:22a	173	43:19b-21	177, 211
41:24a	171	42:22b	173	43:19b	25, 177, 178
41:25-29	157	42:23	173, 174	43:20a	177, 178
41:25	145	42:24	173	43:20b-21	25, 177, 178
41:25a	26, 170, 171	42:24a	173	43:20b	178
41:25b	26, 170, 171	42:25	173	43:21	178
41:26-28	26, 170, 171,	42:26-28	171	43:22-28	153, 158,
	210	43:1-7	153, 159,		178, 213
41:26a	171		174, 177, 178	43:22-24a	180
41:29	26, 170, 171	43:1-4	159	43:22-23a	179
41:29a	171	43:1a	174, 175	43:22	179
41:29b	171	43:1b	174, 175	43:22b	180
42:1-4	145, 157, 173	43:2-3	210	43:23a	179
42:1a	26, 170, 171,	43:2a	174, 175, 211	43:23b-24a	179
	173	43:2b	174, 175	43:23b	179, 180
42:1b-4	26, 170, 171	43:3a	155, 174, 175	43:24a	179
42:5-9	157	43:3b	174, 175, 211	43:24b	179, 180
42:5	170	43:4	174, 175	43:25-26	179
42:6-7	145	43:5-7	159	43:25	179, 180
42:6a	27, 170, 171	43:5a	174, 175	43:26	180, 210, 213
42:6b-7	27, 170, 171	43:5b-6a	174, 175	43:27	179, 180
42:8-9	171	43:6b	174, 175	43:27a	179
42:8	27, 170, 171	43:7	174	43:27b	179
42:8b	171	43:7a	174, 175	43:28	179
42:9	27, 170, 171,	43:7b	175	44:1-5	153, 160,
	210	43:8-13	153, 157,		180, 181
42:10-12	153, 160,		158, 175,	44:1	180, 181
	161, 167,		181, 203	44:1a	181
	169, 170,	43:8	175, 176	44:1b	181
	171, 214	43:9a	175, 176, 210	44:2a	180
42:13-17	153, 157,	43:9b	176	44:2b	180, 181
	167, 169, 172	43:10	176	44:3a	180, 181
42:13	157, 161,	43:10b	176	44:3b	181
	171, 172	43:11	176	44:4	181
42:13a	27, 170	43:12a	176	44:5	181
42:13b	27, 170, 171	43:12b	176	44:6-22	153, 158,
42:14–44:22	33	43:13	176, 210		181, 182,
42:14-17	157	43:13a	176		184, 198
42:14-16	27, 170, 171	43:14-15	150, 152,	44:6-8	158
42:14	231		153, 155, 158	44:6-7	182, 210
42:16b	210	43:14a	155, 178	44:6a	155, 183
42:17	27, 170, 171	43:14b	155	44:8	182, 210
42:17a	171	43:15	155, 178	44:9-20	158
42:17b	171	43:16–46:13	150, 152,	44:9a	182, 184
42:18-25	153, 157,		155, 171, 242	44:9b	182, 184
	172, 174, 175	43:16-21	25, 153, 159,	44:10	182, 184
42:18-19	172, 173, 175		177, 178, 181	44:11a	182, 184
42:19a	173	43:16-17	177, 209, 211	44:11b	182, 184

44:12	182, 184		187, 203	47:5-7	155
44:12b	182, 184	45:14-17	160	47:8-54:17	210
44:13a	182, 184	45:14	187	47:8-15	151, 152,
44:13b-14	182, 184	45:14b	187		153, 155,
44:14	181	45:15	187, 213		159, 190, 210
44:15a	183, 184	45:16	187	47:8	159
44:15b	183, 184	45:17	187	48-54	18
44:16	183, 184	45:18-19	160	48:1-13	150, 151,
44:17	183, 184	45:18a	187		152, 154,
44:17b	183, 184	45:18b	187, 188		155, 158,
44:18-19a	183, 184	45:19	187, 188, 213		159, 190
44:19a	183, 184	45:20-21	160	48:1-11	158
44:19b	183, 184	45:20-21a	187, 188	48:1a	191, 192
44:20a	183, 184	45:21b	187, 188, 210	48:1b	191, 192, 193
44:20b	183, 184	45:22-25	160	48:2	191, 192
44:21-22	158, 183, 210	45:22	187	48:2a	191, 192
44:22b	183	45:22a	187, 188	48:3	191, 193, 210
44:23	153, 161,	45:22b	187, 188	48:4	191, 193
	171, 184, 214	45:23	187, 188	48:5a	191, 193, 210
44:24-45:13	153, 158,	45:24a	187, 188	48:5b	191
	184, 203	45:24b	188	48:6a	191, 193
44:24-28	158	45:25	187, 188	48:6b-7a	192, 210
44:24a	185, 209	46-48	18	48:7b	192
44:24b	184, 185	46:1-2	158, 160	48:8	192
44:25-26a	184, 185	46:1a	187, 188	48:9	192
44:26b	184, 185	46:1b-2	187, 188	48:10	192, 193
44:27	185, 211	46:3-4	158, 160	48:11	192
44:28a	184, 185	46:3-13	153, 158,	48:12-13	158, 159
44:28b	184, 185		189, 206	48:12a	192
45:1-7	158	46:3	189, 190	48:12b	192, 193
45:1	184, 185	46:4	189, 190	48:13	192
45:2-3a	184, 185	46:5-11	158	48:14-22	150, 152,
45:3b	184, 185	46:5	189, 190		155, 158,
45:4a	184, 185	46:6-7	189, 190		159, 190
45:4b	184, 185	46:8	189, 190	48:14-20a	154
45:5a	185	46:9-10	210	48:14-16	155
45:5b	184, 186	46:9a	189, 190	48:14-15	158, 159
45:6	184, 186	46:9b	189, 190, 206	48:16	159
45:7	184, 186	46:10a	189, 190	48:17-19	155, 159
45:8	158, 184, 186	46:10b	189, 190	48:18	231
45:9-10	158, 186, 213	46:11a	189, 190, 206	48:20-22	155
45:9	21, 186	46:11b	189, 190, 210	48:20-21	159, 161
45:10	186	46:12-13	158	48:20	154, 161, 214
45:11-13	158	46:12	190	48:21-22	154
45:11	213	46:13	190	49-54[55]	18
45:11a	155, 186	47	18	49:1-54:17	150, 152,
45:11b	184, 186	47:1-7	150, 151,		155, 242
45:12	184, 186		152, 153,	49:1-12	154, 158, 193
45:13a	184, 186		155, 159	49:1-4	158
45:13b	184, 186	47:1-3	155	49:1a	193, 194
45:14-46:2	153, 160,	47:4	155	49:1b-6	145

49:1b-3	193, 194	50:7	197, 198	51:18a	202, 203
49:4	193, 194	50:7a	197, 198	51:18b	202, 203
49:5-6	158	50:8	22	51:19	202, 203
49:5	193, 194	50:8a	197, 198	51:20	202, 203
49:6	194, 195	50:8b	197, 198	51:21-22	202, 203
49:7-9a	145	50:9a	197, 198	51:22	22
49:7	158, 194, 195	50:9b	198	51:23	202, 203
49:7a	155, 194, 195	50:10-11	145, 158	52:1-2	160, 202
49:7b	155	50:10a	198	52:1a	25, 202
49:8-12	158	50:10b	198	52:1b	202
49:8a	194, 195	50:11	198, 231	52:2a	202
49:8b-9a	194	51:1-8	171, 198	52:2b	202
49:9b-11	194	51:1-2	154, 160, 200	52:3-12	171, 203
49:12	194	51:1a	199	52:3-7	154, 160
49:13	154, 161, 214	51:1b-2	199, 200, 209	52:3-6	160
49:14–50:3	154, 159, 160, 195	51:1b	200	52:3-5	211
		51:2	200	52:3	203, 204
49:14-17	160	51:3	154, 160, 161, 171, 199, 200, 209, 214	52:4-5	203, 204
49:14	195, 196, 210, 213			52:6	203, 204, 210
				52:7-8	160, 210
49:15-21	231			52:7	161, 203, 204
49:15-16	195, 196, 210, 213	51:4-8	154, 160	52:8-9	154, 160, 161, 171, 203, 204, 214
		51:4-5	160, 199		
49:17-18a	195, 196	51:6	160, 199, 200		
49:18-21	160	51:7-8	160	52:8	161
49:18b	195, 196	51:7a	199	52:8a	203
49:19-20	195, 196	51:7b-8	199	52:8b	203
49:21	195, 196	51:9–52:2	24, 171, 200, 203, 242	52:9-10	160
49:22-23	160			52:9	161, 210
49:22-23a	196	51:9-11	160	52:9a	203
49:22a	195	51:9-10	154, 160	52:9b	203
49:23	231	51:9a	25, 200, 201	52:10-12	154, 160
49:23b	196	51:9b-10	211	52:10	161, 204, 210
49:24-26	160	51:9b	201, 202	52:11-12	160, 204, 211
49:24	196, 210	51:10	201, 202	52:13–53:12	145, 154, 158, 204
49:25-26a	196	51:11	154, 160, 161, 171, 201, 203, 214		
49:25	22			52:13-15	158
49:26b	196			52:13	204, 206
50:1-3	160	51:12–52:2	154, 160	52:14	204, 206
50:1a	196, 210, 213	51:12-13	160	52:15	204, 206
50:1b-2a	196	51:12a	201, 202, 209	53:1-10	158
50:2-3	210	51:12b	201, 202	53:1	204
50:2a	196	51:13a	201, 202	53:2	204, 206
50:2b-3	196, 211	51:13b-14	201, 202	53:2a	90
50:4-11	154, 158, 197	51:14-16	160	53:3a	204, 206
50:4-9	145, 158	51:15	201, 202, 211	53:3b	204, 206
50:4a	197, 198	51:16a	201, 202	53:4a	204, 206
50:4b-5a	197, 198	51:16b	201, 202	53:4b	204, 206
50:5	197, 198	51:17-23	160	53:5a	205, 206
50:6a	197, 198	51:17	202, 203	53:5b	205, 206
50:6b	197, 198	51:17a	25, 200, 202	53:6a	205, 206

53:6b	205, 206	55–59	18		224, 232
53:7	205, 206	55:1–56:8	219, 221,	58:1-14	218, 224
53:7a	205, 206		229, 231, 232	58:1-8	219
53:8	205, 206	55	216, 218	58:1-5	224
53:9	205, 206	55:1-3	151, 216, 222	58:1	223
53:10a	205, 206	55:3b	215	58:1b	224
53:10b	205, 206	55:4-5	215, 222	58:2-5	215, 223, 224
53:11-12	158	55:6-7	222	58:2	224
53:11	205, 206	55:8-9	222	58:3a	224
53:11a	205, 206	55:10-11	222	58:4a	224
53:12	205, 206	55:12	222	58:5a	224
53:12a	205, 206	56–66	17, 19, 109,	58:5b	224
54:1-3	231		216, 217, 218	58:6-14	224
54:1-2	160	56:1–66:24	216	58:6-7	215, 223, 224
54:1	154, 160,	56–59	18, 19	58:6a	224
	161, 206,	56–58	217	58:8-9a	224
	207, 214	56:1-9	216	58:8	223
54:1b	207	56:1-8	217, 218	58:8a	233
54:2-17	154, 160, 206	56:1-2	215, 222, 223	58:9a	219, 221, 223
54:2	207	56:3-8	215	58:9b–59:15a	219
54:3	160, 207	56:3a	222	58:9b-10a	215, 224
54:4-6	160	56:3b	222	58:10a	224
54:4a	207, 208	56:4-5	222	58:10b-12	224
54:4b	207, 208	56:6-8	222	58:10b	233
54:5	207	56:7	233	58:12	215
54:6	207, 208	56:9–58:14	217	58:13	215, 224
54:7-10	160, 210	56:9–57:21	217, 218,	58:14	224
54:7	207, 208		222, 232	58:14b	224
54:8	207, 208	56:9–57:13	219	59:1-15a	216, 217
54:9	207, 208	56:9-12	215, 223	59:1-14	217, 218
54:10	207, 208	56:9	223	59:1	210, 212, 224
54:11-17	160	56:10–57:4	217	59:2-8	215, 224
54:11a	207, 208	56:10a	223	59:9-11	224
54:11b-12	207	56:10b	223	59:9-10	233
54:13	207	56:11	223	59:12-13	215, 224
54:14	208	56:11a	223	59:14-15a	224
54:15-17a	208	57:1-2	223	59:15-21	217
54:15	208	57:3-13a	215, 223	59:15-20[21]	217, 218
54:16a	208	57:5ff	216	59:15b-20	217, 219,
54:16b	208	57:13	233		226, 233
54:17a	208	57:13b	223	59:15b-16	226
54:17b	208	57:14-15	219, 220, 223	59:15bff	216
55–66	54, 215, 218,	57:15	216, 230	59:17	226
	221, 224,	57:16-21	219	59:18	226
	227, 228,	57:16-19	223	59:19a	226
	231, 233,	57:16-17	217	59:19b	226
	237, 238	57:16	21	59:20	226
55:1–66:24	20, 55, 151,	57:18-19	216	59:21	219, 221, 226
	214, 215,	57:20–58:14	217	60–66	18
	216, 221,	57:20-21	223	60–62	217
	236, 238	58:1–59:15a	215, 223,	60:1-22	216, 217, 218

60:1-20	215, 227, 228	62:10	219, 220, 229	65:8-66:24	38, 216, 219, 229, 232
60:1-13	219	62:10b	103		
60:1-3	233	62:11-12	219	65:8-10	230
60:1-2	227	62:11	229	65:9	233
60:3-4	227	62:12	229	65:11-12	230
60:5	233	63:1-6	216, 217, 218, 226, 233	65:11	216, 233
60:5a	227			65:12-25	217
60:5b-7a	227	63:1-3	219	65:13-22a	230
60:7b	227	63:1a	226	65:13-16a	230
60:8-9a	227	63:1b	226	65:16b	230
60:9b	227	63:2	226	65:17a	230, 231
60:10-13a	227	63:3	226	65:17b	230
60:10	215	63:3a	226	65:18-22a	230
60:13b	227	63:4	219, 221, 226	65:22b-23	230
60:14-15	219, 220, 227	63:5-6	219	65:25	178
60:16-20	219	63:5	226	66:1-16	218
60:16a	227	63:6	226	66:1-2	230
60:16b	227	63:7-65:7	215, 224, 232	66:1	216
60:17a	227	63:7-64:11	217, 218, 219	66:2	217
60:17b-18	227	63:7-9	225	66:3	216
60:19-20	233	63:7ff	216	66:3a	231
60:19	227	63:10a	215, 225, 226	66:3b-4	231
60:20	227	63:10b	225	66:4-9	217
60:21-61:11	215, 227	63:11-14	225	66:5-16	231
60:21-22	219	63:15-64:11	38	66:5-6	231
60:21a	228	63:15-17	225	66:7-9	231
60:21b-22	228	63:18	215, 225	66:10-13	216
61:1-11	216, 217, 218	63:19a	225	66:10	231
61:1-3	145	63:19b-64:2	225	66:11	231
61:1-3a	219, 220, 221, 227, 228	63:19b	225	66:12-13	231
		64:1-65:10	217	66:12a	231
61:3-11	219	64:1	225, 233	66:14-16	217
61:3a	228	64:1a	225	66:14a	231
61:3b	228	64:2	225	66:14b-16	231
61:4-6	228	64:3-4a	225	66:14b	231
61:4	215	64:3	233	66:17-24	218
61:7	228	64:4b-6	215, 225, 226	66:17	216, 231
61:7b	220	64:7-8	225	66:18-24	217, 218
61:8	215, 228	64:9-10	225	66:18	216, 231
61:9	228	64:9	215	66:19-23	217
61:10	214, 228	64:10	215	66:19-21	231
61:11	228	64:11	225	66:20	233
62:1-12	216, 217, 218, 228	65-66	38, 217	66:22-24	231
		65:1-66:17	217, 218	66:22-23	231
62:1-9	219	65:1-25	218	66:24	31, 216, 231
62:1-2a	229	65:1	219, 221, 225		
62:1	233	65:2-7	219, 229	*Jeremiah*	
62:2b-5	229	65:2-5	215, 225, 226, 230, 233	2:4-9	39
62:6-7	229			2:4	40
62:8	229	65:6-7	225, 230	2:5-37	40
62:9	229	65:7	233	2:5-6	40

2:7-13	40	49:18	45	6:6-7	40
2:10-13	39	50:40	45	6:8	40
2:12	40				
2:14-19	40	*Amos*		*Zechariah*	
2:20-28	40	4:11	45	3:8	90
2:26-28	40			6:12	90
2:29-30	40	*Micah*			
2:31-37	40	6:1-8	39, 40	*Hebrews*	
3:12–4:2	29	6:1-2	40	11:37	244
23:5	90	6:3	40		
33:15	90	6:4-5	40		

Ackroyd, P. R. 201
Alter, R. 201
Alonso-Schökel,
L. 201
van Dijk,

Barth, K.
Barton, J. 5
Berlin, A.
Blum, E. 90, 145
Buss, M. J.

Carroll, R. 160
Childs, B. S.
Clines, D. 7, 38
Conrad, E.

Gadamer, H. 89, 88
Gunkel, H. 64, 88
Gunn, D. 108
Gutiérrez, G. 6, 8, 9, 31
37, 104, 112, 113, 118

Habel, N. 145
Hanson, P. 108
Holmberg, M.
Hayes, J.

Jobling, D.
Jeremias, J.
Johnson, M.
Culler

Barthes, 201, 37, 32
Bakhtin, M. 145
Derrida, J. 89
Derrida, J.
Hawkes, T.
Philman, V.
Dozeman, T. 33, 145
Dozy, R. 72, 84
Dupont-R. 115, 145

INDEX OF AUTHORS

Ackroyd, P.R. 35, 53
Aharoni, Y. 104
Alonso-Schökel, L. 77, 91
Alter, R. 23
Avi-Yonah, M. 104

Baird, J.A. 15
Barr, J. 17
Begrich, J. 16, 39, 156
Bentzen, A. 39
Berlin, A. 15, 16, 245
Birks, T.R. 57
Blenkinsopp, J. 57
Boecker, H.J. 39
Bonnard, P.-E. 156, 217
Bright, J. 102, 103
Brownlee, W.H. 18
Bullinger, E.W. 18

Callaway, J.A. 18
Caspari, W. 149
Cathcart, K.J. 57
Charpentier, E. 216, 217, 218
Childs, B.S. 17, 129
Christensen, D.L. 16
Clements, R.E. 17, 32, 35, 37, 57, 95,
    104, 105, 109, 129, 135, 136,
    137
Clifford, R.J. 19, 156
Condamin, A. 33
Cross, F.M. 42
Culler, J. 21

Daniels, D.R. 39, 42
Davidson, R. 57
Delcor, M. 39
Delitzsch, Franz 35
Dietrich, W. 104
Dillmann, A. 57
Doty, W.G. 15, 17
Duhm, B. 35, 94
Dumbrell, W.J. 17, 53

Eaton, J.H. 17

Eissfeldt, O. 16
Elliger, K. 156
Erlandsson, S. 142
Evans, C.A. 18, 239
Everson, A.J. 66

Fisher, R.W. 162
Fohrer, G. 32, 33, 34, 55, 57
Fullerton, K. 57

Gemser, B. 38, 149
Gileadi, A. 18
Gitay, Y. 19, 165
Graffy, A. 16
Gray, G.B. 35, 109
Gray, J. 66
Greenspahn, F.E. 182
Gressmann, H. 16, 156
Gunkel, H. 16, 39

Hahn, H.F. 16
Haran, M. 19
Harrison, R.K. 18
Harvey, J. 32, 38, 39, 40, 41, 42
Hayes, J.H. 51, 58, 76, 84, 103, 109,
    135, 136, 137, 138
Herbert, A.S. 57
Hesse, F. 38
Hessler, E. 19
Hoffmann, H.W. 57
Hoffmann, Y. 66
Holladay, W.L. 37, 77
Huffmon, H.B. 32, 38, 39, 42

Irvine, S.A. 51, 58, 76, 84, 103, 109,
    135, 136, 137, 138

Jacobsen, T. 245
Jensen, J. 58

Kaiser, O. 31, 32, 34, 37, 50, 57, 81,
    90, 91, 95, 104, 109
Kaufmann, Y. 156
Kiesow, K. 211

Kissane, E.J.   35
Kitchen, K.A.   143
Knierim, R.   15, 17, 19
Koch, K.   15, 16
Kogut, S.   85, 92
Köhler, L.   149, 156

Lack, R.   38, 57, 109, 217
Levine, L.D.   136
Limburg, J.   39
Lindblom, J.   77
Long, B.O.   36
Loretz, O.   33
Lovering, E.H. Jr   17
Lucas, E.C.   32
Lund, N.W.   24

Machinist, P.B.   41
Marti, K.   35
Mattioli, A.   32
McCarthy, D.J.   32
Melugin, R.F.   16, 19, 156, 211
Mendenhall, G.E.   32
Merrill, E.H.   102, 103, 104, 136
Miller, J.M.   104
Moran, W.   32
Mowinckel, S.   16, 156
Muilenburg, J.   19, 24, 156

Nicholson, E.W.   32
Niditch, S.   32
Nielsen, K.   39

O'Connell, R.H.   23, 26, 28, 114, 128
Orelli, C. von   57
Oswalt, J.N.   37, 58, 114, 117, 141

Perelman, C.   37
Platt, E.E.   75
Polan, G.J.   19, 217, 218, 224
Procksch, O.   35

Rad, G. von   66
Rendtorff, R.   17, 35
Richter, W.   15
Ricoeur, P.   23
Rignell, L.G.   32, 33

Robinson, H.W.   42
Robinson, T.H.   16
Roche, M. de   33, 39
Rogerson, J.W.   15
Roth, W.   146

Sawyer, J.F.A.   58
Schoors, A.   16, 104, 156
Scott, R.B.Y.   35
Seitz, C.R.   17
Skinner, J.   35
Sloan, T.O.   37
Slotki, I.W.   35
Stade, B.   129
Sternberg, M.   34, 50, 85
Sweeney, M.A.   35, 58, 71, 77, 109,
    140, 216

Talmon, S.   36
Thiele, E.R.   102, 135
Thompson, J.A.   32
Tigay, J.H.   245
Torrey, C.C.   156
Tournay, R.   216, 217
Tucker, G.M.   34

Vermeylen, J.   31, 35, 50, 57, 95
Volz, P.   16

Wade, G.W.   57
Waldow, H.E. von   39, 156
Watson, W.G.E.   50, 75, 165
Watts, J.D.W.   48
Weiss, M.   66
Welch, J.W.   24
Westermann, C.   16, 31, 37, 39, 156
Widengren, G.   90
Wiklander, B.   29, 60, 70, 75, 77
Wildberger, H.   33, 34, 35, 55, 57, 104
Willis, J.T.   33
Wilson, A.   156
Wolf, H.M.   109
Wright, G.E.   32, 38, 39
Würthwein, E.   38

Young, E.J.   35, 102